AGAINST THE TYRANT

Against the Tyrant

THE TRADITION AND THEORY OF TYRANNICIDE

by Oscar Jászi and John D. Lewis

OBERLIN COLLEGE

THE FREE PRESS
GLENCOE, ILLINOIS

&

JC
495
.J3
cop. 2

Copyright 1957 by The Free Press, a corporation

Printed in the United States of America

Designed by Sidney Solomon

PREFACE

O merciful God! What can this be? What should we call it? What misfortune is this? Or what crime, what miserable crime? To see an infinite number of citizens not obeying but serving; not being governed but tyrannized; not having property, kin, children, even lives to call their own! Suffering the pillages, the debaucheries, the cruelties, not of an army, not of a barbarian camp . . . but of one man alone! Not of a Hercules or a Samson, but of one single little man. . . .

THE WORDS with which the brilliant young sixteenth-century humanist, Étienne de La Boétie, opened his *Discourse on Voluntary Servitude* express the moral revulsion with which noble minds of all ages have regarded the phenomenon of the tyrant. The deeply felt conviction that tyranny is among the most miserable of crimes has often been associated with a reasoned defense of resistance to the tyrant's authority and, less frequently, with the justification of tyrannicide. No one would deny that men who live together in a community must recognize a general obligation to obey their legitimate government and the laws which it lays down. But few would deny that there can be governments so harsh and so unjust that free men will not willingly obey them. Men in all ages have been driven to resist such authority on the basis of their conception of justice or of a higher law.

The concept of the tyrant is an ancient one. It appeared in oriental thought; it was stated emphatically by the greatest of the Greek philosophers; it survived in serious political thought down to modern times. But, with certain important exceptions, the concept of the tyrant was of decreasing importance in modern political theory. The development of constitutional government meant the development of regularized restraints upon rulers for the prevention of arbitrary and tyrannical rule. The growing belief that governments could and should be made to serve the will of the people within the limits of a constitution made it easier to define and recognize tyranny; but the parallel development of constitutional mechanisms made the question of tyranny and of resistance to tyranny seem continually less relevant to practical politics. The impassioned exhortations of La Boétie and the fine-spun distinctions of philosophical discussions of tyrannicide tended to sound like burned-out rhetoric in the ears of the western world. An elaborate theory of individual resistance is unnecessary to those who have a right, insured by regularized procedure, to criticize, oppose, and check the actions of their rulers.

Those who had imagination enough to envisage the possibility that corruptive influences might grow so strong that constitutional mechanisms would be an inadequate safeguard against tyranny tended to believe that a popular right of revolution, as distinguished from a private right of tyrannicide, would be an adequate remedy in case of a renewed era of tyranny. Revolution came to be regarded as the sole alternative to the continued operation of a constitutional system gone wrong. The theory of revolution was thoroughly elaborated in political thought after the events of 1688, 1776, and 1789. But even this doctrine, so closely associated with our democratic traditions, was gradually eroded by the serene stream of constitutionalism; in the countries in which constitutional government had been achieved, it tended to become a theme of merely theoretical importance.

The doctrine of tyrannicide had not even that dignity in modern liberal eyes. At worst, it was the object of an enlightened shudder; at best, of a mild academic curiosity—like totemism, or the state of nature. Many who would justify organized revolution, or the execution of a tyrant by properly constituted authorities, would deny the right of a private citizen, acting on his own responsibility, to kill the tyrant. And that is what tyrannicide means. This is indeed a dangerous doctrine, and many modern men would regard it also as an immoral doctrine. "In our opinion, it is impossible that tyrannicide can, under any circumstances whatever, be morally justifiable." This assertion made by the London *Spectator* (LV, 175) in 1890 undoubtedly expressed the attitude of most thoughtful Americans and Englishmen alike; that attitude could only have been strengthened by the memory of the shocking assassination of two American presidents and of an attempt against the life of the queen whose name has become the symbol of constitutional monarchy.

Certain earlier writers saw clearly that even a recognized right of revolution might be an ineffective safeguard against the arbitrary power of a ruthless tyrant, and that private action against the tyrant might be justified in some cases. For, in proportion to the ruthlessness of suppression, the difficulty of popular revolt increases. This point was less clear to modern democratic theorists. They tended to make the rationalistic assumption, stated succinctly by Bentham, that a community of men would resist "when the probable mischief of resisting" was "less than the probable mischief of submitting." They failed to recognize that such a rational weighing of advantages might be rendered impossible and that any degree of organized resistance by a substantial part of the community might be rendered equally impossible. They forgot the efficient tyrannies of the past and could not foresee the still more effective tyrannies of the future.

The thoroughness and efficiency of totalitarian repression in the dictatorships which appeared in the decades following the First World War were something undreamed of in the philosophy of optimistic nineteenth-century liberalism. These dictatorial governments simply did not play the game in the way in which liberal rationalists had assumed that governments of the future would play it. Organized deceit and organized terror replaced the free give and take of political debate. Therein the modern dictatorships followed the historic models of tyrannical government. But in the thoroughness and machine-made efficiency of suppression and indoctrination they far surpassed the classic examples of tyranny, which had operated without modern devices for mass persuasion and intimidation. And when modern dictatorial governments had reduced the problem of political control to the most brutal terms of violence and deceit, one was forced to ask whether the old concept of tyranny had not become once more a focal point for serious political thought.

In 1936, the distinguished historian Élie Halévy drew attention to the revival of the problem of tyranny. He pointed out that "the World War of 1914 has demonstrated to men of resolution and action that the structure of the modern state puts at their disposal almost unlimited powers" (*L'Ère des tyrannies,* p. 253). He suggested that the new phenomena could best be characterized by the word *tyranny*—a word which came from Greek experience of a similar era—rather than by the Roman word *dictatorship,* which originally applied to a temporary, constitutional expedient. His suggestion was not taken up, and the flood of articles and books which later described the new regimes showed little awareness of the fundamental kinship between the new and the old tyrannies. More recently, Leo Strauss has commented on the failure of modern political science to recognize tyranny when confronted by it, and has insisted that one can not understand modern tyranny before one has understood tyranny in its elementary, premodern form (*On Tyranny: An Interpretation of Xenophon's Hiero,* Glencoe, Ill., 1948, p. 1 ff.).

The revival of tyranny, however misnamed, inevitably brought with it a revival of that moral revulsion against the tyrant on which the old doctrine of tyrannicide had been based. Especially after the establishment of Hitler's rule, one began to hear expressions of despair and rage from the lips of kind and peace-loving people. Philosophers and moralists might continue to regard tyrannicide as unjustifiable, but simple people often said, "Why doesn't someone kill him?" They were pleased rather than horrified at the statement quoted from Sir Neville Henderson, once an apostle of appeasement: "If I were given a gun and told to take two shots, I would shoot Himmler, then Ribbentrop, and brain Hitler with the butt of the rifle" (*New York Times,* Dec. 31, 1942). There were, of course, many unsuccessful attempts on the lives of Mussolini and Hitler, and it is noteworthy that, even before the outbreak of the War, the news of such attempts aroused in the United States no horror comparable to that with which the western world in the nineteenth century had responded to the news of attacks on the autocrats of Russia.

This book was begun just before the Second World War, when actual tyranny or the threat of subjection to tyranny heavily overshadowed the world. The authors were not impelled by an antiquarian interest in remote political ideas; they believed that the old concept of tyranny and the old debate over the legitimacy of tyrannicide had become once again relevant to realistic political thought. Circumstances beyond their control delayed the completion of the project; but meanwhile new events strengthened their conviction of the significance of its theme. In the German Resistance, the old dilemma revealed its terrible and tragic timeliness. And although the Second World War, at an untold cost, put an end to the tyrannies of Mussolini and Hitler, it also led to the expansion of the Soviet tyranny and to an intensification of the pathological social and political conditions from which tyranny arises. In eastern Europe and in China, new dictatorships have appeared as appendices of the Russian superdictatorship; and the maintenance of constitutionalism in some parts of western Europe remains precarious. Tyranny and the threat of tyranny continue to be characteristic phenomena of the twentieth century.

When the danger of tyranny becomes a real danger, the problem of the right of private resistance against the tyrant becomes an

PREFACE ix

urgent moral problem. Thus, the authors suggest, a re-examination of the ancient doctrine of tyrannicide—of the arguments which have supported and opposed it, of the conditions which it assumes as its premises, of the distortions which it has undergone in the course of its history, of its use and its abuse, and of its validity in the modern world—has become, unhappily, a timely problem.

The two authors have worked in frequent consultation and in a general agreement on the importance of the topic. But years of friendly debate have not entirely dispelled the original differences in their approach and emphases, and accordingly in their conclusions. Each is solely responsible for the chapters that appear under his name.

In the first part of the book, attention is focused on the development of the formal theory of tyrannicide from the classical Greek statements through the pamphlets of the English Rebellion. Thereafter, theoretical analyses of the problem became exceptional; thus in the second part of the book attention shifts to a survey of the role played by the tradition of tyrannicide in the successive revolutionary movements of the modern world, and of its distortions, followed by an attempt to restate the traditional doctrine in terms of modern instances and to examine its validity and significance in the context of the modern world.

The authors gratefully acknowledge the generous assistance of those who read part or all of the manuscript and gave helpful criticism or suggestions: Frederick B. Artz, William T. Couch, Andrew Jászi, Recha Jászi, F. W. Kaufmann, Cecelia Kenyon, George Lanyi, Anna Lesznai, Ewart Lewis, Sigmund Neumann, Michael Polanyi, and Robert Tufts. They wish to acknowledge also their great indebtedness to June Wright for her exquisite typing.

The author of the second part wishes particularly to thank Ewart Lewis for her splendid work in the final revision and abridgement of his manuscript—a difficult task, which she carried out with unusual taste and scholarship. He also acknowledges a special obligation to Recha Jászi for assistance in the arduous work of collecting material; to Esther Taylor for skillful improvements in his English style; and, finally, to Emmy Bonhoeffer for valuable material and illuminating comment on the German Resistance.

OSCAR JÁSZI
JOHN D. LEWIS

Oberlin, Ohio
May 1955

CONTENTS

Preface v

PART ONE
THE DEVELOPMENT OF THE THEORY OF TYRANNICIDE TO 1660
by John D. Lewis

I.	Classical and Christian Thought	3
II.	Medieval Theories of Resistance	17
III.	Tyranny and Tyrannicide in Renaissance Italy	35
IV.	From Obedience to Resistance in Protestant Thought	43
V.	Two Sixteenth-Century Humanists on Tyranny	53
VI.	The Theory and Practice of Tyrannicide in the French Wars of Religion	59
VII.	Reappearance of the Theory in Seventeenth-Century England	75
VIII.	Some Comments on the Tradition and Theory of Tyrannicide	89

PART TWO
THE USE AND ABUSE OF TYRANNICIDE
by Oscar Jászi

IX.	Revolution and Constitution: The Tyrant as a System	99

X.	The Invisible Tyrant	111
XI.	The Survival of the Tradition of Tyrannicide	119
XII.	The Era of Putschism: Tyrannicide Distorted	127
XIII.	Tyrants Everywhere: The Ultimate Distortion	133
XIV.	The Stream of Political Murder	149
XV.	Some Case-Studies	167
XVI.	Tyrannicide in the German Resistance	183
XVII.	Private Resistance Reconsidered	199
XVIII.	The Nature of the New Tyranny	205
XIX.	Bolshevik versus Fascist Tyranny	219
XX.	The Function of Tyrannicide	233
XXI.	The Future	247
	Notes	257
	Index	281

PART ONE

*THE DEVELOPMENT OF
THE THEORY OF TYRANNICIDE TO 1660*

by John D. Lewis

1 CLASSICAL

AND CHRISTIAN THOUGHT

THERE IS the sharpest contrast between the usual modern attitude toward tyrannicide and that which characterized the Greek and Roman cultures which contributed so much to the building of our Western mode of thought. In the republican city states the tyrant was a usurper, and it was considered as honorable for a citizen to stake his life on an attempt to remove the domestic usurper as it was for him to sacrifice his life to repel an invader.[1] Among the earliest monuments erected in Athens to the honor of mortal men were those set up to commemorate the first instance of an attempt to slay a tyrant. These were the statues celebrating the deed of Harmodius and Aristogeiton, who had conspired to kill the tyrant, Hippias, and his younger brother, Hipparchus, and who had succeeded in killing Hipparchus.[2]

In a passage which has been described as "the beginning of Greek political philosophy,"[3] the historian Herodotus described the *hubris,* the unbridled, defiant arrogance, of the tyrant, in terms that later became traditional in Greek political literature. Give a man unrestrained, irresponsible power, and he will be driven by pride and envy, Herodotus argued. "But pride and envy together include all wickedness; both leading on to deeds of savage violence." The tyrant was naturally jealous of the virtuous among his subjects and enjoyed the company of the meanest and the basest of them; he destroyed the laws, dishonored women, and killed men without trial.[4] In his dialogue on tyranny, Xenophon recorded the popular attitude when he wrote, "Instead of avenging them, the cities heap honours on the slayer of the despot; and, whereas they exclude the murderers of private persons from the temples, the cities, so far from treating assassins in the same manner, actually put up statues to them in the holy places."[5] Citizens lived in peace and quiet with each other, Xenophon said, and banded together to protect each other from violence. But the tyrant was never at peace with his subjects; he could have confidence in no truce with them.

Herodotus and Xenophon stressed the violent, lawless nature of the tyrant's rule, but the term "tyranny" was originally a word without moral implications.[6] It was sometimes used to designate merely the rule of one man; or, when tyranny was distinguished from monarchy, the earlier distinction was that which emphasized as the characteristic of tyranny, not the abuse of power, but its unconstitutional source. The tyrant was a ruler who had come to power through usurpation.[7]

It is undoubtedly true that some of the tyrants who seized power in the Greek city states were socially useful individuals.[8] And it is also true that in a period of sharpening class struggle, the tyranny of a popularly supported leader could provide a bridge between oligarchic and democratic government. Modern historians are likely to distinguish between "good" and "bad" Greek tyrants on the basis of the record of their achievements. Even Aristotle was willing to acknowledge that Pisistratus, "having seized the government, administered the state in a constitutional rather than in a tyrannical fashion."[9] He "administered the state in a moderate fashion, and his rule was more like a constitutional government than like a tyranny."[10] But Aristotle also observed that the ruler who had seized power by force was likely to maintain it in a manner different from that of a lawful king. Whereas kings "are guarded by the arms of their subjects," "the tyrant, who rules contrary to the will of his subjects, has a [foreign] bodyguard to protect him against them."[11]

Thus the simple definition which had made it relatively easy to distinguish, by the objective test of illegality or unconstitutionality, the tyrant whom it was permissible and honorable to kill, was already giving way to a more substantive definition. In the writings of Plato and Aristotle, the term "tyranny" came to refer not to the method by which a ruler came into power, but to the nature of his rule. Thus for Plato the tyrant was the most wretched of men and tyranny the most miserable of governments;[12] and for Aristotle tyranny was "the worst of governments" and the furthest removed from a well-constituted form."[13] In spite of Aristotle's kind words about Pisistratus, all tyrants were by definition "bad" tyrants, tyranny being the "perversion of monarchy."

To Plato, the distinguishing characteristic of the tyrant was his egocentric and licentious disregard of the welfare of the people he ruled. The tyrant was one who "has run away from the region of law and reason, and taken up his abode with certain slave pleasures...."[14] He was the "protector of the people" who had turned wolf and devoured his own people. Having risen to popularity by lavish distribution of favors, he made himself indispensable by stirring up wars. He must rid himself of his critics, and finally, to secure his position, must purge the state of all who were valiant or high-minded.[15] The tyrant was the personification of ruthless force.

Plato's ideal state was one in which those possessed of perfect knowledge of the true art of statesmanship would govern. Were such a state possible it would matter not at all how the ruler or rulers achieved power. In *The Statesman* Plato went so far as to say that were true statesmen in control it would be irrelevant whether they ruled according to law or without law, with or without the willing consent of their subjects.[16] The restraint of law, necessary in the second-best state which Plato described in the *Laws,* was but an unsatisfactory substitute for the wisdom of rulers. The mechanical test of legality or constitutionality was in Plato's system no longer the fundamental test of tyranny; more fundamental was the character of the ruler himself and the nature of his rule. Thus the distinction between king and tyrant already became an ethical rather than a legal distinction.

Even Aristotle, although he believed that the safest constitution would be one in which democratic and aristocratic institutions were blended, was willing to say that the absolute rule of a single man might be the ideal form of government, provided that that ruler was moved by virtue to use his power for the common good. Thus his definition of tyranny also emphasized the nature rather than the form of government. Tyranny, the perversion of monarchy, "exercises irresponsible rule over subjects ... with a view to its own private interest and not in the interest of the persons ruled. Hence it is held against the will of the subjects, since no free man willingly endures such rule." Tyranny was marked by the arbitrary and irresponsible power of a single individual. That power was used for the good of the tyrant rather than for the good of the whole community. Aristotle constantly repeated this basic distinction between king and tyrant.[17] And, finally, since tyrannical power did not serve the common good, it must exist contrary to the will of the community. This last assumption supplied an additional sign for the recognition of tyranny, but the lack of popular consent was not the basic test of tyranny; it was rather an incidental consequence.[18]

When the quality of the rule replaced forceful seizure of power as the sign of tyranny, the possibility of the dangers and uncertainties inherent in subjective judgments promptly appeared. For who is to decide when a king by ruling contrary to the common good has become a tyrant, and on what grounds is the decision to be reached? A partial answer is suggested in Aristotle's vivid description of the ways of tyrants. With acute perception, he drew his picture from the concrete experience of states that he knew directly or through history. His description reappeared again and again throughout the long story of the doctrine of tyrannicide. For some of his followers it became a convenient formal stereotype, but many others kept the picture alive and meaningful by finding concrete parallels for Aristotle's examples.

These, according to Aristotle, were the traditional methods by which the tyrant kept his power:

"The lopping-off of outstanding men and the destruction of the proud, and also the prohibition of common meals and club-fellowships and education and all other things of this nature, in fact the close watch upon all things that usually engender . . . pride and confidence, and the prevention of . . . study-circles and other conferences for debate, and the employment of every means that will make people as much as possible unknown to one another (for familiarity increases mutual confidence); and for the people in the city to be always visible as they hang about the palace-gates (for thus there would be least concealment about what they are doing, and they would get into a habit of being humble from always acting in a servile way)... and to try not to be uninformed about any chance utterances or actions of any of the subjects, but to have spies . . . wherever there was any gathering or conference; and to . . . cause quarrels between friend and friend and between the people and the notables and among the rich. And it is a device of tyranny to make the subjects poor, so that a guard may not be kept, and also that the people being busy with their daily affairs may not have leisure to plot against their ruler. Instances of this are the pyramids in Egypt . . . and the building of the temple of Olympian Zeus by the Pisistratidae . . . (for all these undertakings produce the same effect, constant occupation and poverty among the subject people); and the levying of taxes, as at Syracuse (for in the reign of Dionysius the result of taxation used to be that in five years men had contributed the whole of their substance). Also the tyrant is a stirrer-up of war, with the deliberate purpose of keeping the people busy and also of making them constantly in need of a leader."[19]

The personal baseness of the tyrant appeared in his distrust of his friends, his love of flattery, and his suspicion and hate of those who were proud and independent. In general, the wishes and devices of the tyrant were directed by three aims: he must keep his subjects humble, "for a humble spirited man would not plot against anybody"; he must prevent mutual confidence among his subjects, "for a tyranny is not destroyed until some men come to trust each other"; he must destroy his subjects' power to resist, "since nobody attempts impossibilities, so that nobody tries to put down a tyranny if he has not power behind him."[20] It appears then, from this description, that the tyrant was usually forced to hold his power by methods which revealed at the same time his lack of concern for the common good and the lack of willing popular obedience. In the method of ruling there appears an objective standard for distinguishing the tyrant. Aristotle's implied suggestion has an obvious bearing upon the problem of modern tyranny.[21]

Thus in early Greek thought and in the writings of Plato and Aristotle the lines were already drawn within which the doctrine of tyrannicide was to develop. The early Greek tradition that the usurper might justly be killed by a private citizen survived without a break throughout the medieval period in the undisputed doctrine that it was permissible for a private person to kill the tyrant who had no legitimate title *(tyrannus ex defectu tituli)*. The concept of tyranny developed by Plato and Aristotle, of which the test was ethical rather than legal, also survived and was further developed in terms of Stoic and Christian philosophy. But whether the ruler who, after gaining power legitimately, showed himself to be a tyrant by his conduct *(tyrannus ex parte exercitii)* could rightly be dispatched by a private person was a far more difficult and disputed question than that of the killing of the tyrant without a legitimate title.

Neither Plato nor Aristotle gave serious consideration to arguments for or against tyrannicide. Plato took it for granted that the opponents of a budding tyrant would attempt to assassinate him,[22] but he expressed no judgment on the action. Aristotle noted as an incidental illustration that "high honors are awarded to one who kills a tyrant" and discussed at length the motives that led men to attack the tyrant.[23] Having noted instances of attacks against rulers which resulted from unjust oppression, fear, or contempt, he distinguished between those who attempted the lives of tyrants from motives of greed or ambition and those who desired "true fame" among their fellow men. "It is true," he continued, "that those who are moved by such reasons [the desire for "true fame"] are only a handful. Their action supposes an utter disregard for their own safety in the event of failure."[24] But Aristotle withheld any personal judgment on the ethical justification of tyrannicide.

The independence of the Greek city states was being destroyed even while Plato and Aristotle were writing. But the younger city state of Rome was at the same time developing vigorous republican institutions, in which executive officers elected for short terms were checked by a delicate balance of plebeian and aristocratic bodies, and, above all, by the elaborate system of law which carefully regulated the relations of men with one another and with their government. Respect for law was a dominant characteristic of the Roman state in the period of the Republic. Even the institution of dictatorship, which was so useful to the Roman Republic in times of crisis, bore no resemblance to the tyranny that Plato and Aristotle had condemned. It is true that the establishing of a dictatorship involved the concentrating of executive authority in the hands of one man. But the Roman dictator was a constitutional officer, appointed by the Senate; he exercised his power according to legal conventions. He was appointed for a temporary emergency, the period of his extraordinary powers was limited, and he was expected to render an accounting when he left his office. Of the eighty-eight dictatorships that existed from the sixth to the third centuries B.C., most were for a very short period and none longer than six months.[25] The tyrant entered Roman history with the decline of the Republic in the days of Marius, Sulla, and Julius Caesar. The traditional constitutionally defined dictatorship of limited duration had not been used since the third century B.C. The power assumed by Sulla and Caesar was unlimited in duration and directed against the constitutional system rather than used for its defense in a time of crisis.

The Roman emphasis on law, which made even dictatorship into a safe emergency device, echoes in Cicero's famous definition of the true state: "The commonwealth is the people's affair; moreover a people is not every group of men brought together in any way, but a group of many men associated by consent to law and by community of interest."[26] For Cicero, the law which bound fellow-citizens into a true commonwealth was not a body of rules arbitrarily made by any particular legislature. On the contrary, he valued the laws of Rome because he thought that he saw in them the embodiment of principles which rested neither on force nor convention, but on a divinely ordered and universal rationality in which men, as rational and social beings, shared. The idea of a natural law which lay behind the laws of particular states had been present in the thought of Plato and Aristotle. But it reached a fuller development among the Stoic philosophers who succeeded them, through whom it became an important part of the Roman culture. It would be hard to find a more eloquent statement of this law of nature than that of Cicero in his *De Republica:*

There is in fact a true law—namely, right reason—which is in accordance with nature, applies to all men, and is unchangeable and eternal. By its commands this law summons men to the performance of their duties; by its prohibitions it restrains them from doing wrong. Its commands and prohibitions always influence good men, but are without effect upon the bad. To invalidate this law by human legislation is never morally right, nor is it permissible ever to restrict its operation, and to annul it wholly is impossible. Neither the Senate nor the people can absolve us from our obligation to obey this law. . . . It will not lay down one rule at Rome and another at Athens, nor will it be one rule today and another tomorrow. But there will be one law, eternal and unchangeable, binding at all times upon all peoples; and there will be, as it were, one common master and ruler of men, namely God, who is the author of this law, its interpreter, and its sponsor. The man who will not obey it will abandon his better self, and, denying the true nature of man, will thereby suffer the severest penalties. . . .[27]

The conviction that the institutions of republican Rome were the reflections of such a law added force to the bitterness with which Cicero witnessed the dissolution of that Republic and the approval which he gave to the desperate attempt of Brutus and Cassius.

The city state, which once had been "the people's affair," proved itself unable to maintain its old constitution when exposed to the temptations and responsibilities of the empire. Even before Cicero wrote, internal class struggles had upset the delicate balance of republican institutions, and imperial conquest had made the general who controlled the victorious army a dangerously irresponsible factor in the politics of Rome. The successive roles of Marius and Sulla had been symptoms of the serious illness of the Republic. Each had drawn his strength from the loyalty of an army eager for spoils. Under Marius the army had ceased to be a militia of land owners and had become a volunteer army recruited from a discontented proletariat. Sulla, who led the conservative reaction of the senatorial class, had surpassed his rival in bolstering his tyranny by massacres of his opponents. The succeeding period of factional struggles and popular unrest had demonstrated the dependence of the Roman government upon military leaders whom it could not control. By 46 B.C., civil war had eliminated most of the contenders for power, leaving Julius Caesar the undisputed victor. A brilliantly successful general, he could rely upon the loyalty of his army; and he also appeared as the champion of the popular faction against the Senate. Caesar's actions showed that he regarded the old Roman constitution as obsolete. He defied it by concentrating all important offices in himself and by having himself named dictator for life. There were suspicions that he planned to institute an hereditary monarchy. But, above all, he aroused the antagonism of the old Senatorial class by his attempt to reconstruct the Senate itself.

Although the assassination of Caesar did not in fact restore the previous constitution, Cicero's eloquent defense of the heroic deed glorified it for later generations as a model for justifiable tyrannicide. His comments, widely quoted in later centuries, became texts for those who sought to enlist the authority of classical tradition in their struggle against arbitrary rule. With obvious allusion to the assassination of Julius Caesar, Cicero wrote:

What can be a greater crime than to kill a man, especially one who is an intimate friend? But is he a criminal who has killed a tyrant, even if the tyrant was his friend? It does not seem so to the Roman people, who regard this as the finest of all glorious deeds.[28]

In another passage of the same work he spoke more generally:

For we have no fellowship with tyrants, but rather are separated from them by the widest gulf; nor is it contrary to nature to despoil, if we can, him whom it is honorable to kill. And this whole pestiferous and impious race ought to be exterminated from the community of men. For even as a limb is amputated when the lifeblood ceases to circulate in it and it becomes injurious to other parts of the body, so that fierce and savage beast in human form ought to be severed from the common body of mankind.[29]

The mild dictatorship of Caesar was followed by the benevolent absolutism of Augustus, and this in turn led quickly to the tyranny of emperors whose names have become synonymous with cruel and arbitrary rule. Cicero had seen the rise of Julius Caesar over the ruins of the Republic; the later Stoic, Seneca, saw the depths to which political degeneration could descend under the tyranny of Nero. He was willing to recommend tyrannicide as the only cure for a desperate situation resulting from tyranny: "For natures like this, exit from life is the only remedy."[30] To Seneca also was attributed the formula frequently quoted in the Middle Ages, "No offering is more acceptable to God than the blood of a tyrant."[31]

These words of Seneca revealed the reaction of a cultivated and sensitive mind to the disheartening political realities of his day. But the traditional view had also become part of the regular stock in trade not only of historians, but also of poets, orators, and professional rhetoricians. Polybius had written the Greek tradition on tyranny and tyrannicide into his *Histories.* "It would not be easy to bring a graver or more bitter charge against a man," said Polybius, than to call him a "tyrant": "for the mere word 'tyrant' involves the idea of everything that is wickedest, and includes every injustice and crime possible to mankind."[32] "The killing of a fellow-citizen is regarded as a heinous crime, deserving the severest penalties: and yet it is notorious that... he who kills a traitor or tyrant in every country receives honors and preeminence."[33] Plutarch's *Lives* dramatized the wretchedness of tyranny and the bloody fate which normally ended the tyrant's career. He referred to the killing of a tyrant as a "remarkable act of virtue," in the same class with valiant feats of arms, and praised Brutus and Timoleon as heroic defenders of liberty.[34] The father of Seneca included in his textbook of rhetorical exercises three problems based upon the familiar belief that anyone who killed a tyrant deserved a reward.[35] Juvenal expressed his sympathy for the schoolmaster who must listen to his numerous students kill cruel tyrants, each mechanically spouting the same old theme.[36]

Far more important to later thought than the persistence of the Greek tradition of tyrannicide was the doctrine, developed and transmitted by Roman jurists, that even imperial power was in some sense subject to law. The most famous statement of this principle in the *Corpus Juris Civilis* is the *Digna vox:* "It is a saying worthy of the majesty of the ruler that the prince profess himself bound by the laws; since our authority depends on the authority of law."[37] It is true that this statement, and others in this vein, were balanced by such statements as the equally famous *Quod principi placuit:* "What has pleased the prince has the force of law, since by the *lex regia* the people has transferred to him all its command and authority."[38] Roman jurists left to later centuries the solution of the dilemma presented by these two passages; but they also transmitted to the scholars of those centuries the distinction between the permanent natural law and the mutable civil law, which was to provide the means of its solution. Thus through the Roman jurists the Stoic idea of a basic law of nature made its way into medieval political thought and, in spite of differing interpretations, became and remained the most important single basis of resistance to arbitrary power.[39]

The sharp distinction between the lawful ruler who sought the common good and the tyrant who, ruling by force, sought first his own ends was, then, fundamental in both Greek and Roman political thought. The idea that in the law of nature could be found a test of legitimate rule was already well established. Aristotle's composite picture of the tyrant and Plutarch's sketches of actual tyrants were on record for later reference. And the proposition that it was permissible and honorable for an individual to slay a tyrant had acquired the sanction of a great tradition. In later periods we shall find examples of Harmodius and Brutus acclaimed together with the Old Testament examples of Ehud and Jehu; and we shall find the authority of Aristotle, Cicero, Seneca, and Plutarch called up as evidence of the rightness of tyrannicide.

From early Christian thought arose two very different attitudes toward the general problem of tyranny and obedience, and these attitudes colored the theory of many following centuries. From the beginning Christian writers assumed that the purpose of government was justice and, following Paul in the belief that government was made necessary by the depravity of man and that the ruler was God's instrument for repressing evil, insisted upon the Christian duty of obedience. Nothing could be clearer than Paul's assertion of this duty in his famous passage on political authority:

For there is no power but of God: the powers that be are ordained of God. Whosoever therefore resisteth the power resisteth the ordinance of God. . . . For rulers are not a terror to good works, but to the evil. . . . For he is a minister of God to thee for good. But if thou do that which is evil, be afraid; for he beareth not the sword in vain: for he is the minister of God, a minister to execute wrath upon him that doeth evil. Wherefore ye must needs be subject, not only for wrath, but also for conscience' sake (Romans 13: 1-5).

Similarly Peter had said:

Submit yourselves to every ordinance of man for the Lord's sake: whether it be to the king, as supreme; or unto governors, as unto them that are sent by him for the punishment of evildoers, and for the praise of them that do well (I Peter 2: 13-14).

Numerous other Biblical admonitions seemed to point in the same direction. In the primitive church this insistence upon obedience may have been necessary to counteract contempt for worldly distinctions and disdain for worldly institutions. Later it was strengthened by the alliance between church and empire, and bolstered by the Old Testament tradition of the king as the Lord's Anointed.[40]

But if the king were obviously cruel and wicked, must he still be regarded as God's agent? The Old Testament had familiarized Christians with the idea that God sent bad kings as punishment for the sins of a people,[41] and Augustine followed the Old Testament tradition when he stoutly maintained that God allotted earthly kingdoms to good and bad rulers alike according to his pleasure, which was always just. "He that gave power to Marius gave it also to Caesar; he that gave it to Augustus gave it to Nero also; he that gave Vespasian power, and Titus his son, both benevolent emperors, gave it also to that most cruel Domitian. And, not to go through the whole list, he that gave power to Constantine the Christian gave it also to Julian the Apostate...." These things were controlled by God, "and if his reasons are hidden, they are not unjust."[42] Augustine described the tyrant as "worse than a beast" but still insisted that Nero himself had "no dominion but from the providence of the great God who sometimes judges that men deserve such rulers. The word of God says plainly: 'Through me kings reign, and tyrants through me hold the earth'" (Proverbs 8: 15-16).[43] Here was the seed of the later doctrine of the divine right of kings, with its corollary of an absolute Christian duty of obedience by subjects. Although Augustine did not state the corollary, he did not deny it, and his words could lend to it the support of patristic authority.

It is true that even Augustine left an opening for later advocates of tyrannicide who were anxious to bring the views of the church Fathers into line with their doctrine. For he could scarcely ignore the Old Testament stories of divinely inspired tyrannicide. In a passage not related to the subject of obedience, he asserted that one was not guilty of sinful murder who killed another in obedience to God's direct command.[44] And Augustine, like every Christian writer, took for granted the duty of refusing to obey any command of a ruler which was directly contrary to the word of God.[45] Yet the dominant influence of Augustine's writings was in the direction of the divine right of kings and the absolute duty of obedience.

The idea was made more explicit in the writings of the last of the Latin Fathers, the sixth-century pope, Gregory the Great. Good and bad rulers alike, having their authority from God, were to be obeyed without complaint or criticism, said Gregory, for to offend a ruler was to offend God himself. "Those who murmur against the rulers set over them speak not against a human being but against him who disposes of all things by divine order."[46]

The conclusion of Augustine and Gregory the Great that God sent good kings as a blessing and bad kings as a punishment could be avoided even by those who accepted the Christian premises. In the Old Testament, Christians could find the stories of such heroes as Ehud, Jehu, and Judith, whose deeds were glorified rather than punished when they freed their people by killing tyrannical rulers.[47] And the words of Paul could be interpreted as permitting resistance to a tyrant. Thus the Greek Father, Chrysostom, writing in the fourth century, explained Paul's passage by saying that the power of the office was ordained by God, but not necessarily the ruler. One might then presumably recognize the kingship ordained by God yet refuse to accept the unjust tyranny of the king who misused the powers of his office. This, as McIlwain points out,[48] was the theory generally accepted in the Middle Ages. It was also the theory of later Protestants, such as Buchanan and Milton, who were to justify resistance to the persecutions of ungodly kings by the claim that Paul's words referred only to the authority of a just king and not to the might of the tyrant.[49] It was a theory that opened the door once more to the concept of the tyrant and reopened the whole question of obedience.

One other of the Church Fathers deserves mention, not because of the originality of his thought but because of his great influence upon later medieval writers. Isidore of Seville, writing in the seventh century, reminded his readers of the distinction made in classical times between king and tyrant. He explained that, although the ancients at first made no distinction between king and tyrant, later the name *tyrant* "came to be applied to the most wicked and unrighteous kings who desired immoderate rule and exercised the most cruel domination over the people." In language often repeated later, Isidore asserted that the name of king belonged to him who governed rightly and was lost by governing unrighteously: "Kings are so called by their ruling *(Reges a regendo vocati)*.... Therefore by doing rightly the title of king is kept, by wrongdoing it is lost."[50]

The implications of Isidore's distinction were drawn sharply by the ninth-century pope, Nicholas I, in a comment on the words of Peter cited above:

But that which you say, that you are subject to kings and princes by virtue of the saying of the Apostle (I Peter 2:13), "... whether to the king, as **supreme**," is correct. However, notice whether those kings and princes to whom you say that you are subject are truly kings and princes. Notice first whether they rule themselves well, then how they rule their subject people. . . . Notice whether they rule lawfully (*iure*). Otherwise they are rather to be considered tyrants than kings: tyrants whom we ought rather to resist and assail than to obey. . . . Therefore be subject to the king "as supreme," namely, in virtues and not in vices; but, as the Apostle says, "for God's sake" and not against God.[51]

Thus we find two distinct lines of development from the early Christian conception of the divine basis of political power as presented by Paul. One leads from Aristotle's distinction between king and tyrant to the theory of the sixteenth-century monarchomachs; the other leads from the idea of a duty of passive obedience, implicit in the remarks of Augustine, to the doctrine of the divine right of kings as expounded by James I of England.

One further aspect of patristic thought was of the greatest importance for the development of the theory of tyrannicide. The Stoic idea of natural law had stressed the equality of all men as rational beings capable of directing their lives in terms of universally valid principles of right. Christianity took over the Stoic theory and gave it added depth through its own emphasis on the value of the individual soul and the moral freedom and responsibility of men. Paul had spoken of the law "written in the hearts" of men; later writers identified this with the Stoic natural law and thus carried into Christian thought the basis for rational criticism of arbitrary authority.

II

MEDIEVAL THEORIES OF RESISTANCE

LORD ACTON, looking back over the long period of the Middle Ages, found that one of the principal achievements of medieval thought was that "the right of insurrection was not only admitted but defined, as a duty sanctioned by religion." The belief in the lawfulness of rebellion against tyrants, he remarked, came down to men like Knox and Buchanan in the sixteenth century "straight from the medieval schools."[1]

In the Middle Ages the problem of private resistance to governmental power became an important object of political thought,[2] not so much because actual tyranny drove men to search for a remedy against it as because it was a logical deduction from the main currents of medieval thought. Medieval men, with very few exceptions, regarded monarchy as the best form of government. The concentration of governing power in the hands of a single man seemed to them the only guarantee of unity and force of action, the only corrective of the decentralization of power which was involved in feudalism. But they saw the king primarily as an executive and a judge. His right to power was correlated with his functions in these capacities, and he had no rights which did not flow from the services which he was expected to render.

Though the king was regarded as absolute in his own sphere, medieval men insisted that that sphere was limited by law. The king "ought not to be subject to any man," said Bracton, "but subject to God and the law.... There is no king where will rules and not law."[3] Bracton, as a lawyer discussing the principles which defined the actual English kingship of his own thirteenth century, was thinking of the body of traditional law, supposedly immutable, which marked out the rights of private citizens and the general form of their government. At his coronation, the king swore to enforce and maintain this customary law, thus acknowledging that his power was a power under the law. For Bracton, as for others

17

who reflected the common medieval view, to say that the king was under the law meant that he must not alter or abolish it; he must not change the traditional form of government; his judgments of right must follow the rules laid down by immemorial custom; and he could not take the property of his subjects—except as a penalty for crime—without their consent.[4]

A somewhat different point of view was expressed by the scholars who through their legal or philosophic studies came under the influence of the old doctrine of natural law. When they agreed that the king was subject to natural law, they were not thinking of specific legal rules so much as of a general group of rational principles which they regarded as rooted in the nature of man and society and therefore as universally valid. Stated in very abstract terms, these principles might look to modern eyes more like a system of political ethics than a system of law; but medieval scholars regarded them as true law and in general were willing to say that if the ordinances of the king clashed with the law of nature they should not be considered to be laws, but to be rather, as Aquinas put it, acts of violence.[5] It is obvious that emphasis on ethical and rational principles rather than on the concrete rules of customary law would allow the king a greater flexibility of action than lawyers like Bracton might have approved; and one result of the natural-law approach was a tendency to set up "the common good" as the most important criterion of the legitimacy of royal actions. On the other hand, as the theory of natural law was gradually developed in the Middle Ages, natural law came to protect, as rational and useful institutions, the rights which simple men regarded as inviolable on the grounds of custom. Rights connected with self-preservation and family life, the variously defined rights implied in the vague notion of freedom, and rights of property and contract were interpreted as guaranteed by the secondary principles of natural law and thus not normally subject to the ruler's discretion. But, since reason rather than tradition was the ultimate standard, most writers allowed exceptional infringement of such rights for the sake of the common good and argued, for instance, that the king might on occasion take property from his subjects to meet a public emergency.[6]

Finally, the king was, of course, regarded as limited also by the principles of divine law set forth in the Bible and interpreted by the church; this divine law not only was expected to guide his actions but also marked off large areas of human life in which he could not interfere. Hence, medieval men thought of kingship as hedged about by law, and by both a natural and a divine order.

The source of royal power was a much discussed problem. In the early days of medieval kingship, ecclesiastical writers strongly emphasized the doctrine that the power of the king came ultimately from God; and this continued to be an unquestioned belief throughout the Middle Ages. Many medieval thinkers did not inquire further into its origin. But from the beginning power was often regarded as coming also from the people. Roman tradition, brought into medieval thought through the study of Roman law, taught that the Roman people had transferred to the emperor the authority which they had held themselves in the days of the Republic; and by the fourteenth century abstract arguments developed by such men as Marsiglio of Padua demonstrated that not merely the power of the emperor but the power of every ruler in every state must have come from the people. It is important to notice that those who maintained a theory of the popular origin of power did not mean to imply that the establishment of governments was an act of the free wills of a multitude of individuals, who might perhaps have chosen to live without a government. They regarded government as natural and as divinely planned; but they insisted that God and nature worked through the reason of man. The theory that government and the fundamental pattern of constitutional law were established by the people was destined to play an important role in the thought of the sixteenth and seventeenth centuries; but in the Middle Ages it had to compete with an alternative theory which described the power of kings as descending from God by way of the papacy.

While the theory of the organized community as the basis of royal power was developing, there developed also the view that the community might act through agents other than its king. The Electors of the Holy Roman Empire and the Estates which met in various countries to grant taxes and to give consent to promulgations of the law came to be regarded as representatives of the community, whose activities supplemented those of the king. This had not always been the case. John of Salisbury in the twelfth century and Aquinas in the thirteenth were typical of their time in regarding the king as the only "public person," the only person who could act on behalf of the community. Consequently, for thinkers in this earlier period, if there was to be any check on the king, it could only be through the private resistance of individuals or groups.

In this medieval body of thought, so thoroughly permeated by the idea of law, it is not surprising that the conception of the tyrant should play an important role. For the non-scholastic lawyers, a king might become a tyrant by interfering with the rights of his subjects or by his failure to maintain peace and justice. His offenses could be measured by the standards of customary law. Thus Bracton declared that the king, so long as he ruled justly, according to law, was to be regarded as the vicar of God, but when he defied law and justice he became the agent of the devil. He was then no longer a king, but a tyrant.[7]

In the earlier *Policraticus* of John of Salisbury, written in England in 1159, the same sharp distinction had been developed elaborately and with colorful illustrations. "Between a tyrant and a a prince there is this single difference, that the latter obeys the law and rules the people by its dictates, accounting himself as but their servant. It is by virtue of the law that he makes good his claim to the foremost and chief place in the management of the affairs of the commonwealth...."[8] The tyrant, on the other hand, brought not justice but oppression and based his rule not on law but on force.[9] The famous maxim of the Roman civil law, "What has pleased the prince has the force of law," was made compatible with the idea of a fundamental law above the king by the argument that the true king would voluntarily follow the law and insure justice. When he ceased to follow the fundamental law he was no longer a king but a tyrant and his word had not the force of law.[10] "The prince fights for the laws and the liberty of his people; the tyrant thinks nothing done unless he brings the laws to nought and reduces the people to slavery." Hence, while the king was "a kind of likeness of divinity," the tyrant was "the likeness of the devil."[11]

It was a standard of this sort that was popularly applied in condemning the tyranny of William Rufus, who was probably killed by the arrow of one of his subjects. And it was King John's violations of customary rights that brought the victorious barons before him in 1215 with their famous demand for a guarantee against further violations. Magna Carta shows how these ideas and ideals could work in practice.

Other standards were particularly emphasized by the Church. The king who violated divine law—for example, by attempting to control the appointment of prelates or by trying to submit the clergy to the jurisdiction of royal courts—could be declared by the pope unfit to rule. The encouragement of heresy or other major sins and in general the flaunting of the precepts of the Bible were sometimes cited by medieval popes as evidence that the offender was no true king. And, of course, political theory in general regarded the violation of divine law as the mark of a tyrant.

But the typical definition of the tyrant among political theorists was in terms of the Greek concept of the "common good." Medieval scholars followed Aristotle faithfully in distinguishing the king from the tyrant by explaining that the king always pursued the common good, while the tyrant neglected and subverted the common good to pursue his private interest. Thus Thomas Aquinas said that tyranny, the worst of all forms of government, was unjust because it was directed not towards the common good, but towards the private good of the ruler.[12] William of Occam explained that tyranny, which was the "transgression" and "corruption" of royal government, was "the first and worst kind of vitiated polity, because the tyrant does not intend the good of his subjects unless incidentally, but principally intends his own good, whether his own good be also the good of others, or their ill-fortune...."[13]

Occam suggested a more specific application of the general principle when he said that "the king can not use his subjects and their goods in whatever way pleases him for his own good; and therefore they are not his slaves but enjoy natural liberty, because it belongs to natural liberty that no one can use free men for the utility of the user; but it is not contrary to natural liberty that someone should reasonably use free men for the common good, since one is bound to prefer the common good to his own private good."[14] An exceptionally systematic explanation of the common good which the king was to foster was developed by Aquinas on the basis of his conception of the ends of man.[15] He said, in short, that with man as the possessor of an immortal soul the state was only indirectly concerned through its obligation to provide the conditions in which religion could flourish; but that the ruler was directly responsible for governing human activities in such a way that an adequate level of material well-being, security from external enemies and local evil-doers, and opportunities for a rational and virtuous life should be available to the citizens.[16]

Most scholars did not go to the trouble of trying to describe the "common good." The norms of the common good were regarded as part of the natural law which was universal in its application and discoverable by human reason. All reasoning men should therefore be able to reach a workable agreement on the meaning of the common good.

Detailed lists of the characteristics of tyranny appeared in the numerous descriptions of the tyrant, which invariably started, and usually ended, with Aristotle's famous description. Thus, in the latter part of the thirteenth century, Aegidius Romanus summarized "the wiles of the tyrant as described by the Philosopher" in ten points: he kills the excellent and noble, including sometimes his own kinsmen; he destroys the wise and keeps his subjects ignorant; he crushes education and study; he forbids social meetings; he scatters spies among the citizens; he tries to break up friendships and social organizations; he tries to impoverish his subjects; he stirs up wars; he relies on foreign guards for his protection; he stirs up dissension and factional strife.[17] Aristotle had said that in general the wiles of the tyrant were directed by three aims; Aegidius named four general purposes: that the subjects should be kept ignorant, that they should be mean-spirited, that they should not trust one another, and that they should be impoverished and afflicted.[18]

The lawyers also accepted and passed on to the future the distinction between king and tyrant. The fourteenth-century civilist, Lucas de Penna, although he went further than many civilists in developing the theory of the absolutism of the ruler, nevertheless followed John of Salisbury in distinguishing between the ruler who governed by law and thus provided liberty and security for subjects, and the tyrant who oppressed his subjects by arbitrary violence.[19] The very influential lawyer, Bartolus, in his treatise, *The Tyrant,* written about the middle of the fourteenth century, simply incorporated Aegidius' description of the tyrant[20] but added a new interpretation. He said that, while all the types of action listed were characteristic of the tyrant, most of the acts, taken separately, might be justified by a particular situation which a ruler faced. Some acts, however, were *ipso facto* signs of tyranny in *all* cases. "All of the above, then, are indications whereby a tyranny can be proved, and especially these two: the promoting of divisions in the community, and the impoverishment of citizens and abusing them in their persons or in their property."[21] It is probably significant that Bartolus selected from Aristotle's description the two characteristics of the tyrant that would have had most meaning in the medieval setting. His practical legal mind thus reworked Aristotle's description of how the tyrant retained his power into an objective test for tyranny.[22]

What could be done about the tyrant? At least five different answers appeared in medieval practice and theory. In connection with each one of these answers it should be remembered that every Christian could confidently expect that even if the tyrant should escape all earthly accountability and punishment, there awaited him still the just punishment of God.

The position stated earlier by Gregory the Great could lead to the simple conclusion that the most wicked and perverse kings must be obeyed since their power came from God. The English reformer, John Wyclif, was one of those who drew this conclusion. Writing in the last quarter of the fourteenth century, he insisted that, although subjects must obey God rather than man in case a ruler's commands were contrary to God's word, they must otherwise obey the most perverse tyrant, suffering in patience and submission whatever ills the tyrant's misrule might inflict upon them. There is in Wyclif's writings the strongest emphasis upon a divinely imposed duty of obedience in everything that affects the worldly welfare of subjects.[23] A similar practical conclusion was drawn by some of the civilists from the principle that, since it was the function of the ruler to interpret natural law, his will must be presumed to be just; this position was most fully stated by the fifteenth-century humanist Aeneas Sylvius, later Pius II.[24] But such a wholesale scrapping of the broad protection to be found in the theory of natural law was by no means typical of medieval thought.

Other answers defended some sort of disobedience or resistance rather than passive submission. Aquinas and Occam expressed a widely accepted view when they asserted the right of disobedience to commands contrary to the fundamental law or outside the scope of the ruler's legitimate authority; and for certain types of commands Aquinas found disobedience to be not simply a right but a duty.[25] Not only was it generally agreed that certain commands might be disobeyed; strong currents of medieval thought supported the view that the king who misused his power might be forcefully resisted.

Feudal revolt against the king could be justified in the same manner as the revolt of any vassal against a lord could be justified by the lord's failure to perform his contractual obligations.[26] The idea of a contractual relationship between king and subjects, implicit in this feudal conception of kingship and its limits and deriving also from the prefeudal theory of Germanic kingships, was sometimes made explicit. The first to state clearly the idea of a contract was Manegold of Lautenbach, a pro-papal writer who discussed the problem of obedience and resistance in the course of the investiture dispute in the eleventh century. Manegold's statement is simple and direct:

For the people does not exalt him above themselves in order that it may grant him an opportunity of exercising tyranny against them, but that he may defend them from the tyranny and unrighteousness of others. Yet when he . . . has begun to foster evil against them, to destroy the good, and himself most cruelly to exercise against his subjects the tyranny which he ought to repel, is it not clear that . . . the people stand free of his lordship and subjection, when the contract for whose sake he was appointed he has been the first to break? . . . For, to draw an example from baser things, if a man should entrust his pigs to be pastured to someone for a fitting wage, and afterwards learned that the latter was not pasturing them, but was stealing, slaughtering, and losing them, would he not remove him with reproaches from the care of the pigs . . . ?[27]

The idea that royal authority rested on a contract between king and people was not fully developed in medieval thought; but the idea that the legitimacy of royal authority depended on the way in which it was used was frequently expressed as a justification of disobedience and revolt.

The right of informal resistance against the king's encroachments upon private rights could also be argued, as it was frequently to be argued in the seventeenth century, from the acknowledged right of an individual, frequently asserted as a principle of natural law, to "repel force with force."[28] The maxim was so well established that in the course of the conciliar debate Gerson could use it against the pope: ". . . . It would be right for any individual in case of violence attempted by the true pope against his chastity or life to repel force with force, instigated by blameless self-defense, and thus he would have a lawful right to lay violent hands upon the pope, or throw him into the sea. Why should it not likewise be lawful for the whole Church to do the same, in her own defense and in the prudent repression of attempted violence?"[29]

There was then nothing remarkable in Aquinas' conclusion that revolt against tyrannic rule was not to be considered sedition. "If the subjects have a government," he said, "which is not just but usurped, or which commands unjust things, they have no obligation of obedience, unless perhaps incidentally, for the sake of avoiding scandal or danger." Sedition was a mortal sin, but resistance to a tyrant was not sedition; it was rather the tyrant who was guilty of sedition.[30] This was entirely in the tradition of his time.

Such tolerance of private disobedience and resistance as we have described might begin to look to modern eyes like utter anarchy. It appears much less anarchic when we remember that this tolerance grew up in a period in which men saw no defense except private action against the anarchy of tyranny, and in a period in which the right to such private action was invariably derived from a law of which "the precepts were definite and uniform and were as accessible to private persons as to officials."[31]

From private resistance to tyrannicide is a long step, but the distance between the two is not so great as the distance between constitutional checks and private resistance. Consequently, we should expect to find that the idea of tyrannicide would be less shocking to medieval men than to moderns. And such indeed was the case.

John of Salisbury insisted that the prince was to be "loved, worshipped, and cherished"; but he was willing to advocate not only private resistance but the slaying of the tyrant.[32] Although he wrote before the recovery of Aristotle and before the systematic development of natural-law theory, John's writings reflect the impact upon early feudal conceptions of his own assimilation of the classical tradition. He cited as authority for his defense of tyrannicide the examples recorded in the Old Testament and in Roman history. He described the careers of the emperors Caligula and Nero and concluded that "it has always been an honorable thing to slay" such tyrants "if they can be curbed in no other way."[33] If a ruler's own moderation would not restrain him, then he must be forcibly restrained or removed. And if the nation as a whole could not overthrow the tyrant because, as we have seen above, the nation had no political agent other than the king, then the tyrant must be removed and law and justice restored through the act of an individual.

Two centuries later, Lucas de Penna, repeating the definition of tyranny in the same general terms as those used by John, also followed John to his conclusion. Tyrannicide, Lucas argued, was justified under human and divine law. Removal of the tyrant was justified as the removal of a public enemy whose presence endangered the very existence of society.[34]

John of Salisbury made two reservations which might seem curious after what he had already conceded, but which were explicable in terms of his own religious background. He warned that no one who was bound to the tyrant by an oath should undertake to kill him, and that poison was not a permissible weapon even against a tyrant.[35] Sometimes John yielded to the views that advocated passive resistance so far as to acknowledge that, God being the final punisher of tyrants, the tyrant should ordinarily be suffered until he was removed by God. "And surely the method of destroying tyrants which is most useful and safest is for those who are oppressed to take refuge humbly in the protection of God's mercy, and lifting up undefiled hands to the Lord, to pray devoutly that the scourge wherewith they are afflicted may be turned aside from them."[36] But the emphasis of his argument was certainly all in the opposite direction. And tyrannicide was found to be entirely compatible with the belief that God would deal with tyrants in his own time and his own way. For "wickedness is always punished by the Lord; but sometimes it is His own, and at others it is a human hand, which He employs as a weapon. . . ."[37] Thus the judgment of God might be executed through the hand of one who slew the tyrant.

John's discussion of tyranny was more than an academic exercise. He had seen a contemporary tyrant in action, and he devoted one chapter of his treatise to a description of conditions under the reign of Stephen, when "all men were provoked to all things, and the only measure of right was force." Of Stephen's son, Eustace, John remarked that when he quitted this mortal life "it was the best deed he ever did."[38]

A far more systematic discussion of the problem of tyrannicide was given by Aquinas. He distinguished two types of tyranny: that arising from the lack of proper title to authority, and that arising from abuse of power properly acquired. This was the first clear-cut statement of a distinction which remained of the utmost importance.[39] The rule of the usurper might be legitimized by the consent of the subjects, but, in default of such legitimation, "when there is an opportunity any one may resist such dominion." Referring to Cicero's praise of tyrannicide in the *De Officiis,* Aquinas gave his approval to the private killing of the usurper, if no other means to remove him were found. The significant section reads as follows:

. . . It should be said that Tullius is speaking of that case in which someone is seizing dominion for himself by violence, the subjects being unwilling or even coerced to consent, and when there is no recourse to a superior through whom a judgment might be made concerning the invader. For in that case he who kills the tyrant for the liberation of his country is praised and receives a reward.[40]

But Aquinas, in a later work,[41] denied the right of any individual to relieve a people of tyrannic oppression by killing a tyrant who had a rightful title. His arguments, although documented with Biblical illustrations, were not based primarily on authority, but on considerations of expedience or utility. To give support to tyrannicide was too risky. "And indeed, if the tyranny is not excessive, it would be more expedient to endure the tyranny for a time, rather than bring about many dangers graver than the tyranny itself by acting against the tyrant." The move against the tyrant might fail, and the tyrant, provoked, would become more cruel. The overthrow of authority might lead to consequent serious dissension and faction among the people. The man responsible for expelling the tyrant might himself become a tyrant, more ruthless on account of his knowledge that tyrants could be overthrown. Finally, if tyrannicide were justified, good kings would be likely to be slain more often than tyrants, for the rule of good kings was hard on evil-doers and evil men were more likely than good men to resort to such a desperate measure as tyrannicide. To allow private judgment to determine whether a ruler should be slain was thus dangerous to society.

Aquinas therefore asserted that "action against a tyrant should not be taken by the private presumption of individuals but rather by public authority." If a people had the right to provide itself with a king, it had the right also to depose or restrain him if he became a tyrant; if some superior had appointed the king, the people should appeal to him for a remedy. But Aquinas' examples of such situations were all taken from ancient times; the latter condition was by no means normal in the Middle Ages; the former, Aquinas apparently regarded as a circumstance which occurred in certain cases but not as a basic presumption of all legitimate government. Aquinas' typical monarch, though subject to natural law, was "absolute" in the sense that he had no human superior to check him.[42] "If no human aid at all can be obtained against the tyrant," he concluded, "recourse must be had to God ... for it is in his power to turn the cruel heart of the tyrant to mercy."

The lawyer Bartolus followed Aquinas in the distinction between the tyrant by defect of title *(ex defectu tituli)* and the tyrant on the ground of performance *(ex parte exercitii),* and cited Aquinas' conclusion that to resist a tyrant was not sedition.[43] The Italian humanist, Coluccio Salutati, proceeded like Aquinas from the distinction to a discussion of whether it was lawful to kill a tyrant. Salutati had no doubt that the usurper might be killed by a private individual. He produced an interesting array of authorities.

... Who will deny that the people as a whole, ... nay, even a single citizen may lawfully resist anyone who attacks the liberty of the people or usurps the government? For if, as the greatest of rulers, the Emperors Diocletian and Maximilian ... decreed, it is right for a lawful possessor, in defense of property to which he has a faultless title, to repel force by force ... and if, as Ulpian, the ablest of jurists, says, one may forcibly resist an armed assailant; and if, according to Cassius, it is a right of nature to repel force with force, who can deny that any person whosoever may lawfully resist one who usurps the government of a city, a province, or a kingdom? ... Shall we not have the right to prevent by force, even to the point of death, one who tries to seize the rule of a city? ... Most unfair would the laws be—or rather no laws at all, if that which is permitted to private persons in case of danger or abuse were forbidden for the preservation of the liberty or life of the community.[44]

Salutati cited from Roman history illustrations of the private killing of even those suspected of aspirations to become tyrants.

But Salutati specifically denied the proposition that a ruler with a lawful title who had become a tyrant by abuse of power might be killed by a private individual. Such a ruler ought to be deposed by his overlord, or, in a community without an overlord, the community itself might banish the tyrant or put him to death. But as for private action:

Let no one, therefore, take his soul in his own hand or make a reason out of his own will and so rise up against his lord, even though the lord be acting as a tyrant! This may be done only with the approval of the overlord or of the people, not through the impulse of an individual.[45]

Of the precedents which John of Salisbury had cited, Salutati said simply, "His illustrations prove, not that the murder of a tyrant is right, but that it is frequent."[46]

After the period of Aquinas, by the fourteenth century, the doctrine of the right of a people to refuse obedience to the tyrannical ruler and the right to depose the tyrant had become a commonplace belief. Recognition that a ruler might lose his right to his office by abuse of power became so completely accepted that the conventional arguments against the tyrant could be borrowed for use against an unsatisfactory pope. But the question of tyrannicide did not become a lively and practical issue until three centuries after Aquinas.

On one important occasion during this interval the question did enter practical politics in France and gave rise to a long-drawn-out dispute. In 1407 the Duke of Orleans, brother of Charles VI of France, was assassinated by the order of his rival, the Duke of Burgundy. Jean Petit of the University of Paris, a protégé of the Duke of Burgundy but apparently neither an important nor a scrupulous scholar, defended the Duke of Burgundy before the King's councillors. Jean Petit defended the thesis that "it is lawful for any subject, without any order or command, according to moral, divine, and natural law, to kill or cause to be killed a traitor and disloyal tyrant. It is not only lawful, but honorable and meritorious, especially when he is in such great power that justice can not well be done by the sovereign."[47] In support of his thesis he cited a long and strangely assorted list of authorities, including Aristotle, Cicero, John of Salisbury, Thomas Aquinas, the Civil Law, Boccaccio, and the Scriptures. Jean Petit presented a poor case. His argument, built upon a *mélange* of authorities rather than upon logical analysis of principles, was marked by flagrant misuse of the authorities to whom he appealed and by strained use of parallels.[48] Furthermore, he tried to apply the doctrine of legitimate tyrannicide to one who could scarcely have been a tyrant, since he was not even a ruler.

Jean Petit died in 1411, but the issue raised by his attempt to justify political assassination survived. Two years later, Gerson, Chancellor of the University of Paris, speaking in the name of the University, denounced the errors of Jean Petit's doctrine. Later he secured denunciation of Jean Petit's position by a Council of the Faith held at Paris in 1414. He then attempted to secure a clear-cut condemnation of tyrannicide by the Council of Constance. The Council, avoiding reference to the particular statement of Jean Petit, and incidentally avoiding trouble with the Burgundians, condemned as heresy a statement justifying tyrannicide, drafted in the broader form in which Gerson had presented the doctrine for condemnation earlier.[49]

Gerson himself, in a sermon before the king of France in 1405, had confronted the king with the tradition of tyrannicide, referring to tyranny as the poison of political life, defending expulsion as an extreme remedy for tyranny, and alluding to the ancient maxim that a tyrant rarely died a natural death. "There is scarcely anyone so weak that, if he wished to expose his life to peril to kill the tyrant, he would not find a way of killing and restoring peace." To determine when an unbearable state of tyranny had come into existence, Gerson, like Mariana later, urged that "wise philosophers, expert jurists, legists, theologians, men of good life, of good natural prudence, and of great experience should be consulted and confidence should be placed in them."[50]

Most of Gerson's later argument was directed against Jean Petit's perverted notions of a tyrant; therefore his emphasis was upon the indefensibility of private assassination when due process of law was possible. However, his discussion did involve an analysis of the general tradition of tyrannicide. Jean Petit's proposition could be called true, he said, only under the following conditions: if tyranny existed notoriously as measured by law or undeniable fact, if there was no possibility of effective action by a superior or through some other pressure or influence, if it was improbable that the removal of the tyrant would lead to a worse situation, if the killing was done with pure intentions—i.e., not out of vengeance, hatred, or ambition, but for the defense of the divine and civil law and in the interest of the common good.[51] Even if in a particular case the above conditions should all be fulfilled, however, Gerson cited the doctrine of Aquinas and others that such a tyrant "ought rather to be left to the judgment of God than killed by private authority or by sedition. . . . It is clear, moreover, that in this matter Catholic doctors are more to be trusted than heathen philosophers."[52]

The episode of Jean Petit loses much of the historical importance that it might otherwise have had because of the fact that from beginning to end the principles involved in the dispute were so clearly subordinated to the exigencies of a highly complicated political situation. But the reasoning of Gerson illustrates the hold that the idea of tyrannicide had acquired upon the minds of thoughtful men. While opposing a perverted use of the doctrine, and while issuing a warning against it, he must still acknowledge that under certain conditions the doctrine might be defensible.

The dominant type of restraint and resistance that men were coming to rely upon to tame arbitrary rule during the fourteenth and fifteenth centuries was not individual resistance but institutional and constitutional resistance. One type of such institutional check was that claimed and occasionally exercised by the papacy. As the final interpreter and protector of the divine law, a determined pope might, as numerous popes did, declare a ruler incompetent, because of his violations of divine law, to retain his rule. Witness the following statement in defense of the excommunication of the emperor, Henry V: "Behold, kings who have done badly, who have been useless, who have made betrayals, who have perpetrated adulteries or perjuries, are to be condemned, are to be excommunicated, are to be disciplined. For Roman pontiffs have as their special privilege to correct the wicked, to confirm the righteous, to perfect the imperfect, and to prohibit the illicit."[53] The role of the pope in these early disputes, as some theorists explained it, was simply to discover and proclaim a situation which *ipso facto* dissolved the allegiance of the people to their ruler. Manegold of Lautenbach explained that by dissolving the people's oath to the emperor, Henry IV, "which was certainly and manifestly, to all faithful possessed of a rational mind, null and void," the Church fulfilled its office; "it did that which was apostolic, when it annulled that which it knew to be inherently dissolved."[54] The condemnation of Frederick II by Innocent IV (1245) proclaimed that the king "on account of his iniquities had been deposed by God"; Innocent then proceeded to absolve Frederick's subjects from their obligation of loyalty and forbade obedience or aid to the king.[55] Aquinas and others had suggested that when a superior authority existed the tyrant might be removed by that superior. As the papal claim developed in the later Middle Ages it took the form of asserting a general superiority over temporal rulers. Papal supporters developed the doctrine of a special papal *plenitudo potestatis*—a kind of universal sovereignty. By the beginning of the fourteenth century, canonists were asserting that while secular and spiritual powers existed separately, the authority of the pope, Peter's successor as head of the Church, was directly from God, and for the administration of his office none but God could judge the pope; but secular power, being of a lower order, was subject to the control of the spiritual power.[56] But this was an interpretation which did not survive; by the middle of the fifteenth century pro-papal writers were returning to the older theory by which the pope had only indirect authority over the king, and could act against him only by virtue of his responsibility for the spiritual welfare of men.

The institutional check that was destined to become important for the future was not deposition by the pope, but the check of the political community itself, acting through agencies that were beginning to share in the authority previously monopolized by the king. The fourteenth century was one of early parliamentary experimentation, beginning in England with the struggle of Parliament against Edward II and ending with the deposition of Richard II, and beginning in France with the first meeting of the Estates General in 1302, followed in the middle of the century by the revolt of the Estates led by Etienne Marcel.

This development was not without its own theory. Even in Bracton's commentary there had occurred a passage asserting the right of the king's council to restrain a king who did not restrain himself: "Thus if the king should be without a bridle, that is, without the law," his *curia,* that is, the earls and barons, "ought to put a bridle on him." The authenticity of this passage has been challenged. But if Bracton did not write it, it was added to the original soon after Bracton. There is a similar passage in another English commentary, *Fleta,* which followed Bracton closely.[57]

By the time that Occam wrote, the conception of the political community had developed to the point where Occam could speak of the right of a kingdom to depose its king. "The king is superior to the whole kingdom," he said, "and yet on occasion he is inferior to the kingdom, since in case of necessity the kingdom can depose the king and lock him up in a castle, for this is derived from the law of nature, just as from the law of nature is derived the principle that it is permitted to repel force with force."[58] Similarly, he said, the successors to the authority of the Roman people might depose a tyrannical emperor.[59] Gerson was of the opinion that it was the right of the whole community to correct and depose princes, and that this right could be withdrawn by no law.[60]

Marsiglio of Padua, in the *Defensor Pacis* (1324), went further than his contemporaries: he not only made a clear statement of the ruler's responsibility to the community but also suggested the necessity for machinery to make that responsibility effective. It is true that modern democracy was far from Marsiglio's thought.[61] But he did express clearly the idea that the authority of the ruler was based upon a law which was derived from the people and expressed by the "dominant part" on behalf of the people. And lest the ruler "become despotic, and the life of the citizens servile and inadequate," the corporate community must have authority to correct or punish the ruler, and the punishment might extend even to removing the ruler from office. The corporate community might discipline the ruler directly, or it might authorize a person or persons to act as its agent.[62] Here, then, we have a conception of monarchy which includes the right of an independent agency of the people to check and judge the king himself when under extraordinary conditions this becomes necessary. We have moved far beyond that more primitive stage of political thought in which it was impossible to conceive the community's acting through any agent except its ruler.

In summarizing the medieval tradition, it should be said that the doctrine of tyrannicide was not a dominant theme in medieval political thought, but it was thoroughly consistent with the main tendencies of medieval theory. Thoughtful medieval writers anticipated and explored almost every important element of the later theory of tyrannicide. It was not that the fact of tyranny directed men's minds to desperate remedies, but that tyranny was so incongruous with medieval thought that direct and simple remedies seemed the natural response to unnatural tyranny. The king was the unifying center of a highly decentralized society, but he held his office and authority for a purpose, and by neglect of that purpose forfeited his authority. The king was the protector of the common good and was necessarily bound by the principles of the law of nature which defined the common good. Since the common good was not what men willed as their good, but rather what men's reason acknowledged as good, the standard for proper kingship could be thought of as an objective standard. Similarly, when the lawyer thought of the restraint of divine and natural law, the standard was still an objective standard existing outside the arbitrary judgment of individuals. Hence the resister or the slayer of the law-defying tyrant could be said to act not for the protection of his own private values but for the protection of values common to the whole community. The medieval case for tyrannicide was primarily a deduction from the deep-rooted medieval belief in lawfulness.

The medieval theory of tyrannicide was, in the second place, a product of the early medieval constitutional system. Because of the lack of effective institutionalized checks upon the power of the ruler, emergency private action had to take the place of regularized public action. Marsiglio was looking toward the future when he described constitutional machinery for making effective the responsibility of the ruler to the community. It was only when theory had come to appreciate the importance of practical constitutional restraints that there could appear a third alternative to the claim that the king must be obeyed were he good or bad, and the claim that the tyrant, having forfeited the right to rule, might be driven from his throne and slain by individual action.

Increasingly important in the background of medieval political thought was the belief that, although authority came ultimately from God, the community or the people was the more immediate source of authority. The idea of the popular origin of authority was a vague idea at best and perhaps of little immediate practical significance. But by the sixteenth and seventeenth centuries it had come to be a central part of the argument used by some to support resistance, by others to support tyrannicide.

To the classical distinction between king and tyrant, medieval writers added the distinction between the tyrant by defect of title and the ruler who became a tyrant by his deeds. This became a commonplace distinction in later discussions of tyranny. Nobody denied that a private person might take the life of the tyrant without title; the important debate after Aquinas was over the right of a private person to take the life of one who became a tyrant by abuse of power. In his argument against tyrannicide in such a case, Aquinas had marshalled the common-sense arguments against tyrannicide in a manner that suggests to a remarkable degree some of the problems of contemporary dictatorship.

Tyrannicide as a practical political issue became important in the early modern rather than the medieval centuries. But the ideas that both inspired and supported deeds in the sixteenth and seventeenth centuries had been nurtured and sharpened by some of the keenest minds of the twelfth through the fifteenth centuries.

III TYRANNY AND TYRANNICIDE
IN RENAISSANCE ITALY

So LONG as medieval decentralization and traditional restraints survived in northern Europe, actual tyranny usually remained outside the direct experience of those scholars who discussed tyranny and tyrannicide. There were exceptions, of course. Although John of Salisbury's account of tyrants was loaded down with classical and Biblical references, he did not neglect to point to the parallel between these and the notorious tyrant of his own land and his own day. But John was exceptional. Most writers, including Aquinas, whose experience was with the Kingdom of Naples and the French monarchy of Saint Louis, relied upon examples drawn from classical history and the Bible. But in fourteenth- and fifteenth-century Italy, tyranny had become something more than an academic question for diligent and conscientious scholars. There the early development of commercial city states and the internal social conflict and intermunicipal rivalry which followed set the stage for a wave of tyrants not unlike that wave which many centuries earlier had engulfed the Greek city states. Nowhere in Europe could the nature of tyranny have been more vividly and frequently illustrated than in the growing and restless Italian city states in the fourteenth and fifteenth centuries. While much of Europe moved towards national unity and an early type of constitutionalism, conditions in northern Italy supported disunity and local despotisms. The later forces which elsewhere led towards national consolidation under increasingly strong monarchies were frustrated in Italy by the early development of the independent commercial city states, by foreign intervention, and by the policy of the papacy. The result in Italy was limited and local consolidation and more intense rivalry among the larger Italian states.

The model of the worst type of Italian tyrant was set as early as the thirteenth century in the person of Ezzelino da Romana, despot of Verona and Padua, a contemporary of Thomas Aquinas and a protégé of the emperor, Frederick II. His ruthless brutality was to make him the legendary tyrant of Italian tradition. He scattered spies among his subjects, held numerous hostages from powerful families, exacted confessions from his prisoners by torture, and protected his position by wholesale slaughters of his opponents. In the city of Padua alone he kept eight prisons full, "notwithstanding the incessant toil of the executioners to empty them."[1] None of his successors, says Burckhardt, not even Cesare Borgia, rivaled his fierce cruelty.[2]

The methods of Ezzelino foreshadowed things to come. In Milan, the house of Visconti distinguished itself in the fourteenth and fifteenth centuries by the treachery and brutality of the tyrants which it produced. Gian Galeazzo Visconti seized control in Milan by tricking his boar-hunting uncle into his power, and for a quarter of a century—while he was building the vast cathedral that has long made Milan famous—he diligently extended his domain and his influence by every type of violence and intrigue. "He seemed to acknowledge himself the enemy of the whole world." No prince kept so many soldiers to guard him, and none took so many elaborate precautions to protect himself against plots, unless it were his son, Filippo Maria, who ruled his domain from the tight seclusion of a citadel as closely guarded as a modern Berchtesgaden, and seldom set foot in the city.[3] Another son of Gian Galeazzo, the dissolute Gian Maria, amused himself by watching his trained hounds tear apart condemned criminals, who were turned over to the prince for the purpose; he denounced and secured the condemnation of his own accomplices in crime to keep up the supply of victims.[4] More familiar to most readers is the murdering career of Cesare Borgia, who sought to found an extensive domain on the basis of his father's possession of the papacy, and whom Machiavelli extolled as "an example to be imitated by all who by fortune and with the arms of others have risen to power."[5] Machiavelli's little handbook for the prince was a synthetic record of the methods of the more successful tyrants of the previous two centuries.

Insane brutality was not a necessary ingredient of the despot's character, but utter ruthlessness and complete repudiation of ethical restraints undoubtedly were. Nor was incompetence necessarily characteristic. Had there been railroads in Renaissance Italy, trains would no doubt have run on time in Milan during the long period of the Visconti and the Sforzas. Nearly all hid their cruelty beneath a lavish patronage of literature and the fine arts. Some would no doubt be classified as "benevolent" as well as capable tyrants. And some by their brilliance and able leadership won the admiration and even the willing loyalty of their subjects. Such a one was the condottiere Francesco Sforza, who made himself master of Milan.

The nineteenth-century liberal historian Sismondi remarked that the spread of tyranny was accompanied by a general moral degeneration. What he said of the early tyrannies of Lombardy and Romagna was no less true of the later tyrannies:

Spies watched and denounced every expression of generous feeling; they insinuated themselves into families to betray them; they abused the sacred ties of kindred, home, and neighborhood, to convert them into snares; they made all feel that the wisdom of the subject consisted in distrusting every one, and not meddling in the affairs of another. Assassination and poisoning were common means of government. Every Italian tyrant was stained with the blood of his kindred; paid murderers despatched the objects of his suspicions; he outraged public virtue, and could maintain order only by fear. Death itself at length failing to inspire terror, he combined with capital punishment protracted tortures, the exhibition of which only rendered men more hardened and fierce. . . . In the fourteenth century it was still worse. . . . Men rose to be princes by crime: their perfidy towards their neighbors, and their domestic treachery, marked the commencement and duration of every reign. Tyrants were so numerous, so constantly under the observation of every citizen, that their example was always operating to corrupt the people.[6]

Contemporary historians would agree that tyranny and the tolerance of tyranny reflected not merely the political confusion that arose from the class struggles and intercity rivalries of overgrown city states, but also the seamy side of that secular atmosphere and hyperdeveloped individualism that was the basis of Renaissance culture. A long period of innumerable tyrants did not call forth a vigorous reassertion of the right of tyrannicide because the common moral standards and accepted moral restraints on which the classical and medieval justifications of tyrannicide could be based were being dissipated in the secular, amoral atmosphere of the Italian Renaissance.

There were, however, a number of interesting exceptions. Galeazzo Maria Sforza, a son of the great Francesco, was noted for his senseless cruelty and vicious debauchery. "There was no crime of which that false and ferocious man was not believed to be capable."[7] On St. Stephen's Day in 1476, Galeazzo was stabbed to death by three young Milanese nobles as he was about to enter a church. The three had been aroused by their humanist instructor, Cola de' Montani, who constantly reminded them of the greatness of the ancient republics and the honor paid to those who delivered them from tyranny. They had rehearsed the assault for some time and had called upon their patron saint for help. But their expectation that when the tyrant had been slain the people would rise to reclaim their liberty was sadly disappointed. Two of the conspirators were killed on the spot by the duke's guards. The third, Olgiati, maintained throughout the most brutal tortures that his deed had been a noble one. "Far from repenting, if I had to come ten times to life in order ten times to die by these same torments, I should not hesitate to dedicate my blood and all my powers to an object so sublime." About to be mutilated, he exclaimed, "My death is untimely, my fame eternal; the memory of my deed will endure forever."[8] Machiavelli relates the story in some detail, and draws from it the twofold moral that princes must secure their own safety by winning the respect of their subjects, and that it is vain to expect the multitude to rise against the tyrant, even when discontented.[9]

The assassination of Alessandro de' Medici (whom the Pope had made master of the Florentine Republic) by his relative Lorenzino de' Medici in 1537), is particularly interesting because of the direct appeal to the tradition of tyrannicide in defense of the act. In an apology supposedly written by Lorenzino it was held that Alessandro had been a vicious tyrant whose excesses during the six years of his authority had surpassed those of Nero, of Caligula, and of Phalaris. He was even accused of poisoning his own mother. The apology then vindicated Lorenzino from any motive other than his desire to free his country from intolerable slavery, and lamented the inability of his countrymen to seize the opportunity and re-establish republican government.[10] Lorenzino, although he was himself a thoroughly dissolute character, was hailed by the Florentine exiles as another Brutus.

It was from Brutus and the classical tradition that the young patriot, Pietro Paolo Boscoli, also drew his inspiration for an abortive plot against the Medici in 1513. While awaiting execution, Boscoli is supposed to have exclaimed to his friend, Luca della Robbia, "Oh, Luca, pray get Brutus out of my head, so that I may make this step entirely as beseems a good Christian."[11] His confessor, who later acknowledged to della Robbia that Aquinas had distinguished between the killing of a usurper and the killing of a tyrant with a legitimate title, apparently chose not to confuse the distinction between pagan and Christian morality by informing Boscoli fully of Aquinas' position on the question.[12]

It seems evident in the few examples of tyrannicide, planned or executed, that it was the classical tradition and the new respect for classical heroes that supported the resolution to destroy the tyrant in the vain hope that tyranny would die with him. One of the first of the classical scholars and enthusiasts, Boccaccio, had declared, "Shall I call the tyrant king or prince, and obey him loyally as my lord? No, for he is the enemy of the commonwealth. Against him I may use arms, conspiracies, spies, ambushes, and fraud; to do so is a sacred and necessary work. There is no more acceptable sacrifice than the blood of a tyrant."[13]

In Florence political morality was not utterly crushed under despotism; the Florentines retained enough spirit to resist the benevolent despotism of the Medici when it fell into incompetent hands. And in Florence the idea of tyrannicide retained wider popularity than elsewhere. After the Medici fled the city in 1494, the statue of Judith and Holofernes was placed before the palace with the inscription, "The citizens have erected this example of the salvation of the republic." The Florentine historian, Guicciardini, perpetuated the classical dictum in these words: "Very few indeed have those been, whose motive for tyrannicide was a pure love of their country's liberty; and these deserve the highest praise."[14] Even Machiavelli repeated the classical judgment against the tyrant. In his *Discourses* he devoted a chapter to the proposition, "Those who set up a tyranny are no less worthy of blame than are the founders of a republic or a kingdom worthy of praise."[15] He observed that men who might have won immortal fame by founding a republic or a kingdom, too often, "either wilfully or ignorantly," "turn their thoughts to tyranny, and fail to see what fame, what glory, tranquillity conjoined with peace of mind, they are missing by adopting this course, and what infamy, scorn, abhorrence, danger and disquiet they are incurring."[16] He contrasted such heroes as Timoleon and Dion with the tyrants of their time. He then contrasted the reputation of Brutus with that of Caesar and pointed out that many of the Roman emperors had reached bloody ends of bad lives at the hands of assassins.[17] In his long discourse "On Conspiracies," Machiavelli dutifully noted that one of the powerful causes that led men to conspire against a prince "is the desire to liberate their fatherland of which a prince has seized possession. It was this that caused Brutus and Cassius to turn against Caesar; this that led to many other conspiracies, against Phalaris, Dionysius, and against other usurpers of their country's rights."[18] In words that suggest the familiar ideas of Xenophon and Aristotle, Machiavelli continued, "Nor can any tyrant prevail over this spirit, except by discarding his tyranny." Then, returning to his familiar realism, and observing that few tyrants chose to abandon their tyranny, he repeated the traditional pronouncement that "one finds few who have not come to a miserable end," and quoted the famous verse to that effect from Juvenal.[19] Having paid his respects to tradition, Machiavelli continued his analysis of conspiracies and assassinations in the same dispassionate manner as that in which, in *The Prince,* he advised the despot on the means by which he could outwit his enemies.

Tyrannicide was a minor theme in the political thought of Renaissance Italy, but the records of the Italian states are bloody with political murder. "Princes and governments," says Burckhardt, "without the faintest scruple reckoned murder as one of the instruments of their power. . . . The imagination of the people at last became so accustomed to facts of this kind that the death of any powerful man was seldom or never attributed to natural causes."[20] Reviewing the violent records of the great families, Symonds writes, "The life of the Despot was usually one of prolonged terror. Immured in strong places on high rocks, or confined to gloomy fortresses like the Milanese Castello, he surrounded his person with foreign troops, protected his bedchamber with a picked guard, and watched his meat and drink lest they should be poisoned. . . . He dared not hope for a quiet end."[21] The churches were favorite places of assassination, since a despot engaged in public worship was somewhat less likely to be on his guard.[22] In the Pazzi conspiracy against the Medici in 1478, one of the conspirators refused at the last minute to commit murder before the high altar of the Cathedral of Florence. At that point two priests were recruited as substitute assassins, since they were "more accustomed to the place and therefore less superstitious about its sanctity."[23] Assassination and poisoning acquired semiprofessional status. The Council of Ten of Venice regularly received bids from those offering their service as poisoners for the removal of inconvenient persons. Those offering such service, which was sometimes accepted, were typically not patriots seeking to serve the state but criminals or exiles. Lamansky cites, from the secret record of the Council of Ten, ninety-one different proposals to make use of assassination. Among the proposals approved by the Council were plans to poison the Emperor

Sigismund, the Sultan, Charles VIII of France, and Pope Pius IV. By the middle of the sixteenth century, the proposals for poisoning had become so numerous that the Council was obliged to institute a separate register for them. A separate poison cabinet was also kept.[24]

In the ruthless struggle for power, political assassination by one method or another was accepted as one of the handiest of political weapons, but appeals to the right of tyrannicide were notably infrequent. Most of the modern literature on Renaissance Italy makes no sharp distinction between tyrannicide, in the technical sense in which the concept is considered in this study, and political murder for personal, dynastic, or other motives.[25] The doctrine of tyrannicide is often described by modern writers as "Machiavellian"—as the result of subverting moral principle to political expedience. In fact, the traditional doctrine of tyrannicide was directly opposed to that type of amoral "Machiavellianism" which characterized the politics of Renaissance Italy. The doctrine of tyrannicide was in its origin the product of unyielding principle, and it never appeared as a doctrine of serious practical importance except in periods or among groups dominated by deeply held uncompromising principles. It has always been the direct antithesis of any doctrine of expediency. Hence the infrequency of tyrannicide during the long period of Italian despotism. It was not that "the demoralization of the age" made tyrannicide popular; but rather that "the demoralization of the age" made self-seeking political murder common and tyrannicide exceptional.

IV   FROM OBEDIENCE TO RESISTANCE
IN PROTESTANT THOUGHT

As REGULARIZED constitutional checks developed in transalpine Europe in the fourteenth and fifteenth centuries, the questions of insurrection and tyrannicide tended to lose their importance and to drop out of political thought. But late medieval constitutional institutions were not allowed to develop without interruption into modern representative parliamentarism. All along the line they were submerged by growing royal absolutism, and in England alone of the important states was there continuity between medieval and modern constitutionalism. The triumph of secular authority over the church was accomplished by the concordats and by the Reformation and in Protestant countries was clinched by the expropriation of church properties. The superior efficiency of royal centralization proved itself in foreign wars. And the wars, in turn, together with national languages and popular vernacular literatures, helped to create an early form of national consciousness which broadened the base of the monarchy.

By the end of the fifteenth century, consolidated national monarchies of varying degrees of stability had been established in England, Spain, and France. The kingship of this period had obviously become something very different from the medieval kingship. The suppression of feudal restraints and the active role which the king began to assume in the promotion and protection of industry and trade were obvious signs of developing absolutism. A further important characteristic of the new monarchy was the increasing efficiency of a permanent royal bureaucracy. And finally, as evidence of royal power, we find the subjugation of the church itself to the demands of national policy.

Three important strands of theory, two of them ancient, one novel, supported the trend towards absolutism. These were the theory of the divine right of kings, the conception of the kingship which was found in Roman civil law, and the open avowal of an amoral power politics which, though described rather than invented by Machiavelli, still goes by his name. It is unnecessary to examine here these three strands of theory, but it is important to note that each denied the basic premises on which individual resistance to authority might be justified. On the other hand, the new absolutism called forth in the sixteenth century a more vigorous and widespread assertion of the rights of insurrection and tyrannicide than in any previous period. Action occasionally accompanied words.

One would expect to find that the Protestant Reformation, with all the weight which it placed on the conscience of individual men, had strengthened the theoretical foundation of individual resistance to authority. And this undoubtedly was one of its ultimate consequences. But the immediate effect of the teachings of the two greatest sixteenth-century reformers was to strengthen the case for authority and to weaken the tradition which supported resistance. Since the doctrine of tyrannicide is logically an extension of a theory of permissible resistance to the ruler, it is necessary to consider briefly the attitude of the leading reformers towards the possibility of individual resistance.

In Luther's writings we do not find any carefully constructed theory about the divine right of the "fools" and "scoundrels" whom he found holding political authority, but we do find the most violent denunciation of those who dared to resist them. Luther had little respect for the dignity of German princes, and he told them so from time to time. He remarked in 1523 that his earlier advice to the German princes had gone unheeded, "for God Almighty had made our rulers mad." "Such people were once called knaves, but now they must be called loyal Christian princes." "They are usually the greatest fools or the worst scoundrels on earth."[1] In 1525, when the peasant revolts were already beginning, he warned the peasants that their claims were unchristian and then turned again to the princes with a warning. God's wrath has sent the peasants against you, he told them; if you do not reform, you will be compelled by violence and destruction.[2] The Scriptures and history should warn you of the fate of tyrants. "As a rule they die a bloody death."[3]

If Luther was little impressed by the dignity of princes, he was even less impressed by the goodness, decency, or self-control of the mass of men. As early as 1522, he was outraged by Carlstadt and the Anabaptists, who carried Luther's belief in the right of private judgment towards conclusions which he abhorred. He saw clearly the social utility of order and stability and, though denying the authority of the Roman Church, was led to insist more emphatically upon the need to obey temporal rulers. He realized, too, that his conception of the freedom of the Christian man, misinterpreted by those more interested in men's worldly status than in men's spiritual salvation, could become an apology for anarchy. In 1522 he expressed his concern about such misinterpretation and condemned resistance to authority: "Those who read and understand my teaching," he said, "will not engage in insurrection. They have not learned it from me." Rather it was inspired by the devil.[4]

In his later treatise *On Worldly Authority* (1523), Luther explained that the true Christian was subject to neither the law nor the sword of authority because he did not need external restraint: "If all the world were composed of real Christians, that is, of true believers, then no prince, king, lord, sword, nor law would be necessary or useful. . . . As Paul says in I Timothy 1, the law is not given for the righteous but for the unrighteous." But since few professed and still fewer led a Christian life, God had commanded obedience to rulers.[5]

Thus, before the peasant revolts Luther was perfectly clear about the duty of obedience to the rulers, good or bad, that God had seen fit to establish. In 1525 he said the same thing that he had said before but said it with unrestrained violence of expression. His vehemence finally rose to the pitch of the short pamphlet, *Against the Plundering and Murdering Hordes of Peasants,* in which he remarked that "there could not be a devil left in hell, since they had all gone into the peasants."[6] "Therefore, let everyone who can, strike, slay, and stab secretly or openly, remembering that nothing can be more poisonous, dangerous, or devilish than a rebel."[7]

Luther rejected the doctrine of tyrannicide not only by inference, but very specifically. He acknowledged that the Greeks, the Romans, and even the Jews had held tyrannicide praiseworthy. But, he said, one should not ask what the heathen or Jews had done, but rather what was right and permissible. Resistance to authority was not permissible. If a prince did not allow the true gospel to be preached or practiced, Christian subjects should move to a land where it was allowed. To the argument from authority, Luther added the utilitarian consideration that, if tyrannicide were sanctioned in any case, men would soon turn the doctrine against good rulers, as was shown by Roman history. Better, he concluded, to bear with one tyrant, however bad, and sustain authority, than to invite the evils of innumerable tyrants—the unrestrained rule of the mob.[8] There is one passage in Luther's *Table Talk* which seems to sanction popular resistance to tyrants. He says that if the tyrant "forcefully take from one his wife, from the next his daughter, from the third his property . . . so that the citizens and subjects can no longer suffer and endure his tyranny, then they might bring him to earth like any other murderer or highwayman."[9] But this statement is balanced by innumerable emphatic statements to the contrary and is immediately preceded by a specific denial of the right of tyrannicide.

Luther was willing to use princes as agents of his religious reform; he was anxious to support princely authority against papal authority; he insisted upon the subjects' duty of obedience. But, like all Christian writers, he had to set a limit to worldly government, for "we must obey God rather than man." Therefore if, for example, a prince should command obedience to the pope, his subjects must refuse obedience to the tyrant. They dared not resist actively, but neither dared they obey.[10] There is here a possible basis for a theory of resistance, but the main force of Luther's thought was in the opposite direction. It served to increase the authority of those princes who were willing to enforce his conception of true Christianity. As the Reformation progressed he became more and more convinced that secular power must defend Christianity against "false prophets" by force. In the end, his teaching contributed, at least in Germany, to the movement towards absolute state authority.[11]

The other great reformer of the century was entirely in agreement with Luther on the question of obedience and more concise in his statement of his position. It is true that the Lutheran influence in Germany, long after Luther, continued to support a tradition of passive obedience and a state-controlled national church, while in France, England, and Scotland, Calvinism supported resistance to authority. But the development of a Calvinist doctrine of resistance was not the work of Calvin; it was the work of Calvin's followers, who could not hope to use rulers as agents of reform as Luther had done in Germany, nor to achieve complete control of political power as Calvin had done in Geneva. Calvinism in control, as it was in Geneva and for a time in the Massachusetts Bay Colony, produced a narrow and oppressive oligarchy that might well be called Christian despotism; Calvinism in opposition produced a vigorous doctrine of resistance and tyrannicide.

Calvin's own views are clear and consistent. "When those who bear the office of magistrate are called gods, . . . it is thereby intimated that they have a commission from God, that they are invested with divine authority, and, in fact, represent the person of God. . . ."[12] Magistrates were the "vicegerents of God"; the vengeance of the magistrate was the vengeance of God.[13] Therefore "we can not resist the magistrate without resisting God."[14] Subjects must recognize the jurisdiction delegated from God and reverence magistrates as God's ambassadors.[15] Calvin acknowledged that in all ages rulers appeared who neglected their duties and lived in luxurious idleness, or pursued their own interests and destroyed the rights of their people, or pillaged the poor and squandered the wealth of the land, and that it was natural to regard such tyrants with hatred. But "if we constantly keep before our eyes and minds the fact that even the most iniquitous kings are appointed by the same decree which establishes all regal authority, we will never entertain the seditious thought, that a king is to be treated according to his deserts. . . ."[16] Even the sacrilegious and unbelieving ruler must be obeyed. Subjects must, of course, refuse to obey if a ruler commanded what God forbade, but even then the subject must endure punishment and persecution passively. He dared not resist actively.

In one section of the *Institute* Calvin hinted at an escape from his doctrine of absolute non-resistance, and the hint was developed eagerly by some of his followers who faced hostile rulers. He said that he had been speaking of the duty of private men, but in some states there had been magistrates especially instituted "to curb the tyranny of kings." Such officials had existed, for example, in Athens, Sparta, and Rome, "and perhaps there is something similar to this in the power exercised in each kingdom by the three orders, when they hold their primary diets." It was not only the privilege, but also the duty of such officials to protect the liberty of the people against a tyrannical ruler.[17] A significant letter written by Calvin to Coligny in April, 1561, carefully restricted any right of popular resistance that might have been implied from the *Institute*. Coligny had inquired about the right of French Huguenots to resist their persecuting king. Calvin warned Coligny that "if a single drop of blood were shed rivers of blood would flow through Europe." He conceded that if the princes of the royal blood acted to protect their legal rights and if the *Parlements* supported them, then subjects might aid them; but action by a single prince of the royal blood would not justify popular support.[18] This interpretation could scarcely meet the needs of the French Huguenots.

It was in Scotland that Calvinists first demanded the right to resist and dethrone unbelieving rulers, and the Scottish reformer, John Knox, was among the first to reject Calvin's doctrine of nonresistance. The views of Knox were a challenge to every non-Calvinist ruler, since Knox maintained that it was the duty of subjects to establish the true religion by force if necessary. And Calvinists elsewhere tended to follow Knox's doctrine of resistance rather than Calvin's doctrine of nonresistance because Calvinists were usually a persecuted or unprivileged minority.

John Knox had become a Protestant in 1547. He had been subjected to nineteen months of penal servitude on a French galley because of his association with the assassins of the bishop and cardinal, Beaton, and, incidentally, he had referred to the murder of Beaton as "a godly fact."[19] He had declined an English bishopric, and spent the greater part of a four-year period in Geneva (1555-1559). In 1554 he consulted Calvin at Geneva and Bullinger at Zurich on the questions: "Whether resistance is to be rendered to a magistrate who enforces idolatry and condemns true religion . . . ?" and "To which party must godly persons attach themselves, in the case of a religious nobility resisting an idolatrous sovereign?" Both Calvin and Bullinger discouraged resistance.[20]

But Knox went his own way. He published in 1588 his *First Blast of the Trumpet against the Monstrous Regiment of Women,* printed anonymously at Geneva. His argument that rule by women was contrary to nature is of no particular importance in our study. But his conclusion is important. It was that "it is the duty as well of the Estates as of the People . . . to remove from honor and authority that monster in nature"[21] whom he called elsewhere "that cruel monster Mary [Tudor] (unworthy, by reason of her bloody tyranny, of the name of a woman)."[22] In the same year Knox made perfectly clear his belief that there was a duty to resist not only a tyrannical or idolatrous woman ruler, but any idolatrous ruler. In his *Appellation,* his defense against the judgment made against him by the Scottish bishops, he spoke of the duty of resistance generally: "For now the common song of all men is, We must obey our Kings, be they good or be they bad; for God hath so commanded. But horrible shall the vengeance be, that shall be poured forth upon such blasphemers of God. . . . True it is God has commanded Kings to be obeyed, but like true it is, that in things which they commit against his glory, or when cruelly without cause they rage against their brethren, the members of Christ's body, he hath commanded no obedience, but rather he hath approved, yea greatly rewarded such as have opposed themselves to their ungodly commandments and blind rage."[23] And, moving a step further, he said in the same tract, "It is not only lawful to punish to the death such as labor to subvert the true Religion, but the Magistrates and People are bound so to do, unless they will provoke the wrath of God against themselves. And therefore I fear not to affirm that it had been the duty of the Nobilitie, Judges, Rulers, and People of England, not only to have resisted . . . Marie [Tudor], that Jezabel . . . , but also to have punished her to the death. . . ."[24]

What Knox was willing to say to the magistrates and people of Scotland about Mary Tudor of England he was willing to say also to the young Mary Stuart of Scotland. He himself recorded his first interview with Mary Stuart in 1561, in the course of which occurred this blunt exchange: "Think you, said she, that subjects having power may resist their princes? If their princes exceed their bounds, said he, Madam, and do against that wherefore they should be obeyed, it is no doubt but they may be resisted, even by power." "At these words," Knox continued, "the queen stood as it were amazed, more than a quarter of an hour. . . ."[25]

For Knox the maintenance of the true religion was paramount over all else, and the ruler who did not support the true religion was to be resisted, dethroned, executed. The question what was the true religion troubled him no more than it did Calvin. As Professor Allen remarks, he had no sense of the difficulty of the question put by Mary when she asked regarding the Catholic interpretation and his interpretation of the Scriptures, "Whom shall I believe?" For he assumed that the correct interpretation, his interpretation, was "manifestly known."[26]

There are a number of excited passages scattered throughout the writings of Knox which might seem to indicate his willingness to support tyrannicide. In an *Admonition* to fellow-Protestants of England, published in 1554, he exclaimed: "God, for his great mercies sake, stirre up some Phinees, Helias, or Jehu, that the bloude of abhominable idolaters maye pacifie Goddes wrath, that it consume not the whole multitude."[27] "A direct appeal to the assassin," says one critical biographer of Knox.[28] But these appeals to the Lord to destroy tyrants are not part of any reasoned defense of tyrannicide.

In the year that Knox published his *First Blast* and his *Appellation,* an English Calvinist, Christopher Goodman, who was closely associated in exile with Knox, published a treatise on *How Superior Powers Ought to be Obeyed,* which expressed essentially the same position as that of Knox.[29] A third Marian exile, writing two years earlier than Knox and Goodman, had gone so far as to justify tyrannicide under certain conditions. John Ponet, formerly Bishop of Rochester and Bishop of Winchester, who had fled to Strasbourg to escape Mary's persecution, published in 1556 his *Short Treatise of Politicke Power, and of the Obedience which Subjects owe to Kings.* . . . Ponet declared that although the authority of rulers went back ultimately to God, it was derived directly from the community and might be revoked by the community. Kings, he said, were subject to the law of God and to the positive laws of the state. The many examples recorded in Scripture of the deposing of kings and killing of tyrants confirmed such treatment to be consonant with God's will. The deposition of Edward II and Richard II and depositions elsewhere added the support of constitutional practice; and furthermore the arguments that supported deposition of an evil ruler "will doe as much for the proofe that it is lawful to kill a tiranne." Ponet cited the honor accorded by the ancients to him who killed a tyrant, and appealed finally for justification to the law of nature grafted in the hearts of men. But Ponet would sanction tyrannicide only under two conditions: first, that the regular judicial process had been subverted or rendered inoperative by neglect; second, that the private slayer was moved by an inspiration from God.

I think that it can not be maintained by God's word that any private man may kill, except (where execution of just punishment upon tyrants, idolaters, and traiterous governors is either by the whole state utterly neglected, or the prince with the nobility and council conspire the subversion or alteration of their country and people) any private man have som special inwarde commandment or surely proved motion of God.[30]

The Calvinist doctrine of obedience to constituted authority was readily converted by Knox into a convenient doctrine of resistance. In Scotland theory accompanied successful action and a Protestant revolution took place. In England the Elizabethan compromise postponed the conflict. But in France Protestantism was still fighting for the right to exist during the second half of the sixteenth century; hence it was in France rather than in Scotland or England that theories of resistance were most elaborately developed.

John Calvin had dedicated his *Institute* to the French king, Francis I, and, clinging to the hope that Protestantism might be allowed to develop peacefully in France, he had declined to sanction Huguenot resistance against a persecuting government. Calvin died in 1564, but even two years before his death French Huguenots were in revolt, and the consequent wars continued intermittently until 1598. At first the Huguenots insisted that they were fighting, not against the king, but to free the king from his Catholic advisers who had usurped the royal power. But the slaughtering of thousands of Huguenots in the Massacre of St. Bartholomew, initiated with the consent of the king and the queen-mother, made this Huguenot pretense unnecessary. After 1572 French Huguenots were driven to the claim that it was entirely lawful to resist tyrants. Their demonstrations of this thesis necessarily involved deeper examination of the basis of political society than the early reformers, primarily interested in other matters, had found necessary.

Even the voice from Geneva changed in response to the desperate plight of the Huguenots. Theodore Beza, Calvin's close friend and biographer and his successor at Geneva, had agreed with Calvin earlier in warning the Huguenots against resistance. In 1563, John of Poltrot had assassinated Duke Francis of Guise, who was besieging the Huguenot city of Orleans, and had defended the deed on the ground that the Duke, who was persecuting the children of God, was a tyrant. Being subjected to torture, Poltrot had accused Beza, Admiral Coligny, and others of instigating the assassination. Beza and Coligny had exonerated themselves of personal responsibility.[31] But in 1574 Beza published a pamphlet *On the Right of Magistrates,* in which he substituted for Calvin's vague suggestion, that in some cases there might be a constitutional remedy for tyranny, a more complete and specific theory of resistance. His argument followed familiar lines of medieval thought and anticipated the still more elaborate theory developed in the well-known anonymous pamphlet, the *Vindiciae contra Tyrannos,* published a few years later.

Although recognizing still a normal obligation to obey, Beza argued that the authority of the ruler was limited not only by the word of God in the Scriptures but also by natural law, which was a part of the law of God. Moreover, there was a mutual obligation between king and people; the authority of the ruler was held conditionally. The tyrant who had broken through the limits of royal authority, and particularly the ruler who persecuted men for following the true religion, might be resisted. The Estates, as representatives of the entire community, had the right and the duty to depose or punish a tyrannical king, even if this involved the use of force; and inferior magistrates (the nobility and municipal officers), although they could not depose the tyrant, "are altogether bound to procure, even by force if they can, against manifest tyranny, the safety of those matters which have been committed to their trust and care." In this resistance they might, if necessary, enlist the support of private citizens, but private citizens had no right to resist tyranny on their own initiative, "except in the case of an extraordinary summons from God, which I do not discuss here." While the private citizen ought not to obey tyrannical commands at the expense of obedience to God, his proper remedy against tyranny was patience and prayer.[32]

All this applied to the case of the lawful superior who lapsed into tyranny, but nevertheless retained "the foundation of his authority in relation to his private subjects."[33] But Beza heartily endorsed the tradition that even private citizens were bound to defend their suffering fatherland with all their force against the usurper without title, "especially when both religion and liberty are at stake." "Wherefore I can never approve the opinion of those who, without discrimination or exception, condemn all tyrannicides, for which the Greeks once ordained so many glorious rewards."[34]

During the short period between Luther and Beza, Protestant thought developed from a theory of passive obedience to one of the right and duty of resistance, in response to the political situations that existed in Scotland and in France. Those who supported resistance continued to build their case upon the traditional body of thought that came to them from earlier centuries, but they naturally regarded as the decisive test of tyranny the attempt of a ruler to subvert the true religion. In Scotland John Knox presented the strongest Calvinist case for resistance; after Knox Calvinists no longer had to resist. In France, on the other hand, the Calvinist minority had need to sharpen the weapons with which it could combat the effort of Catholic leaders to impose religious unity.

V TWO SIXTEENTH-CENTURY HUMANISTS ON TYRANNY

BEFORE turning to the French Huguenots and the Jesuits, we must consider two humanists whose discussions of tyranny had considerable influence upon Huguenot thought. One of these, George Buchanan, was advocating tyrannicide before the principal French works on the subject had appeared. In contrast to Knox, his compatriot and fellow-Protestant, Buchanan was a humanist, educated at Paris, and highly renowned for his scholarship and poetry; Geneva had little influence upon his thought. His attitude was secular and his arguments when he wrote on politics were naturalistic. His earliest semipolitical work was a short tragedy based on the story of John the Baptist and Herod. In describing the tyrant Herod, Buchanan explained, he was thinking of Henry VIII, while the martyr, whose speeches expressed the proper attitude toward the tyrant, recalls Sir Henry More.[1] But Buchanan's important political work was his treatise on the Scottish constitution, *De Jure Regni apud Scotos,* written perhaps in 1568 or 1569, but published in 1579 with a dedication to his royal pupil, James VI. Professor Laski remarks that "it is possible that Buchanan's famous Dialogue was the most influential essay of the century."[2] It was widely circulated in manuscript among Buchanan's friends, and after it was printed four editions appeared in two years. And we must remember that it was written some years before the Massacre of St. Bartholomew and consequently before the flood of Huguenot pamphlets which followed 1572.

Buchanan defended the deposition of Mary Stuart, but his arguments were not those of Knox because he was not primarily concerned about maintaining the "true religion." For this reason, too, his position differed from that of the Huguenots, parts of whose argument he anticipated or shared; indeed, he approached closer to the general view of later writers like Locke.

Buchanan suggested that governments arose because, as Aristotle had maintained, "man is a political animal." He assumed, then, that there was a natural instinct or propensity in all men which drove them toward politically organized society. What was natural must have been ordained by God. Hence political society had God's sanction; but the emphasis here is no longer on the direct institution of authority by God.[3] Because of the equality that existed in a state of nature, kings must have been established by action of the people. Buchanan concluded that the authority of kings rested on a social contract, and that a part of that contract was the king's acceptance of a rule of law. It was the function of the king to maintain justice; he must therefore rule according to law.[4] But law, like the king's authority, was derived from the community. Hence those who conferred authority upon the king could also limit that authority, as well as punish kings who exceeded their authority.[5] Scottish history showed, said Buchanan, that the Scots had always been ready and able to call their kings to account. He cited particularly the case of James III, whose murderers had been exonerated and protected by an act of the Scottish Parliament in 1488.[6]

Buchanan made the obvious distinction between the king and the tyrant. One who had seized power without a true title or who regarded himself as above the law became a tyrant and an enemy of the people. To him no loyalty was due.[7] Paul's admonition to obey established authority did not require obedience to tyrants.[8]

"Therefore the compact between the king and the citizens is mutual. . . . And he who first departs from the agreement and does the opposite of what he had promised, does he not dissolve the compact? Therefore when the bond is broken which united the king with the people no right arising from the compact remains to him who dissolved it. . . . Moreover, if the king dissolves the bonds of human society for the sake of whose unity he was created," he must be called a tyrant. "Now a tyrant . . . is an enemy of the people. War against an enemy on account of grave and unendurable injuries is a just war." And the war that was waged with "the enemy of all mankind, the tyrant," was "the most just of wars." Not only was it just for a whole people to rebel against the tyrant, but any private individual had the right to kill the tyrant. "Once war with the enemy has begun for a just cause, not only the whole people but also individuals have the right to kill the enemy."[9] Buchanan cited the honor paid to those who slew tyrants of Greece and Rome, and concluded that mankind was unanimous in its praise of the deed of tyrannicide.[10]

That Buchanan perceived the obvious danger in the doctrine he asserted appeared from the objection that he put in the mouth of Maitland, his fictitious opponent in the dialogue. Maitland protested, "If it be lawful for anyone to kill the tyrant, see what a fatal door for villainy you open to the wicked; what a danger you create for the good. . . . Any murderer of a good king, or of one not manifestly evil, could claim honorable motives for his crime."[11] To this basic objection Buchanan replied that abuse of a doctrine did not destroy its validity; he was merely explaining the rights that each individual had, and not advising rash use of these rights. The conclusion can not be avoided that his theory permitted responsibility for tyrannicide to rest justly on the conscience of private individuals.

During three centuries, well over a dozen editions of this little book were published, and it had a habit of turning up whenever trouble was in the air. For example, a Dutch translation appeared in 1598 and again in 1610; an English edition appeared in 1680 and was reprinted in 1689; German editions were published in 1796 and 1821.[12] That it was not a book that kings and governments would cherish is indicated by the facts that it was condemned by the Scottish Parliament in 1584, that its circulation was forbidden by the Scottish Privy Council in 1664, and that in 1683 the University of Oxford had it publicly burned.

Buchanan's treatise was notable for its straightforward development of the argument that led directly to tyrannicide, and for the perfection of its Latin style, but the fundamental propositions from which he argued were standard medieval propositions. Far more original in its analysis of tyranny but less obviously related to the troubles of the period was the essay on tyranny written by the young French humanist, Étienne de La Boétie, about 1548. La Boétie was not a Huguenot and his *Discourse on Voluntary Servitude* was not a partisan appeal; neither did he advocate tyrannicide or forceful resistance. His *Discourse* was a bitter denunciation of tyrants and at the same time an explanation of how tyranny arose and how it could be destroyed. It was unique in the literature of the period because of the author's independence from the Aristotelian and medieval conventions in his effort to dig to the roots of tyranny.

In explaining how it was that men who had a natural love of liberty could be made to submit to tyranny, La Boétie presented a psychological interpretation of tyranny which might be amply documented from the practices and attitudes of our own day.

Tyranny, he explained, was founded upon force and deceit, but it could not be maintained by force and deceit alone; it was custom that gradually crowded out of men's consciousness their natural love of liberty and led them to submit to servitude. A man who had known nothing but midnight darkness would not long for the sunlight. The tyrant guarded against the reawakening of the desire for liberty by suppressing scholarship and by isolating those who were more thoughtful than the rest. In short, "under the tyrant the liberty of acting, speaking, and almost of thinking is suppressed."[13] The tyrant sought to degrade his subjects by bread and circuses, and by the circulation of myths and legends he sought to give his power a religious sanction and to create the belief that he was more than a man.

But La Boétie maintained—and this is the novel and significant feature of his analysis—that it was not force nor simple deceit of the masses that supported tyranny; it was rather the hierarchy of those who believed themselves to be personal beneficiaries of the tyrant's system. Five or six had the ear of the tyrant; they were the accomplices of his cruelty and sharers in his plunder. "These six have six hundred under them, who profit by their relation to them. ... These six hundred keep under them six thousand, whom they have raised to eminence. ... They do so much wrong that they can not escape the law and punishment except by their help. ... Not six thousand but a hundred thousand, even millions are attached to the tyrant by this cord, making use of it to further their own ends." The dregs of the country—not necessarily the known criminals and outlaws, but those dominated by unscrupulous ambition and avarice—gathered round the tyrant that they might share in the booty and act as petty tyrants under the great tyrant. In short, the system was based upon legalized plunder; the ruling gang was bound together by vested interest in corruption and by consequent loyalty to the great protector who made the corruption possible. La Boétie here put his finger on one important element of tyranny which earlier writers had neglected and which contemporary writers sometimes neglect. In modern dictatorship this element is dignified by the euphemistic phrase, "the Leadership Principle."

La Boétie mentioned with praise the well-known classical examples of tyrannicide, but his love of liberty and his moral revulsion against tyranny did not lead him to a defense of tyrannicide nor even of forceful resistance. His cure for tyranny was passive resistance, against which, he maintained, no tyranny could prevail. "There is no need to fight this single tyrant; there is no need to defeat him; he is defeated by himself if only his subjects do not consent to be his slaves.... I do not ask that you expel him or shake him off; only that you cease to support him, and you will see how a great colossus, whose base has been taken away, falls of its own weight, and breaks into pieces."

La Boétie was a devout Catholic, but the historical significance of his *Discourse* comes from the role it was to play in supporting the Huguenot cause. After fragments had been published earlier, the full text was brought to print for the first time in a collection of Huguenot pamphlets published in 1576 under the title *Mémoires de l'Estat de France sous Charles IX*. It had been written some years before the earliest of the Huguenot pamphlets; it surpassed the best of them in the novelty of its approach and the vigorous originality of its argument. In the light of the twentieth century, it is one of the most interesting pieces of early modern political literature.

VI THE THEORY AND PRACTICE OF TYRANNICIDE IN THE FRENCH WARS OF RELIGION

THE LONG and bloody struggle between Huguenots and Catholics in sixteenth-century France was not simply a struggle over religious issues. It was also a struggle between rival nobles for the control of the French crown. And, since much of the Huguenot strength was to be found in cities or regions which claimed some degree of autonomy, it was a struggle between royal centralization and medieval particularism. The Huguenot party was just as much a political party as it was a religious grouping; and the Gallican Catholicism of Catherine de Medici, who ruled during the reigns of her sons, Francis II and Charles IX, and the ultramontane Catholicism of the Guises were as much matters of political convenience as of religious conviction. Hence while we may speak properly of the "religious wars," we may expect to find a good deal of secular argument in the pamphlets of the period. And it was perhaps the secular nature of much of the argument that made the literature of this period so useful in later debates in which the dispute was even less religious in character.

The Huguenots did not have to depend solely upon *a priori* principles to justify their resistance. Like the English controversialists of the following century, they could look to constitutional tradition and discover there the proper prescriptions for putting the king in his place. They could combat the doctrine of absolute monarchy, already being stated by the lawyers in terms of Roman law, by giving new emphasis to the medieval belief that the king's authority was always limited, and a more specific interpretation to the vague medieval belief that authority, though ultimately from God, came immediately from the people.

The constitutional argument was developed by Francis Hotman in his summary of French constitutional history, *Franco-Gallia,* published in Geneva in 1573. Hotman was closely associated with the Huguenot leaders and was one of their dependable controversialists. Although little claim for the historical accuracy of the *Franco-Gallia* could be supported today, the book retained prestige for many years. It was quoted with approval in the seventeenth century by Selden, Milton, and Sidney.[1]

Hotman's thesis was that the French monarchy had always been elective and under the control of the Common-Council (Estates-General) representing the people. "... The kings of Franco-Gallia were made such, upon certain known terms and conditions, and were not tyrants with absolute, unlimited, and arbitrary power."[2] "The people reserved to themselves all the power, not only of creating, but also of abdicating, their kings...."[3] His argument can be reduced to the proposition that the people, or more accurately the community, acting through the Estates-General, was above the king and was constitutionally capable of enforcing upon him those limitations, found principally in custom, which by implication or expressly he had undertaken to observe. The idea of an ultimate divine source of authority was simply omitted, and the idea of a social compact, though implicit, was not discussed.

Hotman spoke often of tyranny and sometimes seemed to mean by the term little more than unconstitutionality. However, he showed his acquaintance with the classical concept of tyranny when he remarked that the old French monarchy had none of the three characteristics of tyranny. The people were not ruled against their will, but obeyed voluntarily; the king had no need for mercenary bodyguards; and government operated for the benefit of the commonwealth rather than for the profit of an individual.[4] This ideal state of affairs, Hotman implied, seemed to exist no longer. The conclusion, expressed in the Preface, was that the French must return to the wisdom of their ancestors. Just how this might be done, he left to others to explain.

The best-known and perhaps the most significant Huguenot pamphlet of this period is the *Vindiciae contra Tyrannos,* written between 1574 and 1576 and published in 1579 under the pseudonym Stephen Junius Brutus.[5] The author of the *Vindiciae* systematized the arguments of his colleagues and expressed these arguments with an eloquence which made his pamphlet a reference book for revolutionists for several centuries to come. Hotman found a right of resistance to be inherent in the French constitutional tradition; the author of the *Vindiciae* deduced a right of resistance from general philosophical principles concerning the nature of obedience and then supported his conclusions by references to history and the Bible. The principles were still the familiar medieval principles, but the elaborate development of the contract theory of obedience was new and anticipated the work of important seventeenth- and eighteenth-century writers.

The *Vindiciae* dealt with two main problems. The first was the question whether an heretical ruler might be resisted and, if so, by whom. The king, of course, held his authority from God, the *Vindiciae* explained, and the king, like a vassal, forfeited his authority if he violated the terms under which he had received it.[6] But the whole people were also involved through a contract between God on one side and the king and people on the other. The people became liable jointly with the king for the maintenance of the true religion. The people had, as it were, given surety for the king's Christian behavior. Should the king break his pledge, full responsibility would fall upon the people. They must resist the king lest they share in his sin and risk the punishment which he had earned.[7]

But the writer hastened to explain that when he said that "the people" must resist an heretical ruler he did not mean to justify a spontaneous mass uprising nor condone action by private individuals. The people must follow the officers of the kingdom, who were bound by the compact to resist on behalf of the people.[8] If the officers of the kingdom did not do their duty, then the provincial or municipal magistrates, who were responsible for maintaining the true religion in their own communities, might and must resist.[9] Here is a conception of federal decentralization of authority which seems to be made to order for the Huguenot party. If no magistrate, national or local, was found to oppose the heretical king, true Christians might migrate to another territory, but they might not resist. It was true that in the Bible examples might be found of private persons who delivered their people by slaying unbelieving tyrants; but in each such case, said the *Vindiciae,* the deed was directed by divine inspiration. Although the author did not deny that God might still act through private agents, he apparently thought it improbable. He concluded this section with the warning:

. . . If any, supposing he is inspired by the Holy Ghost, do attribute to himself the before-mentioned authority. I would entreat him to look that he be not puffed up with vain glory, and lest he make not a God to himself of his own fancy, and sacrifice to his own inventions.[10]

What rights existed against the ruler whose offenses were not against the true religion but against the secular welfare of his subjects? More than half the book dealt with this question. The argument was grounded upon the doctrine of popular sovereignty. Kings had their authority ultimately from God, but they were elected by the people, and "after God they hold their power and sovereignty from the people."[11] The king was subject to the law which he received from the people, and the law could be changed only with their consent.[12] The relation between king and subjects with respect to secular duties was expressed in a second contract, which was a contract between king and people. "The people ask the king, whether he will govern justly and according to the laws? He promises he will. Then the people answer, and not before, that whilst he governs uprightly, they will obey faithfully. The king therefore promises simply and absolutely, the people upon condition: the which failing to be accomplished, the people rest according to equity and reason, quit of their promise."[13] Like other pamphlets of the period, the *Vindiciae* referred to particular coronation oaths as evidence of this contractual relationship. In brief, then, the kingship was bound by the purposes for which it was established, and its authority lapsed if these purposes were not furthered. In such a case, the king became a tyrant.

At this point the *Vindiciae* stressed the common distinction between two types of tyrant. The first was the tyrant without title, the invader or usurper who had seized control by force or deceit. Such a tyrant was outside the law; any private person might dispose of him. ". . . The laws of nature, of nations, and the civil law command us to take arms against such tyrants; . . . neither is there any oath, covenant, or obligation, public or private, of power justly to restrain us; therefore the meanest private man may resist and lawfully oppose such an intruding tyrant."[14] The judgment of mankind was vindicated by the praise and honor that had always been rendered to the slayers of such tyrants. The *Vindiciae* did not hesitate to point out that "there be women also who intrude themselves into the government of those kingdoms which the laws only permit to males, and make themselves queens and regents. . . ." or who, "as the queens of the house of Medici in these latter times," educated their sons to dissoluteness, that the royal power might remain in their own hands.[15] Apparently the *Vindiciae* would justify the assassination of Catherine de Medici.

But one must be more cautious in dealing with the second type of tyrant, the ruler who had violated his agreement with the people.

Private persons might not resist him on their own initiative, but they might be called to arms by the officers of the kingdom. "It is therefore permitted the officers of a kingdom, either all or some good number of them, to suppress a tyrant; and it is not only lawful for them to do it, but their duty expressly requires it...." They themselves became tyrants if they did not resist.[16] Here again the particularism of the *Vindiciae* appeared in the assertion that, should the principal officers of the kingdom neglect their duty, a local magistrate, even though he stood alone against other officers, must undertake to free the whole kingdom, "or at least that portion especially recommended to his care," from tyranny.[17]

Since even kings are human, said the *Vindiciae,* we must not expect absolute perfection in their rule, and must be prepared to put up with occasional carelessness. The tyrant, however, was not merely an occasional careless wrong-doer. He was one who persistently perverted legal proceedings and disregarded lawful rights, who made "no reckoning of faith, covenants, justice nor piety," who "subverts the state, pillages the people, ... breaks promises with all, scoffs at the sacred obligations of a solemn oath," and was therefore guilty of the most detestable crimes and vices.[18] The author painted a colorful, although rather conventional, picture of the tyrant, for which he drew much from Aristotle, whom he cited:

A tyrant lops off those ears which grow higher than the rest of the corn, especially where virtue makes them most conspicuously eminent; oppresses by calumnies and fraudulent practices the principal officers of the state; gives out reports of intended conspiracies against himself, that he might have some colourable pretext to cut them off. . . . The tyrant advances above and in opposition to the ancient and worthy nobility, mean and unworthy persons; to the end that these base fellows, being absolutely his creatures, might applaud and apply themselves to the fulfilling of all his loose and unruly desires. . . . A tyrant nourishes and feeds factions and dissentions among his subjects, ruins one by the help of another, that he may the easier vanquish the remainder. . . . A tyrant fills his garrisons with strange soldiers, . . . disarms the people, . . . makes himself formidable with guards of strangers, or men fit only for pillage or spoil, gives pensions out of the public treasury to spies and calumniating informers, dispersed through all cities and provinces. . . . He makes wars abroad; erects idle and needless trophies to continually employ his tributaries, that they might not have leisure to think on other things, as Pharaoh did the Jews. . . . Therefore he always prepares for, or threatens war, or, at least, seems to do so. . . . A tyrant leaves no design unattempted by which he may fleece his subjects of their substance, and turn it to his proper benefit, that being continually troubled in gaining means to live, they may have no leisure, no hope how to regain their liberty. . . . He builds his own, and followers' fortunes on the ruins of the public. . . . He desires much to be esteemed just and loyal in some affairs, purposely to deceive and betray more easily in matters of greater consequence. . . . To speak in a word, that which the true king is, the tyrant would seem to be, and knowing that men are wonderfully attracted with, and enamoured of virtue, he endeavors with much subtlety to make his vices appear yet marked with some shadow of virtue: but let him counterfeit never so cunningly, still the fox will be known by his tail: and although he fawn and flatter like a spaniel, yet his snarling and grinning will ever betray his currish kind.

And if the reader was not satisfied with this description or the more exact representations of tyrants to be found in history, "he may in these our days behold an absolute model of many living and breathing tyrants, whereof Aristotle in his time did much complain."[19]

As the political situation changed, the Huguenots soon detached themselves from the arguments of the *Vindiciae*. It is probable that the book had more influence outside France and in later centuries than within France, where the dominant tendency, in spite of religious opposition, first from one side and then from the other, was toward monarchic absolutism. For the book had a wide popularity, and like Buchanan's dialogue on the law of the Scots had a habit of reappearing in revolutionary times and places.[20] Laski reports that a copy of the edition of 1648 in the British Museum attributes the book to a William Walker, who cut off the head of Charles I. It shared with Buchanan's dialogue the honor of being publicly burned by Oxford University in 1683. Milton, Harrington, Sidney, Locke, Thomas Hooker, and John Adams all refer to the work with respect.[21]

Just when the Huguenots were bringing their case for resistance to its sharpest expression, a new political situation was leading them to doubt their arguments, which then quickly became the property of the Catholics. As early as 1576 the more extreme Catholics under the leadership of the Duke of Guise had formed the Catholic League for the protection of the Catholic religion, which they felt was being imperilled by compromises with the Huguenots. The League was revived in 1584 when the death of the Duke of Anjou, the king's brother, left Henry of Navarre, a Protestant, heir to the throne. And just as the Huguenots had been driven to extreme views by the Massacre of St. Bartholomew, so the Leaguers were pushed to desperate arguments after the assassination of the Duke of Guise and his brother, the cardinal, by order of the king in 1588.

When the Catholics faced a compromising king who declined to persecute heresy, the League writers adopted the Huguenot arguments for constitutionally limited monarchy. When the Catholics faced a king who had slain their most popular leader, and when they later faced a claimant to the throne who was a Protestant and was under the papal ban of excommunication, the League writers began to preach rebellion and tyrannicide. The more systematic of the League pamphlets, such as those of Jean Boucher[22] and the writer who called himself Rossaeus,[23] followed the general theory already outlined in the *Vindiciae*. They assumed, as the writer of the *Vindiciae* assumed in the third section of his book, that political organization was a natural development, the seed of which was to be found in the nature of men. They argued that each community determined its own form of government; that where kings existed, their authority rested on a popular basis; and that the people could change or abolish the kingship. They argued further, as the Huguenots had argued, that a king's authority was limited by the ends for which the kingship existed, and that a king whose acts defeated the purpose of kingship became a tyrant. Boucher described a contract between king and people that was similar to the contract of the *Vindiciae*.[24] And finally they argued in good Calvinist fashion that, since government existed for the good of the subjects, the king, in furthering the good of the community, must maintain the true religion and suppress heresy. The heretical king was *ipso facto* a tyrant.[25] With respect to the problem of having the tyrant properly branded as such, these Catholic writers were assisted by their recognition of the pope's right to excommunicate the king and thereby dissolve the allegiance owed him by his subjects. But apparently resistance and deposition did not require the intervention of the pope; they could be based also upon that conception of the popular source of authority which the League and the Huguenots both acknowledged.

In 1589, about seven months after Henry III had won his freedom from League domination by the assassination of the Duke of Guise and the Cardinal of Lorraine, he himself was stabbed to death by a young Dominican friar, Jacques Clément. Clément, killed on the spot, was promptly honored by the League preachers and by his Order as a martyr. He was proclaimed from the pulpits of Paris as "the holy martyr of Jesus Christ," who had delivered

France from "that dog of a Henry of Valois."[26] Even the pope, Sixtus V, regarded the event as a sign that God still watched over the kingdom of France.[27] Jean Boucher and Rossaeus were among those who found in Clément's deed an example of the proper method for dealing with tyrants.

Boucher, a very influential Paris preacher and an eloquent master of unrestrained invective, published in 1589 his book justifying the deposition of Henry III. He argued that the pope or his representatives had the right to depose Henry because Henry was guilty of perjury, of heresy, of sacrilegious murder, of fomenting schism, of simony, of sacrilege, because he was an assassin, a parricide, and a magician, and, finally, because he was an excommunicate.[28] He then asserted that the people had an independent right to depose Henry because he had been perfidious and guilty of treason against the commonwealth, because he was cruel, useless to the government, guilty of all the vices, and condemned by his own words. It was permissible not only to depose but also to kill a tyrant, said Boucher. It was the duty as well as the right of any individual to execute judgment upon him. History had testified to this by absolving regicides of guilt and recording their names in a roll of honor.[29] When the necessity to be rid of the tyrant was urgent, no formal judgment by the Estates was needed. Before he had completed his work, Boucher could record the news that Clément, that courageous martyr, "inspired by Christ," had put into practice a generally acknowledged doctrine. He had restored peace to church and country and brought joy to the hearts of all good citizens by slaying "that most savage beast." But Boucher was not satisfied by the death of Henry III. Henry of Navarre remained; another execrated tyrant must be chased down and destroyed. Boucher believed that Clément's example and his own advice would not go unheeded.[30]

The arguments that Boucher urged against Henry III, Rossaeus urged, somewhat less violently, against Henry of Navarre. The Protestant doctrine that anyone could kill a tyrant was, he declared, abominable, because the Protestants defined tyranny in terms of their own faith and thus approved the murder of Francis of Guise, Mary Stuart, and the Duke of Parma. But, although the Protestants had perverted and abused the doctrine of tyrannicide, they had, Rossaeus thought, uttered certain truths. For Scripture did approve tyrannicide. Anyone might kill the tyrant who had established his rule by force. And if it became obvious that the commonwealth had come to regard its properly established king as a tyrant, then individuals might kill the tyrant as they would a robber. The opinion of the church was particularly decisive. For Rossaeus also, the deed of Clément was a model to be followed. He spoke of Clément as "that most glorious and innocent young man," "armed by the Holy Spirit," whom God had employed as his special instrument. Henry of Navarre, he asserted, could never be a king; he was a heretic, an excommunicate, and the worst of traitors. Scripture and history taught that all should take up arms against an heretical king; he might be killed by anyone.[31]

Laski has suggested that the "real inheritors of the work of the monarchomachs are in fact the Jesuits and the English thinkers of the seventeenth century."[32] During the sixteenth century, writers in all camps were building their theories of resistance upon medieval foundations. Regarding the origin and nature of civil society there was a remarkable similarity between the basic assumptions of the Huguenots and those of the members of the Catholic League, and these assumptions seem not essentially unlike those of the Jesuits. Two famous Jesuits who wrote at the turn of the century, Suarez and Mariana, gave to these assumptions a sharp and systematic statement which had been lacking in most of the works of earlier impassioned polemicists. The Jesuit statement seems to rest more certainly on a natural-law basis that might be termed in its immediate aspects secular, although the whole system of natural law had, as in Aquinas and throughout the medieval period, an ultimate divine basis.

Both Mariana and Suarez described an original state of nature and explained that civil societies emerged from this primitive state as a result of voluntary delegation of authority to rulers. Such delegation was made because the needs and desires of men could not be satisfied without that cooperation which civil society made possible. The authority of a prince must rest upon the grant made by the community, and this grant could only be construed as conditional and limited. "In my opinion," said Mariana, "royal power, when it is legitimate, has its origin in the citizens, by whose grant the first kings in any commonwealth were raised to the throne. The citizens circumscribe the royal power by laws and sanctions lest it ... degenerate into tyranny."[33] For both Mariana and Suarez, as for the Huguenots, royal power was limited by the purpose for which it was instituted: that is, the welfare of the community. Mariana explained further that the commonwealth reserved to itself power greater than that delegated to the prince, including the specific authority to levy taxes, to give or withhold its approval to changes in the law, and to confirm the succession even to an hereditary throne.[34]

Both Mariana and Suarez then reached the conventional conclusion that the prince who overstepped the limits of his authority became a tyrant and might rightfully be restrained. In explaining what action might be taken against the tyrant, Suarez followed the cautious opinion of Aquinas. The distinction must be maintained, said Suarez, between the tyrant without a proper title—the usurper— and the legitimate king who became a tyrant by abuse of power. The usurper was really not a king, but an enemy of the people, unless after his seizure of power he was accepted by the people. If his power continued to rest upon force without consent, if there was no recourse against him to a superior authority, if the tyranny of the usurper was public and manifest so that no doubt about it could be entertained, and if there was no other means of freeing the community from tyranny, then the tyrant might rightly be killed by any private member of the community.[35] If a legitimate king became a tyrant, the community had the right to depose him, but a private individual might not take action against him. In general, Suarez was sufficiently impressed by the need of order to believe that insurrection was usually worse than tyranny and consequently that submission was wiser than revolt, unless the oppression of the tyrant had become intolerable.[36]

Mariana's doctrine of tyrannicide followed that of John of Salisbury and Buchanan rather than that of Aquinas. His defense of the doctrine has burdened his reputation and that of his Order with a responsibility that should properly be shared by others, both Catholic and Protestant. He was a well-known historian of Spain and an acute political economist, yet because of his detailed analysis of tyranny and his conclusions regarding tyrannicide he soon became known as the outstanding preacher of that "Jesuitical doctrine," and became at the same time a source of embarrassment to his Order. His discussion of the question was bound to stir up heated dispute because he was not discussing, as were Aquinas or John of Salisbury, a fairly academic question, but rather the bearing of theory upon a recent event of grave political importance. Like Boucher and Rossaeus, he went to the defense of Clément, but, unlike the League writers, he was capable of cool reasoning as well as passionate rhetoric.

In Mariana's *De Rege et Regis Institutione,* published in 1599 with a dedication to Philip III of Spain, three full chapters were devoted to a discussion of tyranny and tyrannicide. He agreed with all his predecessors that tyranny was the worst form of government. He then described the characteristics of tyranny as contrasted with kingship, including in his rhetorical description many of the conventional marks of tyranny that were first noted by Aristotle:

> ... Either [the tyrant] has seized by force supreme power over the people, not by his own merits, but by his wealth and his arms; or, having secured supreme power with the consent of the people, he exercises it violently, and his power is directed not to the public utility but to his own profit, his own desires, the license of his vices. ... While he is consolidating his position, he deceives with an appearance of gentleness and mercy. ... When his rule is secure, he promptly turns to the opposite: no longer able to conceal his inherent savagery, he moves against all orders like an untamed and fierce beast. He seizes the property of individuals and squanders it, impelled as he is by the unkingly vices of lust, avarice, cruelty, and fraud. ... Tyrants, indeed, try to injure and to ruin everybody, but they direct their attack especially against rich and upright men throughout the realm. They consider the good more suspect than the evil; and the virtue which they themselves lack is most formidable to them. ... They expel the better men from the commonwealth on the principle that whatever is exalted in the kingdom should be brought low. ... They exhaust all the rest so that they can not unite by demanding new tributes from them daily, by stirring up quarrels among the citizens, and by joining war to war. They build huge works at the expense and by the suffering of the citizens. Whence the pyramids of Egypt were born. ... The tyrant necessarily fears that those whom he terrorizes and holds as slaves will attempt to overthrow him, and he is careful to prevent them from engaging in any arts of skill worthy of a free man or strengthening the vigor of their bodies and the confidence of their spirits by military pursuits. ... Thus he forbids the citizens to congregate together, to meet in assemblies, and to discuss the commonwealth altogether, taking from them by secret-police methods the opportunity of freely speaking and freely listening so that they are not even allowed to complain freely. ... He gathers around him foreign satellites, whom he trusts as outsiders; distrusting the citizens, he develops a mercenary army: which is a great calamity. ....[37]

Mariana then described in detail the assassination of Henry III by Clément. He spoke of the spectacle of the king's body as "a lesson to princes that he who dares impious deeds does not go unpunished; that the power of princes is vain if reverence has departed from the minds of the subjects,"[38] and he spoke of Clément as an "eternal ornament of France." Since many had condemned Clément's act, it became necessary, said Mariana, to examine the arguments on both sides. Those who denied the right of an individual to kill a tyrant argued on the grounds that the king was sacred; that those who tried to change the government often brought chaos or tyranny worse than that which they destroyed; that the harshness of a tyrant could best be mitigated by yielding to him; that to admit the right of private action against a ruler would destroy all reverence and obedience among subjects; and, finally, that there could be no greater calamity than the civil war which would follow insurrection. To these arguments Mariana replied that the people from whom a king received his power might overthrow the ruler who misused that power. Numerous recorded instances of the deposition or assassination of tyrants demonstrated a universal feeling that tyranny justified insurrection and tyrannicide. "Did not every one deem [the slayers of tyrants] worthy of the highest praise? And common opinion is, as it were, the word of nature written on our minds, a law resounding in our ears, by which we distinguish the honorable from the shameful."[39]

About the right of a private person to kill the usurper there could be no question. ". . . Philosophers and theologians agree that the prince who has seized the commonwealth by force and arms can, with no further right, no public consent of the citizens, be killed by anyone whatever . . . since he is a public enemy. . . ." The rightful king who abused his power must be suffered more patiently. "If, however, he destroys the commonwealth, holds public and private fortunes for his prey, holds the laws and holy religion in contempt," then a representative body must warn the king and urge him to return to sanity. If the king refused to mend his ways, a public assembly might depose him and declare him a public enemy whom any private person might kill. A very practical note and one that has a modern ring enters the argument at this point. If the ruler prevented the convening of a public assembly, this in itself became almost conclusive evidence of his tyranny. In such a situation, public judgment being rendered impossible, Mariana "will esteem as having acted in no way wrongly that man who, promoting the public wishes, undertakes to kill the prince." He believed, however, that the liberator should first consult "learned and grave men," as Clément had consulted the theologians before his attack on the king. Mariana did not fear that the doctrine of tyrannicide would be misused, for there would be few individuals in any country with the courage to sacrifice their lives on the chance that they might succeed in destroying tyranny. He believed that the doctrine was a healthy one, since some rulers might be curbed by the fear of assassination.[40]

Mariana's book was greeted in France with great indignation and was burned by the hangman. The General of the Society of Jesus ordered him to delete the offensive passages, but the only change in the second edition, published in 1603, was the omission of the phrase "an eternal ornament of France" in describing Clément. Interestingly enough, Mariana was one of the least "Jesuitical" of the Jesuit writers, since he did not concern himself at all with the right of the pope to absolve subjects from their allegiance. His general theory was at the same time more secular and more national than that of a more conventional Jesuit, Suarez. Yet more than any other Jesuit of the period he became for the non-Catholic world a symbol of pernicious Jesuit influence. His proper claim to fame should rest upon his extraordinarily acute and systematic treatment of those details of the theory of tyrannicide which many of his predecessors had ignored or buried in confusion.

In 1594, after one of the numerous attempts against the life of Henry IV, the *Parlement* of Paris condemned all members of the Society of Jesus as misleaders of the young, disturbers of the public peace, and enemies of king and state, and ordered their expulsion from Paris and from the principal cities of the kingdom. When Henry IV was finally assassinated by the Catholic fanatic, Ravaillac, in 1610, the teaching of Mariana and the influence of the Jesuits generally were held responsible for the act.

In England, Anglicans and royalists regularly condemned Presbyterians and Jesuits together as preachers of the same dangerous doctrine. A popular jingle linked Buchanan and Mariana:

> A Scot and Jesuit, hand in hand,
> First taught the world to say
> That subjects ought to have command
> And monarchs to obey.[41]

The royalist case against the Presbyterians could be supported readily by reference to their actions in Scotland as well as by the words of Knox, Buchanan, and their followers. And to the popular mind the case against the Jesuits seemed to be proved when in 1605 a little group of fanatics tried to blow up king and Parliament together, and three Jesuits were found to be implicated by their prior knowledge of the crime.

The danger inherent in the theory of tyrannicide was illustrated by the assassination of William the Silent just three years after the independence of the Netherlands, which William had done so much to achieve, had been declared. In France also the habit of trying to change governments by tyrannicide became so well fixed during the religious wars that seven attempts against the life of Henry IV were made before he was finally assassinated in 1610. France could perhaps afford to lose the weak and indecisive Henry III, but the loss of the capable and constructive Henry IV could but strengthen the absolutist reaction against all populist theories.

The half-century of bitter civil strife ended in France with the victory going to neither side, but rather to a third group. The *Politiques,* whose members were usually Catholics who despaired of crushing Protestantism by force and who were acutely aware of the desperate situation resulting from continual civil war, advocated toleration for the sake of peace and unity. For the sake of national independence they became strong Gallicans, and for the sake of order they tended to support absolutism. The most important statement of their general position was, of course, the *Six livres de la république* (1576) by Jean Bodin, one of the two most famous books on political theory that the century produced and one of the most significant ever written. With Bodin's general theory we are not concerned here, but we may observe that even the great proponent of the modern theory of sovereignty acknowledged the claim that tyrannicide was a permissible weapon against the usurper. So thoroughly had the doctrine become incorporated into the intellectual tradition of the time.

"A tyrannical monarchy" Bodin defined as that in which "one man treading under foot the laws of God and nature, abuses his free-born subjects as his slaves: and other men's goods as his own."[42] This definition was followed by an elaborate contrast between the king and the tyrant, which concluded, "In brief the one is praised and honored by all men while he lives, and much missed after his death; whereas the other is defamed yet living, and most shamefully reviled ... when he is dead."[43] Having cited the classical tradition, Bodin then declared that one who aspired to take political power by force "may of all the people, or any of them, be lawfully slain."[44] On the other hand, he warned that in the case of the lawful sovereign whose rule had become tyrannical, "it is not lawful for any one of his subjects in particular, or all of them in general, to attempt anything ... against the honor, life, or dignity of the sovereign: albeit that he had committed all the wickedness, impiety, and cruelty that could be spoken. ..."[45] Bodin based his conclusion on practical considerations, as well as upon principle. "Oh how many tyrants should there be; if it should be lawful for subjects to kill tyrants? How many good and innocent princes should as tyrants perish, by the conspiracies of their subjects against them?"[46]

Besides the utilitarian arguments of the *Politiques* and Bodin's argument based on the need for unassailable sovereignty, there appeared also arguments for royal absolutism supported by the conception of the divine right of the ruler.[47] The publications in this class were for the most part aimed directly at the theories of resistance already discussed. Outstanding among them was the comprehensive book of William Barclay, a Gallicized Scot, who undertook to refute in detail the arguments of Buchanan, Hotman, the *Vindiciae,* and Boucher.[48] It was Barclay who first described those against whom he wrote as "monarchomachs." Barclay's essential contentions were that authority could come from God alone, that political sovereignty was incapable of limitation, and consequently that there must exist an absolute duty of obedience by subjects.[49] But once more we find tradition too strong to be denied completely. Although he was certain that the views of the monarchomachs could lead only to constant rebellion and to anarchy, Barclay still recognized that the usurper might be killed by any private person. "Concerning tyrants of this sort," he said, "who in a free state seize dominion over others by force and arms... there is no controversy among men. Indeed all antiquity believed that these as public enemies can with the best right be attacked and killed not only by the whole people, but even by individuals. And the authority of subsequent centuries, agreeing with this perennial assertion, has confirmed it."[50]

There is perhaps no other period in which the doctrine of tyrannicide was considered in such detail, both in scholarly and in popular writings, as in France in the latter half of the sixteenth century. Not only were the traditional arguments and maxims revived once more and applied to contemporary events, but serious attempts were made to relate the doctrine of tyrannicide to general political theory concerning the nature and limits of political authority and to examine some of the problems which advocates of the doctrine had too often been inclined to ignore.

But the flaw that ran through the whole argument, from whichever side it came at the particular moment, was the assumption, implicit or explicit, that a ruler who did not support the true religion must *ipso facto* be a tyrant. Although Huguenots and Catholics dutifully repeated the traditional list of vices whereby the tyrant revealed his tyranny, they made little effort to demonstrate that the rulers they condemned actually possessed these vices. They took for granted that a ruler who subverted the true religion, or allowed it to be subverted, must also be guilty of the other offenses which were traditional marks of the tyrant. Under the doctrine as thus interpreted, rulers whose rule was no more arbitrary and no more subversive of the constitutional system than that of their still-respected predecessors or other contemporary rulers were marked out as properly entitled to assassination. William of Orange, Henry IV, and Elizabeth can be cited as obvious illustrations. Thus the doctrine of tyrannicide, for all the fervor, logic, and subtlety that went into it in the period of the French Wars of Religion, served in this period to justify political assassination in the cause of religion.

VII REAPPEARANCE OF THE THEORY IN SEVENTEENTH-CENTURY ENGLAND

IN SIXTEENTH-CENTURY England there had developed under the benevolent absolutism of the Tudors a doctrine of nonresistance which was not seriously challenged until the eve of the Civil War. In the course of the English Reformation there appeared a simple doctrine of the religious duty of obedience, not unlike that of Luther, which served the necessary purpose of supporting royal authority against the papacy. An extreme statement of the view may be found in Tyndale, who, forgetting the proud assertions of Bracton and neglecting the whole medieval tradition of a fundamental law above the king, went so far as to say, "He that judgeth the king judgeth God; and he that resisteth the king resisteth God and damneth God's law and ordinance.... The king is, in this world, without law, and may at his lust do right or wrong and shall give accounts but to God only."[1] English nationalism, successfully established on the basis of Tudor administrative efficiency and Tudor prosperity, lent popular support to monarchy.

In the reign of Mary Tudor, Catholic persecution of notable Anglicans had driven some of the Marian exiles to extreme doctrines of resistance and even of tyrannicide.[2] But after Elizabeth came to the throne the Protestant need for such doctrines disappeared. The fear of Spain and the warning example of civil war in France developed loyalty to the queen and at the same time created deep suspicion of the one religious minority capable of serious resistance. English Protestantism, English patriotism, and loyalty to the monarchy combined in bitter indignation against the efforts of the pope and of Philip of Spain to make English Catholics the tools of "the enterprise of England," whereby England would be rid of her Protestant queen and the Catholic faith restored. There was ample cause for suspicion. In a papal bull of 1570, Pope Pius V had declared Elizabeth excommunicate and deposed, had absolved her subjects from allegiance, and had forbidden obedience to her laws. In 1580, the papal secretary, in response to an inquiry on behalf of two English Catholics, had justified in advance the assassination of Elizabeth. The opinion from Rome was as follows:

Since that guilty woman of England rules over two such noble kingdoms of Christendom and is cause of so much injury to the Catholic faith, and loss of so many million souls, there is no doubt that whosoever sends her out of the world with the pious intention of doing God service, not only does not sin but gains merit, especially having regard to the sentence pronounced against her by Pius V of holy memory. And so if these English nobles decide actually to undertake so glorious a work, your lordship can assure them that they do not commit any sin.[3]

The most famous of the numerous plots against the life of Elizabeth was the elaborate Babington plot of 1586, just two years after the assassination of another Protestant ruler, William of Orange.[4] Although the execution of Mary Stuart for her role in this plot raised cries of indignation in Scotland and in France, the result in England was to remove a Catholic claimant to the throne and to insure a Protestant succession. It also confirmed once more the general Protestant opinion about the dangers of political Catholicism.

The views of Catholic extremists, like those of the Marian exiles, ran contrary to the now firmly established tradition of loyal obedience. "Perhaps the most striking peculiarity of England in the sixteenth century," writes J. W. Allen, "was the general refusal to admit that any case can be made for a right of rebellion."[5] The *Homilies* prescribed for church reading admonished passive obedience and described the horrors of rebellion. "Such subjects as are disobedient or rebellious against their princes, disobey God and procure their own damnation."[6] One writer summarized the general attitude simply: "Our common teaching is that we ought so to obey princes as sent of God, and that whoso withstandeth them withstandeth God's ordinance. And this is well to be seen both in our books and in our preachings."[7] Jesuits and Scottish Presbyterians were equally abhorrent to the great majority who gave loyal suport to the monarchy. Many would have agreed with Filmer's later statement: "The main and indeed the only point of Popery is the alienating and withdrawing of subjects from their obedience to their Prince."[8] The same crude but convenient simplification served to describe Presbyterians as well.

The first modern statement of a thoroughgoing theory of the

divine right of kings in England appeared at about the same time as similar statements were appearing in France. The book was, of course, the *Trew Law of Free Monarchies,* published in 1598, and its author was the king of Scotland, later king of England. The book reflects James' reaction against the control that Scottish Presbyterians had enforced upon their rulers and against the dicipline that the monarchomach Buchanan had not thought too rigorous for his royal pupil. James' assertions in his *Free Monarchies* reached extravagant heights. Kings appeared as "breathing images of God upon earth," as "God's lieutenants" who "sit upon God's throne"; their commands were "the commands of God's minister"; they were "to be judged only by God"; obviously they might never be resisted. As for the source of the king's vast prerogative, that was a "mystery" "not lawful to be disputed."[9]

Thoroughly familiar with the arguments that had supported the tradition of tyrannicide, James offered systematic arguments against them. It was an axiom in theology, he explained, "that evil should not be done, that good may come of it: the wickedness therefore of the King can never make them that are ordained to be judged by him, to become his judges." Secondly, rebellion would produce effects which would be the opposite of those promised by the rebels, "for a king cannot be imagined to be so unruly and tyrannous, but the commonwealth will be kept in better order, notwithstanding thereof, by him, then it can be by his way-taking." And, thirdly, "it is certain that a king can never be so monstrously vicious, but hee will generally favor justice, and maintaine some order, except in the particulars, wherein his inordinate lustes and passions carry him away; where by the contrary, no King being, nothing is unlawful to none. . . ."[10] James had learned early to distrust the Puritans politically. "If you aime at a Scottish Presbytery, it agreeth as well with Monarchy, as *God* and the *Devill.*"[11] In his *Basilikon Doron* of 1599, he had warned his son against such books as those of Buchanan and Knox and urged him to punish those who were found to have such books in their possession.[12]

After the famous Gunpowder Plot of 1605, which had been designed to blow up king, lords, and commons together and force upon the country a general Catholic insurrection, James' new Oath of Allegiance of 1606 started an international debate in the course of which the whole dispute over the duty of obedience, the grounds of resistance, and papal intervention was renewed once more. The Oath required the king's subjects to "abjure as impious and Heretical, this damnable doctrine and position that Princes which be excommunicated or deprived by the Pope, may be deposed or murthered by their Subjects or any other whatsoever."[13] When the pope forbade Catholics to take this oath, James himself entered vigorously into the debate, arguing against the famous Jesuit, Cardinal Bellarmine.[14] Continuing the argument at a later date in *A Defense of the Divine Rights of Kings,* he roundly condemned those Catholic writers who had encouraged and condoned "parracide": that is, tyrannicide.[15] He attempted to correct the interpretation of Biblical authority as justifying the deposition of kings.[16] He reviewed with contempt the story of Jean Petit[17] and exonerated Gerson of responsibility for the defense of tyrannicide.[18]

English opinion, including the majority of Catholic opinion, might support James, as it had supported Elizabeth, in opposition to resistance based on religious grounds and inspired by foreigners. But James' general political theory was another matter. From the time of Bracton at least, English constitutional theory had combined two fundamentally incompatible ideas: the idea that the king was limited by the rights of his subjects and the law of the land, and the idea that kingship by its very nature must involve an area of absolute, discretionary control over governmental policy. The question of the reconciliation of these two concepts had been postponed by the fact that the policies of late-medieval and Tudor rulers had been on the whole such as their subjects could approve; throughout the sixteenth century, at any rate, no one had had an interest in forcing the constitutional issue. James' insistence on the broadest possible construction of his prerogative had a basis in legal thought and political theory, but it shocked many of his subjects, who could also find good precedents for their emphasis upon the limits of royal authority and a narrow construction of the prerogative.

When James and his successor attempted to put their theory of the kingship into practice, the result was a long series of conflicts with judges and Parliament which led to the development of determined opposition in Parliament and culminated in the Petition of Right and finally in civil war. Evidence of the widening gulf between king and people appeared in the general wave of popular approval that greeted the assassination of the Duke of Buckingham. The young George Villiers, who became the first Duke of Buckingham, had been an influential favorite of James and, when Charles became king, Buckingham practically assumed control of the state. His reckless foreign adventures and his mismanagement of domestic and foreign affairs led the House of Commons to vote, in May,

1626, a formal impeachment of the king's principal minister, an action to which Charles responded by dissolving Parliament. In 1628, the House of Commons drew up a remonstrance setting forth Buckingham's alleged offenses and demanding that he be dismissed. Buckingham, publicly accused as "the cause of all the evils the kingdom suffered, and an enemy of the public,"[19] still enjoyed the full support of the king. It was under these circumstances that he was assassinated in August, 1628, by a former army lieutenant, John Felton. Felton had a personal grievance against the duke, but he claimed that he had been impelled to take the duke's life by reading the remonstrance of the House of Commons.

Although Felton's action had in it a strong suggestion of the traditional doctrine of tyrannicide, it has been generally regarded by historians of the period as an act of personal vengeance.[20] Felton had prepared in advance several short statements in defense of his act[21]; but he did not make a very persuasive case and, before his execution, he publicly repented his deed. Moreover, if Buckingham had governed tyrannically, it was as the agent of the king who had appointed and supported him. Logically, then, Charles rather than Buckingham should have been indicted; but Parliament was not yet ready to call the king a tyrant, preferring to maintain the fiction that, since "the king could do no wrong," misgovernment must be the fault of his minister.

Buckingham was not a tyrant in the traditional sense, but Felton was popularly acclaimed as a "little David," and numerous popular poems and ballads praised him as a benefactor of the nation.

> Live ever Felton, thou hast turned to dust
> Treason, ambition, murther, pride, and lust.[22]

The struggle between king and Parliament in 1628 could still be argued in terms of specific claims and counterclaims about the traditional rights of English subjects and the extent of the royal prerogative, as, for example, in the Petition of Right and the Remonstrance against Tonnage and Poundage, in the king's speech at the prorogation of Parliament in June, 1628, and in his later detailed declaration of the reasons for the dissolution.[23] In 1641, as in 1628, the leaders of Parliament were still attempting to distinguish between the king and his ministers and to make the ministers solely responsible for what they were coming to regard as tyranny. In its original charge against Strafford, the House of Commons declared that he had "traitorously endeavored to subvert the fundamental laws and government of the realms of England and Ireland, and instead thereof to introduce an arbitrary and tyrannical government against law...."[24]

In the long period between parliaments, antagonism against the king for his violations of constitutional tradition had been strengthened by the growing hostility of Puritans, Presbyterians, and Independents to his High Church policy. The execution of Strafford did not save Charles, and his recourse to force in answer to Parliamentary demands issued in civil war. At this point, the revolutionary ideological weapons that had been forged earlier in the religious struggles in Scotland and France began to make their appearance in England. In 1642-43 it was noticed with alarm that Mariana's *De Rege* was "everywhere."[25] The *Short Treatise of Politique Power,* written in 1556 by the vigorous exiled bishop John Ponet, was reprinted. In the confusing *mélange* of ideas that broke forth with the revolution, it was natural that none should appear and reappear more consistently than the old claims that the people or community was the source of authority; that the king was subject to law, and subject further to deposition when he neglected or exceeded his proper office. In the mind of a practical constitutionalist like Selden, the king was stripped of all fantastic pretensions when his place could be described in such simple language as this: "A king is a thing men have made for their own sakes, for quietness' sake. Just as in a family one man is appointed to buy the meat...." As for the mystery surrounding the king, "Prerogative is something that can be told what it is," said Selden, "not something that has no name."[26]

The assumptions on which Buchanan and "Junius Brutus" had built reappeared in the *Lex Rex* of the Presbyterian Samuel Rutherford, published in 1644. All men were born free, said Rutherford; none were born by nature to subjection and none to royal authority.[27] The authority of the king, though ultimately from God, came immediately from the people.[28] The authority of the king, then, rested upon consent, which was expressed through a conditional covenant between king and people.[29] When no written covenant existed, "the general covenant of nature is presupposed."[30] If a king, becoming a tyrant, attempted to abuse his authority "to the destruction of laws, religion, and the subjects," then authority reverted to the people and they might resist the tyrant. Such resistance was in accordance with the principle of self-preservation which was part of the law of nature.[31] In his *Sovereign Power of Parliaments and Kingdoms* (1643), William Prynne also argued, on the basis of the law of nature and of precedents, the superior position of Parliament and the right of the people to resist abusive rulers in defense of their traditional liberties.[32] The general assumptions of Rutherford and Prynne were also those of the Levellers, who drew from these assumptions more radical, democratic conclusions. John Lilburne and his group talked in terms of the original freedom of men, of the contract as a sign of the conventional origin of government, of the conditional grant of political authority by the people to their ruler, and of a natural right of resistance and self-defense against tyrants who violated the law and broke the contract.[33]

But the theory that justified resistance was not an adequate one for the situation that the Parliamentary forces faced after their victory. English kings had been deposed before, but never before had an English king been condemned to death and executed. Even in the case of the king's minister, Strafford, it had been necessary in 1641 for the Commons to resort to the crude instrument of a bill of attainder to secure his execution.[34] How much more difficult would be the execution of the king! But the leadership of the army and the purged House of Commons determined that the country must be rid of the king. Their decision came not from republican principles, but from their conviction that no lasting compromise with Charles was possible and that so long as Charles lived the cause of Parliament remained in danger. Although they regarded the execution of the king as a necessary act, it was clearly not a popular one. "The Royalists were naturally bitterly opposed to the trial and still more to the execution of the king; the Presbyterians were only second in their objection; the people in general were against it...."[35] When the question of proceeding against the life of the king came before the Commons, Cromwell himself apparently put the responsibility upon "the Providence of God." He is reported to have said, "Mr. Speaker, if any man whatsoever had carried on this design of deposing the King and disinheriting his posterity, or if any man had yet such a design, he should be the greatest traitor and rebel in the world. But since the Providence of God hath cast this upon us, I cannot but submit to Providence, though I am not yet prepared to give you my advice."[36]

In fact, what had begun as a defense of constitutional rights had developed into a situation in which it seemed necessary to take action which could not be based upon established constitutional principles. Continuing to insist upon an absolutist interpretation of the English constitution and upon his irresponsibility to men as a monarch by divine right,[37] Charles could also challenge the right of the special high court of justice, established by the purged House of Commons acting with the support of the army, to pass judgment upon him. And he could add that by refusing to plead he was not only defending himself against "the illegality of this pretended court," but also indirectly defending against illegal force the rights of his subjects.[38] To Charles's repeated demands to know "by what power I am called hither," the presiding judge replied, "By the authority of the Commons of England assembled in Parliament on the behalf of the people of England."[39] But this reply could be countered all too readily.

For an action that could not be justified on the basis of traditional constitutional principles, justification had to be found elsewhere. Although the execution of Charles was not an act of tyrannicide, the arguments supporting it relied heavily on the familiar arguments for tyrannicide. The charge against the king asserted that "being admitted King of England," he was "therein trusted with a limited power to govern by, and according to the laws of the land, and not otherwise; . . . being obliged to use the power committed to him for the good and benefit of the people, and for the preservation of their rights and liberties." It was then charged that "out of a wicked design to erect and uphold in himself an unlimited and tyrannical power to rule according to his will, and to overthrow the rights and liberties of the people, yea to take away and make void the foundations thereof, and of all redress and remedy of misgovernment," he "hath traitorously and maliciously levied war against the present Parliament, and the people therein represented. . . ."[40] In the sentence, Charles was condemned to death as "a tyrant, traitor, murderer, and public enemy to the good people of this nation."[41]

There was constant appeal to rough and ready conceptions of the law of nature. The chief prosecutor was prepared to argue that the king had been condemned "by the unanimous consent of all rational men in the world, written in every man's heart with the pen of a diamond in capital letters." There was no more need for a statute empowering the people to condemn a tyrant, he said, than for a law requiring men to eat and drink.[42] And John Goodwin, writing during the trial of the king, asserted that the army conformed "unto a law of far greater authority than any one, yea than all the laws of the land put together; I mean the law of nature, necessity, which, being the law of God himself, written in the fleshly tables of men's hearts, hath an authoritative jurisdiction over all human laws and constitutions whatsoever. . . ."[43]

Once convinced that the necessity of abnormal action against the king was an instance of "the Providence of God," Cromwell himself appealed to the theory of tyranny and resistance to bolster the courage of those who doubted the right of the specially constituted court. Among his followers, he argued vigorously for the king's conviction and, according to one reporter, on one occasion "entered into a long discourse of the nature of the regal power according to the principles of Mariana and Buchanan."[44] Later he spoke of the execution as follows: "The civil authority... did in answer to their consciences, turn out a tyrant, in a way which Christians in aftertimes will mention with honour, and all tyrants in the world look at with fear...."[45]

The most famous defense of the Regicides was that made by John Milton. His pamphlet on *The Tenure of Kings and Magistrates,* written during the trial of the king, appeared two weeks after the execution. The framework of Milton's argument followed a familiar pattern. Men were born free; they united together for mutual protection. Kings might be entrusted with the administration of public affairs, but fundamental power still remained with the people.[46] "... The power of Kings and Magistrates is nothing else, but only what is derivative, transferred and committed to them in trust from the People, to the Common good of them all, in whom the power yet remaines fundamentally, and cannot be taken from them...." To say that kings were accountable to God alone upset all law and government.[47] The contrary was true: the people might reject and depose kings at their pleasure. If it was the people's right to depose a good king, they might obviously rid themselves of a tyrant who had regard for neither law nor the common good but acted only for himself and his faction, as they would rid themselves of any "common pest."[48] Nothing was more agreeable to the law of nature than the punishment of tyrants. Although he regarded this as self-evident, Milton cited the usual authorities, including Greek and Roman tradition, Seneca, the Old Testament, and English history, and concluded with an array of Protestant reformers.[49]

Milton's main purpose was to justify the execution of a tyrant after his conviction by formal procedure, but much of his evidence was evidence pointing toward tyrannicide, and his argument was broad enough to support a limited right of tyrannicide. The subtitle of the *Tenure* reads: "That it is lawful, and hath been held so through all Ages, for any, who have the Power, to call to account a Tyrant, or wicked King, and after due conviction, to depose and put him to death; if the ordinary Magistrate have neglected, or deny'd to doe it." In the course of the argument Milton declared, "The Sword of Justice is above him; in whose hand soever is found sufficient power.... For if all human power to execute... the wrath of God upon evil doers without exception, be of God; then that power, whether ordinary, or if that faile, extraordinary so executing that intent of God, is lawfull, and not to be resisted."[50]

In an incisive passage of the *Leviathan,* Hobbes later called attention to the perennial role of the classical tradition in justifying the killing of a king. "And as to rebellion in particular against Monarchy; one of the most frequent causes of it, is the reading of the books of policy, and histories of the ancient Greeks, and Romans.... From the reading, I say, of such books, men have undertaken to kill their kings, because the Greek and Latin writers ... make it lawfull, and laudable, for any man to do so; provided before he do it, he call him tyrant. For they say not *regicide,* that is, killing of a king, but *tyrannicide,* that is, killing of a tyrant, is lawful." The venom of such books, Hobbes continued, created in a monarchy a disease that might be called *tyrannophobia.* If they were allowed to circulate, their venom should be counteracted by the antidote of the books of "discreet masters."[51]

With the execution of Charles, "the monarchy, as Charles understood it, had disappeared forever."[52] The immediate result, however, was not a new constitutional system but the dictatorship of Cromwell, maintained with the support of the army. In England, as earlier in France, arguments based on the doctrine of the right of resistance to tyranny shifted sides as the political situation changed. It was not long before Cromwell was being assailed as a usurper and tyrant, whose prompt removal, by whatever means, was necessary. In 1654 a group of Royalists issued a proclamation offering a reward to anyone who would kill "a certain mechanic fellow," called Oliver Cromwell, "by pistol, sword, or poison."[53] Royalists and Levellers were linked in their plots against the Protector, especially through the intrigues of Edward Sexby, a former officer in the Cromwellian army, whose agents made persistent efforts to kill Cromwell.[54]

In 1657, shortly after a plot which came close to success, the Protector was vigorously assailed in an anonymous pamphlet, *Killing No Murder,*[55] in which a concise statement of the arguments for tyrannicide accompanied a direct exhortation that they be applied against the Protector. The pamphlet declared that "every man is naturally a judge and an executioner" over the tyrant; "the laws of God, of nature, and of nations expose [tyrants] like beasts of prey to be destroyed as they are met."[56] Cromwell was found to be both a tyrant *sine titulo* (usurper), since his rule rested on "no other title but force and fraud," and a tyrant *exercitio*, since his actions corresponded to the picture of the tyrant drawn by Plato, Aristotle, and Machiavelli.[57] His forceful removal was not only lawful and right, but also thoroughly necessary and expedient. To the well-known argument that tyranny should be borne lest worse tyranny replace the old, the author answered scornfully, "One would think the world were bewitched. I am fallen into a ditch, where I shall certainly perish if I lie, but I refuse to be helped out for fear of falling into another; I . . . let the disease kill me, because there is hazard in the cure."[58] The conclusion was a call to action: "Let every man . . . endeavor by all rational means to free the world of this pest."[59] This conclusion had already been stated with remarkable bluntness in the prefatory letter to Cromwell: "To your Highness justly belongs the honor of dying for the people. . . . To hasten this great good is the chief end of my writing this paper. . . ."[60] Designed to coincide with Cromwell's acceptance of the crown, the pamphlet was received with enthusiasm by the Royalists; but the anticipated popular effect of its circulation was largely nullified by Cromwell's refusal to become a king.

With the Restoration there was a strong reaction against the doctrine of tyrannicide, not only among the Royalists but also among all but extreme religious zealots. The tone of horror that pervaded the charges and arguments of the prosecution in the trial of the Regicide judges was matched by the moderation of the arguments of the defendants, most of whom chose to rely on the legalistic argument that what had been done had been done under the proper authority of Parliament. To this argument, only Thomas Harrison, who had been at least as early as 1653 a member of the extreme sect of Fifth Monarchy Men, added that "I did it all according to the best of my understanding, desiring to make the revealed will of God in his Holy Scriptures as a guide to me. . . . And whereas it hath been said that we did assume and usurp an authority, I say this was done rather in the fear of the Lord." This appeal to conscience was quickly silenced by the court: "Know where you are, Sir; you are in the assembly of Christians; will you make God the author of your treasons and murthers? . . . Christians must not hear this." Harrison thereupon retreated quickly to a reaffirmation of the legal case.[61]

A similar concern to dissociate themselves from theories justifying private, illegal resistance appeared in the statements of prominent Whig leaders when they were on trial in 1683, charged with complicity in the Rye House Plot to assassinate Charles II and his brother James. They not only denied any responsibility for the plot but also refused to defend it in any way; and they maintained this position even on the scaffold, when the last hope of saving their lives had disappeared.[62] In this instance, the issue of tyrannicide was raised only negatively, in the bitter Royalist reaction to the plot.[63]

The situation assumed in the traditional theory of tyrannicide—"manifest" tyranny, as determined by a complex of objective criteria and recognized by collective opinion—is not illustrated in the history of seventeenth-century England. As in sixteenth-century France, religious tests of tyranny resulted only in disagreement. Moral and constitutional tests give conflicting answers—most conspicuously in the case of Cromwell, but neither James nor Charles can be seriously charged with an endeavor to subvert the common good to his selfish interests. Inept, short-sighted, and stubborn they certainly were, but their actions were guided by a genuine conviction that their claims and policies served the common good. The constitutional test, on which the leaders of the opposition to the Stuarts predominantly based their case, really gives no clear-cut answer. The fundamental issue between king and Parliament was rooted in two conflicting but equally respectable views of the nature of monarchy and the structure of the English constitution. This issue was intensified, but not superseded, by the issue that was rooted in the conflicting imperatives of different religious creeds.

Thus the long-range significance of the conflict was not the removal of a tyrant but the clarification of political and constitutional principles: a transition from ambiguity at the beginning of the century to the ultimate victory of the principles of the supremacy of the community and the limitation of monarchy in the Revolution of 1688. In this transition, the concept of the tyrant and the theories that justified resistance to tyranny played a significant, if limited, role. Although the resisters clearly preferred, so far as it was possible, to base their position on specific constitutional arguments, the unyielding opposition of Charles I gradually forced them into a position where they had to appeal to more abstract principles. Thus the concept of the tyrant was applied, first, to Charles' ministers; finally, to Charles himself. The fact that the trial and execution of Charles could not be safely grounded on legal right made the ideology of tyranny necessary; the fact that Charles had been the first to resort to violence made it available.

However, although the concept of the tyrant was used to support the quasi-legal killing of Charles, the idea that a tyrant might rightfully be killed was typically combined with the idea that, in such a case, the appropriate actor was the community from whose consent the rights of kings were derived. The existence of even a Rump Parliament as representative of the community's right made an extreme assertion of the doctrine of tyrannicide unnecessary; and the action of the Regicides was conceived and defended as, in principle, the action of the community rather than the action of private men.

Throughout this period, the symbol of the tyrant continued to be balanced by the symbol of the monarch as the ancient and enduring center of unity and authority. Private tyrannicide continued to be generally regarded with the suspicion evoked by its previous use in the religious strife. And the general seventeenth-century concern for the stability of orderly government, which appeared conspicuously in the Tory doctrine of non-resistance, had its effect also in discouraging, even among those who resisted, any widespread assertion of the right to action of private men.

The revolution begun in 1642 led ultimately to the conclusion of 1688-9, which fixed the constitutional relationship from which modern English parliamentarism could develop peacefully and more or less continuously. With the victory of constitutionalism, the *raison d'être* of the theory of tyrannicide disappeared and the works of English political theorists, while building often on foundations which had supported tyrannicide earlier, made only passing references to the doctrine. In France, on the other hand, the success of highly centralized monarchic absolutism drove doctrines of resistance and tyrannicide out of circulation until, with the degeneration of the French monarchy, they began to reappear in the second half of the eighteenth century.

VIII SOME COMMENTS ON THE TRADITION AND THEORY OF TYRANNICIDE

THE PRECEDING account has traced the continuity of the tradition of tyrannicide in Western political thought from the time of its first appearance in the Greek city states through the period of the Civil War and constitutional reconstruction in seventeenth-century England. From this necessarily brief survey certain general conclusions may be drawn.

In the tradition of tyrannicide there were two original components. The most persistent and most important was the image of the tyrant as set forth by Aristotle and repeated, with various embellishments but no fundamental change, in the writings of many centuries. In this persistent picture, the tyrant appeared as the exact reverse of the rightful ruler; and the essense of tyranny appeared as the subversion of the basic values of the community, on which all rightful claims to authority must be based: its concern for security, for legality and order, and for the basic rights and dignity of free men. Although the violation of constitutional principles was a part of the traditional image of the tyrant, and the particular characteristic of the tyrant by usurpation, the concept of tyranny was fundamentally an ethical rather than a merely legal concept. The tyrant was, by definition, the enemy of the common good.

The traditional image of the tyrant was often, though by no means always, associated with the image of the tyrannicide: a complex of statements and stories that presented in a favorable light the man who put an end to tyranny by killing the tyrant. The image of the tyrant was, from the beginning, closely related to systematic theory about the basis and nature of political authority. It played a part in a considerable body of speculation in which the issue of tyrannicide was not even raised, serving to define, by contrast, the necessary characteristics of rightful government. But the image of the noble slayer of the tyrant frequently appeared simply as a tradition. It had the prestige of its classical and Scriptural origins and could accordingly be cited without much theoretical examination, often with the simple interpretation that the slayer acted under the direct inspiration of God. The rational examination of tyrannicide was, however, an occasional topic for political theorists in the Middle Ages; and in the sixteenth century it became an important topic of systematic political thought, discussed in naturalistic terms.

Discussion of the theoretical problem of tyrannicide occurred in the context of certain fundamental political principles. The general idea that authority was justified by the ruler's service to the common good and the idea that authority was limited by divine and natural law and by the law of the land were basic principles of medieval political theory. Some theorists drew from these principles the corollary of a right or duty of disobedience to specific commands of a ruler when they violated the conditions of his authority. And, toward the end of the Middle Ages, the idea that the ruler's authority existed for the common good had been expanded by many thinkers into the idea that it originated in the consent of the community and could, for cause, be legitimately withdrawn by the community.

The theory of tyrannicide developed in this intellectual context was not an aberration of unscrupulous or irresponsible men invented to excuse a drive for personal power or gain. It was rather the conclusion drawn by certain serious thinkers from their conception of the relations between men and their rulers. It served as a focus for the broader question of the limits of political obedience and the right of resistance to misrule. The general question was here examined in terms of the extreme case: assuming, on the one hand, the existence of a thoroughly bad ruler whose tyranny was manifest; assuming, on the other hand, the absence of any collective institutional means of removing him or limiting his misrule. The crux of the problem was not whether tyrants deserved to die. There was a unanimous recognition that tyranny was among the worst of all crimes. The debate centered on a practical question: was tyrannicide an appropriate means for dealing with tyranny that could not be otherwise abolished, or did its dangers outweigh its probable good results?

The danger of permitting private action against a ruler was recognized by those who approved as well as by those who condemned tyrannicide. But it should be noticed that the reasoned defense of tyrannicide was by no means a doctrine of the supremacy of private judgment. It was not a defense of the individual whose opinion or conscience was his sole guide, or who diagnosed tyranny in terms of the interests of a social group, or who used tyrannicide as a means for the achievement of values not yet accepted in the common thought of the community. The theory of tyrannicide assumed, implicitly or explicitly, a basic situation in which the individual could be conceived as acting on behalf of the community, in defense of values generally shared, against a tyranny generally recognized as such.

Thus the defense of tyrannicide was safeguarded by the ever-present assumption that its purpose would be the re-establishment of the constitutional system which tyranny had destroyed and of the human rights which tyranny had suppressed. The theory of tyrannicide, through the seventeenth century, was conservative theory, in the sense that the object of tyrannicide was to destroy an improper innovation and to restore former values to the community, not to clear the way for new social organization. The nineteenth-century idea of a changing world in which new social values were to be achieved through the revolutionary action of an enlightened minority was not a part of the original theory of tyrannicide; it was completely alien from the presuppositions of medieval and early modern men. Thus the values to which the slayer of the tyrant must appeal for his justification were understood to be values deeply rooted in past experience and in a common social conviction.

The presumption of permanent common values itself reflected a long-continued experience. For many centuries, the Western world was bound—however loosely—into a single community by its common acceptance of certain general principles. It was a single religious community, in which the necessary unity of Christendom was universally taken for granted. It was a community bound together by a common belief that the rights of subjects and the constitutional limits of kingship were clearly defined by custom and reason alike. And it was a single ethical community, whose common moral values were believed to be rooted in the Christian revelation or in the rational law of nature and thus to be also objective, permanent, and generally known.

Moreover, as has been already suggested, the concept of tyranny with which medieval and early modern theorists operated was itself sharply defined in terms of values common to the community.

The tyrant was not seen as the agent of the suppression of one social class by another, nor as the instrument of factional interests or opinions in a divided society. He was, quite simply, a bad man who opposed his private good to the good of the community as a whole. Thus it could be assumed that the whole community or, at any rate, all decent and reasonable members of the community, would concur in the recognition of the tyrant and in a common conviction that he should be destroyed. And it could also be assumed that the cause of tyranny itself would be destroyed with the destruction of the single tyrant.

Within this framework of assumptions, the debate over tyrannicide was a debate on a few practical issues. The practical arguments against tyrannicide itself were summarized by Mariana: attempts to end tyranny by individual action might not achieve their goal but might lead to worse evils—a still harsher tyranny or destructive civil war; and that it was possible to mitigate the harshness of tyranny by bowing before it. Mariana's answer, that there could be nothing worse than incorrigible tyranny and that it would be impossible to appease a tyrant by submission, reflects the absolute terms in which the image of the tyrant was typically conceived. Such an answer is, of course, essentially an evasion of the question. The expedience or inexpedience of tyrannicide must in the end be discussed in terms of particular conditions at particular times.

The practical argument which the defenders of tyrannicide recognized as the gravest challenge to their position was an attack on the expedience, not of tyrannicide, but of the very doctrine that defended it: the argument that to acknowledge the right of individual action in any instance would destroy the reverence and loyalty of subjects to their rulers and thus encourage the assassination of good kings by wicked men. It was on the basis of this argument that Aquinas had condemned the doctrine of tyrannicide; it remains the most persuasive argument against the case for private action. The defense made by Buchanan and Mariana was, perhaps, the best that can be made; and Mariana's answer is particularly significant in making fully explicit the conception of the relations between the tyrannicide and the community which was the premise of the traditional theory.

Buchanan answered that abuse of the doctrine did not destroy its validity. Mariana, on the other hand, began by asserting that there was actually little reason to fear its abuse, for very few men would be likely to appear at any time with enough courage to risk their lives in an attempt against a ruler. Aristotle had made the same point when he said that those who attacked rulers for love of glory "are very few indeed in number, for underlying the venture there must be an utter disregard of safety." But Mariana did not allow the argument to rest there. It was for this very reason that he insisted that, if possible, a representative assembly must first pass judgment upon the tyrant, and that, if the representative assembly had been suppressed, a private individual could kill only in the case of manifest tyranny, certified by the opinion of "learned and grave men": "Nor is there danger that many, by this teaching, will rage against the life of princes as if they were tyrants; for we do not grant this right to the private judgment of anyone whatever, or even of many; unless there is present the public voice of the people, learned and grave men ought to be consulted." Thus the support of public opinion, directly or through those competent to define its interests, was for Mariana an essential and explicit part of the legitimation of tyrannicide.

The community consensus on which Mariana insisted was not available in the sixteenth century. The flowering of the theory of tyrannicide in the sixteenth century was, in fact, primarily the result of the shattering of the long-established religious unity of Europe and of the refusal of religious groups to acknowledge that there could be more than one "true religion." Their use of the religious criterion to test the existence of tyranny was not itself inconsistent with the tradition, which had not been exclusively secular. If tyranny was defined as the subversion of the deepest interests of the community, and if an assured opportunity of salvation was regarded as the most important of those interests, then the subversion or neglect of the true religion could logically be regarded as the most serious offense a ruler could commit. But the basic difficulty in this argument, as it was used by Catholics and Protestants alike, was that, in a country in which the religious convictions of the people were sharply divided, no general consensus on the matter could realistically be said to exist. Similarly, as the course of events in seventeenth-century England conspicuously showed, the medieval assumption of clear-cut and static constitutional principles against which the tyranny of a ruler might be measured had been steadily undermined, as the institution of kingship had developed and the theory of the proper rights of a ruler had become more and more complex and controversial.

In this situation, the recognition of tyranny could not possibly be a recognition by the whole community. It was, in fact, resolved to a question of the opinion of a religious or political group. Adherents of the various schools of non-resistance were quick to observe this and to point it out. But the various restatements of the theory of tyrannicide that appeared in the sixteenth and seventeenth centuries consistently evaded the question of the practical applicability of their doctrine in the circumstances to which they wished it to apply. Their authors continued to reproduce the traditional image of the tyrant without looking to see whether the rulers to whom they objected were actually of that absolute type; and they talked about the voice of the community without really listening to any voices but their own.

Misapplications of the theory of tyrannicide helped to stimulate the extreme development of various theories of non-resistance. Those who were shocked by instances of assassination that purported to be tyrannicides increasingly feared that the whole system of procedural legality and authority might be destroyed if any compromise with its basic principles were sanctioned. They were properly concerned about protecting the structure of authority and obedience which is essential to the civilized life of man, and of which the person of the monarch had become the symbol. But what they, in turn, failed to see was that the maintenance of that structure was itself dependent on the recognition of a difference between the moral claims of a king and of a tyrant, and that in identifying the principle of order with the person of a king immune from earthly control they put in constant jeopardy the values they sought to preserve.

The solution for this dilemma was found in the development of constitutionalism, which, in making government continuously responsible to the community and establishing institutionalized checks against arbitrary rule, provided a stronger moral basis for a doctrine of obedience and seemed to make a theory of private resistance obsolete. Thus, although the symbols of tyranny and tyrannicide continued to play a role in the struggles of the eighteenth and nineteenth centuries, serious discussion of the theory of tyrannicide was scarcely developed beyond the point to which Buchanan and Mariana had brought it.

The survival of a political tradition divorced from any continuously re-examined political theory is likely to lead to its distortion and abuse. The story of the distortion of tyrannicide, and consideration whether the old tradition and the old theory can have any validity in the modern world, lie outside the task of this section of the book. But a final comment may be made.

So far as a reasoned doctrine had been formulated, it was governed by the conviction that an individual attack on the wielder of public authority could be justified only on the ground that the attacker acted on behalf of the whole community in the defense of established values on which a community consensus existed. More recent centuries have demonstrated that on many values there is no consensus and that the pattern of values which a community maintains as essential to the good life is a gradually changing one. The whole complex of principles associated with the values of nationalism and democracy were only rudimentary in the centuries covered in this study; on the other hand, religious unity, so long considered an imperative need, has disappeared from the modern list of the conditions generally regarded as necessary to the fulfilment of men as men. The history of the sixteenth and seventeenth centuries, and of the succeeding period, abundantly demonstrates that, in cases of serious conflict over values held by different groups within a society, the cry of tyranny is likely to be raised and the right of private resistance is likely to be asserted—and not simply by wicked men. What basic principles may arbitrate such claims is not an easy question; but certainly the old theory of tyranny and tyrannicide was not conceived to meet such situations.

To point out the inadequacy or irrelevance of the old theory to many instances of modern conflict is not, however, to deny it a possibility of some contemporary significance. In the historic flux of values, there has remained a core of persistent ethical conviction: a continuing insistence, however variously phrased, on the final dignity of human personality and its claim to be regarded as an end and not a means—a continuing assertion that the free man can not rightly be subordinated to any objective narrower than the common good. This conviction was expressed by classical and medieval thinkers in their absolute contrast between the tyrant and the king; it has not been abolished, but rather strengthened and enriched, by the thought of later centuries. Thus the definition and recognition of modern tyranny may well begin with an investigation of its impact upon the structure of basic human rights which the Western world has come to regard as necessary corollaries of the security and moral dignity of man. Again, the concept of a final reciprocity between private rights and public interest, which was the basis of the old theories of resistance, has not been abolished in more recent political thought, but rather given added meaning. Thus the modern question of the right of individuals to resist tyrannical government can, perhaps, be clarified—though certainly not solved—by the criteria of the old theory: first, through an awareness of what tyranny really means; and, second, through the recognition that claims to a private right of resistance—in any degree—must be made in terms of the established values of the entire community. For a private right of resistance, like every other specific right, must base its justification on its usefulness to what men understand to be their *common* good.

PART TWO

*THE USE AND ABUSE
OF TYRANNICIDE*

by Oscar Jászi

IX REVOLUTION AND CONSTITUTION: THE TYRANT AS A SYSTEM

AFTER THE middle of the seventeenth century, little attention was paid to the formal theory of tyrannicide and very little new was added to the classic doctrine. The traditional ideology survived, in a rather attenuated fashion; it played a part in the symbolism of the American and French Revolutions and of the liberal revolutions of the earlier nineteenth century; it became a literary motif for certain *beaux esprits* who sympathized with the revolutionary struggles. But experience and thought gradually eroded the traditional concept of tyranny as the misgovernment of an individual ruler. As the tyrant came to be conceived as a governing class, as a system of institutions, or as an impersonal social force, tyrannicide seemed a superficial or irrelevant remedy, and attention shifted to the fundamental remaking of institutions as the preventive of unjust and arbitrary power.

The last great period of tyrannicide plots and literature had coincided with the sixteenth- and seventeenth-century struggles between absolutist monarchs and the remains of the medieval structure of power. In England the struggle issued in a transfer of the already-achieved values of monarchic centralization to a new structure of parliamentary government. But elsewhere in Europe monarchs fought step by step toward the establishment of one single authority, one administrative regime, one army, one cultural pattern. What might seem to the holders of traditional privileges to be the arbitrary actions of a new type of tyrant were in reality the foundations of the modern state. What came into existence was not tyranny of the old type, but royal absolutism.

Absolutism, so long as it did not become degenerate, was regarded as a divinely ordered institution bound to law and the interest of the commonwealth. King James I, in his speech to Parliament in 1603, emphasized vigorously the difference between the lawful king and the tyrant. He asserted that "the special and greatest point of difference" between them was this: "that, whereas the proud and ambitious tyrant doth think his kingdom and people are only ordained for satisfaction of his desires and unreasonable appetites, the righteous and just king doth, by the contrary, acknowledge himself to be ordained for the procuring of the wealth and prosperity of his people." And although he asserted that no earthly agency could enforce the obligation upon him, he nevertheless, as in his speech to Parliament in 1609, asserted also the legal limitations of his power. The king binds himself, he said,

... by a double oath, to the observation of the fundamental laws of his kingdom: tacitly, as by being a king, and so bound to protect as well the people, as the laws of his kingdom; and expressly, by his oath at his coronation; so as every just king, in a settled kingdom, is bound to observe that paction made to his people by his laws, in framing his government agreeable thereunto. ... And therefore a king governing in a settled kingdom, leaves to be a king, and degenerates into a tyrant, as soon as he leaves off to rule according to his laws.[1]

The same conception prevailed in France, where some of the greatest thinkers supported the claims of royal absolutism as the only possible expedient to eliminate feudal anarchy and religious civil wars. Bodin and the *Politiques* saw nothing tyrannical in the new power provided it was rightly and conscientiously exercised. The middle class supported the power which was fighting their common enemy, feudal particularism. In 1614, the advocates of the Third Estate asserted:

His Majesty is requested to state and proclaim as an inalienable and generally accepted principle of the state, the following: The king is sovereign in his country. He possesses his crown from God alone. Therefore there is no power on earth, either divine or worldly, which would have the smallest claim upon his realm; even less to rob the holy persons of our kings of their country under any pretext, or to release their subjects from their oath of fidelity.[2]

The power of the king was not regarded as tyrannical until the outburst of revolutionary passion after 1789.

The ill-famed dictum, *l'état c'est moi,* was less the boasting of a despot than the expression of a factual situation generally regarded as desirable, as divinely approved, and as consistent with a basic respect for the traditional laws of France. Rousseau rightly emphasized the legitimate foundation of absolutism:

This hateful system [tyranny] is indeed, even in modern times, very far from being that of wise and good monarchs, and especially of the kings of France; as may be seen . . . particularly from the following passage in a celebrated edict published in 1667 in the name and by order of Louis XIV.

He quoted from this edict:

Let it not, therefore, be said that the Sovereign is not subject to the laws of his State; since the contrary is a true proposition of the right of nations, which flattery has sometimes attacked but good princes have always defended as the tutelary divinity of their dominions. How much more legitimate it is to say with Plato, that the perfect felicity of a kingdom consists in the obedience of subjects to their prince, and of the prince to the laws, and in the laws being just and constantly directed to the public good![3]

Similar conceptions were to be expressed by Louis XVI when he stood before the tribunal of the Convention; and these anti-tyrannical expressions of absolute rulers were not insincere.

Yet even while it fulfilled its function of unification and of laying down the foundation of the modern state, it was in the very essence of absolutism to degenerate and to develop tyrannical traits. The absolutistic system lost touch with the purposes which had justified it; it had a tendency to assume features of personal despotism, and the popular forces which it had accelerated began to revolt against it. It was felt that a new tyranny oppressed the people, and both the English and French Revolutions involved the execution of "tyrannical kings."

However, it became a growing conviction in the minds of sober observers that kings, even if they became "tyrants," were not of the old type, and that killing them would not in itself alter the despotic rule. The tyrant had changed from a person to a system.

The traditional theory of tyrannicide was in its essence a conservative doctrine. There was no revolutionary thought in it, no vision of a better society. The figure of the tyrant was clearly visible, like an inflammation in a human body. Annihilate the tyrant, destroy the small, vicious structure he has created for the oppression of his unhappy compatriots, and the whole regime would collapse immediately. The social organism would regain its former health, like the human body after the lancing of a boil. Thus the typical argument for tyrannicide had run.

But if tyranny were not concentrated in a single person, merely annihilating the king would be no remedy against the despotic tendencies of the system. Not even resistance or revolution against the system would help, without creating institutions which would minimize the possibility of tyrannical action. Thus anti-absolutist thought would come to define its objective as a struggle for constitutionalism: by legitimate means if possible, by revolutionary action if necessary. This tendency was already strong in the Puritan Revolution and became the leading motif of the subsequent centuries.

John Locke, the father of modern constitutionalism, had himself been implicated in the Rye House Plot of 1683 to assassinate Charles II and his brother James. In his *Second Treatise on Civil Government,* written after the Glorious Revolution, he incidentally restated the traditional arguments that had justified tyrannicide, but in a broader context: for his main themes were the analysis of the basic principles of constitutional government and the defense of the community's right of revolution.

He showed that the natural right of self-defense applied to the tyranny of any magistrate who abused his power:

Wherever law ends, tyranny begins, if the law be transgressed to another's harm; and whosoever in authority exceeds the power given him by the law, and makes use of the force he has under his command to compass that upon the subject which the law allows not, ceases in that to be a magistrate, and acting without authority may be opposed, as any other man who by force invades the right of another.[4]

The right of self-defense did not, of course, apply in cases where legal redress was available; but if the tyranny obstructed the possibility of legal remedy, the case was parallel to that of a traveler whose life was threatened by a highwayman, allowing him no opportunity of recourse to the protection of the law:

The law could not restore life to my dead carcass. The loss was irreparable; which to prevent the Law of Nature gave me a right to destroy him who had put himself into a state of war with me, and threatened my destruction.[5]

The argument was an implicit legitimation of tyrannicide. But Locke did not believe that an individual wronged by tyranny would be likely to exercise his right of self-defense in a single-handed attack upon the government that had oppressed him. His statement of these principles was only preliminary to his demonstration that the community likewise had the right of self-defense when either the legislature or the prince, or both, should attempt to pervert the constitution established by the people or abuse their trust by infringing on the natural rights of man to life, liberty, and property. A tyrannical government, he argued, forfeited its claim to authority; political power then reverted to the society, and the people were

> at liberty to provide for themselves by erecting a new legislative.... For the society can never, by the fault of another, lose the native and original right it has to preserve itself, which can only be done by a settled legislative and a fair and impartial execution of the laws made by it.[6]

The public right of self-defense against tyranny included the right to resist the tyrannical rulers:

> Whosoever uses force without right ... puts himself into a state of war with those against whom he so uses it, and in that state all former ties are cancelled, all other rights cease, and every one has a right to defend himself, and to resist the aggressor.[7]

Locke claimed that the right of revolution which he defended would not lay a foundation for constant rebellion. "For till the mischief be grown general, and the ill designs of the rulers become visible ... to the greater part, the people ... are not apt to stir."[8] His whole argument, of course, assumed that in case of "general mischief," the people could and would stir; primarily concerned to defend the already accomplished Revolution, he was not interested in the situation in which collective resistance might have become impossible. He did, however, point out that it was not necessary to postpone revolution until the tyranny had become complete: "This is, in effect, to bid them first be slaves, and then to take care of their liberty, and, when their chains are on, tell them they may act like free men."[9]

Locke's theory of the social contract based the right of revolution partly on the principle that misused authority reverted to the community. But his doctrine of revolution was linked to the theory of tyrannicide in his use also of the argument of the natural right to self-defense, and in his recognition that, when the established agencies of public action were subverted, the community could act only as a collectivity of individual men. Raising the eternal question, "Who shall be judge?" he answered flatly, "The people shall be judge; for who shall be judge whether his trustee or deputy acts well ... but he who deputes?" But he added, "Where there is no judicature on earth to decide controversies among men, God in heaven is judge.... But every man is judge for himself, as in all other cases so in this, whether another hath put himself into a state of war with him, and whether he should appeal to the supreme Judge, as Jeptha did."[10]

The fathers of the American Revolution were the direct heirs of the monarchomachs and of Sidney, Milton, and Locke. A belief in the illegitimacy of tyrannical government and a conviction of the justice of violent action against such a regime were familiar principles to which American revolutionaries naturally appealed in their fight against English domination. The Declaration of Indepence based the justice of the American cause on the claim that "the history of the present king of Great Britain is a history of repeated injuries and usurpations, all having as direct object the establishment of absolute tyranny over these states." Franklin suggested as the motto for the seal of the United States: "Resistance to Tyrants is Obedience to God"; his suggestion was not accepted, but Jefferson had the motto added to the seal of the state of Virginia, and also adopted it for his own seal.[11]

To Jefferson, resistance against tyranny seemed not merely justified but at times positively essential to the maintenance of human liberty. When some of his conservative contemporaries were alarmed by Shays' Rebellion, he wrote the famous words: "God forbid! that we should ever be twenty years without such a rebellion. ... What country can preserve its liberties, if their rulers are not warned from time to time that this people preserve the spirit of resistance? Let them take arms! ... What signify a few lives lost in a century or two? The tree of liberty must be refreshed from time to time with the blood of patriots and tyrants. It is its natural manure."[12] Almost literally the same words were to be used later by Barère in the French Convention when he pleaded for the execution of the king.[13]

But, like Locke, the theorists of the American Revolution had no notion that mere resistance to a tyrant was an adequate remedy for tyranny, which they understood to be rather a perverse system of authority than the mere misgovernment of a single man. Thus the American Revolution issued in the deliberate construction of a constitution based on representative government and a system of checks and balances to restrain what Madison called "the encroaching nature"[14] of power. The American statesmen had learned from Montesquieu to think that separation of powers was of primary importance in the preservation of freedom. "The accumulation of all powers, legislative, executive, and judiciary, in the same hands," Madison declared, "whether of one, a few, or many, and whether hereditary, self-appointed, or elective, may justly be pronounced the very definition of tyranny."[15] He was consciously echoing Jefferson's earlier statement, in his *Notes on Virginia*, that "concentrating these in the same hands is the very definition of despotic government."[16] It was a definition strangely remote from those of classical and medieval tradition.

The French Revolution, like the American, emphasized the familiar symbol of the tyrant. The *philosophes* had kept it alive. Voltaire wrote stirring dramas on *Brutus* and *The Death of Caesar*. His interest was also analytical: he distinguished between the tyranny of the one and that of the many, and listed the tyrants of the past. He declared, however, that in his own day there were no European tyrants of either kind.[17] Diderot was interested in the moral implications of tyranny. "Tyranny," he asserted, "imprints a character of baseness on all kinds of production; even language is not protected from its influence...." "Of all the scourges which affect mankind," he added, "there is none more pernicious than the tyrant.... When war has been declared, so to speak, between the tyrant and his subjects, he is obliged to be continuously on the watch to protect himself; he finds safety only in violence, which he entrusts to his satellites...."[18] In the Diderot-d'Alembert *Encyclopédie,* a special article by the Chevalier de Jaucourt was devoted to "Tyran, Tyrannicide, Tyrannie"; the author came to the conclusion that tyrannicide "should be approved by all people of taste." Another article on despotism found its essence to be the disregard of natural and international law.

One of the most characteristic literary products of the time was the work of Abbé Raynal on the *Philosophical and Political History of the Indies,* which was called "The Bible of two worlds." From its publication in 1770 to the end of the century, the book went through fifty-four editions,[19] and, in its pseudo-historical and pseudo-ethnological fashion, became one of the strongest forces against tyranny. Raynal vehemently attacked tyranny, servitude, and usurpation. To the legislators of 1793, his work "furnished the justification of regicide when he admired the age-old custom of Ceylon which subordinated the sovereign to the observance of the law and condemned him to death if he dared to violate it." He affirmed that this usage existed "in all the countries of the earth, and if the laws are not made for the subjects, they may call themselves what they wish, but they are only slaves...." "The memory of this great lesson," he continued, "endures for centuries and inspires a fear more salutary than death in a thousand other criminals."[20] On a small island in Switzerland, Raynal erected a monument to William Tell.

With this background of literary tradition, and with the classicism that was a prominent part of eighteenth-century French culture, it was natural that symbols of tyranny and of noble resistance to tyranny should play a leading role in the Revolution. In particular, the Jacobins and left-wing revolutionaries felt themselves to be the successors of the old Romans who had fought for the liberty of the Republic. Babeuf, most extreme of the revolutionaries, added to his own name the name of Gracchus, who had fought for the liberty of the Roman peasants; his gesture was symbolic of the revolutionary ideology. "Romans" and "Republicans" were identical expressions, and many of the Jacobin clubs were adorned with busts of the "heroes of liberty," Brutus, Cincinnatus, Seneca, and Cato. In many public and private acts, Roman analogies were used by preference.[21] In the patriotic spectacles arranged by the Jacobins, the fall of the Bastille and the death of Caesar were characteristic themes. The story of Brutus had especial symbolic importance for this later age.

But the Jacobins did not have a monopoly of the tradition that glorified the destruction of the tyrant. One genuine case of tyrannicide—the assassination of Marat by Charlotte Corday—appeared in the period of the French Revolution. Charlotte Corday was a great-grandniece of Pierre Corneille; the daughter of a royalist family, she was herself a convert to the Republic. In the dreamy solitude of a small Norman town, she read with enthusiasm Voltaire's *Brutus* and drank in the ideas of her admired masters—Plutarch, Rousseau, Montesquieu, Raynal. The wave of terror that broke out in Paris in 1793 horrified her. In her opinion, Marat was the originator and presiding demon of the terror; and as she discussed the tragic situation of France with proscribed Girondins who had fled from Paris, the idea grew in her that it was her duty to liberate the Republic from his bloodstained rule. She came to Paris—with a small dressing-case and a volume of Plutarch—and calmly carried out her fatal design.

Arrested and imprisoned, Charlotte Corday showed not the smallest sign of trepidation or remorse. The Jacobins attempted to involve the Girondist leaders in responsibility for her action; she denied that she had had accomplices. At her trial, her advocate did not dare to plead insanity, so logically and persistently did she explain her grim resolution. "I saw civil war ready to rend France to atoms; persuaded that Marat was the principal cause of the peril and calamities of the land, I have sacrificed my life for his to save my country." In a message written in prison she asserted, "I desire that my last sigh may be useful to my fellow-citizens ... that my head borne through Paris may serve as a rallying point of all friends of the laws; that the tottering Mountain should behold its destruction written in my bood."[22] Her courage at the execution was so great and serene that a murmur arose among the crowd: "She is greater than Brutus!"

Charlotte Corday considered Marat a tyrant; but the Jacobins of course applied the traditional ideology to the counter-revolutionaries and in particular to Louis XVI. Revolutionary change and the fight against the tyrant seem closely connected, almost inseparable. No mass action is imaginable without the feeling of personal injustice suffered by innocent peoples. A revolution cannot be depersonalized. It must always show to the people who will bear the sufferings and the risks of the uprising that their exploiters will be punished and removed. This feeling was always prominent in the French Revolution. Even Mathiez, who has a tendency to explain the main developments of the Revolution in terms of exclusively economic and class motives, concludes:

Mankind has need, in the course of its trying and discouraging march forward, to have its illusions rekindled by the warm rays of the past. The revolutionaries of 1789 drew sustenance for their struggles from the memory of the republics of antiquity or from the more recent example of the American Revolution. Plutarch was before their minds and his spiritual elevation served to exalt their courage, to increase their faith in the Revolution. They imitated the heroes of Greece and Rome and like them they gave up their lives for their faith—becoming in their turn heroes.[23]

But this small concession to an ideological interpretation is not enough. Men are not led simply by illusions, but by the feeling of right and wrong, the eternal source of the Law of Nature. The same economic and class background can have different effects under different ideological structures of mind. The singular deficiency of fighting *élan* and revolutionary spirit in later German Marxism was primarily due to the elimination of moral issues and to the conception of an automatic economic evolution leading inevitably to socialism. The unheard-of fighting *élan* of revolutionary France was deeply rooted in the moral conviction of the Revolution, the chief symbol of which was the tyrant.

Among many instances, we hear that the Jacobin Club of Eymoutiers took, amidst an "indescribable delirium," an oath which was ordered by the department of Haute-Vienne: "I call down anathema upon kings and tyrants, anathema upon dictators, upon triumvirs, upon false defenders, upon false protectors of the people: anathema upon any who under the title of chief, general, stadtholder, prince, or any other name whatsoever, would usurp a superiority, a pre-eminence over his fellow citizens; and I swear to pursue him to death." And their so-called "philanthropic prayers" not seldom burst into anti-tyrannical effusions: "Let thy lightning execute justice on our enemies, known and hidden! They are thine, God of vengeance!"[24]

Thus, the more the actors of the Revolution felt themselves menaced by the intrigues of the counter-revolutionaries, the more the feeling grew that a new tyranny was imminent—a tyranny which could be fought only by the annihilation of the coming tyrants. The massacres of September, 1792, when many suspected counter-revolutionaries were taken from the prisons and executed summarily, were felt to be a defensive act of mass tyrannicide.

It is interesting to reread in this context the debates of the Convention on the question of the execution of Louis XVI. The execution itself was surely not a tyrannicide, since it was not the secretly prepared act of an individual but the open decision of a then sovereign body. Its motive was the fear of Louis's treason and of internal and international complications should he continue to live —the same motive as later led the Bolsheviks to the assassination of the czarist family. As Barère stated in an influential speech, the whole trial was "an act of the commonweal, a measure of general security."[25]

However, in spite of its foundation in political expediency, the whole debate was dominated by the idea of the tyrant. This was the symbol that justified the execution in the eyes of the revolutionary masses. Robespierre, indeed, proclaimed, "... There is no need whatever for a trial. Louis is not before any tribunal, nor are you sitting in judgment. The trial of the tyrant is the insurrection, the judgment is the fall of his power, his punishment that which is demanded by the liberty of the people. Peoples do not pronounce sentences, they launch the lightnings; they do not condemn kings, they plunge them into nothingness...."[26] Danton's explanation of his vote seemed to express the dominant current: "I do not belong to that crowd of statesmen who do not know that one can not make compromises with tyrants, who do not know that one can not strike kings except on the head, who do not know that one can hope for nothing from the kings of Europe except by force of arms. I vote for the death of the tyrant."[27] Fayau, the deputy from Le Vendée, expressed a mystic faith in tyrannicide: "The despot must be forgotten; our successors must be ignorant of the existence of kings; everyone who breathes must die and be reborn at the very moment when the head of the tyrant falls. The offspring of a great people are entrusted to you."[28]

The historian and idealistic socialist leader, Jaurès, has attached the greatest importance to this act of regicide in the drama of French history: "Still the stroke endures which the Revolution administered to the monarch and to the past; a profound and decisive stroke; and the emotions of pity, the transitory returnings of counter-revolution will not avail against the force of this sovereign act. The kings may return for a moment, but, whatever they may do, from this time on they will be only phantoms. France, their France, is forever regicide."[29] A similar judgment has been expressed by Mathiez: ". . . The divine right of kings had received a fatal blow in the proclamation of the principles of 1789. The idea of sovereignty had undergone a change of meaning. From the king it had passed to the people, and the scaffold of January 21 had shorn it of all supernatural prestige. When Charles X at his coronation made for the last time the gesture of touching the scrofulitic, he was greeted with laughter."[30]

But even those who used the old ideology of the tyrant saw themselves as attacking not a single man but the whole complex of abuses and antiquated privileges with which the French monarchy, forgetful of the historical bases of absolutism, had become involved. In the heyday of the French Revolution, the ideology of the Convention found the following characteristic expression:

Beginning with this moment the French nation proclaims the sovereignty of the people, the suppression of all civil and military authorities which have governed you until this day, and all the taxes which you bear, the seigneurial rights, both feudal and based on copyhold tenure, fixed or casual, the banalities, the servitude real and personal of the privileges of hunting and fishing, of the statute labor, of the excise, of the tolls, of the grants and in general of all kinds of contributions with which you are charged by your usurpers. The nation proclaims also the abolition among you of all corporations nobiliary or sacerdotal and others, of all prerogatives and privileges contrary to liberty. . . .[31]

Those who felt these burdens could not but recognize that personal tyranny did not explain this situation, that tyranny had become immensely complicated and ubiquitous. From this point of view, tyrannicide had become an antiquated idea. It was felt that the anachronistic and corrupt constitution, even more than the tyrant who supported and symbolized it, should be annihilated.

At the very Convention which condemned Louis XVI to death, Condorcet and Thomas Paine, opposing this measure, declared, "Execute the king but not the man!"[32]

This was not a humanitarian outburst or rhetorical formula for Paine; it was his scientific conviction. Nobody has stated more deeply the ubiquitous nature of tyranny than he:

When despotism has established itself for ages in a country, as in France, it is not in the person of the King only that it resides. It has the appearance of being so in show, and in nominal authority; but it is not so in practice and in fact. It has its standard everywhere. Every office and department has its despotism, founded upon custom and usage. Every place has its Bastille, and every Bastille its despot. The original hereditary despotism resident in the person of the king divides and subdivides itself into a thousand shapes and forms, till at last the whole of it is acted by deputation. This was the case in France; and against this species of despotism, proceeding on through an endless labyrinth of offices till the source of it is scarcely perceptible, there is no mode of redress. It strengthens itself by assuming the appearance of duty, and tyrannizes under the pretence of obeying.[33]

Thus at the end of the eighteenth century, anti-tyrannical thought tended to turn from ideas of tyrannicide and individual resistance to theories of revolution, and the eighteenth-century idea of revolution assumed an activistic and optimistic color. It meant the application of the force of the whole commonwealth to eliminate unbearable abuses, to increase individual and social happiness by the crushing of a whole corrupt regime, and to create a new and better constitution in which representative government, separation of powers, and the definition of inalienable human rights would serve as institutional checks against the very possibility of tyranny.

X THE INVISIBLE TYRANT

THOUGH THE constitutionalists' theory of tyranny undermined the idea of a single tyrant, it left a personal interpretation of tyranny still possible. But certain currents of thought of the late eighteenth and nineteenth century ran deeper than the constitutional analysis and revealed the remoter causes of tyranny, thus making the problem more and more impersonal.

One current of thought, prominent in the French Enlightenment and developed further by the English philosophic radicals, tended to demonstrate that tyranny was primarily a matter of human stupidity. Bentham rejected practically all the categories that were dear to the constitutionalists. He rejected natural rights as "simple nonsense; natural and imprescriptible rights, nonsense upon stilts";[1] he rejected the contract theory of the origin of the state;[2] he criticized the idea of separation of powers.[3] His system was a system of universal egoism, mitigated and reconciled with the public interest by human reason, which was the only real guarantee of human progress.

From this point of view the problem of the tyrant had very little meaning. Tyrant and subject were equally motivated by the "self-preference principle." It was perfectly natural and logical that kings should try to exploit their subjects for their own self-gratification, whereas subjects would obey them "so long as the probable mischiefs of obedience are less than the probable mischiefs of resistance."[4] Testing human institutions simply by their immediate utility to "the greatest happiness for the greatest number," he had no fundamental objection to concentrated power, if guided by reason toward the common welfare; denying the validity of natural law and of traditional constitutional principles, he had no clear objective standard by which to define misrule. Tyranny could be defined only in terms of the quantity of human unhappiness; when pain sufficiently overbalanced pleasure, revolt would occur. Thus, in effect, the existence of tyranny would be proved by the occurrence of revolt; and the problem of the moral right to resistance was resolved into a mere instance of the hedonistic calculus.

Power, to Bentham, was in itself morally neutral. What mattered was the ways in which it was used. This was the essence of the Benthamite message. Its deepest meaning was clearly stated by Sir Frederick Pollock:

The state bears not sovereignty in vain. *Non est potestas super terram quae comparetur ei.* There is no power on earth which could be compared with it, says Hobbes: therefore fear the sovereign and obey. True, says Bentham, obedience is good; but while I "obey punctually," I will "censure freely." What is sovereignty for, if it is not to be directed by every light of reason towards the attainment of the common happiness? The formula of the greatest happiness is made a hook to put in the nostrils of Leviathan, that he may be tamed and harnessed to the chariot of utility. Indeed, if Leviathan will haul the chariot, it matters little whether he has one head or many.[5]

In the first period of his philosophic career, Bentham showed a certain predilection for enlightened despots: they would more easily follow the road of the philosopher than the masses who had been kept for centuries in ignorance and superstition. And, though he later adopted most of the program and procedures of radical democracy, his guiding purpose was always the same: the fight against abuses created by ignorance and superstition. Nobody has emphasized this fundamental mission of Benthamism more eloquently than Bentham's heretical pupil, John Stuart Mill:

If superstition about ancestorial wisdom has fallen in decay; if the public are grown familiar with the idea that their laws and institutions are in great part not the product of intellects and virtue, but of modern corruption grafted upon ancient barbarism; if the hardiest innovation is no longer scouted *because* it is an innovation—establishments no longer considered sacred *because* they are establishments—it will be found that those who have accustomed the public mind to these ideas have learnt them in Bentham's school. . . .[6]

Thus, although Bentham came to believe that representative, constitutional government was a useful device for harmonizing the self-interest of the ruler with the self-interests of the ruled, he was by no means certain that the unenlightened masses might not become tyrannical themselves.[7] No form of constitutionalism will work so long as the masses misunderstand their fundamental interests. Thus Benthamism put its greatest emphasis on reason and education as the most important correctives of tyranny. In the Benthamite system, the true tyrant was the invisible one: human ignorance, stupidity, and superstition.

A second current of thought that tended to transform the idea of the tyrant was a continuation of an old human conviction, entertained mostly by people of great religious sensitivity: the conviction of the wickedness of all kinds of force and violence. In their minds, the problem of the tyrant remained a moral problem; but this moral problem was extended beyond its traditional meaning. Tyranny in government was simply one aspect of the intrinsic tyranny of any society founded upon force. And it was not the tyrant only that broke the foundation of human morality; the exploited people were also guilty. No kind of tyranny would be possible in a society in which people knew their rights and refused to cooperate with any man who tried to undermine the genuine foundation of a free society. The essence of conscientious objection, so widely spread in the religious tradition of many sects, under the most various forms of civilization, means, if rightly interpreted, not only the repudiation of war but the categorical refusal of all cooperation in any unlawful action or immoral enterprise. The trend of this conviction leads inevitably to the conception which found its first fully developed expression in La Boétie's theory of *Voluntary Servitude*[8]: you and I are all responsible for the tyranny which torments us, and it lies with you, with all of us, to make an end to the abominable consequences of tyranny, not by revolt or tyrannicide but simply by not cooperating with the tyrant.

This was to be the kernel of the whole political philosophy of Leo Tolstoy, the greatest of the moral anarchists. He condemned not only war and every form of human exploitation, but our whole Western civilization—its revolutions included—which had abandoned the basic Christian principles upon which alone peace and justice could be established:

If people would at last comprehend that no parliaments, no strikes, no trade unions, no cooperative societies, no discoveries, no schools, no universities and academies, no revolutions can benefit man who lives in a false religious atmosphere! Should this be the case, all forces of better men could be directed not towards the consequences, but towards the cause, not towards state-functions and revolutions, not towards Socialism, but towards the unveiling of the false doctrine and the restoration of the true one.[9]

It can scarcely be doubted that the philosophic radicals' emphasis on human stupidity and the ethical anarchists' doctrine of collective moral responsibility contributed greatly to the discarding of the idea of the tyrant. Yet these were refined and sophisticated generalizations which the broader masses did not grasp. There was, however, a third school of thought, growing continuously in importance after the end of the eighteenth century, which pointed to a common cause of tyranny which was concrete, massive, apparently a general experience of all the toiling masses. This was modern socialism, steadily proclaiming that the deepest cause of human degradation and servitude was economic: that the tyrant was only the synthetic and ultimate expression of the injustices of the capitalist system.

This experience was so close to the proletarian multitude that it did not need much theorizing. In the first stage of the Industrial Revolution, the following Luddite song, denouncing the demoniac power of *King Steam,* was widely spread among the workers:

> He has an arm, an iron arm,
> And though he has but one,
> There is magic in that single arm
> That crushes millions down.
>
> Destroy King Steam, the Moloch wild,
> You toiling thousands all!
> Bind him his hand, or else our land
> Will over night down fall.[10]

The tyrant was replaced here by a suprapersonal power, almost a cosmic force; and though later socialism rehabilitated King Steam, practically all schools of socialism maintained the conception which was behind the Luddite song: that only unjust economic power, which created extreme wealth and extreme proverty, could lead to all the manifestations of servitude and tyranny. The advantages of constitutionalism were minimized; the essential problem of human freedom and servitude was located in the economic framework of society.

Long before the advent of modern socialism, Jean Jacques Rousseau had placed this truth in the very center of his system. Though not a socialist in the Marxian sense, but a convinced anti-communist, he foresaw the fundamental problem of modern socialism. The old ideology of the tyrant was meaningless for him when he inquired into the causes of inequality and servitude. The central problem for him remained always this:

If the object is to give the State consistency, bring the two extremes as near to each other as possible; allow neither rich men nor beggars. These two estates, which are naturally inseparable, are equally fatal to the common good; from the one come the friends of tyranny, and from the other tyrants. It is always between them that public liberty is put up to auction; the one buys and the other sells.[11]

As he did not believe in the possibility of communism, he could only propose drastic state control as a remedy:

My thought is not to destroy private property absolutely—because this is impossible—but to restrict it to the closest limits, to give it a bridle which reins it, which directs it and keeps it always subordinate to the general will.[12]

The tendency to depersonalize tyranny and to replace moral values and considerations more and more by economic categories reached its culmination in Marxian socialism. It was not only the idea of the tyrant that became a naive and antiquated problem, but the idea of right and wrong itself. It became a purely relative matter, a kind of repercussion in the mind of the masses of the changed forces of production. Exploitation and servitude depended not on individuals but on the laws of economic evolution, which were regarded as dialectically determined. Thus, although the *Communist Manifesto*, and all Marxism thereafter, was—in opposition to its ultimate theoretical foundation—deeply colored with moral indignation, Marxism became a strong influence against acts of individual violence and all forms of *putschism*. In spite of Marxist harangues against the usurpers and for the "expropriation of the expropiators," the more highly developed and more rationalistic labor groups of the West, especially those who expected a democratic transformation, looked with a certain contempt on the old "legend" of the tyrant and believed in the immutable laws of economic determinism.

When, at the end of the nineteenth and the beginning of the twentieth century, many Marxist leaders emphasized the anti-terroristic character of the Marxian creed, they were indeed prompted partly by political opportunism—for at that time violent anarchist plots were frequent, and conservative leaders such as Bismarck began to use these plots as pretexts for crushing the labor movement. But they could also base their assertions on the "scientific" foundation of their school. No action of individuals or of groups, it was argued, could change the existing relations of power. The only chance of radical transformation was either constitutional political action, if possible, or widespread political revolution, if necessary. And even revolution was less and less imagined in the old forms of street fights and barricades; the idea of the General Strike assumed more and more the role of a myth of liberation.

Engels' introduction to a new edition of the *Class Struggles in France* (1895), though surely somewhat distorted by its cautious editors, was without doubt the expression of a new spirit, which tried to check disorderly individual action and strongly emphasized the preponderant importance of the political action of the masses. This antagonism between outright violence and—as far as possible —peaceful reformist action was to become the main line of difference between the Second and the Third International.

When the assassination of the poetic figure, Elisabeth of Austria, by the Italian anarchist Luccheni at Geneva in 1898 aroused world-wide indignation, August Bebel, the leader of German parliamentary socialism, exclaimed in a speech at Berlin: "Change the social order from the foundation up, give it a corresponding political superstructure, and you can leave the enemies with their heads in peace." As a special remedy against Italian anarchism he advised "the transformation of the Pontine Marshes into flourishing fields."[13] What an irony of history is the fact that Bebel's suggestion was carried out by Signor Mussolini to strengthen his tyranny!

Similar ideas were expressed by Karl Kautsky after the victory of Bolshevism, when the orgies of bloodshed and arson in Russia made the rupture between the western and eastern labor movements final. Kautsky, who before the First World War had been the leader of the orthodox Marxists against the Revisionists, now insisted that Bolshevism was a perversion of the true gospel of Marx. He tried to show the growing humanitarian spirit of the labor movement and its growing abhorrence of violence. All the economic and intellectual forces of the nineteenth century, he believed, were leading inevitably to this result. The brutal violence of the French Revolution, and of the beginnings of the English labor movement, was disappearing, and the causes of the reign of terror were vanishing simultaneously. Under the influence of Marxism, the more advanced proletariat of the world had learned that "the realization of socialism ... could not be the work of a *coup;* it could only be the result of a long historical process.... The socialists were always admonished to undertake only such tasks as could be solved under the existing power-relations and material conditions...." Ever since Marxism had been the dominating force of the socialist movement, "the idea of effecting [socialism] by a reign of terror had disappeared completely in its ranks." At the same time, the increasing possibilities of democratic action made the proletariat more conscious "of the economic conditions and the power-relations between classes. In this way phantasmic adventures were avoided, and civil war as a method of class struggle was eliminated."[14]

In this spirit the revolutionary wing of the labor movement tried to tone down the revolutionary appeals of the past. It quoted, with growing consent, the casual and not very sincere statements made by Marx in 1872, that there was a possibility that the proletarian revolution in America, England, and Holland could assume peaceful forms.[15] It also quoted an early assertion of Engels to the effect that "no communist thinks of committing an act of vengeance against any individual person, or believes that the individual bourgeois could act otherwise under existing conditions.... Therefore, the more the English workers assimilate socialistic ideas, the more their present resentment will become ... superfluous, and the more their actions against the bourgeois class will diminish in wildness and brutality. Were it possible ... to make the whole proletariat communistic before the final struggle begins, [the transformation] would pass peacefully."[16]

All these explanations of tyranny undermined the traditional foundation of this concept. When the philosophic radicals had replaced the concept of right and wrong by that of utilitarian expediency, when the ethical anarchists had eliminated strict personal responsibility and substituted for it a general collective responsibility, when the Marxists had proclaimed an all-pervading economic necessity in human action and in the structure of society, there was no longer any argument against the One. The dictatorship had become impersonal. Its cure was either slow political and social reform as with the Benthamists, a radical religious-ethical reform as with the Tolstoy school, or an economic evolution leading automatically to socialism, as with the latter-day western Marxists. The moral enthusiasm of the old fighters against tyranny seemed to belong to the past.

XI

THE SURVIVAL OF THE TRADITION OF TYRANNICIDE

THE TRADITION of tyrannicide was not completely dissolved by the theoretical tendencies which presented the tyrant as a particular system of concentrated and irresponsible power or as an impersonal structure of social or economic relationships. Moral responsibility can not be ignored in human affairs. In spite of modern emphases on impersonal causation and collective responsibility, it remains true that those who occupy positions of authority, whether hereditary, appointive, or elective, must bear the brunt of responsibility for conditions which the majority or an influential minority of citizens feel to be obnoxious and degrading. Moreover, the spread of democratic ideas had a twofold effect: although it tended to submerge the individual man in the crowd, it also increased the average man's individual consciousness and sense of his own importance; thus even among the masses social injustice was felt to be an offense against the individual man. It was, therefore, quite natural that the old hatred of the tyrant should continue deep into the nineteenth century, and that men of sensibility and courage should sometimes echo the old philosophy of tyrannicide. This especially occurred, of course, in those countries in which a corrupt absolutism continued to dominate, and in which there might seem to be no other hope of getting rid of the accursed system.

In Italy, especially, the hatred of tyrants was continuous. One of the most eloquent representatives of the Italian spirit in the late eighteenth century was Count Vittorio Alfieri, tragic poet, dramatist, political writer, and precursor of Italian unity. He wrote a long ode to *Free America;* he admired the early stage of the French Revolution. His book *On Tyranny,* written in Siena in 1777, expressed the idea that the whole of Europe was sighing under the yoke of the tyrant:

The term "tyranny" must be applied without distinction to every government in which the men who direct the execution of the laws can make them, destroy them, infringe upon them, hinder them, suspend them, or frustrate them. Therefore, whether this law-breaking be hereditary or elective, usurped or legitimate, good or bad, of one or of many, in any case, anyone who has power to do this is a tyrant; every society which allows this is a tyranny; every people which supports it is a slave people. . . .[1]

Alfieri analyzed the causes of the tyrannical system and asserted that it would collapse when it had reached the extreme limit of its infamies; therefore, if a good man should happen to become the minister of a tyrant, the best thing he could do would be to encourage the tyrant to the greatest excesses in order to make his rule generally odious. A revolutionary conspiracy, he argued, must be directed not against the tyrant only, but against tyranny itself; its motive should be not merely private revenge, but the will to create true liberty. The fall of the tyrant would always cost enormous suffering and bloody sacrifice. In his poem, *Etruria Avenged (L'Etruria vindicata)*, Alfieri described the killing of the Renaissance tyrant, Allessandro de' Medici, by his cousin Lorenzo. He exalted tyrannicide and defended the "theory of the dagger" as one of the most effective means of destroying oppression.[2]

Alfieri's ardent hatred of tyranny arose not only from his love of personal liberty, but also from his zeal for the unification of Italy. The many Italian tyrants, who made the life of free men miserable, were also the chief obstacles to national unity.[3] As his recent biographer aptly says, "In Alfieri we find the development of ideas which historically prepared the way for modern Italian nationalism: hatred of tyranny, lay and religious; love of freedom, individual and national. . . ."[4]

Even in a country so little inclined to revolutionary upheavals as eighteenth-century Germany, there was a widespread feeling against the tyrant and an enthusiasm for republican institutions. This revolt was quite natural under the despotism of the small principalities. Wilhelm Röpke has reminded us that a margrave of Anspach, who wanted to show off his skill in shooting before his mistress, shot a worker from the tower of his castle and graciously handed a florin to the widow; that a duke of Mecklenburg put to death his privy councillor in order to make the widow his mistress; that a prince of Nassau-Siegen had a peasant killed, only to prove that he had the power to do so; that in Swabia a jurist was beheaded because he had quoted Voltaire in a tavern.[5]

H. A. Korff has admirably shown that the spirit of the *Sturm and Drang* was to a large extent a protest against the corruptions of the despotic system. It was, however, characteristic of the German situation that this literary revolt did not attack the system directly, but, so to speak, by analogy. Poets took their themes from the dramatic episodes of the history of the Italian republics and from the Dutch struggle for independence. The first Brutus-drama came from the circle of Lessing: the greatest of the tyrannicides was still a favorite motif in this period.[6] But the most enduring expression of this revolt came from Friedrich Schiller, who combined lyrical enthusiasm with deep philosophical insight. He used the motif of tyrannicide several times, realizing clearly that the problem of tyrannicide was ultimately a moral problem and a conflict between antagonistic moral obligations. In *Wilhelm Tell,* he emphasized the fundamental difference between common murder and the killing of a tyrant. Johannes Parricida, who had murdered his royal uncle as an act of dynastic rivalry, was indignantly repudiated by the Swiss tyrannicide when he claimed that they had both committed the same crime:

> Unhappy man! Dare you confound the crime
> Of blood-imbued ambition with the act
> Forced on a father in mere self-defense?
> Had you to shield your children's darling heads,
> To guard your fire-side sanctuary, to ward off
> The last, the direst doom from all you loved?
> To heaven I raise my unpolluted hands
> To curse your act and you! I have avenged
> That holy nature which you have profaned,
> I have no part with you. You murdered, I
> Have shielded all that was most dear to me.[7]

Hatred of tyranny did not remain a purely literary matter. At the beginning of the nineteenth century, a liberal student movement denounced despotic rule, and the *Burschenschaften* became the centers of subversive activities. As in Italy, hatred of tyranny was organically connected with the growing feeling of nationalism. The petty tyrants were hated not only as the annihilators of "ancient freedom," but also as the main obstacles to German unity. A revolutionary wing of the students openly adopted tyrannicidal ideas. When a student from Jena, Karl Sand, murdered August von Kotzebue, a former Russian spy, Metternich was so alarmed by the growing spirit of rebellion that he instigated the issuing of the Carlsbad Decrees. These enactments, sanctioned by the Germanic Confederation in 1819, bound sovereigns to control universities through special commissions, introduced strict censorship of all publications, and created a center for the investigation of secret societies.

This transitory movement of juvenile revolt produced a more independent thinker in the person of Karl Follen, who later became a refugee in America and for a time a professor at Harvard. The sincerity of his lifelong devotion to freedom was demonstrated by the fact that, in his exile, he became an ardent supporter of the anti-slavery movement. According to a tradition, Follen had induced Sand to commit his fatal act and had contributed a famous incitement to tyrannicide, the *Great Song,* written for the radical student group at Giessen:

> The knife of Liberty drawn!
> Hurrah! The dagger through the throat pierced!
> In purple dress, adorned
> With crown and frills
> Stands the victim before the altar of vengeance![8]

This was not, for Follen, simply the expression of an ephemeral emotion; he was the author of a theory of tyrannicide which some of his contemporaries have transmitted to us. He was convinced that men "would not hesitate to defend themselves against a highway robber by shooting him down, but they are afraid to draw the dagger against the great robbers and murderers of popular freedom. If men were only consistent, all of us would have been free long ago."[9] On another occasion he said, "The tyrants know how to protect themselves against legal acts, therefore they must learn to tremble before our daggers. Whoever resorts to these measures in the full conviction that he is sacrificing all that is dear to him for the welfare of the Fatherland is morally all the nobler, the harder he finds it to overcome his aversion to such deeds."[10]

A generation later, in the tempestuous period of the forties, similar ideas agitated advanced public opinion in many European states. The exasperation of this period found expression in the extreme and distorted tyrannicide doctrine of Karl Heinzen (1809-1889). An exile in various European countries and finally in America, a militant radical, republican, atheist, and abolitionist, he felt that, so far as Germany was concerned, the social and political evils of his generation originated in Prussianism and in the "thirty-four German slave-drivers"—"crowned ne'er-do-wells and good-for-nothings." He advocated tyrannicide as the chief means of historical progress. And, in spite of the enormous difference between the Czarist environment and that of the rather *gemütlich* petty German states, Heinzen anticipated the later Russian Nihilists in making practical suggestions for a policy of widespread assassination. After the mass murders of war, Heinzen argued, why should one hesitate to use the blood of kings and aristocrats for the cause of social progress? "If you have to blow up half a continent and pour out a sea of blood in order to destroy the party of the barbarians, have no scruples of conscience." Mere admonition was not enough; Heinzen became very practical. He suggested the need for new inventions: explosives, underground lethal chambers, bombs planted under pavements, containers filled with poison. He advocated prizes to encourage research in these fields. "By these means not only the tyrants but the supporters of tyranny should be exterminated." As his biographer says, he saw the problem in simple terms: "Kings and princes were the greatest obstacles to progress, so have them removed by the quickest and most practical methods."[11]

The chief poetic exponent of the growing tension of the forties was Ferdinand Freiligrath, who sometimes gave moving expression to the popular revolt against tyranny. In a poem written in 1846 called "Up from Below" *(Von unten auf)*, he described how the king of Prussia was travelling on the deck of a Rhine steamer, while down below, in coal soot and sweltering heat, the proletarian mechanic for a moment played with the idea that it depended only on a slight pressure of his hand to cause a volcanic explosion:

> We are the force! We hammer anew the old decrepit thing, the State,
> We who are by the wrath of God still the proletariat. . . .[12]

In another poem, "The Ice Palace," he glorified "the holy flood of the peoples" which "sweeps away what it has long carried, the Ice Palace of despotism."[13]

These expressions of revolt were cast in rather symbolic terms; the same spirit burst out in brutal proletarian language in a popular revolutionary song of 1848. Its first two lines give an idea of the whole:

> Drag from the royal bed the concubine,
> Grease with royal fat the guillotine. . . .[14]

The same spirit again, with even greater emotion, characterized the left wing of the revolution of '48 in Hungary, where social oppression was coupled with the absolutism of the Habsburgs.

The denunciation of tyrannic rule was an often-repeated theme of the greatest poet of the period, Alexander Petőfi. Here is one of many representative passages:

> A knife in the heart of Lamberg, a rope around the
>   neck of Latour,
> And after them others may follow;
> You begin to be mighty, O people!
> This is all right, this is perfectly fine,
> But this has achieved you little—
> Hang the kings![15]

The refrain is repeated throughout the poem. It is obviously assumed that every king is a tyrant and the cause of all the miseries of the people.

It was natural that the most numerous and most violent expressions of the tyrannicide theme should come from absolutist countries; but even in England, where constitutional liberty had been most fully attained, the voice of tyrannicide was not completely dead. There were some ardent poetic souls who sympathized with the continental struggles for freedom and were ready to agree that under tyranny tyrannicide might be the only possible remedy. Walter Savage Landor, republican admirer of Cicero and Milton, of Manin, Mazzini, Garibaldi, and Kossuth, was so excited by the despots of France and Austria, whom he compared with the Renaissance tyrant Ezzelino, that he composed in 1851 a poem "On Tyrannicide," accompanied by an address in prose. The poem exalted the glory of tyrannicide.[16] In 1857, in a letter to Emerson, Landor referred again to tyrannicide:

We English are the most censurable of all.... The ministers of England have signed that Holy Alliance which delivered every free state to the dominion of arbitrary and irresponsible despots. The ministers of England have entered more recently into treaties with usurpers and assassins. And now, forsooth, it is called *assassination* to remove from the earth an assassin; the assassin of thousands; an outlaw, the subverter of his country's, and even of his own laws. The valiant and the wise of old thought differently.

He contended that tyrannicide involved less misery than war and argued that "the removal of an evil at the least possible cost is best."[17] His enthusiasm for tyrannicide was so real that he promised to one of Mazzini's friends ninety-five pounds for the family of "the first patriot who asserts the dignity and fulfills the duty of tyrannicide."[18]

Earlier, in 1808, he had written to his friend Southey with reference to Napoleonic Spain, "When Joseph gets back to Madrid, it would not surprise me if Spain were to produce a tyrannicide. He who should do the deed, should stand next to Brutus in my calendar."[19]

Landor's friend and publisher, John Foster, deprecated such ideas as "the bad habit... of applying heathen doctrines and precedents in a manner alarmingly unsuitable to a Christian Commonwealth." But Swinburne, one of the most enthusiastic admirers of Landor, fell again into the heathen habit when, after reading an account of the Russian prisons, he wrote his "Russia: An Ode," in which are the following lines:

> Love grows hate for love's sake; life takes death for guide;
> Night hath none but one red star—Tyrannicide.[20]

It would be easy to fill a volume with examples of the same theme reiterated with obvious sincerity and force. But these emotional and literary outbursts added nothing new to the great thought of previous centuries.

Only one man in nineteenth-century Europe can be regarded as really contributing to the long-established theory of tyrannicide. This was Giuseppe Mazzini, the great philosopher of democratic nationalism and forger of Italian unity. For him the problem of tyranny was intimately connected with the task of liberating Europe from those despots who stood in the way of the unification of the young nations still suffocating under foreign and absolutist rule. He openly advocated tyrannicide; and in 1833, when the young Antonio Gallenga, a member of the *Giovine Italia,* confided to him his resolution to assassinate Carlo Alberto, king of Piedmont, Mazzini gave him money and a dagger. At that time—fifteen years before he granted a constitution to Piedmont—Carlo Alberto was regarded by Italian patriots as a traitor and a hangman. That Mazzini later also approved of Orsini's attempt on the life of Napoleon III is supported by a good deal of circumstantial evidence. But Mazzini's significance for us does not lie in his encouragement of these regicidal adventures. From the point of view of the pure theory of tyrannicide, their wisdom may be doubted; it may even be argued that Carlo Alberto and Louis Napoleon were not tyrants at all.[21] The real significance of Mazzini lies in his theoretical analysis of tyrannicide.

For Mazzini, the act of tyrannicide was not primarily a matter of political expediency, but a revindication of the moral order on which the despot had trampled. It could be justified, therefore, only if it came from an unselfish conscience. He tried to dissuade Gallenga—"as I always did in such cases"—from his contemplated deed. He questioned him to discover whether there might not be a motive of personal interest and vengeance in his resolution:

I discussed the matter with him, I put before him all the reasons which would deter him from his intentions. I told him that I hold Carlo Alberto worthy of death, but that his death would not save Italy; that in order to assume a mission of retaliation he should feel himself clean of any sense of cheap vengeance, and of anything which was not in his mission; that he should feel himself capable, after having fulfilled his fate, of folding his hands on his breast and surrendering himself as a victim; that at all events he would die in the attempt, he would die dishonored by men as an assassin; and so I continued for a while.

But the answers of the young man were so sincere and genuine, so animated by the passionate desire to free his country that

... he convinced me at the end that he was one of those beings whose resolutions stand between conscience and God, and whom, from Harmodius on, Providence sends from time to time upon the earth to teach the despots that it is in the hands of a single man to make an end to their power. And I asked him what he wished of me. A passport and some money, he said. I gave him a thousand francs and told him that he would find a passport at Ticino.[22]

Mazzini several times discussed "the theory of the dagger." He stated his ideas most clearly in a letter to Daniel Manin in 1856:

Holy in the hand of Judith is the sword which cut the life of Holofernes; holy is the dagger which Harmodius crowned with flowers; holy is the dagger of Brutus; holy is the poniard of the Sicilian who initiated the Vespers; holy is the arrow of Tell. When justice is extinguished and the terror of a single tyrant denies and cancels the conscience of the people and God who wished them to be free, and when a man unblemished by hatred and base passion, solely for the Fatherland and for the eternal right incarnate in him rises against the tyrant, and exclaims: "You torture millions of my brothers, you withhold from them that which God has decreed theirs; you destroy their bodies and corrupt their souls; through you my country is dying a lingering death; you are the keystone of an entire edifice of slavery, dishonor, and vice; I overthrow that edifice by destroying you,". . . I recognize in that manifestation of tremendous equality between the master of millions and a single individual the finger of God. Many feel in their hearts as I do, and I express it.[23]

XII THE ERA OF PUTSCHISM: TYRANNICIDE DISTORTED

THE REMARKABLE continuation of the complex of ideas and emotions that centered on the old theme of tyrannicide did not manifest itself merely in sentimental literary outbursts and occasional acts of symbolic vengeance and despair. It also furnished a part of the ideological motive-force for a variety of revolutionary movements: not only those which aimed to extend the constitutional achievements of the French Revolution to other countries where absolutism still flourished, but also those which sought to carry revolutionary reconstruction even further, to achieve a complete remolding of society through fundamental economic and social change. Some of the more radical leaders of the era of the French Revolution and of the nineteenth century attempted to adapt the tradition of the personal tyrant and the noble tyrannicide to the necessities of revolutions conceived in these more drastic and more dynamic terms. In this attempt, the traditional doctrine was distorted: it was transformed, first, into a doctrine of conspiratorial violence and, finally, into a doctrine of mass terrorism. These misapplications of the classic theory served further to discredit the once-respected doctrine, especially in the eyes of those who had already attained the security and freedom of constitutional government.

This tendency toward a perverted application of the doctrine of tyrannicide can be observed even in the French Revolution, in a by-product of Jacobinism, the movement initiated by Francois-Noel Babeuf. Babouvism can be properly regarded as a connecting link between Jacobinism and Bolshevism. Babeuf—who called himself, in the classicizing fashion, Gracchus—felt that the objectives of the Revolution were falsified and therefore advocated a doctrine of absolute equality, permeated by the conviction that the unequal distribution of property was the cause of servitude. This equality would extend to every manifestation of life. All citizens should wear the same clothes; all children should be educated in the same institution, irrespective of their mental gifts; all the performances of science and the arts should be kept on a level understandable by all; all the great cities should be dissolved, as they represented a sickness of public life.

Babeuf's movement was directed primarily against the Constitution of 1795, which set up the Directory of Five. He regarded this new constitution, which substantially retreated from the democratic extreme of the Constitution of 1793, as a restoration of the old tyranny. In his eyes it was the rule of a small gang of "starvers, bloodsuckers, tyrants, hangmen, rogues, and mountebanks."[1] His paper, *The Tribune of the People,* was suppressed in February, 1796; its last issue described the rule of the Directory in these terms: "All is finished. The Terror against the people is the order of the day. It is no longer permitted to speak; it is no longer permitted to read; it is no longer permitted to think; it is no longer permitted to say that we suffer; it is no longer permitted to say that we live under the reign of the most abominable tyrants."[2] The only solution would be the final elimination and extirpation of this gang.[3]

Babeuf assumed the leadership of the revolutionary association called The Society of the Pantheon; after its suppression in 1796 he took the lead in organizing an inner committee of the movement, the "Secret Directory," which proceeded to make detailed plans for a conspiratorial insurrection. In the *Act of Insurrection,* the program drafted by this secret committee, the revolutionaries declared, "Those who usurp sovereignty ought to be put to death by free men.... The people shall take no rest until after the destruction of the tyrannical government."[4] The goal of political liberation was combined with the goal of immediate economic equalization. "All the possessions of emigrants, of conspirators, and of all the enemies of the people, should be distributed without delay to the defenders of the country and the unfortunate. The unfortunate of the whole Republic shall be immediately lodged in the houses of the conspirators. The objects belonging to the people left in the public pawn-office should be immediately returned gratuitously."[5]

The leaders believed that the restoration of the old constitution could be attained only through an act of armed conspiracy, and Babeuf conceived practically the whole repertory of Bolshevism: a well-organized spearhead of professional revolutionaries, a small armed force gained by the demoralization of the official army, a seminary for propaganda to educate leaders for the revolution, appeal to popular passions against a regime of exploiters and usurpers, a suffrage which would exclude all the unreliable elements of the people. In short, the dictatorship of the proletariat was foreshadowed in his mind. The whole ideology and practice of revolutionary putschism, against which later orthodox Marxism had an embittered fight, was elaborated here. In Babouvism one finds also that feeling of creative violence of which Bakunin spoke later, and which Sorel made the foundation of his doctrine. "Let everything return to chaos," he declared, "that out of chaos may arise a new and regenerated world."[6] But Babouvism was also "the natural outcome and the last expression of Jacobinism."[7] Without the ideology of natural rights, of the liberation of mankind, of the fight against tyrannical power, the whole movement would be incomprehensible.

The Conspiracy of the Equals was easily suppressed. Babeuf and some of his colleagues were executed, facing death with the courage of their ancient precursors. But the vitality of Babouvism remained extraordinary. In the eighteen-thirties, a number of secret revolutionary organizations came into existence, advocating the same principle of equality and the same method of violence. Their ideology was sometimes more communistic, sometimes more republican, but the symbol of the tyrant was always present. The attempt of the Corsican Fieschi on the life of Louis Philippe, in 1835, supplemented the idea of armed insurrection with that of regicide. Between the fall of 1834 and the next summer, seven projects of this crime, "at that time new," were discovered and frustrated by the authorities. In a proclamation of May, 1839, we read, "The cowardly tyrant of the Tuileries laughs at the famine which torments the bowels of the people; but the measure of his crimes is full; he will at last receive his punishment."[8]

The movement lost ground after 1842, but the spirit of Babouvism gained new force in the revolutionary activities of Auguste Blanqui, whose whole life was a series of armed plots and imprisonments. Between 1837 and 1870 he took part in thirteen uprisings, was condemned to death several times, and spent thirty-seven years in prison. In a way he can be regarded as the last Jacobin of the violent type; he and his adherents sought to gain power by armed riots and then, in the spirit of the Encyclopedists, to realize their aims by education and legislation. His program mixed elements of Babouvism with vague ideas of communism and an ardent atheism; his ideas also anticipated many essential elements of Bolshevism.

In the mind of Blanqui and his fellow-conspirators, violence was the foundation of servitude. "The world belongs to force," Blanqui declared; "the regular destiny of the weak, their providential mission, is to serve as pasture to the strong. Society is nothing else than an organization of cannibals."[9] This artificial order of violence and corruption must be broken down by force before the communist society of equality could develop. In this life-and-death struggle, there could be no compromise or gradual reform. The Blanquists were not particularly interested in the specific daily problems of the workers. Their main endeavor was, first, to seize power through the armed revolt of a conscious minority and to establish "the dictatorship of the proletariat." The victorious revolutionaries would repudiate all cooperation with the liberals, would repudiate the idea of a national assembly, would expel God, would suppress any publication having an antagonistic ideology, would introduce universal instruction and the necessary economic reforms.

Even unsuccessful revolutions were to be greeted: "Revolution! This is the only relief of their ulcerous souls, the only relief from their mortal pains, the always too short moment which uplifts their foreheads bowed to the ground! Oh, I understand today one hour of victory and of power, one hour of being upright, after so many prostrate years!"[10] Only so could the proletarians be educated to use armed force efficiently to establish their dictatorship and make an end to the state of exploiters. In a message of 1851 denouncing the failure of the Revolution of 1848, he insisted, "In the presence of armed proletarians, obstacles, resistances, impossibilities will disappear. But for those proletarians who allow themselves to be amused by ridiculous promenades in the streets, by the planting of liberty trees, by the sonorous words of an attorney, it will be holy water at the beginning, injuries afterwards, and, finally, gunfire and always misery. Let the people choose."[11]

These ideas, so opposed to the dawning philosophy of economic or evolutionary socialism, had a tremendous revolutionary force. They animated the extreme left wing of the Commune, which was under the leadership of the Blanquists. In the critical hours of opposition to the government of Thiers, it was the Blanquists who propagated the idea of a *"marche sur Versailles."* The head of the Versailles Government said to a delegate of the Commune that "to return Blanqui to the insurrection would mean to send it a force equal to an entire army corps."[12] In pre-Marxian Russia, also, Blanquism was for a time popular, and the revolutionary leader Tkatchev called Blanqui "our inspirer and guide in the grand art of conspiracy."[18]

The first great English movement toward equality and socialism, that of the "physical force Chartists," though far less ideologic and revolutionary than the corresponding French movement, was animated by the same conception that tyrannic rule should be crushed by violence. In the *Manifesto of the General Convention of Industrial Classes* (1839) we read: "The mask of Constitutional Liberty is thrown forever aside and the form of Despotism stands hideously before us. For let it no longer be disguised; the *Government of England is a Despotism* and the industrial millions slaves."[14] A Chartist handbill circulated in Manchester proclaimed: "Nothing can convince tyrants of their folly but gunpowder and steel, so *put your trust in God, my boys, and keep your powder dry.* . . . Be ready then to nourish the tree of liberty with the *Blood of Tyrants.* . . ."[15]

In his discussion of Jacobinism and early revolutionary socialism, the historian Beer asserts:

The whole democratic and socialist movement, which is based on considerations of the law of nature, considers the evil of the existing order of things to be the result of bad laws based on usurpation. Certain cunning despots are supposed to have gotten hold of society in order to oppress and to exploit it for the benefit of a small minority. The whole system of government is, therefore, a misuse and violation of the social contract and natural equity. This conception appeared with classic clearness in the conspiracy that is connected with Babeuf's name. The people are justified and in duty bound by all great principles to do everything in their power to sweep away the unnatural, unjust, and pernicious state of things. The fight against this condition is a holy war for the restoration of the law of nature, the social contract, the ancient constitution, innate rights and liberties. . . . A holy war against usurpers, who destroyed and subverted the old conditions. . . . This existing order is full of manifest evils; each of the evils is an indictment against usurpers and an argument against the minority who gained their power by robbery and destruction. Nature created man in a state of freedom, the rulers threw them into chains.[16]

With the beginning of Marxism, in its different shades, the older conception lost ground continuously, until Lenin revitalized certain elements of it. There were two souls in the genuine Bolshevik breast, only one of which was Marxist in the orthodox sense. The other was the revolutionary activism of Lenin, who knew the independent force of an ideologic penetration of the masses. There can be no revolution without the popular conviction that a just cause is frustrated by usurpers. And although the tradition of tyrannicide, still so fervent in Babouvism with its heritage of natural-law theory, was far paler in Bolshevism, yet one who studies the Bolsheviks' propaganda can not doubt that a concept of tyrannical injustice was always prominent in their minds.[17] The continuity between the Jacobins and the Bolsheviks was vividly felt by some Bolshevik leaders. Lenin himself called the Bolsheviks "the Jacobins of Socialism."[18] In the development of theories of revolution, there is a remarkable continuity from Babeuf to Lenin. "Babeuf, Blanqui, and Lenin all pinned their faith on a compact group of convinced and determined revolutionists, certain of the necessity of destroying by force the agencies of existing government. All were convinced of the necessity of a dictatorship, individual or collective, during the period of transition between the old order and the new. . . ."[19] They were equally persuaded of the necessity of terrorism, of making "a just example, capable of frightening the traitors and of securing to those whom the people honored their confidence in the future."[20]

The conspiratorial socialism of Babeuf and Blanqui was a kind of distortion of the original ideas of tyrant and tyrannicide. Impatient groups of revolutionaries, outside the stream of constitutional thought, felt themselves betrayed by later developments and identified the new regimes simply with "tyrants," against whom they or their fathers had fought. They felt that by crushing a comparatively small group of usurpers, the new tyrants, a daring spearhead of determined revolutionaries could restore freedom, the "general will" of the people so basely misused. In contrast, Marxism, at the same evolutionary and revolutionary, emphasized the inevitable development of the economic forces, rejected the problem of right and wrong, and found no place for the tyrant. As the greatest mass-party of socialism, it thus became a factor of stabilization, of gradual prudent reformism. It became the creed of the better organized and better trained elements of the proletariat.

However, elements of the conspiratorial and terroristic thought of the putschists found a propitious ground in the backward parts of the world, under the yoke of feudalism and despotism. Here the logic of the old creed paved the way to a last distortion of the idea of tyrannicide: to the tyrannicide of the mob.

XIII TYRANTS EVERYWHERE: THE ULTIMATE DISTORTION

THE VARIOUS FORMS of putschism analyzed in the preceding chapter did not reach broad popular masses. They were the activities of individual leaders or of small groups of professional revolutionaries. In the West, the crushing of the Commune and the growing trend of liberalism created an atmosphere unfavorable to violent action in the conquest of power. Marxism itself, in the thought of the prophet's followers, assumed more and more what Lenin later called "legalistic" tendencies, and the task of organization and of economic reform tended to replace the former revolutionary *élan*.

There appeared, however, new revolutionary movements in which the old problem of oppression and tyranny was faced by extreme violence. A radical left-wing movement came into existence, revitalizing on a far broader basis the traditions of Babouvism, Blanquism, and the Commune. This movement had three different aspects, which mutually supported one another. One was a product of Russian autocracy; the second arose in the feudal, absolutistic atmosphere of Central Europe; the third resulted from the growing dissatisfaction, especially in the Latin countries, with the more moderate trends of socialism.

After a short period of hopefulness following the liberation of the serfs by Alexander II in 1861, a wave of utter pessimism overcame the more active minds of Russia. This led to a complete distrust of reforms and to a conception that a violent destruction of the old society was inevitable. This conviction animated the Nihilist movement. Young intellectuals, many "conscience-stricken noblemen,"[1] ardent clerics shocked by the soulless rigidity of the Greek Orthodox Church, and enthusiastic women disgusted by the many signs of class and national oppression of the minorities were attracted by a philosophy which later, in different forms, led to bloody terroristic explosions. The uniqueness of the Nihilist ideology lies not in its ultimate foundation but rather in the forms which it assumed under the impetus of the Russian messianic temper and amidst the crude barbarism of Russian political life. It was a Russian form of materialism, positivism, hedonism, atheism, and naturalism, plus certain political consequences which impatient and ardent intellectuals attached to those ideas. In the West, the same moral and political ideas were checked and tempered by centuries of political thought, by centuries of warfare between antagonistic philosophical systems, by a sound distrust of purely abstract ideas, and by opportunities for debate in an increasingly liberal atmosphere. In the world of Czarist absolutism, of police brutality and the continuous menace of Siberia, the utmost and crudest consequences were drawn from the newly imported philosophy.

Nihilism was, above all, an internal revolution, the rejection of the whole ideology of the *Fathers* by the *Sons*. In the famous description by Turgenev, the originator of the term *Nihilist,* the *Fathers* seemed to the *Sons* to be antiquated faddists, hypocritical *beaux esprits* who tolerated the further development of the age-old abuses of Russia while reiterating obsolete moral, aesthetic, and constitutional formulas. To the ardent souls of the new generation, whose vaunted amoralism hid a profound moral conviction, there was no remedy for the sins of the past and the present except the total destruction of all the values which respectable people had accepted. This work of destruction must be begun in the individual conscience. As Pisarev, the idol of the school, put it, "Here is the ultimatum of our camp: what can be smashed must be smashed; whatever will stand the blow is sound, what flies into smithereens is rubbish; at any rate, hit out right and left, no harm will or can come of it."[2] The extreme political consequences of such a doctrine were soon drawn by overexcited and unbalanced individuals. Dostoyevsky, in his wonderful novel, *The Possessed,* powerfully analyzed this type of mind in the figure of Verkhovensky, a portrait of the extreme anarchist Nechaev, who was a connecting link between theoretical Nihilism and active anarchism.

The annihilation of the contemporary world-order was intimately connected with the romantic belief, held by both the Pan-Slavists and the Narodniki, in the creative forces slumbering in the Russian peasants, which should be liberated in order that the degenerate world of Western capitalism might be supplanted by a new cooperative system, which would continue the traditions of the Russian *mir*. Similar ideas were maintained by the later Socialist Revolutionary Party. Its slogan, "to go to the people"—to give revolutionary leadership to the popular masses—was accompanied by propaganda for terroristic deeds which would undermine the whole ruling class of exploiters. The idea of the existence of an all-pervading tyrannical system was at the bottom of the whole conception.

The Russian anarchist school gave the most elaborate theoretical expression to this idea of a popular struggle against all the oppressors and drew the most dangerous practical conclusions from it. Its doctrine[3] had an enormous repercussion on later revolutionary thought in the West. The teachers of European anarchism were the rebellious Russian noblemen, Bakunin and Kropotkin.[4] They were strongly influenced by their study of Western socialist thought, and especially of Marxism, but they passionately repudiated its ultimate conclusions. The essence of their teachings could be not inaccurately described as a new form of universalized tyrannicide. They accepted the doctrine of the economic foundation of human servitude. They denounced the state as the citadel of private property and of the capitalist system. Therefore, they argued, the fight must be directed primarily against the state and the economic system. But, since these were pure abstractions and there was no possibility of putting an end to them by law, and since even the right of revolution could not be used by degraded masses, it was necessary to resort to individual action against all who were interested in the maintenance of the present order—not only against czars, kings, and presidents, but against anyone who seemed to exercise obnoxious power or who simply irritated the masses through the ostentation of his wealth or privileges.

Bakunin said, "The urge of destruction is at the same time a creative urge."[5] In the old Narodnik fashion, he believed that the common people, even the despised rabble, were a depository of the creative forces of nature and that out of unorganized violence the new world would come into existence. The rationalistic construction of Marxism was replaced here by a highly emotional and even mystic conception, in spite of its author's rabid atheism.

To Bakunin, God was the Devil, the source of enslavement and violence. The tyranny of the oppressors was put under the protection of religion:

It is not without good reason that governments hold the belief in God to be an essential condition of their power. . . . There is a class of people who, even if they do not believe, must necessarily act as if they believe. This class embraces all mankind's tormentors, oppressors, and exploiters. Priests, monarchs, statesmen, soldiers, financiers, officeholders of all sorts; policemen, *gendarmes,* jailers, and executioners; capitalists, usurers, heads of business, and house-owners; lawyers, economists, politicians of all shades—all of them, down to the smallest grocer, will always repeat in chorus the words of Voltaire that "if there were no God it would be necessary to invent Him; for must not the populace have its religion?" It is the very safety-valve.[6]

Bakunin hurled destructive flashes of lightning from his exile; but his disciple and emissary, Nechaev, gave ultimate expression to the doctrine. He personified all the devastating potentialities of the anarchistic philosophy. His whole individuality was submerged in the passion to destroy all the enemies of the oppressed. In his *Catechism of a Revolutionary,* he thus described the revolutionary temper: "The Revolutionary knows only one science—destruction. For it and only for it he studies mechanics, physics, chemistry, even medicine; for him there is only one pleasure, one consolation, one remuneration and satisfaction—the Revolution. Day and night he may have only one thought, one purpose: merciless destruction."[7] Nechaev was merciless towards the state and the entire system of privileged educated classes. Then in a pseudo-scientific way, for the doctrine always claimed to be experimental and scientific, his secret pamphlet asserted that "the whole ignoble social system must be divided into several categories. In the first category are those who are condemned to death without delay. The association should draw up a list of persons thus condemned in the order of their relative harmfulness to the success of the cause, so that the preceding numbers may be removed before the subsequent ones.... Thus, first of all, those men must be destroyed who are particularly harmful to the revolutionary organization, and also those whose sudden and violent death may fill the government with the greatest fear and shake its power by depriving it of its clever and energetic men."[8] Then follows in six categories a kind of inventory of the enemies of the people and of the methods for their elimination. One has the feeling that a new Machiavelli has appeared: reason of state is here totally transformed into reason of the exploited class.

Though Prince Kropotkin conspicuously enlarged the foundations of the anarchist doctrine by showing its pretended connection with the natural sciences, its deepest, often hidden, motive-force remained the same: the fight against despotism and the new tyrant, a "declaration of war against present-day society." He denounced all Western parliamentarism as futile: "Precisely like any despot, the body of representatives of the people—be it called Parliament, Convention, or anything else; be it appointed by the prefects of a Bonaparte or elected with all conceivable freedom by an insurgent city—will always try to enlarge its competence, to strengthen its power by all sorts of meddling, and to displace the activity of the individual and the group by law.... The six-hundred-headed beast without a name has outdone Louis XI and Ivan IV.... Parliamentarism is nauseating to anyone who has seen it near at hand."[9]

Some of the anarchists, in their exact scientific ardor, were even precursors of the Nazi racial science, though of course with a different application. Thus a certain Pavlov, a theorist of the extreme radical wing of the anarchist movement, asserted in his pamphlet, *The Purification of Mankind* (1907), that the exploiters who were in power possessed "organic negative characters, profoundly rooted to such an extent that one must regard them as a special race. This race distinguishes itself by being worse than our animal ancestors; the repugnant qualities of the gorilla and orang-utang have progressed in it to such an extent that they have assumed a power unknown in the animal world.... Their children in an overwhelming majority will show the same ill-will, cruelty, cowardice, voracity, and avidity...." Pavlov asserted that all the representatives of this race, women and children included, should be annihilated.[10]

The popularized tyrannicide advocated by the anarchists had several functions. It would refresh the revolutionary *élan* of the masses. As Kropotkin said, "In the midst of the complaining, talking, discussing, comes a mutinous deed by one or more persons, which incarnates the longings of all."[11] It would concentrate the attention of the rulers, the oppressors, and the oppressed on the central injustice of society. It would induce the legislators to act and to introduce at least a minimum of reform. These principles were almost codified in the program of the *Narodnaya Volya* (The People's Will Party), which later was continued by the Socialist Revolutionary Party:

Terroristic activity, consisting in destroying the most harmful person in the government, in defending the party against espionage, in punishing the perpetrators of notable cases of violence and arbitrariness on the part of the government and of the administration, aims to undermine the prestige of the government's power, to demonstrate steadily the possibility of struggle against the government, to arouse in this manner the revolutionary spirit of the people and their confidence in the success of the cause, and finally to give shape and direction to the forces fit and trained to carry on the fight.[12]

But the chief driving force which made the last quarter of the nineteenth century so bloody with attempts and conspiracies against many leaders of the condemned state was the eternal motif of the rebellion against tyranny, which always needs deeds and symbols if no remedy is in sight. Amidst the theoretical dogmatism of the anarchists a distorted version of the old moral impulse of tyrannicide always appeared. This fact explains why the anarchistic outburst very often found wide popular support. When Vera Zassulich made an attempt against the life of General Trepov because he, as president of the St. Petersburg police, had ordered the lashing of the imprisoned revolutionary student Bogyljubov, she was not only absolved but assumed the role of Charlotte Corday in liberal public opinion and was openly praised by an influential part of the daily press, to such an extent that the Minister of Justice was compelled to resign.[13] This happened at the height of czarist absolutism; if one compares the political morality of that period with the ethics of totalitarianism, it is impossible not to see the abysmal degradation of European moral values.

That moral indignation was the cause of anarchistic action was sometimes openly recognized by the very leaders of the terroristic movement. In 1881, after the assassination of President Garfield, the *Narodnaya Volya,* the organ of the Russian terrorists, published the following declaration:

The Executive Committee, expressing its profoundest sympathy with the American people on account of the death of James Abram Garfield, feels its duty to protest in the name of the Russian revolutionaries against all such deeds of violence which have just taken place in America. In a land where the citizens are free to express their ideas, and where the will of the people does not merely make the law, but appoints the person who is to carry the law into effect: in such a country, political assassination is the manifestation of a despotic tendency identical with that to whose destruction in Russia we have devoted ourselves. Despotism, whatever may be the parties or whoever may be the individuals who exercise it, is always blameworthy, and force can only be justified when employed to resist force.[14]

A member of the Socialist Revolutionary Party once declared, "Never will history forgive autocracy for making terrorists of us."[15] Alexander Ulyanov, a brother of Lenin, interpreted in the following words the terroristic plot against Alexander III in which he was involved: "Terror is the sole form of defense left to a minority that is strong only in spiritual force and in the consciousness that it is right, against the physical force of the majority. Among the Russian people there will always be found scores who are so devoted to their ideas that it is no sacrifice for them to die for their cause."[16]

A second current of popular revolt against tyrannic rule came from the semi-absolutist and semi-feudal atmosphere of Central Europe. The revolutionary movements of 1848 did not bring real improvements for the masses. No system of liberalism evolved. The rigid class structure and the alliance between the state and the church still remained to support the political privileges of the rulers. And, though Social Democracy tried for the first time to canalize the growing revolutionary temper of the masses into political and economic organization, and to avoid anarchistic outbursts, public opinion in Germany was aroused by a series of anarchistic attempts which were the more alarming because they found considerable popular support. When, in May, 1878, Emile Hödel tried to assassinate Kaiser Wilhelm I, and, in June, Dr. Karl Nobiling tried to assassinate and in fact badly wounded him, no fewer than 563 persons were tried, from the beginning of June until the middle of August, for insulting the Kaiser and approving these attempts. Some of them openly regretted that the attempts had failed. Such persecutions occurred not only in Berlin, but also in Breslau, Bonn, Bochum, Mannheim, and Halle.[17] The mood of the people seemed so menacing that Bismarck found it necessary to introduce his anti-Socialist bill; or, at all events, he used the popular mood as a pretext. In 1883 a conspiracy against the Princess was discovered: two revolutionaries had been ordered by the anarchist Reinsdorf to dynamite the illustrious assembly which gathered at the Niederwald monument.

One of the extreme German revolutionaries, Johann Most, who later played a conspicuous role in American anarchism, was scarcely less radical than his Russian colleagues. He wrote a handbook on *Revolutionäre Kriegswissenschaft* "for the extermination of the bourgeois vermin." On one occasion he wrote, "Surely it would be better if one could eradicate the whole reactionary breed at the roots like poisonous herbage; but, for the moment, isolated executions are not without value."[18]

The belief in violent anarchistic action became so universal that around 1880 even the good-natured Austrian workers resorted to such methods, and the order of the state seemed seriously endangered until the growing strength of socialist organization of a Marxian type gave a new outlet to popular dissatisfaction.

Even in France a serious wave of anarchistic action spread. Here the common elements of anarchist thought were mingled with the more rationalistic attitudes of Western Europe. The leading anarchists of the West were not the emotional, culturally backward, underground revolutionaries of Russia; from the end of the eighteenth century they had had a continuous training in materialistic metaphysics and revolutionary politics. In Western thought, relativism and expediency, universal physical causation, and strict determinism of human actions, excluding personal responsibility, became the guiding stars of modern men. It followed that, as a simple member of the animal kingdom, man should act only with reference to the category of pain and pleasure; he should not feel himself bound by antiquated religious doctrines or nebulous ethical speculations.

In the imagination of the impatient masses, the figure of the tyrant assumed a new form: practically everyone who was supposed to enjoy a privileged position in the social hierarchy was regarded as a noxious and pernicious creature. With the growth of the capitalist system and the popularization of the Marxian ideology of the class struggle, the bourgeoisie assumed the role of the tyrant, whose greedy head appeared everywhere. This led to a naive identification of all the functions and activities of social life with the underlying economic structure. The existing social, political, economic, and intellectual hierarchy was regarded as a single *bête noire,* as a compact hydra whose very life was based on the exploitation, conscious or unconscious, of the proletariat.

Benedetto Croce has pointed out[19] that this whole conception of bourgeois society was a demagogic abstraction, and that the term was applied to what was in fact an agglomerate of very divergent and often contradictory historical forces. Yet when the class struggle became the leading symbol of all the revolutionary forces, the most active elements were not satisfied to regard it as a pragmatic generalization, a tactical principle to be employed carefully; on the contrary, all the hatred and exasperation typical of the antityrannic tradition were mobilized against a single usurping class.

It was ridiculous to believe, the revolutionary asserted, that this Moloch of bloodsuckers and exploiters, with their priests and hangmen, armies and prisons, brothels and universities, could ever be eliminated by peaceful and evolutionary activities. A new society could be created only by a total revolution which would destroy the whole edifice of class rule before building up the new structure and spirit of society. And this mighty revolutionary upheaval could not be brought about by the press, by propaganda, and by parliamentary debates, for the bourgeoisie was sufficiently powerful to suppress or falsify all serious resistance; the true revolution could be fostered only by the violent revolutionary actions of small, class-conscious, determined groups of individuals.

And here the revolutionary mind of France and the other Latin countries collided, at the end of the nineteenth century, with Marxism itself; for the responsible leaders of Marxism had begun to repudiate violence and all forms of putschism, and to explain Marxism in purely economic and evolutionary terms. Revisionist Marxism gave new force to anarchist thought. The successes of the peaceful parliamentary and trade-union methods were ridiculed as the betrayal of the working class, as the selling of their glorious revolutionary birthright for a dish of porridge. An extreme left wing of Marxism appeared, which found the peaceful atmosphere of continuous compromise disastrous. One could not put the revolutionary ardor aside until the high priests of the Marxian creed declared, "Now, Comrades, the forces of production have been sufficiently developed, and the necessary concentration of industry has been achieved; now, therefore, go on and make your final revolution." Furthermore, the anarchists argued, a revolution led, organized, and carried out by a single party would inevitably lead to a new state: that is, to a new armed minority which would necessarily subjugate and exploit the majority of the proletariat.

Thus, at the end of the century, the same antagonism as that which, a generation before, had separated Bakunin from Marx became again the center of controversy. Bakunin, as is generally known, had dreaded the Marxian state socialism as much as the existing capitalist system; and this difference had been the main theme in the vehement struggle between his Alliance of Socialist Democracy and the International Workingmen's Association, led by Marx, until Bakunin was expelled from the International at the Hague Congress of 1872.

One of the chief aims of the anarchists of the West became to restore to the masses, in the epoch of fully developed capitalism, the revolutionary ardor of their Babouvist, Blanquist, and Communard ancestors. Thus Ravachol exclaimed, after a series of bombings, before his judges, "I wanted to terrorize in order that people should become attentive to us and understand that we are what we are, namely, the real defenders of the oppressed."[20] After throwing a bomb into a plenary meeting of the French Parliament in 1893, August Vaillant shouted, "Let the ministries and the deputies know that there is a bomb of Damocles over their heads. I shall be followed by another who will succeed better than I have done."[21] A year later, President Carnot was stabbed by anarchist Caserio; and in 1898 Luccheni's assassination of a kind and poetic lady, remote from politics, Empress Elisabeth of Austria, showed that anarchistic bloodshed had become a purely symbolic act, though occasionally heated by personal motives of frustration.

This was the last chapter in the tyrannicide of the mob. A careful student of the doctrine of tyrannicide says rightly, "In this way, the doctrine of tyrannicide ... ends in the thesis that not only the people as a totality, but everyone, every member of it, is sovereign as soon as it pleases him. Every anarchist according to his convenience puts himself outside the social order of which he is a member, and impudently negates the morality which the collectivity acknowledges."[22] But the anarchist thesis was a perversion of the traditional doctrine of tyrannicide rather than a logical conclusion from it.

The anarchist movement soon collapsed because of vehement governmental persecution, the manifest impossibility and absurdity of its methods, the growing force of trade unionism, the organized life of the political party, and the achievements of legal parliamentary action.

Yet the leaders of the radical left felt that something was lacking in the labor movement. Peaceful evolutionary socialism seemed to them a betrayal of the working class. The early fear of Marx that the movement would degenerate into the continuous haggling of a trade-union bureaucracy for petty compromises became, at the end of the nineteenth century and the beginning of the twentieth century, a strong conviction among those who stubbornly stuck to the old ideal of a wholesale revolutionary transformation of society. Millerandism in France and Bernsteinism in Germany were for them signs of a petty-bourgeois narrowness of outlook or, what was even worse, a moral corruption of the proletariat. Therefore various forms of syndicalism and guild socialism appeared as a protest against purely parliamentary action and as an attempt to revive the original great aims of socialism.

The most significant theorist of this leftist trend of thought was Georges Sorel, who, in several works, analyzed the crisis of the labor movement. The newest and most hopeful symptom in the situation was, he thought, the mingling of anarchism with syndicalism: "Some day the historians will see in this entry of the anarchists into the trade unions one of the greatest events produced in our time...."[23] The essence of the transformation was the intentional use of violence and the systematic preparation of the working class for the final destruction of the capitalist system through a political General Strike.

In the revolutionary rebirth of the working class, violence was for him an indispensable element: "Today I do not hesitate to declare that socialism could not survive without the apology of violence."[24] He tried to show the heroic nature of certain criminal acts in various types of revolutionary movements. Only heroic action involving risk, discipline, self-sacrifice, mortal combat could bring about a proletarian leadership fit for the magnitude of the task. Yet Sorel's thesis was still surrounded by certain formulas of dialectical materialism. He did not explain why the workers should resort to violence and adopt the supreme danger of class war. He was satisfied to draw analogies between war and civil war: both, if conducted in the right way, would sublimate human nature.

It is clear that violence, in the thought of Sorel, is a phenomenon related to the moral order. We can not speak of violence against nature. Violence, as an outburst of self-sacrifice and heroism, must be based on some mighty emotion of human nature. Without reason, ideas, and sympathy with the sufferers no such emotions can be produced. But in the thought of Sorel the necessity of symbols for collective revolutionary action remained vague since he failed to show how these symbols would be motivated. If one rejects natural law, self-evident human rights, all those values which have animated the revolutionary movements of the West, symbols can be only emotional constructions open to mystic self-deception or propagandistic manipulations. Marxism had ridiculed or rejected these values as pure accidents and, therefore, continually deprived itself of the ultimate source of revolutionary transformation. Sorel and his collaborators sought a remedy, but revolutionary violence was manifestly only a symbol for them. Thus they avoided the real issue. Fight against tyranny has been and will always remain the ultimate motive that urges heroic men to open towards freedom and potential equality the roads blocked by abuses and monopolies. But Sorel and his friends were still too deeply rooted in Marxism to accept such an interpretation.

The same difficulty was faced by Lenin. With the powerful emotional life of a true revolutionary and with deep insight into the life of the common people, he attacked what he called the corruption of socialist consciousness by post-Marxian opportunists, by Bernstein and the evolutionary socialists, by the legalists of the movement, by the economists, by all those who regarded the movement as more important than the ultimate aims and who persuaded the working class that they were primarily interested in the economic reform of the existing system. "There can be no strong socialist party," he declared, "without a revolutionary theory which unites all socialists, from which the socialists draw their whole conviction, which they apply in their methods of fighting and working."[25] And, in an illuminating essay which belongs among the most important contributions to collective psychology, *What Is to Be Done*, first published in 1902, he powerfully demonstrated that a one-class struggle based primarily on the economic interests of the participants could not produce a really revolutionary movement. In this connection, he was the first in the Marxian camp to emphasize the enormous importance of the intellectuals, whose real function was to demonstrate to the workers their true situation in this world, showing that their true servitude was not only an economic one. The appearance of a literature performing this task was, he said, a turning point in the labor movement.[26]

The essence of this propaganda was, according to Lenin, the unveiling of the tyrannical system under which not only the workers but other classes were also suffering. "Is it true," he asked,

that in general the economic struggle "is the most widely applicable method" of drawing the masses into the political struggle? It is absolutely untrue. All and sundry manifestations of police tyranny and autocratic outrage, in addition to the evils connected with the economic struggle, are equally "widely applicable" as a means of "drawing in" the masses. The tyranny of the zemstvo chiefs, the flogging of the peasantry, the corruption of the officials, the conduct of the police towards the "common people" in the cities, the fight against the famine-stricken and the suppression of the popular striving towards enlightenment and knowledge, the extortion of taxes, the persecution of religious sects, the severe discipline in the army, the militarist conduct towards the students and the liberal intelligentsia—all this and a thousand other similar manifestations of tyranny: though not directly connected with the "economic" struggle, do they in general represent a *less* "widely applicable method" and subject for political agitation and for drawing the masses into the poltical struggle? The very opposite is the case. Of all the innumerable cases in which the workers suffer . . . from tyranny, violence, and lack of rights, undoubtedly a relatively few represent cases of police tyranny in the economic struggle as such.[27]

This unbearable tyranny was not simply a tyranny over the proletarian class. It was universal in its application. The true revolutionary slogan, consequently, should not be "go among the people" but "go among all classes of the people." Therefore, "the Social Democrat's ideal should not be a trade union's secretary, but a *tribune of the people,* able to react to every manifestation of tyranny and oppression, no matter where it takes place, no matter what stratum or class of the people it affects; he must be able to group all these manifestations into a single picture of police violence and capitalist exploitation . . . in order to explain to *all* and everyone the world-historical significance of the struggle for the emancipation of the proletariat. . . ."[28]

Therefore, Lenin was driven to the conclusion that a universal fight must be waged against tyranny: "Is there a single class of the population in which no individuals, groups, or circles are to be found who are discontented with the state of tyranny, and, therefore, accessible to the propaganda of Social Democrats as the spokesmen of the most pressing general democratic needs?"[29] "Political exposures are as much a declaration of war against the *government* as economic exposures are a declaration of war against the employers. And the wider and more powerful this campaign of exposure will be, the more numerous and determined the social *class* which has *declared war in order to commence the war,* the greater will be the moral significance of this declaration of war. . . . Only a party that will *organize* real all-national exposures can become the vanguard of the revolutionary forces in our time. . . "[30]

Lenin's thesis had nothing to do with the "scientific" theses of Marxism. It was the old creed of the Jacobins and their successors, that all the suffering masses of mankind were faced by a common tyranny. The indignation of the masses must be aroused against the autocratic system; otherwise no revolutionary will could be produced. Yet, like Sorel, even Lenin did not go to the core of the problem. He attacked only the falsification of the later Marxists; he did not see that the so-called objective economism of the Marxian system itself tended to neglect the moral side of the problem. What he had in mind was simply the creation of a revolutionary will and of a wave of efficient violence. In a way, he remained a class man even more rigidly and narrowly than some of the Revisionists. He did not see that the main problem of socialism, as an active historical force and not simply a compromise for economic reforms, was the restoration, not of violence, but of the conviction that the ultimate issue still remained the decision between right and wrong. Though he returned to the traditions of the previous revolutions, his position was a purely tactical one: the training of the masses for revolutionary action, not the continuation of the old moral struggle for freedom against tyranny. He did not grasp the fact that what really menaced the labor movement was not its lack of revolutionary *élan* but the narrow class-consciousness that tended to separate the workers from the common interest of society. The danger was, and is, that a purely economic adjustment between capitalists and labor tends to make labor as egotistic and monopolistic as capital. The real need, therefore, is not violent revolution, though occasionally it may be necessary, but a fight imbued with the idea of human rights, a moral solidarity with all the sufferers against all forms of exploitation, injustice, and monopolistic positions. The ultimate motive of the struggle against the thousand-headed tyranny of the modern state remains the same as it has always been against all former manifestations of tyranny. It is the consciousness of this that must be made clear to the masses; revolution or violence can only serve as occasional means.

We have now seen how the spirit of the anti-tyrannical tradition persisted in recent times as a stimulus to many types of men and groups who opposed oppression that they regarded as unbearable tyranny. But we have seen, too, how tyrannicide as a method of action was gradually transformed in modern times from the primitive but austere remedy of the ancient doctrine to putschism and terrorism and finally to the anarchist program of almost promiscuous assassination, to Sorel's revolutionary myth of violence, to Lenin's calculated tactics for revolution. These distortions retained some relation to the original tradition of tyrannicide because the persistent drive behind them was the hatred of oppression and the dream of freedom. But anarchist assassination or syndicalist or Bolshevik revolution were also clearly remote from traditional tyrannicide. From an act of conscience, of an heroic revolt of the individual against an unbearable and unjust oppression, it was transformed to a calculated act of political expediency in order to destroy, not a specific tyrant, but a hated political and economic system.

The distortion and perversion of the original doctrine of tyrannicide which was involved in this development helped to create the modern revulsion against tyrannicide. But more significant in creating this revulsion, and in confusing the whole issue, was the tendency to identify tyrannicide indiscriminately with the age-old practice of political murder, which, in its motivation and procedure, has little relation with tyrannicide. To the long and brutal story of political murder we must now turn.

XIV THE STREAM OF POLITICAL MURDER

POLITICAL MURDER is one of the oldest and most widespread of social phenomena. Whenever it has seemed likely to go unpunished, whenever the restraints of watchful public opinion, of free political institutions, or of moral and religious convictions have been lacking, ambitious and unscrupulous men have never hesitated to kill their opponents. Bergson has sadly alluded to the capital importance of this problem:

... It is certain that nature, at once destructive of individuals and productive of species, must have willed the ruthless leader if she provided for leaders at all. The whole of history bears witness to this. Incredible wholesale slaughter, preceded by ghastly tortures, has been ordered in absolute cold blood by men who have themselves handed down the record of these things, graven in stone. It may be argued that such things happened in very remote times. But if the form has changed, if Christianity has put an end to certain crimes, or at least obtained that they be not made a thing to boast of, murder has all too often remained the *ratio ultima*, if not *prima*, of politics. . . .[1]

Machiavelli, Hobbes, Nietzsche, and Spengler all conceived man as fundamentally a "Beast of Prey" and made this conception the basis of their political philosophies; and, however crudely simplified and one-sided this interpretation may be, it comes nearer to reality than the sentimental humanitarianism that regards all criminal and unsocial action as the conditioned consequence of economic and social situations. Both extreme views have undoubtedly contributed to the present catastrophe of our race: the former, by intensifying the animal greed of the aggressors; the latter, by softening the resistance of the naive and peace-loving.

There is a tendency in the historiography of assassinations to confuse extremely different types of political murder with tyrannicide. Tyrannicide has, indeed, one trait in common with political murder: both try to achieve changes in the possession or exercise of state power through the killing of an individual or group of individuals who are regarded as the chief obstacles in the way of the realization of certain aims. This has led certain writers to apply the same moral and political judgment to tyrannicide as to any other form of political murder. In fact, they sometimes single out tyrannicide as an exceptionally dangerous form of political murder because it is directed against the ruler; on the other hand, they do not sufficiently analyze those political murders that are instigated by so-called legitimate rulers in order to eliminate persons and groups dangerous to them.

It is a pity that our whole political and sociological literature has not produced a single work devoted to a careful analysis of the various types of political assassination and to the causes of their continual recurrence. In the lack of a systematic treatment of political murders,[2] all that can be done in the limited space available here is to show the main types of political murder and their relation to the problem of tyrannicide. We shall see how tiny the rivulet of tyrannicide has been among other streams that have flowed into the enormous river of political murder.

The "Beasts of Prey" particularly assert themselves in two types of political situations. The first may be called "oligarchic," because the fight goes on between small groups of men at the top. This situation assumes a state which, lacking the safeguards of public opinion and balance of powers, can be conquered or held by the extermination of one man or a small group of men. In such a structure, getting power is the simple mechanical problem of capturing the central organ and the few key positions connected with it. When a new political dynamo is put in the place of the old one, the machine immediately functions as if nothing has happened. This was the situation in the cases in which assassination became almost a normal phenomenon.

A second type of situation, that of widespread revolution or devastating war, has always been fertile soil for political murder, because it destroys orderly government, creates misery and famine, and heats human passion and hatred to the boiling point. This can be called the "plebeian" type, since in it common men may join the action.

The classification of types of political murder is a difficult one, partly because the very term "political murder" is ambiguous. Strictly speaking, political murder means the premeditated killing of an individual or group of individuals in order to get, maintain, or extend the power of the state in the interest of an individual or group. When the killing is directed to well-defined individuals, it would be more correct to speak of "political assassination." But the assassination can be an indirect one: when, for instance, the possessor of power uses packed tribunals for the elimination of hated and dangerous opponents, or when riots or frontier conflicts are instigated by the organs of the state or by revolutionary propagandists. In such cases, the term "political murder" seems more appropriate.

On the other hand, it shows the common good sense of the people that the enormous amount of killing committed in international and civil wars, in spontaneous riots, and in racial conflicts is not felt to be political murder. In these cases masses are fighting with masses; killing is not directed against certain individuals. Though recently an effort has been made to designate war itself as an act of political murder, it is very doubtful whether this policy can be supported by the genuine moral forces of the warring communities, in the present state of international consciousness and organization. This policy would give the conqueror almost unlimited power to make of every vanquished war leader a murderous criminal; it is very doubtful whether in the long run such exuberance of moral motives would create a more genuine international solidarity.

The following classification of political assassinations and of some other political murders will necessarily be schematic and simplified, since in all cases several motives are intertwined. Yet it remains true that the types show certain dominant tendencies. No systematic enumeration of cases is possible, but a few instances of each type will serve to illuminate certain historical situations.

The first type may be called assassination for personal motives, without any concrete political aim in the action, which assumes a political character only by the fact that it is directed against the head of the state or some other prominent person connected with the state. Hatred, revenge, jealousy, and other passions may be the cause of such acts, although they are sometimes hidden by a thin veil of ideological pretext. Perhaps the clearest example of this category was the assassination of President Garfield by the disappointed office-seeker, Guiteau.

The second type is murder to seize power for the gratification of power or for the advantages with which power is connected. In the ancient oriental despotisms, where a dominant military monarchy ruled over loosely integrated agglomerates of territories, to destroy the supreme possessor of such power was always an alluring idea to ambitious and ruthless men. In the spreading disintegration of the Roman Empire, the practice of assassination became almost a political institution. There is no need to recall the horrors described by Plutarch and Gibbon. The emperors became, more and more, the tools of the strongest legions, and the natural death of an emperor was almost regarded as an unusual occurrence.

Political murder of this sort was characteristic also of the period that followed the German migrations. "The closest ties of nature are here disregarded; fratricide, the murder of the nearest relatives, becomes an everyday event."[3] This situation lasted until the strong rule of the Carolingians enforced a certain order and unity.

The various forms of the city-state were also permeated by analogous phenomena. As was previously shown,[4] the classic doctrine of tyrannicide arose when vehement class struggles destroyed the former solidarity of the ancient community. The lust for power became a dominant motive in the struggle of tyrants and would-be tyrants; and in this struggle assassination played a considerable role. An analogous social and political situation led to an almost continuous series of assassinations in the Italian city-states of the fourteenth and fifteenth centuries. The use of paid assassins was widely practiced both in political and private relations. The *bravi* became an indispensable element of the Italian social structure; even regular courses in the use of the dagger were offered for would-be assassins.

A third type of political murder is diplomatic assassination: the use of assassination in international relations for the elimination of dangerous opponents. The original "assassins" were a Mohammedan sect which formed highly organized military groups which skillfully carried out political murders; the name was derived from the fact that many of these murders were committed under the intentional influence of hashish.[5] During the Crusades, they terrorized Christians and other enemies. Their services were often used by both Western and Eastern princes, including Byzantine emperors.

From the fifteenth century, the Council of Ten in Venice used assassinations as a carefully organized political institution, menacing the life of many outstanding statesmen of Europe. A long list of diplomatic assassinations collected by von Bezold[6] shows that several leading Christian rulers, for instance, the emperors Charles V and Ferdinand II, did not despise this method. The involvement of the papal courts in many gruesome assassinations has become a favorite topic of anti-clerical historiography.

A diplomatic assassination of very modern flavor is mentioned in the correspondence between the grand duke Cosimo of Tuscany and his ambassador in France (1577-78), planning the murder of some Florentine exiles who had found refuge in France under the rule of Henry III. The method has remained popular down to our own time, when the Italian Fascists used hired *bravi* at Bagnoles, in France, to kill Carlo Rosselli, whose growing influence among the Italian exiles had become disagreeable to Mussolini.[7] In the foreign policy of the Nazis, the extradition of political refugees was systematically forced upon the governments of conquered territories. A borderline case can be found in the assassination of the noted philosopher Theodor Lessing, when he was a refugee in Czechoslovakia, by an armed guard of Nazis sent across the frontier for this purpose; though without any political influence, he was hated as a Jew, a Communist, and a severe critic of President Hindenburg.

A fourth type of political murder is that committed for reason of state. It is perhaps the most widely used and the most dangerous, because the rationalization of a quasi-moral motive is always at hand. In reason of state, as first presented by the amoral genius of Machiavelli, the age-old power motive is coupled with the consideration of maintaining or expanding the power of the state. The *salus publica* does not know religious or moral considerations. If the interest of the state demands it, any illegal or criminal method may be used. Machiavelli extolled many cases of assassination in the interest of the state and praised the ruthless methods of Cesare Borgia as applications of real statesmanship. The author of *The Prince* had only contempt for the tyrant of Perugia who did not use the opportunity to kill his enemy, the pope, when he was in his hands. It is well known that this new philosophy aroused a wave of righteous indignation, but the same method had been used long before Machiavelli,[8] and has been continuously used up to the present time. Assassination for reason of state is the more ominous because the wielders of concentrated and uncontrolled political power can commit murders by so-called legal methods, by using intimidated or packed tribunals for the extermination of their opponents.

The cases are so numerous that special instances are scarcely needed. One of the most spectacular was the murder of Alexis, son of Peter the Great, in 1718, after a mock trial in which one hundred and eighty-one judges unanimously condemned the prince, who was the exponent of an old and still dangerous party. The assassination of Wallenstein by the generals of Ferdinand II liberated the monarch from a possible rebel. The killing of the brothers John and Cornelius De Witt by a mob infuriated by the Orange party made the ascendancy of William III easier. The execution by Austrian absolutism, in 1849, of thirteen Hungarian generals who fought for the constitutional rights of their country was only partly the revenge of the *soldatesca,* deeply humiliated by its many defeats; it was also motivated by fear of similar rebellions in the future. The extirpation of the whole czarist family by Bolshevik underlings under orders from the government was surely not a revengeful revolutionary act, but rather one committed from fear of a counter-revolution under the leadership of the Romanovs. The assassination of Matteotti by the Italian Fascists, the blood purges of dangerous or hated political opponents by the Nazis, by the henchmen of Horthy, by Franco, and by Stalin tell the same story. Often the extermination has been directed against those who had been protagonists of the new revolutionary system but later became disgruntled with its achievements.

One of the bloodiest and most cruelly perpetrated mass murders of the Nazis was directed against Captain Röhm and a great number of other members of Hitler's private army, when reason of state made it imperative that Hitler avoid a conflict with the old army. Hitler acknowledged seventy-seven victims, but more reliable reports have put the figure at several hundred. The words with which the Führer legalized the cold-blooded slaughter of his former friends can be quoted as the last authoritative statement of the theory of reason of state: "In that hour I was responsible for the fate of the German nation, therefore the supreme court of the German people during these twenty-four hours consisted of myself."[9] The role of the supreme judge and the hangman coincided in this most complete form of totalitarianism.

A fifth type of political murder involves religious issues, often connected with racial fanaticism and the struggle for power. In certain cases, existing powers, lay or ecclesiastic, have found their political interests endangered by the unshakable religious convictions of certain individuals and have silenced them by murder or mock trials. The names of Thomas à Becket, John Huss, Girolamo Savonarola, Thomas More, and Joseph Mindszenty will remain landmarks in this struggle between conscience and power. In other instances, religious conviction has been a motive, or a contributing motive, for murder. This motive assumed its greatest intensity in the sixteenth and early seventeenth centuries, when religious interests were closely interwoven with the combat between absolutism and particularism.[10] It was also combined with the power motive or reason of state in the history of the Inquisition.

With the decrease of religious fanaticism and the consolidation of the nation-state, the religious motive for assassination virtually disappeared, but when the severities of Bismarck's *Kulturkampf* aroused the indignation of the Catholic masses in Germany, Eduard Kullman, a member of the Catholic apprentice association, made an attempt on the life of the Chancellor in 1874. In a debate in the Reichstag, Windhorst, the leader of the Catholic Party, openly stated that the act of violence was a result of the unhappy situation which the attacked statesman had created.

In the Ottoman Empire, religious opposition was one of the factors in the frequent killing of Turks by the conquered Christian population. And religious fanaticism, coupled with a strong sense of racial antipathy, was also the source of repeated massacres on the side of the Turks. In a six-week period in 1895, some 30,000 Armenians were killed; the next year an organized massacre, sometimes called the "Turkish St. Bartholomew," was carried out in Constantinople; some 6,000 persons perished in the horrible carnage.

In the sixth type of assassination the driving motive is nationalism, often connected with struggles for constitutionalism, especially republicanism. In Germany, the unrealized promises of the French Revolution gave place to national enthusiasm in the wars against Napoleon, who appeared as a tyrant in the minds of the fighters. Friedrich Stapsz, the young son of a pastor, haunted by religious visions, tried to kill the emperor in Schönbrunn, and after the failure of his effort exclaimed, "To kill you is not a crime but a duty! You are the misfortune of my Fatherland!" The later assassination of Kotzebue by Karl Sand has already been mentioned.[11] Sand, like Stapsz, was possessed by the feeling of a supernatural mission; Kotzebue was regarded as a spy of the czar and an intriguer against the national cause. Before his execution Sand shouted, "I take God for witness that I am dying for the freedom of Germany."

In France, the period of restoration and reaction and the succeeding period of pseudo-liberalism caused the reappearance of a strong wave of Jacobinism and republicanism. No less than eighteen attempts were made on the life of Louis Philippe. On one occasion the revolutionary paper, the satirical *Charivari,* to which the cartoons of Honoré Daumier gave added importance, wrote, "Yesterday, the citizen-king came to Paris with his superb family without being in any way assassinated." After the sanguinary plot of Fieschi[12] against the king, in which an infernal machine, used for the first time, killed fourteen men, an opposition paper remarked, "At this time the Republic failed only by a fraction of a minute of being born."[13] It was a period of scarcely masked appeals for assassination; revolutionary legions were organized with the special purpose of regicide.

The dictatorial tendencies of Napoleon III also aroused a deep discontent at home and abroad. In 1853 Victor Hugo urged the assassination of *"Napoleon le petit":* "You can kill that man with tranquillity." Italian patriots regarded him as the chief cause of Italian disunity. Felice Orsini, inspired by the theories of Mazzini, tried with others to assassinate the emperor and empress in 1858. From his prison he wrote to Napoleon, "I conjure Your Majesty to render Italy its independence. May you not miss the petition of a patriot on the steps of his scaffold! Liberate my fatherland and the blessings of twenty-three millions of my brothers will follow you into posterity."[14]

Not only kings, but popular leaders as well, have been menaced by the passion of nationalism. Jean Jaurès, the great exponent of humanitarian socialism, was assassinated at the very outbreak of the First World War by a fanatic aroused by the nationalistic propaganda of the reactionary press.

Vengeance for national or constitutional grievances was a frequent motive for political assassination. Eugen Schaumann assassinated the Russian general Bobrikov in order to avenge Finland; a Ukrainian student murdered the Polish governor Potocki; Magyar absolutism in Croatia led to a series of political assassinations. Serb history is especially full of murders of princes and kings. Of eight Serbian rulers between 1904 and 1934, four were murdered, three were exiled, and only one died a natural death while on the throne.[15] The terroristic campaign of the Fenian Brotherhood against English rule and landlordism culminated in 1882 in the Phoenix Park murder of the Irish Secretary of State.

The most conspicuous and tragic case in the history of assassination motivated by a desperate national particularism was the murder of Abraham Lincoln by John Wilkes Booth. In spite of the insufficient analysis and documentation of the story, it seems to be clear that he acted under a false concept of tyrannicide. The lost war of the South, the tremendous sufferings of the people, its economic disaster, and the intrusion of the carpetbaggers appeared in his romantic and passionate heart to be the work of a tyrant, and he felt himself an avenger of crushed freedom. The conspiracy he organized, his words after the carrying out of his terrific act, *"Sic semper tyrannis!"* and "The South is avenged," and his last message, "Tell Mother... I died for my country!" suggest the fatal sincerity of his conviction. His act remains the classic example of a distorted conscience, which completely misunderstood the essence of the historical conflict and imagined that Lincoln, the hero of democratic ideals, was a tyrant.

The attempted assassination of President Truman on November 1, 1950, by two Puerto Ricans is an instance of an utterly naive and distorted nationalism. The motivation of these criminals had no connection with the ideology of tyrannicide; they appear to have acted simply under a confused notion that the killing of the president might create a revolution in the United States, and that "in the upheaval Puerto Rico might break free."[16] Needless to say, the role of the American government in Puerto Rico, especially under recent administrations, has been the reverse of tyrannical; and although the contrast between extremes of wealth and poverty in Puerto Rico may foment a fantasy of national independence in some unbalanced minds, such a fantasy is completely remote from any conception of the actual situation of Puerto Rico or of possible alternatives.

It is not necessary to expatiate on the seventh type of political murder, the main motive of which is class struggle, predominantly but not exclusively economic. The previous chapter has shown how the oppression of the masses, combined with a revolutionary dynamism, produced an outburst of assassinations fostered by anarchism, syndicalism, and Bolshevism.

These various currents of political murder were accentuated and intermingled in the period after the First World War, when the long suffering of the masses, the breakdown of orderly government, the revival of tribal solidarity and national exclusiveness, the great number of neuropaths produced by the war, and the acute class-struggle between the proletariat, the landless peasantry, and the former privileged classes caused a new wave of bloodshed and terrorism.

According to the estimate of Kerensky, there were ten times as many Russian victims in the Civil War as in the World War. Nobody can reliably estimate what proportion of these were victims of street fighting, of counter-revolutionary plots, of individual action, or of hunger. Nationalist revolts of the Cossacks, the Ukrainians, the White Russians, and the Baltic peoples contributed to the total. After a short period of consolidation, the attempted assassination of Lenin aroused a new wave of terrorism, which was renewed whenever reason of state made the purging of the Communist Party or of the military forces seem necessary.

In other countries, too, there was a wave of riots, assassinations, and execution of revolutionaries by counter-revolutionary tribunals. In Ireland, the bloody Easter Rebellion of 1916 was followed by assassinations committed by rival Irish factions which desired different solutions of the constitutional issue. In 1922, Michael Collins, and in 1927, K. O'Higgins, a dominant Republican figure, were murdered. The republican revolution in Spain set off hundreds of political murders, followed by the court-martialling of the revolutionaries at the orders of the military dictatorship. In Finland, the upheaval of the Communists, the White Terror of Baron Mannerheim, and the uprising of the fascist *Lapua* produced terror and insecurity. In Hungary, the excesses of the Communists were cruelly avenged by courts, concentration camps, and the hunting expeditions of counter-revolutionary officers against workers and Jews. The perpetrators of these crimes were called by Admiral Horthy "his best officers." In Yugoslavia, the growing antagonism between Croats and Serbs led to shooting in Parliament, in which the peasant leader Radich and some of his associates were gravely wounded. Continuous border raids by Macedonian revolutionaries from Bulgaria made the political atmosphere even more tense. Bands of dissatisfied Croatians, the so-called *Ustashi,* were armed and equipped by the Italian and Hungarian governments. This underground movement resulted in the assassination of King Alexander and the French foreign minister, Barthou, in Marseilles in 1934. In Greece, the murder of General Tellini and his staff on the Albanian frontier caused serious complications. In Bulgaria, Alexander Stamboliski, the far-sighted peasant statesman, was killed by Macedonian revolutionaries at the behest of reactionary bourgeois elements. An abortive Communist insurrection later caused widespread bloodshed. As a reaction to this came the bomb outrage in the Sofia cathedral, which caused the death of 123 persons. In Rumania, too, a latent civil war, especially against workers and Jews, became more and more conspicuous. The fascist Iron Guard organization, originally favored by King Carol and later used by the Nazis, was involved in countless murders. In 1933, the foreign minister, Jan Duca, of the so-called Liberal Party, was assassinated by the Iron Guard. In order to escape the growing pressure of the terrorists, the government executed the leader of the Iron Guardists, Codreanu, with thirteen of his underlings, on the pretext that they had tried to escape while being transported from one prison to another.

The atrocities of the well-organized Fascist terror of Italy have often been described. Giacomo Matteotti, later the victim of a murder initiated by Mussolini himself, condensed in his book, *A Year of Fascist Domination,* on forty-two octavo pages the list of assaults committed from November, 1922, to October, 1923: here are over two thousand cases of murders, woundings more or less severe, beatings, forcible administration of castor oil, decrees of exile, illegal seizure and burning of newspapers, wrecking of private houses and offices.[17] When the Fascist sovereignty was established and terror became a state institution, the "individual actions" were condoned by amnesties on the theory that political crimes in the interest of Fascism were dignified revolutionary actions; they were replaced by the judgments of extraordinary tribunals and by Lipari.

But nowhere did political murder as a form of political activity become so efficient and so thoroughly rationalized as in Germany. This happened even before the Nazis came to power. E. I. Gumbel showed in two pamphlets published in 1922,[18] presenting a large array of documentary evidence, that in the period 1918-1922 at least four hundred political murders were committed in Germany. Most of them were perpetrated by the extreme right, some of them against leading personalities such as Liebknecht, Rosa Luxemburg, Paasche, Erzberger, Gareis, and Rathenau. At a time when the press was still relatively free, Gumbel asked the government of the Republic to investigate the murders, most of which remained unpunished. Professor Radbruch, on becoming Minister of Justice, did his best to clarify the situation, and, after a thoroughgoing investigation, sent a memorandum to the Reichstag in which Gumbel's assertions were fully supported. Yet the Minister was unable to publish his own account because of the obstruction of his own ministry. Similarly, the governments of the *Länder* neglected to prosecute the criminals.

Some of the murders were systematically organized by the various secret associations and the *Fehme* tribunals, in which the extreme right was preponderant; some were committed by armed units under the pretext of suppressing leftist riots; some involved putsches fabricated for the purpose of getting rid of hated and dangerous persons, called *Schädlinge* (social pests). The concept of killing the *Schädlinge* was propagated by the loudest terrorist means. Though none of the assassinated persons could be called tyrants and though many of them were men without a particle of public power, their "obnoxious" character or their "anti-patriotic behavior" was regarded as enough to invite crime. Gumbel enumerated more than sixty secret or semi-secret organizations as the sources of the rising wave of criminality. Some of them had considerable financial means, furnished by certain industrialists connected with the heavy industries or by the owners of large Junker estates. Murderers were sometimes hired, or paid *agents provocateurs* were used to trap the *Schädlinge*. Although the Communist revolts had been quickly crushed, legally or illegally, and there was no real danger from the extreme left, the hunting of the radicals went on unabated.

Why was there this enormous preponderance of the rightists in political murders? Gumbel's answer is that the adherents of the leftist parties had behind them decades of trade-union schooling, which condemned individual action, not so much for moral reasons as because of the conviction that economic and technical factors were preponderant in history. In contrast, "the Right was the follower of the heroic conception of history, according to which the hero is the maker of history...." But this seems only a secondary cause. It was of far greater importance that individual responsibility had been blurred by continual mass agitation and that it had become evident that the rightist perpetrators of political crimes would remain unpunished. The documents show that police organizations and tribunals did not function. In some cases the connivance of public authorities with the murderers was clear. Even escape or refuge was offered to them. Some of them enjoyed foreign protection: for instance, some of the murderers of Rathenau found refuge at the estate of the Hungarian premier, Gömbös. It was evident that the Weimar Republic was unable to maintain order and security against its enemies, who occupied many important positions. In 1923 the situation was so poisoned that a conservative politician who had been prime minister of Bavaria for a decade called the country, in a public speech, a state "in which no honest man can be sure of his life."[19]

There were two other efficient means for the protection of political murderers. One was the theory of an *übergesetzlicher Notstand* (supralegal necessity), which the German *Reichsgericht* elaborated even before the advent of Hitler. Although it condemned political murders in general, the High Tribunal acknowledged "extraordinarily difficult situations" in which murder "out of love for the Fatherland" was the "only" means for the defense of the interests of the state. The situation in Upper Silesia in the time of the "defensive fight against Poland" was explicitly mentioned as such a case. By this alone hundreds of political murders were legalized.[20]

When such artificially construed loopholes seemed to the Nationalists to be not quite sufficient for their political purposes, several laws of amnesty provided another welcome opportunity. In a law of 1928, death sentences and sentences of life imprisonment inflicted for crimes against life were reduced to imprisonments for a term of seven and a half years. This measure was supported by the Communists in order to alleviate the punishment of certain of their comrades who had been involved in crimes against life. Nationalists and Communists continued to agitate for a complete amnesty for all crimes against life. In 1930, when 107 Nazi deputies were elected, the pressure of this propaganda induced all the parties except the Social Democrats to vote a law giving full amnesty for political murders committed before September, 1924.

As is well known, the Nazis' use of political murder was one of the most effective means of their rise to power. In the last years of the demoralized Republic, the Nazi terror became increasingly unrestrained and unconcealed. When, in 1932, in the Upper Silesian village of Potempa, five Nazis invaded the home of a worker at night and killed him in a horrible manner, they enjoyed the enthusiastic protection of the Nazi press. When the criminals were condemned to death by the proper tribunal, Hitler sent his famous telegram to the five men, calling them "comrades," assuring them of his "unlimited fealty," and asserting that their liberation was "a question of our honor."[21] Under the pressure of an aroused public opinion, the death sentence was commuted to imprisonment. After Hitler became Chancellor, a new general amnesty law passed in March, 1933, released his Potempa "comrades," and other comrades.

Thereafter the risks of political murder were largely eliminated. The concentration camps gave a welcome opportunity for such deeds in legalized form. In one of them, Camp Lichtenburg, the disciplinary order practically gave *carte blanche* for the extermination of the *Schädlinge,* enumerating seventy-two types of cases in which the death sentence was provided as a "disciplinary punishment." The cases varied from "political activity designed to incite the camp" to "refusal to work at the assigned place."[22]

The era that began with the establishment of the Nazi dictatorship was a kind of golden age of political murders, rising to a culmination in the Second World War and its aftermath. Almost all types of political murder showed a horrid accentuation: individual assassinations, organized assassinations in the concentration camps, elimination of unreliable elements by order of the dictators or by specially appointed tribunals, mass extermination of national and racial groups, and the innumerable deaths that resulted from the introduction of slave labor on a gigantic scale and from the compulsory migration of peoples. The overwhelming motive in these hecatombs, in which human dignity and the value of the individual person were radically denied, was the fight to establish new sovereignties on a world basis.

Our Western world is inclined to regard all these horrific facts as primarily the outcome of the Nazi system and ideology or as a personal work of "war criminals." The Nürnberg Trial, carefully organized by the victorious nations, was a mighty popularization of this conception, which, however, distorts the actual situation through its disregard of the part played by native patriots in the occupied countries and of the parallel activities of the Russian empire-builders and the Russian satellite states.

The statement with which Justice Robert H. Jackson, speaking for the United States, opened the Nürnberg Trial was a devastating indictment against the Nazis. For the first time, the picture was presented to mankind in its apocalyptic dimensions and with a clear revelation of the Nazi perversion of all the values that have always been cherished by decent human beings. "The catalogue of crimes," said Justice Jackson, "will omit nothing that could be conceived by a pathological pride, cruelty, and lust for power. These men created in Germany, under the *'Führerprinzip,'* a National Socialist despotism equalled only by the dynasties of the ancient East. They took from the German people all those dignities and freedoms that we hold natural and inalienable rights in every human being. The people were compensated by inflaming and gratifying hatreds toward those who were marked as 'scapegoats.' "[23]

In accordance with Nazi racial doctrine, the super-scapegoats were the Jews. Their extermination surpassed, in number and organization and "scientific" method, all the cruelties which had previously been committed against that unhappy people. "The conspiracy or common plan to exterminate the Jews," said Justice Jackson, "was so methodically and thoroughly pursued that despite the German defeat and Nazi prostration this Nazi aim largely has succeeded. Only remnants of the European Jewish population remain in Germany, in the countries which Germany occupied, and in those which were her satellites or collaborators. Of the 9,600,000 Jews who lived in Nazi-dominated Europe, sixty per cent are authoritatively estimated to have perished. 5,700,000 Jews are missing from the countries in which they formerly lived, and over 4,500,000 can not be accounted for by the normal death rate nor by emigration, nor are they included among displaced persons. History does not record a crime ever perpetrated against so many victims or one ever carried out with such calculated cruelty."[24]

The systematic campaign against the Jews can not be explained as the simple result of German racial passion. In the occupied countries also—in Slovakia, in Hungary, and in Rumania—the Nazis easily found groups of native patriots, such as the Hlinka guardists, the Arrow Cross "socialists," and the remnants of the Iron Guardists, to carry on the murderous job against the Jews with the same atrocity.

In the Middle Ages the chief motive in the persecution of the Jews was a religious one, hatred of the "murderers of Jesus Christ." But the atheistic and anti-Christian Nazis used anti-Semitism, as they used their confused social and economic ideology, as a tool in their struggle for power. The fanatical motive of hatred of the Jews was a propaganda pattern systematically calculated, more than it was the essential motivating force of the Nazi crimes. Similar methods were used against their other European enemies. Hitler told his officers on August 22, 1939, that "the main objective in Poland is the destruction of the enemy and not the reaching of a certain geographical line." Rosenberg approved the project of deporting promising youth from occupied territories on the theory that "a desired weakening of the biological force of the conquered people" would be achieved. A similar idea was expressed by Himmler: "Either we win over any good blood that we can use for ourselves and give it a place in our people, or ... we destroy this blood."[25] Similar atrocities in the same mood and with analogous theories were committed in the concentration and slave labor camps; and a vast deportation of prisoners of war was carried out with total disregard not only of the dignity but also of the biological needs of the individuals. "Germany became a vast torture chamber," as Justice Jackson put it.

How flimsy the pretext of the racial dogma was is suggested also by the behavior of the Nazis against their own people. One must remember that in 1933 there were about 525,000 Jews in Germany; by the end of the Nazi regime, 295,000 had emigrated, 215,000 perished. Thus the 300,000 people who were in concentration camps at the beginning of the war included huge numbers of "Aryan" Germans; and the estimated total, based on figures of the Reichsministry of Justice and the records of army court martials, of 32,500 persons formally executed from 1933 to 1945, is a clear index to the extent of the political murder of "Aryan" Germans by the Nazis. These figures, of course, do not include the many who were more informally dispatched.[26]

The expulsion of native populations by the Germans for the sake of national security, frontier regulation, or Germanization exposed millions of human beings to hunger and death. And this was not only, or primarily, the Machiavellian action of the great power driving for world empire; it was also the action of the smaller states under Nazi domination, which tried to secure for themselves all the advantages which they could, as obedient instruments of the German invaders.

The other side of the story, the atrocities committed by the Russian empire-builders, has not yet been systematically investigated; but there is enough evidence to show that the picture there was no less horrifying, except that the ignominies of gas chambers and "scientific experiments" were unknown. When the Russian liberation came, the satellite countries in turn tried to build up their own little sovereignties under the rule and protection of the Bolshevik world empire. But the Russian penetration was far more effective than the Nazi penetration had been. Whereas the Nazis were satisfied by having in their hands the economic and military key positions, themselves eliminating only occasional opponents of the new system, the Russian Communist rulers were driving at the systematic extermination of the middle classes or that part of the peasantry that tried to maintain its independence. Social Democrats were expelled or coerced into unity with the Communists.

This process was carried out by a long series of violent actions, imprisonments, and murders in the satellite countries. Any independent voice was strangled in the new sovereignties under Russian tutelage and control. As a witness of the Yugoslav proceedings put it, "Since the 'liberation,' the Communists themselves admit that—by detention, disappearance, or death—they have got rid of 500,000 Yugoslavs.... [Their] purpose is to 'liquidate' the entire agricultural, commercial, and industrial middle class.... The new men will take their place quickly enough."[27] The old economic and political relations and the relations of classes were broken down; even family solidarity was often intentionally wiped out.

The small states accepted eagerly the Nazi and Communist lesson and imitated it. They wanted as advantageous frontiers as possible and compact homogeneous nation-states, formed by the wholesale wiping out of national minorities, which were denounced as traitors. A terrible wave of persecution directed against the Germans in Hungary, Czechoslovakia, Rumania, and Yugoslavia, and against the Hungarians in Slovakia, cost the lives of many thousands. This wave of intolerance originated in two main currents. One came from above: even some formerly liberal statesmen, such as Benes and Jan Masaryk, thought the time propitious for a final solution of their nationality problems by the elimination of their minorities through compulsory expulsion. The other current came from below: wider circles of the population became interested in the new policy, which gave them excellent opportunities to rob those who were expelled or sent to forced labor, to occupy their homes and other properties under the honorable disguise of a patriotic effort to secure the national unity of their countries or to avenge former oppression.

The end of World War II was marked also by a wave of political assassination, sometimes sporadic, sometimes planned by the various underground movements, directed against collaborationists, against Nazi intruders, or against leading figures in the dictatorial regimes when their power began to totter. The gruesome liquidation of Fascism in the killing of Mussolini impresses one almost as a symbol of the whole system. In the general uprising in North Italy, he and his mistress were captured and executed by partisans. Their bodies, suspended by the feet in the market place of Milan, were beaten and abused by the vindictive crowd. The Duce and his fugitive ministers had carried with them the Fascist government's reserves, besides Mussolini's personal fortune and other treasures in gold or jewels. These remnants of the Fascist glory became a bone of contention between those partisans who were loyal to the state and the Communists, who ultimately stole the booty.[28]

The postwar picture of gloom and blood was not restricted to Europe but appeared in Asia and Africa and the Near and Middle East as well. Space forbids detailed discussion of the bloodshed connected with the conscious and organized movement of nationalism in India, where, for instance, the great saint and man of peace, Mahatma Gandhi, lost his life by the bullets of a Hindu terrorist nationalist in the bloody struggle between the Hindu government and the government of Pakistan; or in South Africa, the land of patient "voluntary servitude," where the new spirit created by world transformations has sharply intensified the racial conflicts; or in Egypt, where patriotism and racism led to the assassination of the prime minister, Nokrashy Pasha, by the Moslem Brotherhood,[29] and to the Cairo riots of 1948, in which "the number of those killed ran into three figures."[30]

The Jews, decried by the anti-Semites as cowardly and incapable of violent action, developed in Palestine a most terroristic nationalism, which was fully reciprocated by the Arabs. This militant Jewish nationalism was partly a struggle for the independence of the Jewish state against the Arab world; it was also partly motivated by the agony of European Jewry. Excessive nationalism coupled with fanatical racism was seen in the "punitive military actions" that followed the publication of the British White Paper of 1939;[31] in the assassination in 1944 of Lord Moyne, the British resident minister in the Middle East, by two Palestinian Jewish youths, probably connected with the terroristic Stern Gang;[32] and in the assassination of Count Folke Bernadotte, the official representative of the United Nations, in Jerusalem in 1949 by members of a terrorist group as an action of vengeance and of propagandistic repudiation of international control. It is significant that neither the United Nations nor the Israeli government was able to capture the criminals involved in the latter act.

This desultory sketch[33] of political murders includes many different types, varying from individual, planned assassination to murders committed during mass riots where the victims were mostly not even known by name to the perpetrators of the deeds. The cases mentioned are only a fraction of all that might be cited; but they will serve to show the terrifying frequency of political murders in the history of the Western world. This is a good lesson for those who shudder at the very idea of tyrannicide and forget the enormous majority of political murders which were by no means tyrannicides. Pure tyrannicides, as the next chapter will show, have been extremely rare.

XV SOME CASE-STUDIES

MOST OF THE CASES of political murder mentioned in the preceding chapter have manifestly nothing to do with tyrannicide. Tyrannicide requires, first, the existence of a man, or group of men, whose tyrannic power crushes all personal liberty and makes it impossible to undo unbearable evils either in a constitutional way or by revolution. In this situation, an individual (or a group of individuals) resolves to annihilate the central organ of tyranny on his own responsibility. He has good reason to believe that this act will serve to liberate the constructive forces of the community and to restore the opportunity of free institutions. Moreover, he is motivated by altruistic considerations, by a desire for what he believes to be the good of the whole community. No personal ambition for power, to be gained directly or indirectly, motivates him; personal grudge or vengefulness does not play a dominant role in his determination.

On the contrary, he is, in most cases, aware of overwhelming odds against his own survival. He is thus a man with "the ability to die," with the conviction of a martyr. This characteristic, of course, the tyrannicide shares with certain religious or political fanatics. But the tyrannicide is not the instrument of the particular interests of a political or religious group. He thinks of himself as a free, independent, and responsible individual. As he is determined to perpetrate a crime against the moral order summed up in the commandment, "Thou shalt not kill," he must act in the interest of the entire community; and he must follow the voice of his own conscience—neither that of popular passion nor of factional interest groups.

In the circumstances of modern tyranny, public opinion can not be organized. Modern tyranny is not, like the tyranny of the traditional theory, a mere excrescence upon an otherwise healthy society; it disintegrates and demoralizes the society itself. Thus only through the voice of his conscience can the modern tyrannicide interpret what the real voice of the community is. Of course, the "voice of conscience" should not be interpreted as separated from or opposed to the "real voice of the community." The tyrannicide is not a hermit; he is intensely, nay, passionately connected with the woes and tortures of the society in which he is living, with its cultural heritage, with the moral and constitutional traditions which the tyrant has perverted and submerged. His relation to society is something like that which Nicolai Hartmann, in his profound *Ethics,* has described as the role of the individual in the great ethical revolutions of history:

> Here the great ethical leaders come into evidence: the spiritual heroes, prophets, founders of religion—the champions of ideas. From them the movement proceeds; they revolutionize the crowd. It is natural enough to think that such leaders are "inventors" of the new forms of value, that the birth of values themselves takes place in the thought of the champion of ideas. Even that is a great mistake. The champion himself invents nothing; he only discovers. Indeed, even his discovery is conditioned. He can only discover what already lives darkly in the valuational sentiment of the crowd, and presses forward to expression. He it is who, as it were, reads in human hearts the values newly felt; there he gleans them, draws them into the light of consciousness, lifts them onto his shield and invests them with speech.[1]

The difference between the tyrannicide and the leader described by Hartmann is simply that what the tyrannicide discovers is not new values to be formulated, but old values, almost forgotten or annihilated in a corrupted society, to be restored.

Believing himself to be the executor of the higher moral will of the community, the tyrannicide must explore this higher will, so far as this is possible in the disruption of public life. For this reason Mariana, followed by some other serious thinkers, advised the future tyrannicide to consult "learned and grave men" before acting.[2] But his conscience must still be the supreme judge, in an issue which may put an end to his life, perhaps also to the lives of people whom he loves; which may inflict catastrophe on his community, on his nation, on mankind. In any moral dilemma, conscience can not be eliminated as the source of final decision. The "learned and grave men" can not be a *deus ex machina* to be followed blindly. The tyrannicide must, in fact, take the responsibility of choosing whom he will consult. He must distinguish for himself between the real moral leaders of the community and those who are only rhetoricians, professors, or gang-leaders. And, as the story of the German resistance shows,[3] the wise men may disagree, even on important points. Thus, among the different values with which he is confronted, the conscience of the tyrannicide must be his final guide. The genuine moral leader and the part of the community that is still morally alive must be complementary to each other.

These tests obviously exclude from the category of tyrannicide most of the cases of political assassination which have been described in this book. The overwhelming majority of these murders were not directed against tyrants; and in nearly all cases the motivation of the deeds was connected with personal interests or with the interests of a group or class. For instance, when the nihilists, anarchists, or other terrorists killed heads of states or other prominent dignitaries, their acts—even though sometimes revealing a remarkable lack of self-interest and readiness for self-sacrifice— were not tyrannicides but carefully planned acts of ill-guided expediency. They did not regard their victims as the only or the chief obstacles to the liberation of the community; rather they saw their own actions as merely links in the chain of permanent revolution.[4] Nobody could have thought that the assassination of even such a powerful figure as the "Czar Liberator," Alexander II, could emancipate the masses from the yoke of czarism. *A fortiori,* only mad men could have imagined that the assassination of Empress Elisabeth or of President Carnot or of President McKinley, or even of powerful administrators like Plehve or Stolypin, much less the attempted assassination of Queen Victoria, would change the situation in the respective countries.

Moreover, acts of revenge and despair without any hope of bettering existing conditions, although sometimes committed in a genuine spirit of self-sacrifice, have nothing to do with tyrannicide. In Berlin in 1921, the Armenian student Teilirian shot Talaat Pasha, the Grand Vizier of Turkey during the First World War, as responsible for the murder of his father, mother, brother, and sister; the Russian counter-revolutionaries, Conradi and Palunin, killed at Lausanne in 1924 the Soviet dignitary, Vorovsky, to avenge the victims of the Red Terror; Salomon Schwarzbard shot in 1926 the Ukrainian leader Simon Petliura in Paris in retaliation for the Jewish massacre in the Ukraine. All four were absolved by their juries.[5] All these deeds showed a tragic determination and a certain immunity from base motives. However, one can not but conclude that the killing of their victims were not acts of tyrannicide. And when, in Paris in 1938, the seventeen-year-old Polish Jew, Herschel Grynszpan, killed Ernst von Rath, a member of the German Embassy, avenging, through the killing of an unimportant person, the disgrace imposed on his race by the Nazis, it is manifest that the deed was rather one of symbolic vengeance than of tyrannicide.

However, we find some borderline cases in recent history which bring us nearer to the characteristics of tyrannicide. One of the most important was the assassination of King Alexander and Queen Draga and several members of their court in the royal palace of Belgrade by a group of army officers in June, 1903. The deed, accompanied by ghastly outrages of passion and barbarism, was vituperated by the official press of Austria and Germany as simply the crime of a military junta against the legitimate ruler. However, the degenerate Alexander and his despicable consort had many of the qualities of irresponsible tyrants. They had annihilated all vestiges of personal and political liberty. The king had arrested his ministers when they dined with him, had annulled or changed the constitution arbitrarily, had gagged and intimidated the press, and had ruthlessly persecuted his political antagonists, the friends of Russia. There was a growing conviction that Alexander and his *bon vivant* father, the former King Milan, had surrendered all the legitimate interests of their country to Austrian anti-Slav imperialism. The army and the government officials were irregularly paid and graft polluted the whole bureaucracy. The queen was generally believed to be a former prostitute. Her brothers exercised a disastrous influence at the court. And when, physically incapable of motherhood, the queen simulated pregnancy in order to substitute another's child as successor to the throne, the existence of the regime was felt to be a nightmare of scandal and shame. The character and rule of Alexander had many resemblances to those of some Renaissance tyrants, lacking, of course, the culture and refinement which often illuminated the Renaissance courts. An historian of the period compares Alexander to Borgia in his complete lack of moral restraint. He made plans for the assassination of hated political leaders and promised large sums of money to the murderer-to-be. When his father had opposed his marriage with Draga, he had even plotted against the life of the former king.[6]

The English historian Temperley affirms, "Indeed, under Alexander's rule it is strictly true to say that insurrection was the only means of protest that offered a real chance of safety. As insurrection had been tried and failed, the extremists fell back on conspiracy.... Political revolution was justified on every ground, and a deposition and peaceful deportation of this unfortunate pair would have been condemned by no impartial observer."[7] But it is exactly the lack of the possibility of such a procedure that drives men to tyrannicide. So it was in Serbia. Yet one would hesitate to call the tragedy in the palace a true tyrannicide. Eighty-six conspirators were involved in the assassination, a few of them men of great integrity, others blind fanatics (many of them drunk) or implicated in the envenomed political struggle of the country. Such an action is rather a political-military revolt than a tyrannicide. It is not purely the result of a dilemma of conscience.

The assassination of Archduke Francis Ferdinand, in 1914, by the exasperated Serb student Princip, while several other young men with the same purpose waited in ambush, also had certain elements of genuine tyrannicide. However, the victim was not only not a tyrant but also a man without actual power, who sincerely intended to liberate the Slavs of the Monarchy from the yoke of German-Magyar domination, although in a way that was incompatible with the Yugoslavs' dreams of a Greater Serbia. In the minds of these fanatic young men, he symbolically represented, as heir apparent, the imperial structure which kept the Yugoslavs in dependency and made their national unification impossible. And the pressure of Vienna and Budapest undoubtedly was an insurmountable obstacle to Yugoslav freedom and unity.

One must acknowledge that Princip and some of his fellow-conspirators were of the stuff of which tyrannicides are made. R. W. Seton-Watson, who condemned the assassination, recognized that "from first to last they gloried in it, unhesitatingly accepted the consequences, and repudiated all idea of external influence. This proud and self-conscious attitude never varied, even though some of them were cruelly mishandled in prison, and on more than one occasion were bespattered with mud by Tyrolese soldiers as they entered the courthouse. Almost without exception they affirmed their belief in Yugoslav unity as the motive of their action."[8] Some of them declared that with all of them "national belief" had become a religious conviction.

There was behind the deed a widespread popular conviction. "The outrage of Sarajevo was the sixth in less than four years. All six were the work of Serbs or Croats from within the Monarchy, while one had come all the way from America for the purpose."[9] In June, 1913, a young man named Jukić had made an unsuccessful attempt on the life of the "Satrap" of Croatia, Banus Cuvaj, an instrument of Magyar domination. On the first anniversary of his deed, an influential newspaper of Belgrade, *Pravda*, wrote, "It must grieve us to the utmost that not everyone has acted the same way as our Jukić did. We have no Jukić any longer but we have the hatred, we have the wrath, we have today ten million Jukićs."[10]

Another case which one is tempted to describe as an attempt at "vicarious tyrannicide" is that of Fernando de Rosa, who tried to kill the Italian heir apparent, the Prince of Piedmont, in Brussels in October, 1929. This young man of twenty saw in the Prince one of the chief representatives of the Fascist regime. "I regret very much," he said before the judge of investigation, "that I broke the laws of Belgium, but I broke them in order to obey the laws of my conscience."[11] Later he said before the tribunal, "You live in a free country, you can not understand me. In a country like Belgium, I condemn violence. I can not make an apology for insurrection here, but I think it is legitimate in a country in which the people have no right at all." Then he added, "I am not a criminal before the law. I pity my country, I pity all those who sigh in prison. There was a struggle in me. I willed to kill the prince and I willed not to. It was reason that drove me and instinct that restrained me. I committed an intellectual crime. I felt that my crime was necessary for my country."[12]

Several distinguished scholars, writers, and statesmen of pre-Fascist Italy appeared before the court to testify that the most elementary rights of men were unknown in Italy. They described the system of lawless brutality and affirmed the complicity of the king and of Prince Humbert in the Fascist movement. One of them, a member of the Christian Democratic Party, Dr. Francesco Ferrari, asserted that the king had lost all his prerogatives and was then "only the Chancellor of the Fascist Dictatorship."[13]

Another similar case of a "vicarious tyrannicide," which, however, came nearer to the original meaning of tyrannicide, was the assassination of Wilhelm Gustlof by a fanatical and exasperated Jewish student, David Frankfurter, at Davos, in February, 1936. Gustlof was surely not a tyrant in the proper sense. He was a foreigner in Switzerland enjoying, like Frankfurter, the hospitality of the Republic. But very soon he assumed an aggressive role and began to organize Nazism in that free country. He issued orders to his German co-nationals in Switzerland and his activity became so impudent that a member of the Council of the States, Dr. Thalmann, said in a public meeting, "Some of the leaders behave as if they were perfectly at home here, issuing orders.... Gustlof is for Switzerland what Habicht was for Austria.... Let the Federal

Council take severe measures against a spy system which is execrated by the whole Swiss nation."[14]

The passionate young man, embittered by the Nürnberg Laws and deeply concerned for the future of Switzerland, a country which he adored, killed, symbolically, in the person of the gauleiter the arch-enemy whom he could not reach. "I am a medical student," he said in an interview with a Swiss paper, "and he gave me the impression that he was a bacillus through whom a virulent pestilence might be introduced into Switzerland. It was the pestilence I aimed at, not the person."[15]

One should add four other cases which seem to constitute real tyrannicides, both in their motivation and in the objective conditions which prompted the deeds, though in some of them full evidence is not yet available. Their analysis will further show us the complexity of the phenomenon of tyrannicide.

One was the assassination of the Austrian premier, Count Stürgkh, by the left-wing Socialist leader, Friedrich Adler, in October, 1916. It was at the peak of the war crisis. Large masses were suffering cruelly from malnutrition and were disgusted by many acts of war profiteering. Austrian parliamentarism, never very strong, was totally paralyzed; the press was completely silenced; and an irresistible, often irresponsible, military dictatorship had been established. The war had never been popular among the workers, who regarded it as an extension of German imperialism. The right-wing leaders of Austrian Social Democracy had tried in vain to give the war a popular appeal by calling it a war against czarist autocracy. In the conviction of the masses, the Austrian regime assumed, more and more, the aspects of absolutism. No help could be expected from the Hungarian feudal parliament, a bulwark of the German imperial policy against the Slavs of the Monarchy, who vainly tried to put an end to the dualistic system and replace it by a federal constitution.

Adler felt that the deadlock must be broken by executing the head of the system. His intention was to create a psychological explosion which would shake the system, give more force to the workers, and compel the complacent elder labor leaders to listen to the underground murmur of the masses. Count Stürgkh was surely not a tyrant; yet, in his official capacity and by his extraordinary powers, he was the visible head of the system; everyone knew that the old emperor was already a living corpse. Undoubtedly Count Tisza,[16] the Hungarian premier, was far more responsible for the situation than was the Austrian bureaucrat. As a matter of fact, Adler hesitated for a time whether to choose the Austrian or the Hungarian as his victim. But he came to the conclusion that for the Austrian masses the person of the Austrian premier would have a far greater significance and that the imperial palace would be far more upset if the shooting occurred in its immediate neigbhorhood.

From a psychological point of view, Adler was a pure type of tyrannicide. No personal calculation of power entered his mind. He was a sensitive intellectual prompted by moral and philosophical considerations. His father, Victor Adler, had been the first organizer of the Austrian Social Democracy, and thus his whole life was inseparably connected with the working class. Though he was a Marxian, the idealistic traditions of German philosophy remained strong in his mind.

Before the court which tried him the murderer stated his case with great courage and precision. Among the working masses of central Europe, his apology[17] became the most widely read document of the period. In no other case have the traditional motives of tyrannicide been so clearly restated.

Adler emphasized the sacrificial character of his deed: "It is not an act which arose from a momentary urge, but a clearly and fully considered action. I have committed this deed in the perfectly clear comprehension that my life would come to an end through it." He also recognized the illegal character of the act: "I am in full accord with the Attorney of the State that in an orderly community murder can not be a political weapon...." But he argued from a great number of facts that Austria had ceased to be such a state: "Therefore, the moral justification of my deed is in my eyes, as a citizen, a perfect one. The Cabinet has torn asunder the Constitution, the Cabinet has ceased to care for the laws of Austria, and so there remained for me no other road than the road of violence." "Freedom has its ethical grandeur in the maxim, 'Don't do to anybody what you would not want done to yourself.' " But this "moral of democracy" had been annihilated in Austria.

Adler had also a well-defined conception of the practical expediency of his aim. In a time when the "government-socialists of Germany and Austria are going to Stockholm as traveling agents of their foreign offices," he felt that the public opinion of the workers should be aroused. "Of course I did not think for a single moment of unloosing mass action at this time, but what I wanted was to create the psychological conditions for future mass action in Austria, to restore the disposition for such mass action. I did not want to make revolution by my deed, but I wanted to obtain the possibility of a revolution." Therefore, he considered his act as a "symbolical deed.... It should show that one is under the obligation to risk his life for his conviction." Yet his motivation was by no means influenced by the anarchist philosophy. He did not intend to prepare for a new society. He wished only to make an end to the Austrian deadlock by liberating popular forces for action.

Adler insisted that the utility of his deed could not be proved for lack of an historical precedent. "But I can say that I have never regretted this act, and I was always convinced that it was a useful one; that I had done what a single man could do.... I am satisfied that I have spent my life in this way...." And he added, "I declared in the preliminary investigation ... that the first play that I saw was *Wilhelm Tell,* and since then I have never had a doubt that one is morally justified in killing an Austrian petty-tyrant *(Vogt)*."

The president of the court, before pronouncing the death sentence, looked firmly into the eyes of the accused; and could not speak. Only when Adler averted his face was he able, with tears in his eyes, to pronounce the sentence.[18] In the course of the whole trial, there was not uttered a single brutal word which could have offended the personal dignity of the accused. The silent pressure of public opinion, representing very heterogeneous groups of society, was so strong that the death sentence was commuted to life imprisonment. Austrian absolutism was surely not of a totalitarian type.

A second case which, if we knew the whole truth, might measure up to the tests of tyrannicide is the assassination of Huey Long. For lack of complete evidence only a hypothetical analysis is possible.

Whereas Count Stürgkh was only a symbolic tyrant—one might say, a tyrant against his own will—the creature of Austrian absolutism under the iron heel of the war machine, Huey Long seems to have been a true tyrant of the ancient type, with all its ruthlessness, vitality, ambition, greedy appetite, and low jocularity. He created his autocracy intentionally, bit by bit, as a purely personal accomplishment. Always in his mind was the insatiable greed for more power. Dreams of domination, the vision of the Presidency of the United States, haunted his shrewd intellect, tool of an unbridled dynamism. He was far nearer to the classic than to the present-day type of tyrant. He did not have in his state the obstacles of a broad popular culture and of a traditional distrust of despots, such as the other contemporary dictators had. He did not need a new ideology: his Share-the-Wealth Program was simply the old classic method of bribing the hesitant and of expropriating his enemies. It was pure demagoguery adjusted to the demands of the moment. The Kingfish had also the well-developed sense of the old and the new dictators for ostentatious building programs, for glamorous festivals, for *panem et circenses;* but these were bluntly offered without any hocus-pocus of *Kraft durch Freude.*

He had a profound disrespect for men of thought. When asked whether he had read Adam Smith or Karl Marx, he answered, "No, I never read a line of Marx, or Henry George, or any of the economists. It is all the law of God; a people which transgresses against the law shall be bruised and confounded. If we follow the law of God we can end this depression in twenty-four hours."[19] His appetite for power and enjoyment of life had, for him, the driving force of a mission.

A genuine tyrant of the classic type! This is the impression one receives on reading the voluminous literature about him, especially the solid presentation of his story by Harnett T. Kane.[20] The large poor white and Negro population of his state constituted an appropriate basis for uncontrolled demagoguery. He did not need to gain power, as his forerunners had done, by the armed force of his praetorian cohorts; but after he had destroyed a superficially rooted constitution by ruse and corruption, his security rested on the bodyguard which watched over all his steps.

The new tyrants of Europe could create a brilliant ideology which fascinated, at least at the beginning, younger men of high idealism and occasionally of a remarkable talent for organization. In contrast, the dictatorship of Louisiana, like those described by the classics, showed clearly its criminal features:

Absolutism came to Louisiana with a grin on its lips, a jest on its tongue . . . ; a gallery of engaging rogues, of highly diverting rascals, is the result; Cajuns of a smiling amorality; Italians of underworld background that did not bar them from public honors; Jews who grew wealthier by the process of special favor that speaks all languages; plain Anglo-Saxon thieves, fat men who grew fatter, lean and hungry men as dangerous as they looked. They advanced from rank as barbers and hot-towel men to masters of great estates; from show-clerks to connoisseurs of expensive living. They invested in gold toilet-fixtures. They dug private lakes. They named airports after themselves. . . .

They built steam-heated shower baths for their cattle and pigs, ordered air-conditioning units for their own bathrooms. "Share the Wealth" was a slogan they understood well. . . .[21]

What is strangest in this whole story is the fact that, as in the tyrannies of the past, large masses of the population, for whom the constitutional process and human rights were only abstract generalizations, supported the despot. Even now his renown seems to be unabated in a large sector of the population. Their democracy had not cared for their interests, whereas the absolutism of Huey Long gave them public entertainments and some participation in the booty. The people of the "independent nation of Louisiana," as the dictator occasionally called his domain, did not realize that they themselves were being exploited.

On September 8, 1935, a young doctor of Baton Rouge, Carl Austin Weiss, a silent, thoughtful, modest, scholarly man, remote from politics, shot Huey Long as he was finishing a usual night meeting in the capitol, surrounded by friends and by his bodyguard. After the deed the guards fired immediately. Not a word left the lips of the slayer; sixty-one bullet holes were found in his dead body. The machine had worked with the utmost precision.

And now we come to the most unbelievable episode of this unbelievable story. We are informed by a competent writer[22] that a third of the population did not believe that Dr. Weiss had assassinated Huey Long, in spite of the revolver which he grasped in his dead fist, in spite of his closeness to the wounded dictator, in spite of the sixty-one bullet-holes in his body. We are told that a considerable part of public opinion held that a man in the bodyguard had begun shooting, and that Dr. Weiss had gone to the capitol at an unusual hour, with his revolver, only for a chat. And, indeed, strange things happened: the official investigation, so loudly announced by the successors of the Kingfish, was supressed; not even an autopsy was held; and the father of the accused denied that his son had intended a murder.

And—what is even more curious—among the many writers and reporters who were fascinated by the tragedy, there were none who were interested in the intentions and motives of the assassin. Of course, there was probably no "scientific" evidence to explain his motivation; and perhaps younger Americans, following the precepts of current psychology, have lost interest in things that can not be measured exactly. They felt it more important to investigate the measurable details of corruption and fraud. But we know that Dr. Weiss had been a graduate student in Vienna when Dolfuss crushed the labor movement and machine-gunned the workers' apartment houses; that he had been disturbed by these experiences and knew the consequences of dictatorship; that a few of his friends had suffered from the ire of Huey Long; that the dictator had made unfounded remarks about his father-in-law, alleging that he had Negro blood in order to drive him from office.[23]

Why were these paths of psychological inquiry not followed? Why did nobody question the doctor's intimate friends? Why was nobody interested in the books which the young man read? Why was his correspondence not scrutinized? Perhaps the terror was too great for this; perhaps family interests were involved. At all events, it seems that the hypothesis of tyrannicide was dismissed as improbable because of the fact that no really serious personal interests of the murderer were involved. One author explicitly states that public opinion disbelieved in the criminality of the physician because no sane man would kill somebody in an affair in which his strictly personal interests were not involved.[24]

Perhaps we shall never know the authentic story of the murder at the capitol of Louisiana.[25] But it is a fact of great historical and moral importance that a great part of present-day public opinion can not even reconstruct the essence and motivation of tyrannicide. From a purely utilitarian and personal point of view, it is, of course, absurd.

More significant is another reaction. The role of Long was defended, even glorified, not only by his friends and personal beneficiaries, but also by several intellectuals and leaders of American culture. A noted novelist, Robert Penn Warren, then associate professor at the University of Louisiana (one of Long's most advertised achievements), in his novel *All the King's Men,* elaborated a complete theory of the legitimacy of political criminality on the basis of expediency. He called it "the theory of the moral neutrality in history. . . . Process as process is neither morally good nor morally bad. We may judge results but not process. The morally bad agent may perform the deed which is good. The morally good agent may perform the deed which is bad. Maybe a man has to sell his soul to get the power to do good."[26] Such theories give a safe conduct to fascism, bolshevism, and any other "process" for crushing the moral dignity of the individual. In these movements the responsibility of confused intellectuals has been considerable: even of those who hated tyranny. They have accentuated the moral collapse of society.

A third case which seems to point towards tyrannicide was the attempt, in 1941, against the life of Pierre Laval and Marcel Déat, the two principal collaborators with the Nazis. A young unemployed stoker, Paul Collette, tried to shoot them during a parade of the "French Legion of Volunteers to Combat Bolshevism" at Versailles. The details of the attempt were suppressed, but it was stated that the young man steadfastly declined to admit affiliation with the Communists, rather professing De Gaullist and pro-British sympathies.[27]

The moral significance of the act was scarcely noticed in the American press. Curiously enough, only a conservative of broad vision, Walter Lippmann, commented upon its importance:

There can be little doubt . . . that what Laval and Déat have been organizing is not a crusade against Russian Communism but a revolutionary conspiracy to enslave France, to save their own lives, to raise themselves to power. Nor will there be many in France or elsewhere who think that Paul Collette sacrificed his life merely in order to protest sending a handful of troops to Russia. They will know that he died that he might strike a blow at the betrayers of his country's honor and independence. . . . The effects will be far-reaching. For this shooting at Versailles is the climax of the first chapter in the popular uprising which was inaugurated by British resistance last summer, then carried forward by the heroic stand of the Greeks and then confirmed by the suicidal rebellion of the Yugoslavs. . . . There is little doubt that the resolution has been taken, deep down among the masses of the people, that they will not accept Hitler's new order. When men have come to the point where they are resolved to die rather than submit, there is loose in this world a force which will make history.[28]

A later case which seems to have strong elements in common with tyrannicide was the assassination of Admiral François Darlan in the office of the High Commissariat in Algiers by a twenty-year-old soldier, on Christmas Eve, 1942. The details of the crime were covered by intentional mystery. Not even the name of the assassin was revealed, and no official explanation of the deed was given. The Germans, of course, propagandized it as a murder plotted by the English. As Darlan was a traitor both to the France of Vichy and the France of de Gaulle, others interpreted the assassination as an act of vengeance from one of the two camps.

This much was acknowledged, however, even by the official sources: that the young man was "a French citizen whose mother lives in Italy," and that he had shown complete calm after the act and, hearing that his attempt had been successful, said, "So much the better.... You may kill me now." It was also made public that he refused to admit having had accomplices and that he "faced the firing squad as calmly as he had confessed his crime on Christmas Eve."[29]

These facts seem to indicate that the deed was either a crime of passion or an act of conscience. Nobody could believe that the tottering system of Vichy, or that of the renegade Communist Doriot, a Nazi henchman, could have produced a martyr. There were only two French movements which might have had enough dynamic drive to lead a young man to self-sacrifice: the group of extremely nationalist Royalists, and the very different types of patriots united around de Gaulle. Both were animated by the same hatred of Vichy, shame for the humiliation inflicted on France, and an ardent desire to restore the independence and dignity of their country. Both not only hated Darlan, but regarded him as dangerous to the future struggle against the Germans. It could scarcely be doubted that the assassin belonged to one of these camps. Under either hypothesis, the act of the young soldier is manifestly related to the type of tyrannicide.

Without evidence about the motives which drove the young man to his final decision, it is significant how the de Gaullist Frenchmen interpreted it. In all probability they were living with feelings and emotions akin to those which incited the anonymous soldier to his fatal deed. Therefore, a broadcast of a Fighting Frenchman from Brazzaville in French Equatorial Africa, arguing against President Roosevelt's condemnation of the act as a "first degree murder," is surely worthy of attention. Though recognizing that political murder is a crime, he declared that the assassin was "entitled to all the extenuating circumstances possible" and that "never has an assassination been more similar to a punishment from the sky." He went on to say that although they could not identify the assassin—they did not even know whether he was a Frenchman—they could "envisage thousands of reasons the assassin might have held as legitimate."

If he were a Frenchman what could he say? ... He could say: "I wanted to avenge my country of two years of treason and shame brought upon it by Darlan."

Maybe he is a sailor. Then he will have specific reason to say: "I wanted to avenge so many of my comrades massacred at Dakar, Casablanca, Toulon. I wanted to avenge all these splendid ships, needlessly sunk in harbors, the whole fleet of France, the best and last of its kind, and shamefully left inactive."

Maybe this twenty-year-old assassin is a soldier. He would also have specific reason to say: "I wanted to avenge so many of my comrades needlessly killed on the battlefields of Syria, in order to prevent our British friends from taking over the airports of Syria which Darlan had given to our German enemies. I wanted to avenge so many of my comrades needlessly massacred at Madagascar to prevent our friends the British from saving the island from a government which was going to hand it over to our enemies, the Japanese."

Maybe our assassin is a worker and he will have specific reasons for saying: "I wanted to avenge so many of my comrades who today live a convict's life in German factories, as a consequence of the economic collaboration, the foundation of which was laid by Darlan."[30]

These or similar motives may have been in the mind of the young man at that tragic hour when he threw away his life for the liberation of France.[31]

A year after the execution of the young Frenchman, the untiring effort of Eugène Bonnier de la Chapelle, a newspaperman, won partial vindication of the man who killed Darlan: his son, a frail university student, Fernand Bonnier de la Chapelle. The Ministry of Justice of the French Committee of National Liberation issued a statement announcing that a re-examination of the case had revealed that the young man had not been connected with the Axis, as had been alleged by General Jean Marie Bergeret, then Darlan's chief assistant, later charged with treason by order of the National Committee. "Through the year," the statement said, "these facts have become apparent: the idealism of the young student, an ardent follower of General Charles de Gaulle, was used by older men who never have been brought to trial. These men supplied the gun and the opportunity to shoot Darlan."[32]

A week after the communiqué of the Ministry of Justice, the French resistance movement issued this statement:

A year ago Bonnier de la Chapelle, who had just killed Darlan, was shot. The group of resistance parties in France, some of whom are members of the Assembly, on the invitation of the French resistance movement will go tomorrow at 11 A.M. to lay flowers on the tomb of young Bonnier de la Chapelle. All patriots are invited to take part in this pious act.[33]

XVI TYRANNICIDE

IN THE GERMAN RESISTANCE

THE PREVIOUS cases of tyrannicide are surpassed in significance, in clarity of vision, and in the feeling of moral responsibility by the attempt on the life of Adolf Hitler made on July 20, 1944. The case is important, also, because it shows the enormous difficulties of tyrannicide in a modern totalitarian state, in which the tyrant has accumulated in his own all-embracing organization all political, military, and spiritual powers.

Anyone who has had direct or indirect contact with the events in Nazi Germany, studied the material presented at the Nürnberg Trial, and read the literature on Hitler and his movement, will have no doubt that Hitler was no mere military and political dictator but a real tyrant.[1] But, to appraise his tyranny rightly, it is not enough to show, as has often been shown, that it originated in national defeat, economic disaster, class struggle, and the perverted political ideology of a systematically misled people. His tyranny had also a personal aspect; and without understanding this, one can not understand his utter misuse and abuse of the great majority of the German people.

Lacking any religious, constitutional, or traditional ties, the former housepainter and hungry art student used his power with the *hubris* of an unbalanced upstart. Surrounded by astrologers and quack physicians, by mediocre intellectuals and artists who shamelessly cajoled him, and suppressing any sober criticism or independent opinion, he became more and more convinced of his supernaturally ordered destiny. This he identified with that of Germany and the German race, to which the whole world should be subordinated as inferior creatures destined to serve the superman and his people. His formula, "world-power or ruin," became the supreme policy of the state.[2] Disregarding the advice of his best military leaders, he drove millions to unnecessary death; he systematically planned the annihilation or expulsion of native populations; he introduced slavery into the concentration camps, where, in the name of science, thousands were tortured as objects of experimentation. Under his rule, as has been aptly said, a new science of "thanatology" was developed.

"The passions which ruled Hitler's mind," says a recent biographer, "were ignoble: hatred, resentment, the lust to dominate and, where he could not dominate, to destroy."[3] One of the greatest German experts in psychiatry, Professor Karl Bonhoeffer, was convinced that Hitler's bloodthirst was pathological. He mentions that Hitler repeatedly enjoyed seeing films of the executions he had ordered. It was "in accordance with his true self," Bonhoeffer asserts, that "millions of Jews, Poles, and of Germans, too, were tortured to death in the concentration camps."[4]

Other traits of his rule also developed on the lines of the traditional pattern of the personal tyrant. Though he played the role of a puritan of modest taste, despising meat, alcohol, tobacco, and women, his household was far more luxurious than that of most of the legitimate monarchs. His undertyrants also lived in luxury, scarcely trying to hide their extortions and robberies. They continuously intrigued against each other, trying to monopolize the favors of the dictator. To this Hitler reacted by using a system of "divide and conquer" among his underlings. In the last days before his final collapse he expelled even Goering and Himmler from his government. The famous words of Lord Acton became literally true: "Power tends to corrupt and absolute power corrupts absolutely."

Thus, when the catastrophe was approaching, even the final annihilation of Germany seemed to him justified, because the defeat showed that the people were not worthy of him. He began to operate more and more by *Vernichtungsbefehle* (orders of extermination). On March 19, 1945, he ordered all the gauleiters and army groups to continue the struggle without any consideration of the German population. All industrial plants, all means of transportation, all food provisions were to be destroyed; populations were to be forcefully evacuated. He had previously declared to Speer, his Minister of Armament, "The nation has proved itself weak, and the future belongs solely to the stronger Eastern nations. Besides, those who remain after the battle are of little value; for the good have fallen."[5]

He advocated the same philosophy of destruction for the defense of his own life. At a tea party with Mussolini and his staff, immediately after his escape from the attempted assassination of July

20, 1944, Hitler shouted in a fit of frenzy, with foam on his lips, that he would have revenge on the traitors. "Providence had just shown him again, he screamed, that he had been chosen to make world history; and he ranted wildly about terrible punishments for women and children,... an eye for an eye, and a tooth for a tooth...; none should be spared who set himself against divine Providence."[6] He introduced "the abominable institution" of *Sippenhaftung,* by which a great many innocent members of the families of those who had conspired against him were condemned to death.[7] An eyewitness mentions that after the attempt on Hitler's life he met at Buchenwald ten Stauffenbergs, eight Goerdelers, and so on.[8]

Until the final collapse, the unlimited power which Hitler had accumulated seemed, to most people, irresistible. It was secured by the enormous resources of the organization and iron discipline of the Third Reich. Its ultimate foundation was twofold: on the one hand, it rested on the rapid development of technological equipment which might seem to make Germany undefeatable in war; on the other hand, it rested on the complete domination of a whole nation by a network of continuous propaganda and terror, against which no independent thought and feeling could be mobilized. No decent man who did not howl with the wolves could feel safe from spies and the torture chambers of the Gestapo. In the intellectual and spiritual field, any glimmer of independent thought was suppressed. The famous German universities had become training-schools for Nazism. Religion was tolerated only on the condition that it remain silent on all political and social issues.

Yet it is no wonder, but almost the result of moral law, that against this tyranny all the still living spiritual energies of the German nation revolted more and more passionately.

A final history of the German resistance is still lacking,[9] but books, articles, official records, and private documents now at our disposal demonstrate that it displayed at least as much heroism and self-sacrifice as any of the undergrounds of other peoples who became victims of Nazism. One must remember that in other countries the fight went on against foreign aggressors and usurpers, whereas the German resisters had to combat their own national forces; and this is an enormous difference. The underground movements in the conquered countries were national affairs, in which the combatants could count on the support of hundreds of thousands of anonymous sympathizers. In Germany, through an absolutely poisoned propaganda, Nazism was haloed as the struggle of the entire German people for *Lebensraum* and National Socialism, whereas those who fought against Nazism were decried by the totalitarian state and party machine as traitors and spies against their own country.

And there is another difference which should not be forgotten in assessing the difficulty and the heroism of the German resistance. The penetration of the conquered countries remained superficial, a police-and-spy affair. The penetration of Germany became something like a moral cancer. Count Moltke, one of the heroes of the passive resistance in Germany, wrote to English friends in 1942, "Can you imagine what it means to work as a group, when you can not use the telephone, when you are unable to post letters, when you can not tell the names of your closest friends for fear that one of them might be caught and might divulge the names under pressure?"[10] We can not talk of an underground in Germany in the same sense as in the occupied countries; the German resistance necessarily was the loosely co-ordinated effort of many groups. Yet its many rivulets, some of them originating as early as 1932, grew into a broad river of collective despair and indignation and a profound concern for the salvation of Germany.

The first resistance of workers' organizations under Catholic, Social Democrat, or Communist leadership was suppressed and driven underground; but as the atrocities of the Nazi tyranny became more and more apparent, a reorganized workers' movement was supplemented by a new movement of resistance from all walks of life, bound together not by party affiliation but by a common moral revulsion which, in many instances, was also a religious revulsion. The resistance, whose new structure had taken form by the end of the thirties, was based on the silent, man-to-man co-operation of many thousands of persons scattered throughout the country. It was a many-sided structure of small, overlapping groups, some merely local, some nationwide, whose interconnections were achieved largely through a network of personal relationships. Its activities varied from simple refusal to participate in any support of the tyranny to distribution of anti-Nazi literature, transmission of information, aid to Jews and to political fugitives, recruitment and training of new members, building contacts in the world outside, and the gradual construction of an organization of influential leaders to plan for the overthrow of Hitler and the restoration of a decent and purified Germany. Its extent and activities were apparent neither to the world outside nor to the German people themselves. The movement, of course, sought to protect itself by secrecy. Official propaganda, in a country thoroughly atomized by totalitarian control, was highly successful in concealing the fact that there was substantial opposition to the regime. In the prewar period, the governments of other countries, uncertain whether to oppose Hitlerism or to appease it, had no interest in calling public attention to indications of opposition within the Nazi state; and during the war intelligence work required that its contacts with the resistance be protected by secrecy, while at the same time the Allied propaganda line was based on an assertion of the absence of significant resistance and an insistence on the collective guilt of Germany.

Some occasional instances of opposition, such as the outspoken condemnation by courageous churchmen of Nazi assaults on Christianity, could not be concealed. But when the Gestapo gave publicity to the execution of a group of students at the University of Munich in February, 1943, this admission of the existence of opposition to the regime came as a shock to the general public in Germany and abroad. The little group of students called itself "The White Rose." Under the inspiration of Professor Kurt Huber, a Kantian for whom the categorical imperative had become the rule of life, they had been distributing leaflets condemning Nazism and calling for the resistance and atonement of the German people.[11] The next public revelation was still more impressive: the news of the attempted assassination of Hitler on July 20, 1944.

There had, indeed, been a number of earlier attempts to assassinate Hitler; some were the result of group action, others the work of isolated individuals—as was the planting in a Munich beer cellar in November, 1939, of a bomb from which Hitler narrowly escaped,[12] convinced, as he said, that "the fact that I left the Bürgerbräu earlier than usual is a corroboration of Providence's intention to allow me to reach my goal."[13] The attempted assassination of 1944, however, was the climax of the work of a group of extremely distinguished soldiers and civilians, whose ability, prestige, and contacts with various aspects of the resistance movement had given their project considerable promise of success. Among members of this group, plans to assassinate Hitler had been made as early as January, 1942,[14] and some actual attempts had failed only by a narrow margin of bad luck. One plan, for example, came near to success when Fabian von Schlabrendorff, a Berlin lawyer before the war, placed a time bomb in Hitler's plane. The bomb failed to explode, but Schlabrendorff escaped. He became one of the organizers of the final conspiracy and one of the few to survive the slaughter that followed on its failure; his own narrative is one of the sources from which we know its details.

In the final plan, the assassination of Hitler was to be followed by organized military revolts throughout Germany, a summons for a civilian uprising, and the establishment of a provisional government which would initiate the recovery of Germany under a liberal, decentralized constitution. The conspirators had made, from 1938 on, several efforts to win recognition and support of their movement by the English and American governments,[15] which had, however, refused to negotiate with them and, in the Casablanca meeting of 1943, had announced their commitment to the formula of "unconditional surrender." Without any encouragement from the leading democracies, the leaders of the resistance remained convinced that a German effort to overthrow the tyranny of Hitler must be made. "We have tested ourselves before God and our conscience," said the man who was to be the chief actor in the final scene; "it must happen, for this man is the Devil himself."[16]

Colonel Count Claus von Stauffenberg was chief of staff to General Fromm, the commander of the Home Army. He was a man of high culture and intelligence and of extreme heroism. Since he had lost in the war one eye, his right hand, and three fingers of his left hand, he was unable to use a revolver and attack Hitler personally. He had previously been a key figure in two other plans for attempts on Hitler's life; both had had to be abandoned because of unforeseen difficulties.

On July 20, 1944, Stauffenberg took part in a conference at the Führer's headquarters in East Prussia. He deposited a time bomb in a briefcase, starting the mechanism of the bomb, and left the room immediately under a pretext. Scarcely had he left the conference when the detonation followed. Four participants in the conference died of their wounds; the others escaped with their lives, though wounded more or less severely. Hitler was hurled out of the room through the wooden wall of the building. His escape was due to the fact that the meeting, in the warm season, was held not in the usual concrete bunker but in a wooden hut with open windows, which diminished the force of the explosion.

When Stauffenberg left, he hurried to Berlin to give the signal for the military revolt. He was convinced of the success of the attempt and learned only in Berlin that the whole plan had been frustrated by Hitler's almost miraculous escape.

The revenge of the Gestapo was terrible. Under the command

of Himmler, a nationwide manhunt was organized against the conspirators, officially called "the Potsdamers" or "blue-blooded swine." Unheard-of tortures and brutalities were used to extract confessions. Schlabrendorff's description of the methods used against him surpasses even the most evil imagination. Stauffenberg and almost all the conspirators were executed.[17] Some committed suicide. A special category of the persecuted was the so-called *Schade Verbrecher,* those who, when they heard that the attempt on Hitler's life had failed, uttered the words, "It is a pity." They were hounded all over the country.

The events of July, 1944, and the following months shook not only Germany but the whole world. The revelation of the widespread German resistance to Hitler came as a great surprise to many of us, so successful had been the official war propaganda which described the whole German people as a single band of criminals. Nazi propaganda attempted to minimize the effect of the revelation by explaining the conspiracy as an aristocratic military revolt, a kind of Junker plot against Hitler and the National Socialist rule of the new Germany; and this interpretation was immediately echoed in the propaganda of the Allies. It was, however, a complete distortion of the truth, though it can not be denied that the conspiracy had to some degree an aristocratic and military character.

The group which planned the tyrannicide and the revolution that was to follow was made up of some high-ranking army officers, some politicians and administrators, a few diplomats, labor leaders, and religious leaders, who shared the conviction that the physical annihilation of Hitler was necessary to put an end to the tragedy of Germany. Some, but by no means all, belonged to the titled nobility. Many were men of deep religious conviction, Catholic or Protestant. A major part in the early liaison work of the conspiracy was played by the noted Protestant theologian Dietrich Bonhoeffer, who had said at a secret church meeting in Geneva, in 1941, "I pray for the defeat of my nation. Only in defeat can we atone for the terrible crimes we have committed against Europe and the world";[18] he was arrested in the spring of 1943 and killed in 1945 by drunken SS men in a concentration camp, shortly before American troops reached it. Another important figure was Adam von Trott zu Solz, a former Rhodes Scholar and an expert student of the Far East; he used his position in the German Foreign Office as cover for successive attempts to open negotiations with foreign powers. Through such labor leaders as Wilhelm Leuschner and

Julius Leber, the conspiracy had contact with the skeleton organization of the workers' resistance. Noted economists, lawyers, historians, political scientists gave their help in the drafting of proclamations to be issued after the tyrannicide and in the planning of the political and economic structure of a liberated Germany.

Karl Goerdeler in the political field and General Ludwig Beck in the military field were the outstanding leaders of the group. Goerdeler had been mayor of Königsberg and of Leipzig and commissar for price control under Brüning and under Hitler until 1936, when he resigned to devote himself to the organization of what he called "the front of decent men."[19] A member of the conservative Nationalist Party, he was permeated with a devotion to the traditional principles of liberalism; an experienced organizer and administrator, he grew in intellectual and moral stature, through his work in the resistance, to the dignity of a great statesman. For a long time his religious convictions led him to oppose the assassination of Hitler; but he was finally convinced that this must be the essential first step in the destruction of the tyranny.

Beck had been Chief of Staff of the German Army from 1935 until the summer of 1938 and was regarded by many as the best mind in the army. In July, 1938, he had attempted to organize among his fellow generals a military revolt against Hitler to prevent the Czechoslovakian adventure, which he regarded as certain to lead Germany to disaster. The essence of his argument was summed up in these words:

The final decision on the position of the nation is at stake. History will burden the leaders of the army with bloodguiltiness if they do not act in accordance with their professional and political knowledge and their conscience. Military obedience has a limit where the knowledge, conscience, and responsibility of the leaders prohibit the carrying out of a command. If, in such a situation, their advice and warnings find no hearing, they have the right and the duty to the people and to history to resign their offices. If all act in common, the execution of a military action will become impossible. They will have thereby saved their fatherland from disaster. It is a failure in greatness, and in his concept of his office, if a soldier in the highest position considers his duties only in the narrow frame of his military task, unconscious of his supreme responsibility to the whole people. Uncommon times demand uncommon actions.[20]

Such a revolutionary doctrine was, of course, completely opposed to the traditions of the German army; nevertheless Beck won considerable support among the generals and, in co-operation with

Goerdeler, prepared to carry out a military revolt against Hitler which would culminate in his capture and formal trial. The plan was frustrated by the announcement of the forthcoming Munich conference. The British policy of appeasement made it impossible to brand Hitler as a warmonger. In retirement, Beck continued to work closely with Goerdeler and became one of the strongest exponents of tyrannicide as the essential prelude to a military revolt.

Although it is incorrect to regard the German resistance as primarily the resistance of top army officers at a time when the defeat of Germany in the war was already evident, it can not be denied that without the participation of a number of military leaders there could never have been the final attempt at tyrannicide. In the first place, under a total dictatorship only men in the closest contact with the tyrant can come into a position in which they can attack or kill him. Hitler was so thoroughly guarded by his private army, by his police and spy organization, that no common mortal could approach him. "One can not even realize the protective measures around the person of the Führer. No armed officer could any longer enter his room of audience. His arms were taken away from him by SS men, even if he had been called to receive a decoration."[21] Only such circumstances as those utilized by Stauffenberg could allow an opportunity of tyrannicide. A second consideration also made the cooperation of influential military men essential. Even in case of a successful tyrannicide, nothing would be gained so long as the supreme command remained in the hands of generals obedient to Hitler. Therefore the plan of tyrannicide was necessarily combined with that of a military revolt, which would create a new supreme command in sympathy with the resistance. As early as 1941, Ludwig Beck, discussing the difficulties of resistance, asserted categorically, "This Gordian knot can be solved only by a single stroke with the sword. However, he who performs this stroke must both know and rule the mighty machine of the German army."[22]

The application of this final stroke appeared to many members of the active resistance to be not only a tactical and strategical necessity but above all a moral one. Many of the best observers agreed that the oath of allegiance to Hitler remained, until the end, the chief hindrance to mobilizing the armed forces against Hitler, a hindrance that affected both the higher ranks and the common soldiers. Even among those who condemned Hitler's military and political leadership, the tradition of the time-hallowed oath of allegiance was so deeply rooted that it paralyzed a number of plans for revolt. Many of the best minds of the resistance were heavily burdened by the question: who would be authorized to give an order for a military action against Hitler? Therefore, a free and spontaneous act of tyrannicide, which would let loose all the energies of despair and revolt, appeared essential for the "creation of an oath-free situation."[23] And beyond these practical considerations lay the conviction expressed by another intrepid general, Henning von Tresckow, in the summer of 1944: "The assassination must be attempted at any cost. Even should that fail, the attempt to seize power in the capital must be undertaken. We must prove to the world and to future generations that the men of the German resistance movement dared to take the decisive step and to hazard their lives upon it. Compared with this object, nothing else matters."[24]

In their conception of the goals of their revolt, the military leaders shared the general ideas of the civilians. They were vehemently opposed to the very idea of a new "Kapp putsch" or the establishment of an anti-Nazi military dictatorship. On the contrary, all agreed that an independent civil government must be established. Moreover, in spite of the frequent emphasis on the restoration of Christian values, no kind of institutional clericalism was contemplated. Those who can think only in terms of class struggle and Marxian revolution are unable to understand the gist of this movement, which was in no sense counter-revolutionary, and at the same time was not revolutionary, since ideas of social revolution did not enter into it. As in the classic cases of tyrannicide, the main effort was to be, not a social upheaval to put a new ruling class into power, but rather an attempt to re-establish traditional human rights and to restore the moral basis of society.

We know this from several contemporary documents, especially from the draft of a proclamation which Goerdeler formulated, which was destined for publication after the revolt against the Nazis had succeeded. The fundamental intention of the program was to restore their moral foundations to a people thoroughly demoralized by the Nazi philosophy of power, race, and cruelty. Thus, instead of the Nazi "caricature of a true state ..., the Reichsgovernment will establish a state sympathetic to Western Christian ideals, based upon the principles of civic duty, loyalty, self-sacrifice, and efficient service to the commonwealth, as well as upon respect for the individual as a human being." For the realization of this aim, the proclamation called for "the dissemination of genuine information and the freedom of public opinion and its expression.... The German people must be allowed to pierce the fog of propaganda and learn the truth and nothing but the truth...."

Judges, freed from bias and police dictation, must become the undismissible servants of the community. "All schools are at once set free from the pernicious part they were forced to play in faking facts, ... in teaching phrases in place of knowledge, hypocrisy instead of courage, brutality instead of high endeavor.... The Reichsgovernment refuses to recognize any exclusively state-sponsored Youth organization...."

In another appeal to the German people, which Beck was to issue, all stress was laid upon the ignominies committed by the previous regime. All those crimes must be atoned for by "free men" who wanted to regain "tranquillity of conscience." The restoration of the "majesty of law" should be the supreme effort, in order to achieve the main task of "washing off the stains.... We Germans alone can and shall do that."[25]

In all their planning the main ideas were the restoration of the rule of law, the formation of independent tribunals, punishment of the war criminals through an international court, denazification of all the key positions, democratic self-government, reorganization of the Reich on the basis of the equality of the federal states and the dismemberment of Prussia, creation of a world organization, nationalization of the key industries, and a healthy agrarian reform.[26]

The active resistance group that centered on Goerdeler and Beck was in contact, through an overlapping membership, with a group led by Count Helmuth von Moltke, who rejected the very idea of assassination and active revolt. He and some of his followers were afraid that the violent elimination of Hitler would lead to the formation of a new political myth, a glorification of Hitler and a kind of new *Dolchstosslegende* ("stab-in-the-back" legend), which would hinder forever the process of purifying Germany of the Nazi ideology. They were convinced that Germany could be cured only by complete defeat, when the people might clearly see the devastating effects of Hitlerism. They felt that the pagan amoralism of the Nazis was the real venom which corrupted the people. Therefore they advocated the spreading of a moral and spiritual revolution and the elaboration of a governmental program on a Christian basis.

The Kreisau Circle, as the group around Moltke was called because his followers often met on his estate at Kreisau in Upper Silesia, resembled the active resistance group in its inclusion of men from very different walks of life. Some bore names famous in Prussian and Germany history; some were professional men and intellectuals. There were Protestants and Catholics, a few outstanding clergymen, militant Socialists and men of the Right. Not all of them rejected the idea of tyrannicide and active revolt, but their main concern was to debate and think through all those problems, national and international, that the country would be compelled to face after its liberation. They wanted to find the right men to carry out the work after the defeat and the elimination of Hitler. They developed plans for a group of commissioners who could be the local leaders of the liberation. They discussed in a broad spirit the moral and political structure of the new Germany. The movement was in the best sense a progressive one, and not a timid passive resistance trying to avoid the real issues.[27] All of them felt real comradeship for anyone who was willing to cooperate toward the elimination of the Nazi rule. Their general principles and goals were not far from those of the active resistance group, although they could not agree that those goals should be reached through violence.

Thus in that period of moral tension when hundreds risked their lives for the liberation of Germany, when so many brave men committed suicide or were executed and so many families lived in continuous agony, the problem of tyrannicide was discussed in broader circles and with more desperate earnestness than, perhaps, in any other crisis caused by tyranny. And some theoretical conclusions were reached, which can stand comparison with the best thoughts expressed in the history of that age-old doctrine.

The widow of one of the most heroic fighters against Hitler wrote in a letter to a friend the following recollections, which cast a beam of light upon the moral atmosphere of those tortured years:

From conversations with my husband on this topic, which naturally recurred time and again, I am entitled to say that the assassination of Hitler was no longer a moral problem for him, after the moment when he realized the thousand-times murderer in Hitler. This happened very early, before his becoming Chancellor. The more the facts supported him in his conviction, the more intensely he worked for this aim. Count Moltke, as you know, was of an opposite opinion: whatever it might cost, the story must come to its logical conclusion, Hitler must perish as the consequence of his *Weltanschauung,* otherwise humanity would not learn the lesson. My husband respected this widespread opinion, but he could not accept it. He thought that people do not get wiser in this way. One must attack the evil principle right at the beginning. *Principiis obsta.* That the assassination of Hitler would cost him his life never occurred to him. What troubled him was to be put in the torture-chamber of the Gestapo, to lose his command over his senses and to expose other comrades. . . .

On the other hand, he did not regard it as morally necessary that the tyrannicide himself should perish during the attempt, as the critics of Stauffenberg often claimed. On the contrary, he had very concrete plans about settling the European problems after the elimination of the devil. . . . He said once, "To whom has the thought ever occurred that Wilhelm Tell should have sacrificed himself!"[28]

Such statements of moral dilemmas abound in the history of the resistance.

The principles which the conspirators asserted were not mere ideologic declamations. Many of them died for those principles, which they maintained even in the hours of the last agony. Many intimate documents from several leaders show convincingly that they thoroughly realized their moral responsibility and knew that they had risked their lives. Nicolaus von Halem, an industrialist and idealist philosopher, wrote to his mother two days before the main trial, "He who is prepared need have no fear of death. . . . You are one of the few who have won the fortitude that comes from inward detachment from the world and can therefore meet the death of your son with courage. You too will be able to smile as freely as I shall on my last way. . . ."[29]

Another of the military conspirators, Count Heinrich Lehndorff, wrote in his last letter to his wife, who, together with his children, had been repeatedly arrested, released, and rearrested, "I have always had the definite impression that you were walking at my side, and this feeling will be with me to the last hour. You must keep always in mind that I have not wantonly destroyed your future, but have been serving an ideal that, I believe, does not allow consideration of family or private interests."[30]

Count Moltke, the leader of the nonviolent resisters, found before his execution deep religious satisfaction in the fact that the Nazi tribunal could not find any political implication in his activity, but that he was condemned for having been the "moving spiritual force" against National Socialism. Alluding to this, Moltke wrote in his farewell letter to his wife that he had carried out the mission imposed upon him by God. "And through this your husband stands before Freisler [the bloodhound of the People's Court] not as a Protestant, not as a great landholder, not as a noble, not as a Prussian, not as a German, even," but "as a Christian and nothing else."[31]

Before committing suicide, Henning von Tresckow told his friend Schlabrendorff, "Everybody will now turn upon us and cover us with abuse. But my conviction remains unshaken—we have done the right thing. Hitler is not only the archenemy of Germany, he is the archenemy of the whole world. In a few hours' time I shall be before God, answering for my actions and for my omissions, and I shall uphold with a clear conscience all that I have done in the fight against Hitler.... Whoever joined the resistance movement had to realize that his life was doomed. A man's moral value begins only when he is prepared to sacrifice his life for his conviction."[32]

Looking at these and many other cases of heroism and self-sacrifice, it is disconcerting and almost humiliating to hear the opinion that the whole resistance movement was something immature and lacking in seriousness. This thesis has been advocated by two unconnected, even antagonistic, groups. One is made up of certain left-wing radicals, who, fed with party dogmas and slogans, are unable to understand the very essence of the movement for tyrannicide because they do not hear in it their class-struggle catchwords and the promise of social revolution, or the dictatorship of the proletariat, but rather an emphasis on the moral and religious basis of society and even, from some of the conspirators, an advocacy of monarchy as the only escape possible at that time from tyranny, bolshevism, and anarchy. These left-wing ideologists identify the movement with counter-revolution or timid conservatism. For this line of thought, tyrannicide is simply a special type of political murder, which is almost senseless unless it is connected with what they call "social revolution."

The other group which underrated the German resistance consisted of certain practical men, specialists in public affairs, economic advisers, a few connected with the intelligence service.[33] As the resistance was not solidly organized, as it lacked generally recognized leaders and a clear-cut program for action, they regarded it as an action of despair, doomed to failure from the beginning, without historical importance. However, some of these critics were themselves partly responsible for the tragic collapse of the movement. It was partly their fault that the leading statesmen of the victorious democracies had not the least understanding of those deep and widespread moral forces that had agitated Germany. The German underground was the only underground that got no support from the Allies, not even moral encouragement. The sinister slogan of "unconditional surrender" discouraged resistance by making no distinction between the resisters and those who were responsible for the war.

As a summary of the German resistance movement one may

quote representative opinions from three witnesses, who regarded the tragic events around them from viewpoints that differed with their social position and individual sensibility.

Friedrich Meinecke, dean of the German historians, after a detailed analysis of the German resistance, came to the following conclusion: though there would never be a consensus in judging the attempt on Hitler's life, "as an accessory in the broader sense I can only say that I consider the motives pure and high-minded. The revolutionaries have proved to the world that, in spite of all, there were still men in the German army and among the German people who did not will to submit themselves like mute dogs and who had the courage for martyrdom."[34]

Countess Marion Dönhoff was primarily affected by the spiritual efforts of her friends. In a commemorative essay full of life and intuition she wrote the following appreciation:

For this was the inexorable claim of those men: the spiritual transformation of the individual, the refusal of materialism, and the overcoming of nihilism as the form of life. The human being should be again placed in a world of Christian order, which has its roots in the metaphysical; he should again learn to breathe in the whole largeness of space between heaven and earth; he should be liberated from the narrowness of a world which made itself absolute, because blood, race, and causality were its last wisdom. And exactly this made these revolutionaries far more than the antipodes of Hitler and of his accursed system: their struggle, aside from its significance for the history of our days, was on a higher plane, was the attempt to overcome the nineteenth century in its spiritual foundation.[35]

Ricarda Huch, historian, novelist, and poet, in her appeal for the collection of materials for a comprehensive history of the German resistance, wrote:

From our midst came wicked, brutal, and unscrupulous men, who dishonored Germany and brought about its ruin. They dominated the German people by a system of terror so shrewdly planned that only heroes could dare the attempt to overthrow it. There were many such courageous men among us. Destiny did not allow them to save Germany; they could only die for Germany. . . . But they did not die in vain. As we need air to breathe, as we need light to see, so we need noble men in order to live. . . . They tear us from the swamp of triviality; they enflame us to fight against evil; they nourish in us faith in the divine in man.[36]

XVII PRIVATE RESISTANCE RECONSIDERED

THE SIGNIFICANCE of the German resistance and of the attempted tyrannicide can not be rightly estimated exclusively, or even mainly, on the ground of its practical achievements. The essence of tyrannicide, as has been shown in previous chapters, is ultimately an effort to liberate the moral energies of a society utterly muzzled by tyranny, under conditions where there is no other possibility of making an end to universal degradation. This point of view was clearly expressed in German political literature after the end of Hitler. Three representative opinions, all by Catholic writers,[1] seem particularly significant; in at least one of them we find a precise restatement of the traditional controversy over the bases of tyrannicide.

Reinhold Schneider, a well-known poet, emphasized in his commemoration of the victims of the conspiracy the moral and heroic nature of their revolt:

The men who entered the conspiracy in order to restore the law, to help the people to truth, to liberate the world from the ruin which started from our country, could have no doubt that in case of failure all the torments of torture and death, slander and shame, would fall upon their names, upon their relatives, and upon their graves. . . . Robbed of all their decorations, delivered to every kind of degradation, they staked their faith, their human dignity, the command of their conscience, against the miserable knaves of injustice who called themselves judges. . . . Above conscience there is no power of men, no duty; if it is not listened to, all life becomes sick and the enemy of men gets despotic power. . . .

But Schneider's answer to the problem of tyrannicide is somewhat hesitating: "We consider that it is not permissible. And yet under tyranny the holy certainty may develop in a man that the tyrant must at all events be felled."[2]

Let us now compare this rather emotional answer with the point of view of a man trained in international law. Looking back at the event of July 20, 1944, and the causes which led to it, Dr. Paulus von Husen has tried to determine the right attitude of German Catholics towards tyrannicide.[3] After a careful analysis of the religious traditions and the situation which his compatriots faced under Hitler, he finds the legitimacy of an active and, if necessary, a violent fight against tyranny in the right of self-defense, generally accepted by both laymen and churchmen. He quotes the widely used Catholic People's Catechism of Spirago[4]: "The right of self-defense enters when we are menaced by violent action against our life or against the property that is absolutely necessary to our life.... In the same way, it is permissible for us to defend, out of charity, the life of another person." Von Husen comments, "Did not Hitler and his accomplices continually, time and again, kill innocents without any legal basis, and did they not destroy the property that was absolutely necessary to the life of the whole people, to such an extent that they are not able to exist by their own resources?" And although, as a layman, von Husen does not venture a final judgment in a theological controversy, he thinks that in accordance with the principle *in dubio libertas* (in a doubtful case there is freedom) man can follow his conscience without hesitation. He comes to the conclusion that

> those who died because of July 20 had examined their responsibility earnestly. They were, almost without exception, believing and devout Christians. Count Stauffenberg himself was a highly trained and devout Catholic.... He was also the opposite of a military bravado: a very spiritual man with the courage that emanates from this attitude.... The world is inclined to judge according to the success or failure of a deed! But, when some time has passed, history will honor the dead of July, 1944, as the only men in the great German people, for twelve long years, who dared to risk life and limb by active deeds in order to spare their people and the world unspeakable ruin and another million deaths, and to save by this action a little honor for Germany.

The deep moral crisis of Germany also produced a systematic treatise asserting the living actuality of the age-old dilemma: a treatise which, in breadth of knowledge, in depth of argument, and in independence of judgment, can be favorably compared with the best products of the older literature of tyrannicide. This is the essay of Max Pribilla, S.J., "On the Limits of the Power of the State."[5] Pribilla's discussion is primarily rooted in theological considerations; but they sharpen his understanding of the German tragedy. His opening shows the realistic orientation of his essay:

> Spiritually and politically, the most oppressive question which burdens the Germans, especially since the collapse, is this: Was the German people compelled to follow its way of passion and erring to the bitterest end? Was it compelled to empty to the dregs the cup of poison offered it by the Nazis? Or did there exist the possibility or, at least, the right of overthrowing this wicked system before it fully accomplished its work of destruction? In other words, what could or should have happened in order to oppose this sinister development, which brought nameless misery upon us and upon other peoples?

This is the problem of the right of resistance against the encroachments and abuses of the power of the state. The Catholic doctrine of the state, Pribilla asserts, has remained unclear and is often, with fatal results, misunderstood even by Christians. On the one hand, the state is for Catholics an institution divinely ordered in the interest of the community; on the other hand, it never approaches its ideal, it is full of the weaknesses of human nature, and it may develop into a criminal tyranny, a dangerous instrument against the common weal.

What are the rights and the guarantees of citizens against this possibility? There is perfect agreement in Christian thought concerning the right and duty of passive resistance. And passive resistance, in the hands of respected men who use it with prudence and perseverance, can be a mighty weapon. But, in the time of terror which always accompanies the corruption of the state, this weapon is often used with hesitation and without conviction. It can become "a pretext of cowardice and a pillow for its rest."

Therefore, the question is inevitable: whether, under exceptional conditions, the use of violent means for the elimination of evil and even for the overthrow of the government may be permissible. This question, which "millions of men ask at the present time," must, Pribilla argues, be answered clearly and unequivocally. After a careful discussion of the Christian tradition and especially of the much commented words of the apostle Paul, "Let every man be subject to the higher powers...,"[6] he concludes that Christian revelation gives only scant guidance and that, therefore, the problem must be clarified on the basis of natural law with the help of reason. This investigation leads him to the fundamental thesis that the common weal is the supreme law. In accordance with Thomas Aquinas and with Hugo Grotius, he declares that the ruler who does not care for the best interest of his people, but becomes its enemy and corrupter, abandons the basis of law upon which his power is built: "It is contrary to the rational order, and therefore to the law of nature, to demand from the tortured and oppressed people that it should continue to be submissive to its enemy, especially since the ruler exists for the people and not the people for the ruler. . . . In any case, it appears contrary to reason to grant to the individual, without scruple, the right of self-defense, but to deny to the community the only legal means which, under existing conditions, can effectively remove their extreme predicament: namely, to render harmless and to deprive of his power the ruler who abuses his might."

Though Pribilla is convinced of the justification of active resistance from the point of view of morality and natural law, he knows very well that it is "a dangerous weapon" which "must be protected from blunder and misuse. Therefore, certain conditions must be fulfilled before it is put into application. First, there must exist an extraordinary abuse of the power of the state," demonstrated by the suppression of all liberties, the supersession of law by force, and the perversion of the common weal by partisan control. "The essential point is not the personal unworthiness of the ruler, but the abuse of the power of the state. Second, active resistance can be used only as the very last resort in a critical case, after all peaceful and constitutional means have been exhausted. Third, there must be a moral, that is, a reasonably grounded, certainty that active resistance can be successfully carried out, since . . . the supreme principle of the common weal commands that nothing be undertaken that would increase the evil instead of diminishing it."

This important consideration leads Pribilla to a substantial limitation of the right of active resistance: "The decision in such matters should not be entrusted to the small man who can not survey the real situation and the possible means, and who has no contact with the organization of the resistance." This was, according to Pribilla, the element of truth in the point so frequently emphasized in the historical literature on resistance: that it should be decided and carried out, not by individuals, but by estates or similar representative corporations. However, Pribilla recognizes that the certainty of success which he requires is not absolute, but only a reasonable or moral certainty, because of "the opaqueness of human affairs, especially in an extremely tense situation." "Active resistance will always remain a venture and will demand courageous men who do not falter before the danger."

Fourth, "only so much force should be applied as is necessary for the purpose, the abolition of the abuses.... As a deep interference with the structure of the state is contemplated, the disturbance of public order should be limited to a minimum in order not to drive out the devil by a worse one and to push the people from tyranny into anarchy.... The revolt that is justified by the crisis of the state should be itself an act of justice, and not of unchained violence."

After building up his theory of resistance, Pribilla takes a further step, seldom considered in the literature on the subject. He inquires about the duty of resistance, and comes to the conclusion that, in cases of extreme urgency "he who has the necessary vision and power to help the people is obliged to put the right of resistance into action, regardless of his personal security and comfort.... The duty of resistance is the more urgent, the higher the social position, the personal authority, the capacity for effective action, of those who are qualified to initiate it and carry it through...."

Pribilla opposes the position held by the Evangelical Bishop of Berlin, Otto Dibelius. Dibelius avoided a direct answer to the dilemma of active resistance, concluding that the resister would never go through this dilemma without involving himself in guilt, but that there was not only guilt but also the great grace of God. Pribilla repudiates the point of view of this Protestant leader, asserting, "the theory of the guilt to be repented but forgiven is a lukewarm compromise, self-contradictory and therefore untenable. In reality it could only confuse those who act."

Pribilla regrets that the struggle of opinions, over the centuries, did not produce clarity and agreement in such important controversy. This was due partly, he thinks, to the inner complexity of the problem, partly to changing historical conditions. "The great theologians of the Middle Ages ... could expect, in the case of extreme popular distress, the interference of the pope, who would excommunicate the unworthy ruler and release the subjects from their duty of loyalty. The possibility of this solution blunted the acumen of their analysis of natural law."[7] After the Reformation, the problem was tangled in the muddle of religious and confessional passions. Later, a denial of the right of resistance was a part of the struggle of the Catholic Church against the revolutionary movements of the nineteenth century. And many Catholic thinkers were confused by the fallacious hope that constitutional guarantees had made the whole problem anachronistic.

Meanwhile, we all—Catholics, Protestants, and Jews—have witnessed such an extraordinary abuse of the power of the state as no previous theologian or jurist anticipated or could anticipate; and in the face of this abuse we have been both theoretically and practically helpless, almost to self-annihilation. With this, a new problem has come into existence: that not a ruler only, but a party or an ideological system has exercised the terror and misused the power of the state. The whole problem of the right of resistance has been presented anew by the new evolution and must therefore be thought through again. There is scarcely a doubt that the defenders of the right of resistance will increase considerably in the future.

Pribilla regards it as a religious duty to give, without timid reserve, guidance to believers concerning the right and the limits of active resistance. "At all events, morality has no reason to burden with a moral stain the active resistance that is justified by the extreme crisis of state, and to brand it as an outrage against a divine command. This would be equivalent to tying the hands of the brave and self-sacrificing defenders of right and freedom and offering even to the most criminal tyrant the quieting assurance that, at least from his Christian subjects, he would have nothing to fear. This would only strengthen him in his crime."

It is interesting to notice that in the whole remarkable essay the word "tyrannicide" is never mentioned. However, it seems clear that the whole logic of Pribilla's argument should lead to the inclusion of tyrannicide under the more general heading of active resistance.

XVIII THE NATURE OF THE NEW TYRANNY

THE AMAZING tyrannical systems which were established in the twentieth century have not been fully understood by the general public, nor by many scholars. One cause of this lack of precision has been the confusion created by the ambiguity of the terminology which has identified the new structures by such terms as absolutism or dictatorship. In vain did the distinguished French historian, Élie Halévy,[1] point out that what was happening could be more adequately described by the Greek term *tyrannis;* almost all the writers on the subject have used the more familiar term, "dictatorship."

This word, however, has many different connotations, some of which have no connection with the reality we are studying. Dictatorship in the form which Carl Schmitt[2] has aptly called "commissary dictatorship" was an honored Roman institution by which, in a national emergency, the power of the state was vested in a single individual for a strictly limited time and for a well-defined purpose. This type of dictatorship has not the smallest connection with the rule of the twentieth-century dictators. But even the other main type of dictatorship, which Schmitt has designated "sovereign dictatorship," a dictatorship called into being in order to create the conditions for a new constitution, typically has only a few elements of the kind of despotism and arbitrary power that has characterized the modern tyrannies.

Another confusing explanation has described modern dictatorships as the continuation of divine-right absolutism. But there is no real analogy between the two structures. Sixteenth- and seventeenth-century absolutism was the culmination of a natural process through which the modern state came into existence. Though the concentration of power in the hand of the monarch sometimes led to despotic distortion of the royal authority, its very nature was alien from the claims and practices of totalitarian dictatorships.[3]

The authority of the absolute monarch was based on alleged divine right and well-defined hereditary right; it was limited by remnants of medieval constitutionalism; it was typically exercised in the form of law. Except in a few periods of anarchistic civil wars, even Russian czarism could scarcely be identified with the autocracies of our own day. Thus, in general, the absolute monarchs, even when they achieved almost complete personal rule, were strongly bound by the moral, religious, political, and legal traditions of their time. They were driven, so to speak, towards the realization of some fundamental needs of the community.[4] And Edmund Burke could affirm without exaggeration that "this comprehensive scheme virtually produced a degree of personal liberty. ... That liberty was found, under monarchies styled absolute, in a degree unknown to the ancient commonwealth."[5]

Liberal thought in the middle of the nineteenth century regarded the absolutism of the Habsburgs and of some German princelings as tyranny. Yet these governments were not unbridled tyrannical structures; they were the continuation of old, time-hallowed institutions, and the feelings connected with them always exercised inevitable checks on the central government. Even the system of Metternich was embedded in certain general values of Christianity and liberalism. Human dignity, freedom of conscience, and the independent sphere of private life and family relations were never denied in principle. The dungeons of Spielberg were not systematically planned instruments of torture and of debasement of the condemned person. The imprisonment, for instance, of Lovassy, the liberal Hungarian patriot, by Habsburg absolutism aroused nationwide indignation. It was surely an odious case of political persecution. Yet the official reports of the case, now at our disposal, show no effort to annihilate his honor or personality.[6]

Torture chambers, concentration camps, castration, and moral humiliation were exceptional in the repertory of absolutism of the old type. There was still enough respect for traditional authority and for divine right to guarantee a sufficient amount of obedience to rulers without the physical and moral destruction of their opponents. Their spy systems, although growing with the growing menace of liberalism and socialism, never became an open military organization with extraordinary tribunals and executioners unbound by law. A moderate display of armed force and secret service protection was enough to guarantee the security of Francis Joseph and Wilhelm II during their public appearances. It never occurred to them to give each other such presents as the bomb-proof railway train that Hitler gave to Mussolini. It never occurred to them to live as Hitler lived on the Berghof: in an armored castle equipped with bomb-and-gas-proof cellars, surrounded by fortified posts, guarded with anti-aircraft guns embedded in the adjoining mountainsides, and furnished with the most up to date surgical laboratory in case of an attempted assassination.

Even those unconstitutional dictatorships of "usurpers," which come the nearest to the category of the medieval writers, *tyrannus ex defectu tituli,* the rules of Cromwell and the two Napoleons, show no true analogy with the totalitarian dictatorships of our own days. As Cromwell and the two Napoleons emerged from revolutionary situations when the conflicting power of society could not yet create adequate constitutional forms for compromise, they were necessarily obliged to use a certain amount of intimidation and coercion. Nevertheless, they made continuous efforts to build governments wrapped in traditional values, respecting and accepting widespread moral currents of public opinion. Though sometimes assuming features of tyrannic policy, Cromwell always remained faithful to the principle of religious and parliamentary liberty, even when he came into conflict with both. He did not wish to impose upon society a newly excogitated revolutionary order, but to restore what he felt was the true spirit of constitutionalism. He was rightly called a "dictator in spite of himself."[7]

Napoleon Bonaparte himself was surely not a totalitarian dictator: that is, a tyrant. Coming to power after the bloody period of Jacobinism and the unsavory period of the Directory, he was acclaimed by the greater part of public opinion as the restorer of order. He established a gifted and public-minded bureaucracy. He was the chief promoter of the Civil Code which was "at once the summary and the correction of the French Revolution" and "the abiding symbol of that unity of law which was first made possible by the meeting of the Estates General in 1789."[8] Some of the best minds of the period eagerly co-operated with him. Though in his passionate nature there were some elements of a Renaissance tyrant, his personality was filled with the traditions of the French Revolution, and what he tried to accomplish was the saving of that part of the French Revolution which he regarded, not as Utopian, but as the real need of the century.

And though his rule became increasingly autocratic and military, the words which he spoke to O'Mara after his downfall are not without a ring of truth:

In the first place, France required a strong government. While I was at the head of it, I may say that France was in the same condition as Rome when a dictator was declared necessary for the salvation of the

Republic.... We had to strike down others or to be ourselves struck down.... Between the parties that so long agitated France I was like a rider seated on an unruly horse, who always wanted to swerve either to the right or to the left.... In quieter times my dictature would have finished, and I should have commenced my constitutional reign.... Even as it was, with the coalition always opposing me, either secret or public, avowed or denied, there was more equality in France than in any other country in Europe.[9]

This is not a mere apology, but the expression of the very dilemma created by Thermidor.

The rule of Napoleon III was based on a large popular vote. The greatest of the French socialists, Proudhon, admitted, "We ourselves, republicans, have repeated..., 'The voice of the people is the voice of God.' Well, the voice of God has named Louis Napoleon. As an expression of the people's will he is the most legitimate of sovereigns."[10] He was not the emperor of the peasantry and of the Church only: many Saint-Simonians, including *père* Enfantin himself, wholeheartedly served a regime which showed many signs of a sincere social policy. And though, through his support of the principle of nationality, Napoleon III became involved in dangerous foreign wars, for a time his empire meant peace for the people. Occasionally he applied severely repressive measures, but nobody can talk seriously of a reign of terror during his rule. Albert Guérard concludes that the regime of Napoleon III was "mildness itself compared with the conditions which prevailed at the time in Naples, Rome, Austria, or Russia," and that "if government by consent be the criterion of political liberty, no regime in France was more 'liberal' than that of Napoleon III," and that "to call Napoleon III a tyrant would be a ludicrous distortion of the facts."[11]

Both Napoleons, then, were supported by mighty popular forces; both were the continuators of certain important traditions of the French Revolution, both worked with the Catholic Church. Neither tried to eliminate class struggle by dictatorial pseudo-constitutional frameworks. Neither leaned on an organized party of his own, nor had a private army. Both were supported by the real national army. Neither was the advocate of an exclusive national or racial theory; on the contrary, they were protagonists of democratic nationalism. Neither aspired to a divinely ordered leadership, and neither felt himself the creator of final moral values.[12]

The true analogy is that between the totalitarian dictators of our own day and the tyrants in the city-states of antiquity and of the

Renaissance.[13] The traits which the opposers of tyranny have always emphasized as its essential characteristics have reappeared in the modern dictatorships: personal rule unbound by law, military despotism based on private armies, continuous ventures into dangerous diplomatic situations with the risk of war, luxury and ostentation in the surroundings of the dictator and his gang, bounteous remuneration of the obedient servants of the system, intimidation of the people, suppression that leaves no possibility of expressing opinions contrary to the dictatorship nor of organizing popular forces to effect a change. All these are characteristic both of the new and the old tyrannies.[14]

However, these analogies are only symptoms of a deeper congeniality between the old and the new tyrannies. The old tyrannies were rooted in the small city-states, which could be easily caught by military power or demagogic activities. Then, for a long time, because of the continuous growth of states in territory and population, there was no possibility of the recurrence of the tyrannical structure. Now again, as Alfred Cobban rightly emphasized, "the press, the cinema, and broadcasting have re-created the demagogic possibilities of the ancient city state in the modern nation state...."[15] At last there are again almost unlimited opportunities for the corruption of politics in the interest of one man or a small group of men.

And here is the real essence of tyrannical rule. All the great thinkers who have tried to explain this phenomenon have agreed that tyranny is necessarily a rule based on corruption, a rule devoid of any genuine moral content. The depravity in the moral structure of the old tyranny, based on the rule of one man and his clique, and in that of the new, based on a totalitarian synthesis, is the common element. Both arose in crises in which dissatisfied or hungry masses had lost their traditional values. Both disregarded the interest of the people and the moral dignity and natural rights of the individual, though the new tyrants hid their greedy *hubris* by a cloak of high-sounding and irrational theories. Both regarded men only as instruments for their own selfish ends. This analogy in the moral and social situation explains the similarity in methods between the old and new tyrannies.

Were Plato or Aristotle, Aquinas, Locke, Jefferson, Mill, contemporaries of the twentieth-century tyrannies, they would not have had the smallest doubt of the moral depravity and final ignominious failure of these ventures. Their judgment would have been uncompromising, because they viewed expediency from the point of view of fundamental values. The law of nature or divine law or a strong feeling of common-sense morality would have made them impervious to the propaganda of the new tyrants. Modern statesmen and scholars, with less faith in abstract principles of right and wrong, were slow to feel the intrinsic immorality of the modern tyrannies; some tended to welcome them; some were even fascinated by the new "experiments." Thus, for instance, the late Nicholas Murray Butler, speaking in 1927 at the University of Virginia in celebration of the 184th anniversary of Thomas Jefferson, spoke of "the amazing movement which under the leadership of Premier Mussolini has brought new life and vigor and power and ambition to the great people of the Italian peninsula." "There is no contradiction," he added, "by any responsible authority, to the stupendous improvement which Fascism has brought in the order, the safety, the health, the education, the comfort, and the satisfaction of the Italian people."[16] At this time Italy was already permeated by a flood of bloodshed and terror.

In the absence of moral corruption we can not truly speak of a tyrannical system. Thus many dictatorships are not tyrannies because, in spite of occasional self-gratification and abuse of power by the ruler, there remains the fundamental conviction, based on religion, natural law, or time-honored tradition, that the ruler is an instrument and agent of the welfare of the people.

Certainly some modern dictators, who came to power in grave national crises, tried to put an end to anarchy, to establish order, and to lay foundations for a rebuilding of popular forces. Though dictatorship always drifts toward a system of personal favors and the interests of the most powerful groups—usually of the armed force which maintains the dictatorship—it has not seldom happened that men of high quality have used dictatorial powers in the real interest of the community. Though, from the point of view of legitimist interests, their powers were originally "usurped," they have tried to create a new legitimacy based on the consent of broad popular masses. And in this effort naked power and violence have played only a subordinate role. Their rule has corresponded to the widely felt general interest of a community long distorted by the continuous struggle of greedy factions. They have not wished to establish a totalitarian rule over all the manifestations of individual life; they have not tolerated the terrorism of criminal gangs; they have not needed to establish a noisy, artificial, and arbitrary ideological structure. In a word, there has been a moral purpose in their actions.

One or two examples will suffice to substantiate this distinction. The dictatorship of Kemal Atatürk, though occasionally crude and sometimes too extreme in its reformist ardor, aimed to rebuild a country disorganized by war and inner convulsions. He was surely not a totalitarian dictator, a tyrant. It was aptly said:

Kemal Atatürk . . . was certainly a dictator in the sense of being the head of a state which he governed practically without opposition. However, it would be quite false and a grave injustice, alike to that great man and to the Turkey he created, to place him, as so many unreflecting journalists have done, among the modern usurpers risen from the masses. His historical role is much more that of the "Dictator" of ancient Rome, as opposed to the real tyrants. . . . Thus, after Kemal's death, the direction of the state could indeed pass without any breach of continuity into the intelligent, moderate hands of Ismet Inönü. In the Turkey of Kemal there is no praetorian guard, no hierarchic, exclusive party alone allowed to bear arms and insolently identifying itself with the state. Neither is there any high-pitched self-advertisement, no striving after new ways of stimulating the masses so as to prevent their slipping back to the humdrum daily round, to the balanced, normal, steady community life. . . .[17]

In spite of the great differences in the social and economic conditions of Portugal, there seems to be a similar moral and political atmosphere about the dictatorship of Salazar. After the collapse of the monarchy in 1910, there were twenty-one revolutions and many military revolts. Events after the First World War accentuated these anarchic conditions. In 1920, nine governments succeeded each other, in accordance with the game of rival factions. One lasted only twenty-four hours, another only six days. Extreme illiteracy and the poverty of the rural population provided fertile ground for the selfish fight between "attorneyism and militarism." After a number of factional revolts, General Carmona established his dictatorship in 1926, and it was approved by a plebiscite. Though the final support of the new regime was primarily military, with disproportionate participation of the officer caste in politics and administration, the guiding spirit of the dictatorship became Salazar, a former professor of the University of Coimbra. He was first minister of finance, later prime minister. His moral and political influence grew continuously, and General Carmona himself liked to speak of a "dictatorship without a dictator." Between a weak extreme right and extreme left, Salazar was successful in gaining wide popular support and in carrying out a conspicuous work of reconstruction and reform. Though a modicum of occasional violence is still required, it would be entirely erroneous to regard Salazar as a relative of the totalitarian dictators.

His whole philosophy, deeply rooted in his Catholic religious convictions, is different from that of fascism. In his speech of June 30, 1928, which is considered the charter of the new state, he said, "Both to the one and the other extreme we must oppose the strong state, but limited by morality, by international law, by . . . the liberties of the individual, which are superior exigencies of social solidarity. . . ." In a later interview he stated explicitly the difference between fascism and his system: "The fascist dictatorship has a tendency towards a pagan caesarism, towards a new state which does not know juridical or moral limits, which marches to its purpose without meeting complications or obstacles. . . . In contrast to this, the new Portuguese state can not avoid, and does not think of it, certain limits of a moral nature which it considers indispensable to maintain, as a basis for its reformist action. . . . Our laws are less severe, our customs less indoctrinated, and the state is less absolutist and we do not proclaim it omnipotent. . . ." The supreme aim is "that the state should be strong enough not to need to be violent."[18] On the whole, the record of Salazar's dictatorship has been consistent with these statements.

In spite of certain analogies between the old tyrannies and those new dictatorships that deserve the same name because of their similar moral corruption, there are also notable differences, especially in the techniques of maintaining power. The new tyranny is totalitarian. Its main claim is the regimentation of all the manifestations of human personality in the exclusive interest of the state. This claim was expressed by Mussolini in the following words:

The Fascist conception of the state is all-embracing; outside it, no human or spiritual values can exist, much less have value. Thus understood, Fascism is totalitarian, and the Fascist State—a synthesis and unit inclusive of all values—interprets, develops, and potentiates the whole life of the people.[19]

This claim of the totalitarian dictators was perfectly new. Previous tyrants never proclaimed such a doctrine, though their despotisms might be as oppressive as those of the new tyranny. They did not proclaim it because they did not need it.

The old tyranny was a tyranny without a doctrine. The rule of the old tyrants was far more mechanical: it was based on the simple coercion of comparatively few individuals by intimidation or promises. The repertory of ancient tyrants, as described by Aristotle,[20] has been unconsciously imitated by their present-day totalitarian successors. But the crude methods of the old tyrants, using a small armed gang and a certain accumulation of wealth under their control, are not enough for the maintenance of tyranny in our present-day societies, in an age of mass democracy, of industrialization, of the supremacy of natural science. The new tyrants must secure not only passive toleration by the people, but also their active participation in the system. They must be driven to a clamorous activity in numerous formidable organizations directed against those who maintain moral sanity and independence, to secure the complete acceptance of the new order by every group within the nation.

The new tyrants could not permit themselves the luxury of arousing the antagonism of the classes, because the main groups of society were so well organized and so conscious of their interests that there was no single class that could give adequate support to the tyrants. Therefore they needed a unifying symbol, a myth which would silence the interests of the various classes and combine them in an imaginary unity. A few days before marching on Rome, Mussolini said, "We have created our myth... the myth is a creed, a passion. It is not necessary that it should constitute a reality.... Our myth is the Nation...."[21]

This unification by myth alone, however, was not enough, because the real interests of the masses would ultimately destroy the myth. Therefore the tyrants had to destroy, by false formulae and by terrorism, the existing class structure of society. What happened in both Italy and Germany was the establishment of a new state power annihilating the social as well as the constitutional framework of the previous states. All the rights of men which were at least timidly acknowledged in the era of liberalism were crushed and ridiculed. The former class structure was discarded in favor of corporations or *Stände,* which became powerless instruments of an almighty state bureaucracy. This bureaucracy, dependent solely on the will of the dictators, was not only the wielder of political power but the chief instrument of terrorism. As we have seen,[22] both Fascism and Nazism rose to power with the aid of systematic political murder. Both systems were soaked in blood. When their sovereignty was established, terror became an institution of the state in the form of the Ovra and the Gestapo.

The remolding of the state and society through propaganda and terrorism needed an extremely unscrupulous and arbitrary leadership. The Fascist and Nazi movements recruited great masses of ruthless and ambitious men to do the dirty jobs. Thus the new tyranny, as in the penetrating description of La Boétie,[23] developed a complete system of undertyrants. The party organization became an omnipotent and omnipresent hierarchy extending from the Leader to the janitors of the apartment houses in the big cities.[24] In the party bureaucracy, with its thousands of appointed underlings, each responsible for his actions to his superior alone, the only road to self-realization and power was the support and acknowledgment of the Leader and of the ever changing possessors of his confidence.

The lack of a free and spontaneous political life, the absorption of the state by the party bureaucracy and the secret police, the continuous waves of intimidations, terrorizations, and blood purges inevitably corrupted all the manifestations of the totalitarian dictatorships. Corruption in a democracy is often unveiled by parties and other competitive groups, and there remains always a healthy flow of ideas; but the dictatorships made politics, in a decent sense, an impossibility. Everything depended on the ultimate decision of the Leader and the small inner circle around him. Instead of the conflicts of ideas and personalities, there were only the intrigues and plottings of the followers of the dictator.

Under such a system, the head of the state must assume the supernatural quality which Max Weber has called *charisma*.[25] The greatest achievement of the National Socialist propaganda was the creation of a legend around the Führer, by which his character and exceptional qualities were extolled to a degree unattained even in Byzantine practice.[26] The totalitarian Leader did not follow existing rules, he created new ones. As public opinion had no means of organization, the intuition of the Leader was the only source for determining the aims of the community. Faith in the Leader became a religion. Thus Goering boasted, "When was there ever deeper and more passionate faith in Germany than there is today? What faith was ever aroused more strongly than our faith in the Führer? Never has a greater miracle happened in our time. The Almighty made this miracle through Adolf Hitler."[27]

Myth, regimentation, and terror were not enough; the necessities of the new tyranny required also a systematic assault upon the individual personality. It is not necessary to describe in detail the techniques of mechanistic unification by mass demonstrations, glaring symbols, and exciting music; the use of anti-Semitism as a means of mobilizing the fighting instinct of the dissatisfied masses against a scapegoat supported by the irrational emotions of many centuries; the continuous repetition of a loud and shallow propaganda based on the distortion of two great ideas, nationalism and socialism; the control and regimentation of religion, and of every church which attempted to exert an independent moral power; the control of children through an all-comprehensive system of state education, filling their drilled and servile minds with a nationalistic vainglory, the main tenet of which was that their dictators were the greatest men in the world, who could do no wrong.

To make their rule impermeable, the new tyrants cleverly manipulated some of the deepest foundations of human nature. They understood, much more clearly than the advocates of economism or jural constitutionalism, that the promise of bread and abstract liberty alone would not solve the social problem.[28] Their symbol specialists used abundantly the dynamic and heroic elements of the human soul. What they promised was not simply bread, but a higher importance for the life of the average man through a more intense feeling of community. Not only were jobs distributed among the unemployed, but there was a strong appeal for the ambitious and energetic in the feeling of *hubris* (the wanton violence of ruthless men), so well known to the philosophers of the ancient states. They organized also vast movements for *Kraft durch Freude* and *Dopolavoro,* giving new vistas of nature and beauty to the average man. These important beginnings, however, were not used for the development of human personality but only as implements for the intensification of their propaganda of war and glory.

The Nazis gave special attention to the emotionality of women, who were systematically driven back to the trinity of *"Kinder, Kirche, Küche"* with sonorous appeals to their natural instincts as breeders of soldiers and heroes. Hitler shouted with profound conviction:

Reason can treacherously deceive a man, emotion is sure and never leaves him. . . . It is not for nothing that you see so many women here in this hall. . . . In the woman emotion dominates and rightly tells her that the future of her children is at stake. . . . Our adversaries may talk as much as they like about our hysterical women. In former days women brought Christianity to the countries. In the end she will also lead our movement to lasting victory.[29]

Extramarital sexual relations were encouraged for the augmenting of population, the ultimate foundation of power.[30]

From the depths of his religious intuition, Christopher Dawson has forcefully summarized the nature of the tyranny thus created:

In the new States not only a man's property and his work, but his family, his leisure and his thought are controlled by the immense and complex machinery of party and police and propaganda which are gradually transforming society from a commonwealth of free citizens into a hive or an ant-heap. For the new tyranny is not merely a matter of subjugating the people by force to the rule of a master, like the tyrannies of the past; it uses the new techniques of psychology and behaviorism to condition the personality and to control the mind, as it were, from within. By continued repression and stimulation, by suggestion and terrorization, the personality is subjected to a methodical psychological assault until it surrenders its freedom and becomes a puppet which shouts and marches and hates and dies at its masters' voice, or in response to their unseen and unrecognized stimulation. . . .[31]

And Franz Neumann has rightly said:

National Socialist propaganda has other aims than the mere penetration of soft spots. Through its synchronization of all the general activities, National Socialism subjects the German people to unceasing tensions. The insistence upon activism in place of thinking means that men shall never have the freedom and time to think for themselves. Action without thought is possible only if it is directed and controlled action, except for short periods of genuine mass spontaneity. Thus controlled, it is pseudo-action, for it is not man who acts but a bureaucratic machine. . . . National Socialist propaganda is thus the expression of the same two phenomena that appear in every aspect of the regime: the destruction of whatever remnants of spontaneity are left and the incorporation of the population into a super-machine. . . .[32]

Totalitarian tyranny is, indeed, a further intensification and conscious organization of a sociological situation which Max Scheler diagnosed long before the advent of the Nazis. This situation is the state of war which unites all men and all groups in an indivisible reality.

It makes the individual heroic at the same time that, to a large extent, it lulls all spiritual individuality to rest. It pulls him out from every care for the problems of the corporeal ego. But it makes the spiritual personality terrible and lawless! Revolutionary masses and their movements show the same states of collective ecstasy, in which the corporeal ego and the spiritual ego are submerged in a passionate life-movement of the whole community.[33]

The very essence of the totalitarian system is to make permanent this annihilation of the individual personality and of self-conscious groups and to mobilize the masses exclusively for the aims of the system.

At the bottom of all these various aspects of the new tyranny lie two factors of overwhelming importance. The one is in the nature of every society in which military activity has become the exclusive or predominant function of the state. The other is connected with the social structure of the capitalist state. The generalizations of Herbert Spencer concerning the "militant type of society" have not only remained true in their essential elements but throw new light on our experiences with totalitarian dictatorships. The truly militant type of society has always been totalitarian in its character. It can not recognize any individual sphere of human rights, must emphasize the supreme divine character of the tribe or the state, must subordinate individual morality to state morality, individual or spontaneous group action to tribal or state action. The present century's totalitarian dictatorships have been unconscious followers of all the social, moral, religious, and economic patterns of the "conquering states," whose life is exclusively concentrated on military exploits.[34]

Such a society, moreover, has no confidence in an international division of labor and in the spontaneous forces of market economy. When war is always considered near, autarchy seems to be the only real guarantee of the survival of the state. Such a society also needs a high birth rate in order to secure a supply of future warriors. But encouragement of a high birth rate leads to overpopulation, for which, in the lack of an international division of labor, there is only one remedy: the conquest of new territories, foodstuffs, and raw materials. The very idea of limiting the population seems suicidal to rulers motivated by the idea of constant war.

The tendency toward autarchy assumed colossal dimensions in the totalitarian dictatorships. Whether it originated in a proletarian revolt against capitalism or in an anti-proletarian revolt against "liberal plutocracy," modern tyranny was bound to develop a more or less collectivist form of economic life. This drift was both natural and inevitable. In a world in which small business, small industry, and independent farmers predominated, the active participation of the state in production and distribution was only secondary, and the aims of dictators could be secured simply by military and police pressure. Quite different is the situation in the modern capitalist states. The growing concentration of capital and industry in mammoth concerns and the relative degeneracy of independent producers, always inherent in the periods of grave social crimes, compelled the new tyrants to subordinate the whole economic life of the country to a fixed plan of war economy. Whether they eradicated the whole capitalist class, as happened in Russia, or used the capitalists as their instruments and administrators for their aggressive purposes, as was done in Italy and Germany, they regarded the free market as the ultimate enemy, which must be coerced in the name of a higher value: the creation of a strong military state for the winning of their "total wars." The consumers would no longer determine the quality and quantity of production; the almighty state would decide what the consumers might enjoy after satisfying the needs of the war machine.

The other mighty force which drove the dictators in the same direction was the emergence of an organized and self-conscious proletarian class which could not be dominated by the old tyrannical methods of *panem et circenses* alone. Since they always felt the danger of revolution and since they were unable to expand their economic system by growing division of labor, by the elasticity of the world market, and by adequate reform of their forces of production, they were compelled to militarize labor and to combat unemployment by a general decrease in the standard of living of the working classes. The tyrants and the under-tyrants assumed more and more personal responsibility for the important fields of production. Their foreign competitors were restricted through tariffs, falsification of currency, arbitrary exchange regulations, police measures, and other well-known instruments of economic nationalism. The individual became a slave, not only in politics, in spiritual life, in education, in morals, but also as producer and consumer.

All these tendencies concurred in the annihilation of the moral and rational personality in man.

XIX BOLSHEVIK VERSUS FASCIST TYRANNY

INTERPRETATION of the Fascist and Nazi systems as a new type of tyranny will scarcely be denied by any competent student of these dictatorships. However, when one asserts that the Communist dictatorship in Russia is equally tyrannnical, one may expect some opposition, although much less than a decade ago. For some people insist that, in spite of certain tyrannical elements caused by historical necessities or by the personal influence of Stalin, the Russian dictatorship has a quite different character and different aims.

There are three different approaches to such a position. Bolshevik propaganda has maintained that the Russian system is a new form of democracy, distinct from and superior to the decadent democracies of the West. According to this view, which won the support of a considerable number of Western liberals before and during the Second World War, the tyrannical features of the Russian system were merely a necessary by-product of its unique democracy, a kind of self-defense against the imperialistic tendencies of the capitalist countries.

A second line of argument calls attention to the historical origins of the Communist rule. In its origins, Russian Communism was intimately connected with the liberal revolutionary movements of the West. Anarchism, socialism, even Marxism, were, in some of their aspects, logical continuations of the Western spirit that emphasized the dignity and equality of human beings. In Bolshevik propaganda even now, the promise of bread is less important than the assertion of human rights to be achieved after the triumph of the revolution; the slogan is still "liberation."

A third argument comes from the ideologic arsenal of the left-wing Bolsheviks, led by Trotsky, who violently and unsuccessfully fought the growing dictatorship of Stalin. According to their reasoning, the totalitarian tyranny of Stalin had nothing to do with the work and values of Lenin. How could there be a real relation between the thoughtful, self-effacing founder of the revolution and the cruel tyrant who built up on hecatombs of victims his omnipotent state machine and established himself as a kind of Communist czar with the aureole of a charismatic leader? From this point of view, the rule of Stalin was a true tyranny. Bukharin called him a modern Genghis Khan; Trotsky described him as a super-Nero and super-Borgia.[1] But the thesis of the ousted Bolsheviks always was that Stalin had transformed "soviet democracy" into his own teroristic absolutism, exercised through his subservient party bureaucracy, his spy system and secret police.

None of these arguments, however, invalidates the claim that the dictatorship established by Stalin was a full-fledged tyranny. The first is a purely propagandistic concoction obviously contradicted by the facts. The second, although mainly correct from a historical point of view, presents only one side of Marxism. For Marx and Engels themselves abandoned the idealistic foundations of modern socialism and cut themselves off from the liberal tradition by their ridicule of human rights as bourgeois values. The communist system that they elaborated still presented liberty and equality as its remote goals, but it was based exclusively on economic determinism, on ruthless class struggle, on the dictatorship of the proletariat over and against all other classes, and on the use of violence to achieve the final outcome.

This consideration also invalidates the Trotskyist argument. It is not true that Stalin, as a power-thirsty villain, falsified the main ideas of Marxian socialism and sacrificed democracy to his subservient party machine. The truth is that the Marxian ideal of the communist state could not be realized by the method and spirit of democracy.[2] Lenin's application of the communist revolution to Russia had already involved an unscrupulous undermining of the beginnings of democratic institutions in Russia in order to achieve Bolshevik power; and he had frankly transformed the Marxian "dictatorship of the proletariat" into the still narrower dictatorship of the party that was its "vanguard." With Marx, he regarded the state as "the centralized organization of force and violence,"[3] and he had no hesitation in using it as such. Thus it never occurred to Stalin that in his attack on the Trotskyist wing of the party he was opposing "democracy" in the traditional, Western sense; and when Trotsky and his followers emphasized "intraparty or proletarian democracy," they were quite conscious of the fact that such a democracy would remain the privilege of a small, class-conscious minority. Dictatorship and violence would remain an essential element in their system.

Every true Bolshevik, and above all Trotsky, has been in complete agreement with the principles of dictatorship and violence.[4] What Stalin did was simply to put these principles more thoroughly into practice, in a way that was repugnant to the aesthetic and moral sensibilities of those intellectuals who were in closer contact with the Western tradition. Both Lenin and Trotsky had remained, to some extent, theorists who followed the heroic, uncompromising ideology. But with "intraparty democracy" only chaos could follow; and, although there can be no doubt that his chief motive was a drive for personal power, there can also be no doubt that Stalin faced an iron necessity in organizing the communist state.

The dictatorship of the proletariat is, necessarily, the rule of the dominant elements of a bureaucracy directed by a supreme dictator. Of course, certain forms and shades of this dictatorship are determined and colored by the character and antecedents of the man who controls the state machine. Thus one need not deny the significance of the personal role of Stalin in the tyranny that he perfected. His ultimate motivation was the same as that of Hitler: the *hubris,* the greed for personal power, the dogmatic belief in an historic mission to which he was willing to sacrifice his opponents and even his people. But the essence of the process was strictly determined by the ideology and ethos of the communist movement, which has remained unchanged since the Communist Manifesto. Only a man with the shrewd and ruthless practical genius of Stalin, making and breaking compromises according to changing conditions, assimilating his thirst for power with the fundamental traditions of the Bolshevik religion, could carry out the conceptions of Marx and Lenin. He had every reason to regard himself as the executor of that testament.

There is, of course, truth in the accusation of the left wing that Stalin's system was Thermidorian. Every successful revolution must have its Thermidor, because extreme radicalism of the genuinely revolutionary spirit must necessarily undermine the state without creating the institutions necessary to maintain it in the struggle of hostile factions and international enemies. In Russia, a certain compromise with old nationalism, militarism, and the church became a necessity. Stalin's work, from one point of view, was the partial reconstruction of the czarist state, but with an incomparably higher degree of concentration of power, of terrorism, and of irresponsibility. Fainsod has summarized the process with acumen: "The great *tour de force* of Stalinism was the construction of a totalitarian edifice which bestrides the revolutionary and authoritarian heritage of Leninism, the dynamic nationalism of Tsarism, the stabilizing equilibrium of conservative social institutions, and the rigid bureaucratic hierarchy of a full-blown police state."[5]

The machinery of the Soviet state was deliberately and skillfully constructed to secure the complete control of Stalin through preventing the possibility of any rival focus of power. He developed "a system of competing and overlapping bureaucratic hierarchies in which both the Party and the secret police, penetrating and watching each other, simultaneously pervaded and controlled the administration and the armed forces. He reserved his own ultimate authority to direct and co-ordinate the system by permitting no point of final resolution for differences and conflicts among the hierarchies short of himself."[6] The centralized structure of the organization was supplemented by ruthless elimination of any independent group or individual. After the liquidation of the Old Bolsheviks had put an end to the possibility of an organized ideological opposition, subsequent purges, reaching their climax in the bloodstained trials of 1935-1938, secured the dictator against the possible ambitions of his under-tyrants. "The top command of the MVD (ministry of Internal Affairs) lives with the knowledge that even such powerful figures as Yagoda and Yezhov were eliminated."[7] Thus the status of the new Soviet elite, consisting of Party functionaries, top administrators and managers, senior army officers, and the most prominent of the literary and scientific intelligentsia, was made completely dependent on their subservience to the will of Stalin. As Fainsod rightly says, "The security of the totalitarian dictator is built on the insecurity of those who surround him." By this regime of "institutionalized mutual suspicion"[8] Stalin secured his own position and at the same time kept himself alone above suspicion.

The development of the centralized and intimidated bureaucracy was combined with a development of the charismatic aura of the supreme leader. Stalin prepared the way towards his own deification by deliberately building up the figure of Lenin into a superhuman being. Lenin had protested against even the public celebration of his birthday, but Stalin well understood how to transform Lenin's revolutionary reputation into a veritable hagiography which he could use to support his own position. As early as the Fourteenth Party Congress in 1925 he was greeted with shouts of "Hail, Stalin!" Soviet propaganda gradually increased his stature from that of "the most faithful disciple of the great Lenin" to that of a Communist and Russian saint by his own merits. When the victories in the Second World War showed that Stalin had been triumphant not only against "the enemies of the people" within the Soviet Union, but also against the mighty armies of foreign foes, the cult of Stalin became gigantic. It reached its culmination in the celebrations of his seventieth birthday on December 21, 1949, which lasted for several days, obliterating completely in the East European satellite countries the observance, until then universal, of Christmas.

In the Soviet press Stalin now figured as *Vozhd,* a word far broader than the English "leader," and close to the German *Führer* and the Italian *Duce.* The official monthly of the Central Committee of the Communist Party, *The Bolshevik,* summarized in January, 1950, all the facets of the worship with which Stalin was surrounded:

There is no significant creation of popular folklore which is not inspired by the thought of Lenin and Stalin and the grandiose transformations of our country which the Soviet people . . . realized under the leadership of genius. In the images of Lenin and Stalin the peoples of the USSR see the very incarnation of the most deep and progressive ideas of our contemporary era. . . . The peoples of the Soviet Union glorify the great Party and its leaders in various languages. Lenin, says a folklore songster, "has awakened people like powerful thunder . . . the weak have become strong, thanks to him." "Stalin raised us from the dead," echoes another songster. ". . . His wise look made of men the true men." "The sun in the sky shines only in daytime," says a Georgian song, "but Lenin's and Stalin's teachings and their great images shine for the people day and night." The light emanating from Lenin and Stalin "penetrates deeply into souls" and "has a healing power for friends, and strikes thunder at enemies". . .

A widely-known popular song inspiringly says:

"From border to border,
Above the mountain summits
Where soars the free eagle,
Resounds the beautiful song of the people
About Stalin, the wise, the dear and the beloved. . . .
The leader who, like sun, has cleared away darkness,
Who is the conscience of the world, the light of ages,
Stalin, Stalin, Glory to Him!"[9]

Stalin also succeeded in linking his own cult with a massive new nationalism, and even with a revival of Russian nationalism, which had been suppressed after the revolution as a remnant of czarist autocracy and bourgeois prejudice. Even though himself a Georgian, he established himself as the infallible judge of controversial points in Russian history and as the supreme scholar of the Russian language.

That Stalin should be a supreme scholar in the field of Russian history and philology is in keeping with a regime in which the criterion of artistic and intellectual accomplishment and truth is its conformity with the party line as interpreted by the leader of the party. Stalin, who in 1912 said that "full conformity of views can be achieved only in a cemetery,"[10] made tremendous efforts to achieve this very goal, once it served his tyrannical interests. Thus complete conformity of beliefs has been demanded from the most celebrated writers, artists, or scientists as well as from the masses of simple citizens. It is not their own integrity but the decision of the party and its leader that determines whether their poems or musical compositions or scientific articles are good or bad. Those who deviate from the party line are forced to recant abjectly. Even those who have faithfully followed the tyrant's commands may be instructed to denounce their own views because in the meantime the tyrant has changed his mind; what was true yesterday becomes untrue today. "No sector of Soviet life is more jealously guarded by the ruling group than the ideological realm."[11]

In the early years of Stalinist rule, even those Western liberals who recognized its totalitarian control over intellectual life and culture in general sometimes counted among the virtues of the Soviet state its respect for the cultural autonomy of national minorities. As the Stalinist regime increasingly identified itself with the nationalist drives of czarist Russia, the hollowness of this Soviet virtue became increasingly apparent. After the Second World War, collective punishments were meted out to whole nationalities within the USSR for "having failed to oppose" when some of their young men joined volunteer detachments organized during the war by the Germans.[12] A number of autonomous republics were dissolved; their citizens were deported and presumably scattered in Siberia.

Below the insecure and subservient elite of the Soviet System lie the rigidly disciplined and systematically indoctrinated masses of the people, cut off so completely from the outside world that they have no standard for measuring the extent of their slavery. It was Trotsky who first advocated the militarization of labor. According to his sympathetic biographer, Deutscher, "Trotsky planned to combine the soldier's service book with the worker's labor book."[13] In this regard, also, Stalin outdid his former rival. Soviet workers, members of the allegedly triumphant and liberated proletariat, operate today under a multiplicity of rigid controls. Young people are drafted for the State Labor Reserve and are compelled to work in the factories to which they are assigned. If they leave their jobs they are punished. Workers regarded as politically unreliable are deported to distant places. Labor discipline has become a supreme value in the moral code of the Soviet citizen. Offenses against it are harshly punished.

Even more oppressed is the situation of the peasant. No act of czarist *raison d'état* compares in cruelty and in systematic violence with the Stalinist extermination of the *kulaks*. Under Stalin the peasants sank from the comparative freedom and prosperity of the period of the New Economic Policy to a condition of serfdom in no way less repressive than was the serfdom in Old Russia before the Emancipation Edict of 1861. Today, while traveling, for workers, is subject to severe restrictions, the peasant is simply prohibited to leave his farm and native village unless recruited for other employment by his superiors. "If the collective farmer quits the collective farm in order to seek some other work, he violates collective farm discipline with all the consequences which result therefrom," states a standard Soviet work on the collective farm system.[14]

But the most miserable victims of the Stalinist system are the many men and women from all walks of life who spend much of their lives in the slave labor camps, under conditions far surpassing the worst brutalities of Siberian exile under the czarist rule. The hardest manual labor under the harshest climatic conditions is performed by the forced labor of those who are punished for failure to collaborate with the demands of the dictatorship. Only by sending many millions of resisting, reluctant, or merely lazy workers, peasants, and intellectuals into forced labor camps was it possible for the Stalinist tyranny to enforce discipline and keep its subjects in permanent insecurity. While Hitler rather exterminated his victims, Stalin made sure that he would "at least derive some advantages from this process."[15]

In these ways all the elements of despotic totalitarianism attained a fuller development in Russia than even in Fascist Italy or Nazi Germany. In the repertory of the Fascists and Nazis, which has aroused the indignation of the world, there is almost nothing that has not been evinced with even greater systematization and ruthlessness under the dictatorship perfected by Stalin, and, so far as the evidence goes, not clearly changed by his successors. In Russia, too, there is no division of political power, no independent judiciary, no human rights; there is terroristic suppression of individual opinion in all fields, annihilation of opponents of the system, blood-purging of hated or feared individuals, the expulsion of national or cultural minorities for reason of state. And the fundamental analogies of both systems are overwhelming. Both were born of interior convulsions; both rejected conscience and the traditional values of right and wrong; both drove aggressively toward world domination; both used fifth columns in their drive for conquest; in both, national humiliation was converted into a superiority complex; both claimed to build a radically different world-order, the one based on a superior race, the other on a superior class.

Nothing shows more clearly the enormous propagandistic vigor of the Bolshevik system than the fact that for a long time it was welcomed by many liberals and humanitarians, blind to these resemblances. A decade ago, the Russian exile, Victor Kravchenko, bitterly complained about the naive credulity of Western liberals: "I can not expect the average citizen of a democratic nation to understand the true character of totalitarian tyranny. Those who drafted the indictment of Nazi war criminals came close to that understanding when they described the Nazi regime. Reading this document, I could not help exclaiming, 'Here, at last, is an adequate summary of the Soviet regime! We need only change a few names, substitute Soviet for Nazi, and we have a picture of the Kremlin set-up.' "[16] The essential likeness among all the totalitarian dictatorships is now more frequently recognized. But even today the proselyting force of Bolshevism is formidable, not only in the East, but also in the West.

Even if one recognizes the common pattern of all totalitarian tyranny, one must still ask whether there are inherent differences between the two systems which may be significant for the future.

One must first emphasize the far greater strength of the Russian system. It is based not only on greater natural economic resources and larger population, but also on the age-old attitudes of obedience and servitude which the czarist system firmly established in the minds of the Russian people, and which have been further accentuated by the greater concentration and more ruthless mechanism of suppression in the Bolshevik system. Such a system could not develop fully in Italy or Germany, where far larger masses were penetrated by the spirit of individualism and the idea of political liberty. This becomes evident when one compares the blood purges of Stalin with those of Hitler. The Russian purges were incomparably more extensive than those of Hitler; and in this competition Mussolini, of course, comes in a very poor third. The executions of Hitler, moreover, were of a chaotic nature. At the climax of the purge, Hitler was obliged to kill Röhm on his own responsibility and to ask later for the authorization of the Reichstag; he did not even know what had happened in the purge, since his underlings had their own private proscription lists.[17] Stalin's purges worked far more smoothly, under his own personal, though hidden, control. He carefully considered which of the purges needed solemn publicity, and which—the overwhelming majority—could be carried out without notice to the public; which could be brought to an end in the concentration camps, and which were best done secretly by the special poison chest of Yagoda, with the help of his special laboratory and group of toxicologists.[18] The extent of Stalin's power, even in 1925, and the utter absence of any regard for the rights of individual personality, are significantly illustrated in the story of the death of Frunze, who had succeeded Trotsky as War Commissar. Against his own will and the advice of his physicians, Frunze was formally commanded by Stalin to undergo a surgical operation in the interests of the state; he died under the knife.[19]

On the other hand, the Bolshevik system has been comparatively free from the ugliest trait of Nazism: its sadistic joy in torturing, the experimentation with prisoners of war in the name of science, the whole abjectly ambitious scheme of "thanatology." The Russians have killed more people, have expelled at least as many people as the Nazis, but Russian cruelty rests on a ruthless expediency and a sort of crude indifference to suffering rather than on a sophisticated sadism. This more human aspect of Bolshevism is difficult to explain. It may be partly due to its nature as an international religion and its belief in a mission to save the world: even at the time when the Bolsheviks adopted the worship of natural science, rejecting traditional ethics and metaphysics, the very nature of their dialectics had an implication for the future which showed values higher than experimentation. But there is a more important factor. Russia has not been "civilized" to such an extent as the Western countries, especially Germany. In the Russian character, as described by the great classics of Russian literature and by more recent observers, traditions of a simple neighborly kindliness have been coupled with a direct and primitive brutality. The cult of an amoral "scientism," which became an important trend in the German universities, has remained only a superficial veneer in the Russian mind. Thus Bolshevik ruthlessness has not depended on a particular role of pathological individuals, so conspicuous in the Nazi tyranny; and it has not been glorified by the dignity of science.

Another obvious difference between the Bolshevik and fascist tyrannies lies in the fact that the Russian system is based on an elaborated ideology a century old, discussed in a worldwide literature. This ideology became an almost religious conviction for a great many people, including some with unusual mental powers. Many of the Bolsheviks, even Stalin himself, continued to be influenced by the traditional conception of the communist state and world revolution. However often the Russian leaders may reinterpret their doctrines, whatever immediate concessions they may make to practical necessities, they are still somewhat bound by the traditions of their heroic period. Their compromises are pseudo-compromises with the mental reservation that they can be revoked when the circumstances change. Their dogma is still stronger than their *hubris,* and their future deeds can accordingly be foretold with some degree of probability.

This type of ideological determination was absent from the Fascist and Nazi systems. Theirs were the occasional improvisations of political adventurers, without any real theoretical foundation. Trotsky made the point with biting irony: "The Roman She-Wolf was not the grandmother of Mussolini. The swastika is not the family coat-of-arms of Hitler, but only a symbol stolen from the Egyptians and the Indians."[20] Thus, although for a time the fascist leaders were able to arouse the enthusiasm of fanatical masses, the ardor of their creed easily evaporated as their defeat drew near. What remained was, for the leaders, simply the effort to maintain power; for the followers, the effort to secure their jobs and their booty. There had been no ideological or moral conception to give them unity: nothing but a common dependence on the leader.

Moreover, the Bolshevik system has not abandoned its international origin. Though the Bolsheviks have persecuted racial or religious minorities as ruthlessly as the Nazis did, and though they have used the nationalistic formula of "collective responsibility" in destroying national autonomies, their persecution has been motivated rather by a crude practical expediency than by a perverted mystical nationalism. Even in their most nationalistic utterances, they have avoided the glorification of war. Their cruelties have been typically directed, at least verbally, not against a special category of mankind but against categories of society: the bourgeois, the aristocrat, the *kulak*. Thus they can give all peoples an invitation, although, of course, a deceitful one, to join the common fold of the proletariat. This difference between the two totalitarian religions has safeguarded the Bolshevik aureole of internationalism in the eyes of uncritical observers or even of shrewd fellow-travellers. They are cruel and terrible, but they can pretend to maintain the ultimate values of humanism.

And these considerations lead us to what is the most ominous difference between the two systems and the most conspicuous in practical consequences: the appearance of a number of totalitarian dictatorships which have carried out by proxy, as it were, the spirit and the methods, the aims and the achievements, of the sacrosanct Russian model. Though the Nazis also operated with fifth columns, they remained impotent imitators in the field of undermining the mentality and the resistance of enemy countries. The fascist fifth columns were mostly bands of adventurers, jobless soldiers, or intellectuals, greedy for gain and command, whereas the Russians had in every occupied and "liberated" country real comrades in the Marxian creed, who were enthusiastic in spreading the world revolution and the dictatorship of the proletariat. And though they were soon outnumbered by fellow-travellers and by people terrorized to "co-operate or perish," there remained everywhere, as in the mother country, a nucleus of convinced and determined men.

When the new Yugoslav constitution was discussed, Dragoljub Jovanovitch, a Yugoslav scholar and peasant leader, declared, "I am afraid that this unifying element [the Communist Party] may become as much a barrier to our existence as was the other unifying element in old Yugoslavia: the Monarchy.... If we strangle other social and political forces, if we beat down their leaders and make their activity impossible, [we] may bring disaster to new Yugoslavia.... We have separated Church and State. It would be desirable to separate Party and State also, and thereby liquidate all resemblance between our New Order and Fascism...."[21]

But of course just the opposite happened. All the satellite states developed all the essential features of the Bolshevik dictatorship, with the one exception that they remained conscious of their lack of sovereign power. Those sincere democrats who tried at first to co-operate with the "people's democracies," trusting in the original promises of Moscow and of the satellite leaders that all the parties of liberation would have an honest share in the government, soon realized their mistake and paid for it with their lives. The difference was only in the tempo with which the pattern of Bolshevik fascism was realized. Hungary, Czechoslovakia, and Poland, countries of pre-eminently Western culture, showed a tougher resistance than the Balkan countries. But ultimately the same thing happened in all the countries under Soviet domination. The situation was ably described by an independent writer: "In the days of pre-war despotism, one could at least shut one's eyes and ears, keep still, and not be molested. Now this was no longer possible. Now the system was totalitarian, not merely slipshod exploitation by a remote clique which took the profits but left at least the spirit free. The new regime hunted down the silent, demanded that they proclaim and parade their allegiance, because all who were not for the creed of the current messiah were judged to be against it, and therefore candidates for liquidation."[22]

It seems that there is an inherent, almost immanent, logic in the nature of all tyranny. Having established an absolute power with an overwhelming military backing, and either disregarding all commands of morality and religion or using them only as useful superstitions for the maintaining of arbitrary rule, the system will always be driven towards the same consequences. One common characteristic basically unites all the countries inside the Iron Curtain: the Russian leaders and their followers in the satellite states are men without conscience. In the West, there is a general conviction, though a conviction not always followed in practice, that in cases of fateful decisions, in the turmoil of conflicting facts and dissenting opinions, the moral individual must follow the inner voice of his conscience, even if the state or public opinion tries to coerce him into a certain course. Just the opposite is the fundamental maxim and conviction inside the Iron Curtain. The individual has no choice. He must follow blindly the reason of the state, which means the final victory of the proletariat in the supreme fight for the world-state. How the action should be performed in individual cases the supreme government of the proletariat, now residing in Moscow, will decide. As long as it survives, the spirit of this proletarian utilitarianism, anchored in a materialistic dialectic, will make all compromises based on right and justice impossible.[23] This is the supreme strength of the Bolshevik tyranny, which, of course, may turn to a supreme weakness.

The immanent logic that tends to drive all modern dictatorships along similar paths is strikingly suggested by two books that were by-products of the dictatorships of the two Napoleons. While their systems, as has been shown,[24] were by no means fully developed totalitarian tyrannies, they yet had aspects which revealed to sensitive observers where such systems, if expanded and accentuated, would lead. The little pamphlet of Benjamin Constant, published in 1813, astonishingly anticipated the contemporary effects of what he called "the spirit of conquest":

Compulsion must make up for the insufficiency of sophism . . . ; the supreme authority must hire a covetous crowd destined to break the general opposition. We shall see spies and informers, those eternal resources of force, encouraged and rewarded . . . ; myrmidons let loose like wild dogs in the cities and villages to persecute and chain fugitives who are innocent from the viewpoint of morality and nature; a class prepared for all crimes, accustomed to the violation of the laws; another class familiarized with infamy, living on the misfortune of their fellow men; fathers punished for the faults of their children; the interest of the children separated from that of the fathers. . . .[25]

In 1865, Maurice Joly was condemned to fifteen months of prison and a fine of two hundred francs for writing a little book, once famous, now almost forgotten: a protest against the system of Napoleon III, in the form of a dialogue between the ghosts of Machiavelli and Montesquieu.[26] It, too, reads like a prophecy. "I can affirm," says Machiavelli,

that the people will not feel bored in my kingdom; their minds will be occupied without interruption by a thousand different things. I shall give to the people the spectacle of my equipage and the pomp of my court, great ceremonies will be prepared, I shall open gardens, I shall offer hospitality to kings, I shall invite the embassies of the remotest countries. Now there will be rumors of war, now diplomatic complications about which to gossip during whole months; I shall go further, I shall give satisfaction even to the monomania of liberty. The wars which will occur under my rule will be enterprises in the name of the liberty of the peoples and the independence of nations, and whereas on my appearance the people will applaud me, I shall whisper secretly in the ear of the absolutist kings: Don't be afraid, I am one of you; like you I bear a crown and I am eager to conserve it; *I embrace the liberty of Europe, but only to strangle it.* . . .[27]

And when Montesquieu argues that the tyranny will be only temporary since even under a corrupt government the love of virtue will continue to live in the heart of the people, Machiavelli answers,

There is only one fault in what you are saying, and that is that in the mind and soul of my people I personify virtue, and what is more, I personify the Revolution, progress, the modern spirit, all that is best in contemporary civilization. I do not say that they respect me, I do not say that they love me, I do not say that they venerate me, I say that the people adore me; that if I wished I could induce them to raise altars for me, because—explain this—I have the fatal gifts that stir the masses. . . .[28]

XX

THE FUNCTION OF TYRANNICIDE

BEFORE THE ADVENT of modern tyranny, the idea of tyrannicide not only appeared anachronistic to most people in advanced countries but was generally condemned from the viewpoints both of expediency and of morality. From the viewpoint of expediency, it seemed superfluous to those who basked in the free air of Western democracy, where constitutional mechanisms gave ample opportunity to correct abuses. From the viewpoint of morality, any bloodshed was abhorred. For Christians, humanitarians, and pacifists, the sanctity of human life was becoming the supreme moral axiom.

Now it is perfectly true that once real constitutional government has been achieved, all acts of violence signify a return to barbarism; but the theory of tyrannicide, correctly defined, does not apply to such situations. The argument based on the sanctity of human life, however, requires close examination. It can not be doubted that the recognition of the ultimate value of human life, the abhorrence of brutality and bloodshed, the growing condemnation of war, the fight against capital punishment, and similar trends of public opinion constitute the promise of a more humane civilization. A democracy which negates the value of human life is necessarily a sham democracy.

But the conception of the supreme value of human life needs qualification. In its purely vegetative sense, life itself has no supreme value, though it is the prerequisite of all other values. Its value derives only partly from the well-being of the individual; it is dependent also on the qualities that are attached to it through the process of growing perfectibility. Only this growth brings mankind nearer to the realization of certain fundamental values, whose perfection is called "the good life" or the *summum bonum* by philosophers, or God by people with religious insight. A life which can not develop these values—a life exclusively rooted in animal functions—can not be regarded as the first principle in either our individual or our collective existence.

Contented bourgeois and worldly-wise proletarians alike too quickly forgot this all-important qualification. Thus a grossly simplified doctrine of humanism and pacifism came into existence, assuring men that civilization meant that under no conditions would they be compelled to sacrifice security and prosperity, under no conditions would they be summoned to kill and to risk their lives. The memorable thoughts of the best of mankind concerning just wars, legitimate insurrection, and the moral basis of tyrannicide were easily forgotten. A loud chorus of voices glorified the supreme value of individual life under all conditions; it was suggested that one need only eliminate fighting, struggle, and violence —and universal peace and security would spread their bounty over an eternally prosperous humanity.

But there are tragic moments of history when we can live only by dying for our ideals. It may be that these tragic moments can ultimately be eliminated by an immense increase, almost unimaginable, in the moral qualities of our race and the adequacy of our institutions; but they can not, unhappily, be eliminated by the doctrine of the absolute sanctity of individual life.

To put the problem of tyrannicide into its proper perspective, we must recall its strong connections with two other phenomena of human history: with war and revolution. All three have one common element: men of moral sensibility feel in all three a kind of evil, a moral guilt, an offense against the categorical imperative, "Do not kill," and yet they assert under certain conditions the moral obligation to accept the responsibility of the guilt for the sake of a higher value.

This conviction is strongest in regard to war. For centuries, war was so intimately connected with the symbol of tribe, city, state, or nation, so strongly supported by tradition, drill, and education, that its legitimacy was not even questioned. But even enlightened individuals—individuals who, in Henri Bergson's sense,[1] have liberated themselves from the fetters of the *closed society* and begun to think in terms of the *open society,* more and more approaching an all-embracing humanitarian point of view—have had to admit that there are just wars, in which all decent persons must be ready to fight and take upon themselves the guilt of sacrificing human lives. It has become a widespread conviction that a defensive war against a ruthless aggressor is a just war. And there is a growing agreement that war may be just when, in the absence of an adequate international organization, a people can not liberate itself otherwise than by war from the unbearable oppression of foreign despotism.

Revolution, too, has a strong backing in the feelings of modern men. There is a strong public opinion that revolution is justified whenever, for lack of constitutional institutions, a people is otherwise unable to make an end to tyrannical conditions and achieve the possibility of a decent, orderly development. The teachings of Locke and of the American and French Revolutions have remained so clearly engraved upon the souls of men that the right of revolution has been generally accepted even by some of those who condemn other sorts of violence. The right to apply the force of the community against illegal force imposed by violence seems almost axiomatic.

Yet even those who acknowledge the right of revolution and the possibility of just war agree with men of the opposite philosophy in condemning tyrannicide. It has been said, and rightly said, that, given the embittered passions of political leaders and given the large mass of uncultured and hungry people, political assassination can easily lead to the complete demoralization of society. The same verdict has usually been pronounced against anarchistic plots and tyrannicides alike, as being only special cases of political assassination.

The general condemnation of anarchistic plots is fully justified. To preach murder against anyone whom a political doctrine regards as obnoxious to society, to use murder as a kind of political education, to make a large-scale terrorism the means of moral and political emancipation, is manifestly a procedure which can only further demoralize an already corrupted society.

And is not tyrannicide itself an act of anarchy? So those who condemn it will ask. Although the intention of the perpetrator of a tyrannicide may be honorable, it remains an individual deed of a person acting on his own responsibility. An individual assumes the authority of the judge and the power of the executioner, which in civilized societies are justly considered to be strictly public functions of duly constituted authorities. This is the main reason why tyrannicide is far more abhorred than war or revolution, in which people feel far more clearly the will and the decision of the community.

This argument of those who oppose tyrannicide would be perfectly sound if the individual faced an orderly society in which the public will could be asserted. But the chief claim of the defenders of tyrannicide has always been that tyrannicide is justified when, and only when, tyrannical power so completely absorbs all the organs and functions of political society that no other remedy can be found to correct unbearable abuses against human rights and human dignity. Individual lawlessness is directed here against lawless despotism in order to destroy it and to restore the constitutional system which existed before the advent of tyranny. It is based on the age-old principle of natural law, *vim vi repellere cuique licet* ("it is permissible for anyone to repel force by force"); on the principle of the legitimate defense of human rights, both individual and collective, against an unlawful power which can not be changed by peaceful constitutional means or by collective revolution. It stands even higher than individual defense, because the act of tyrannicide is not, or is only very secondarily, an act of personal self-defense; it is primarily the defense of the collectivity in a situation where the all-pervading tyrannical power makes collective action hopeless. It is a special case of revolutionary insurrection, perpetrated by an individual when revolution has become impossible. Buchanan, as has been seen,[2] compared tyrannicide with a just war, declaring that the war waged against "the enemy of all mankind, the tyrant" was "the most just of all wars."

Whether tyrannicide is justifiable in practice is another question, which must be analyzed later; but the moral justification of tyrannicide, at least in principle, seems unassailable. From the moral point of view, there seems to be only one truly weighty argument against tyrannicide. This is a part of William Godwin's refutation of the theory of tyrannicide. Assassination, he asserted, would destroy the moral foundations of society. The tyrannicide must carry out his fatal work in secret. Sometimes, as in the case of Brutus, he must use deceit, guile, and duplicity, which are abhorrent to our consciences. And, though Godwin admits that "... no man will deny that the case of the usurper and the despot is of the most atrocious nature" and that "in this instance all the provisions of civil policy being superseded, and justice poisoned at the source, every man is left to execute for himself the decrees of immutable equity," yet he concludes that "wherever there is assassination there is an end of all confidence among men. Protest and asseverations go for nothing.... The boundaries that hitherto served to divide virtue and vice are gone. The interests of mankind require, not their removal, but their confirmation."[3]

Godwin was surely right in declaring that the confirmation of the boundaries between virtue and vice is absolutely necessary for civilized society; but in the case we are assuming those boundaries have been already destroyed by the tyrant. The history of tyranny has always been accompanied by a torrent of bloodshed, by coldly planned and arbitrarily legalized political assassinations, by "the end of confidence among men." One must conclude that assassination will always remain a crime against the principle of the sanctity of human life; it is therefore, manifestly, even apart from the deceit that may be connected with it, an act which hurts the wholesome and deep-rooted feelings of good men. There are deeply tragic dilemmas, which involve conflict between duties of greater and less moral significance: the sacrifice of a lower for a higher value. A man commits a wrong in the name of a higher good which otherwise would perish. It is because of this element of tragic conflict that the act of tyrannicide must never be a simple act of expediency but an act of conscience.

As a matter of fact, the responsibility of the tyrannicide is far greater and more overwhelming than the simple dilemma of killing the tyrant. The tyrant is always guarded by an intricate protective mechanism of his state, and the perpetrators of the act necessarily risk many other innocent lives. More than this, they may risk destruction of the state demoralized by the tyrant. Some of the actors in the German resistance were conscious of risking the defeat and the collapse of Germany; but even this seemed to them a minor consideration compared with the supreme aim of liberating the moral life of their country. Finally, the circumstances of modern tyranny put a far heavier burden on the individual conscience than was assumed in the traditional theory of tyrannicide. Tyrannicide is pointless and therefore unjustifiable unless, as Pribilla emphasized in regard to active resistance in general,[4] it is based on a seriously considered evaluation of the regenerative forces of the community and on a reasonably grounded expectation that a decent and orderly society can be restored. The danger that tyrannicide might lead to a worse situation was considered in some of the classic discussions of the theory: it was an argument in Aquinas' case against insurrection.[5] But, in the traditional theory that defended tyrannicide, tyranny was assumed to be focussed in the one tyrant who had distorted clearly known and generally accepted principles to serve his own ends; the simple killing of the tyrant might be expected to result in an almost automatic restoration of the system. Modern tyranny is a far more complex and deeply-rooted matter; the tyrannicide can not assume that his convictions coincide with the silent consensus of the community; he can not be sure of the practical results of his action. Thus the obligation of basing tyrannicide on a full appreciation of the moral issue and on a realistic appraisal of the practical potentialities of the situation is far more imperative than it was in the tyrannies of the past—and far more difficult.

The obligation to relate the decision of tyrannicide to an evaluation of its probable results does not abolish the role of conscience. But it serves to distinguish the rare cases of justifiable tyrannicide from the many cases of assassination which were expected to have no significance except a symbolic one and from the cases in which pure and disinterested motives were not combined with an adequate appraisal of the situation or the probable results. Mazzini was wrong in the grounds on which he based his approval of Gallenga's projected assassination of Carlo Alberto, which he admitted "would not save Italy."[6] A modern mystic, seeing "in that manifestation of tremendous equality between the master of millions and a single individual the finger of God," he overvalued the symbolic gesture of retaliation and failed to see that mere freedom from personal aims does not make a genuine tyrannicide; there must also be intelligence and knowledge.

On the other hand, an act of conscience is not a mere matter of intelligence and knowledge. Modern psychology has been so successful in destroying the original meaning of conscience by its "*id* drives" or "visceral reactions" or "conation" that an explanation of conscience seems to be necessary. Conscience is not equivalent to expediency, either individual or collective. As long as an act follows practical reason *alone,* measuring the advantages and disadvantages of the consequences, it remains outside the sphere of conscience. There is always an element of conflict in a situation where conscience enters. The phenomenon of conscience begins when there is a conflict between values and when the traditional rules and norms and *mores* of the closed society do not satisfy us. An act of conscience means the obeying of a higher law which we feel to be above the practical expediency of the moment. An act of conscience is a resolution inspired by our feeling of unity with the moral order, with the pattern of values that religious men call God or philosophers the good life. Conscience in this sense is the deepest spiritual foundation of our personality; it is the "daemon" of Socrates, the "here I stand and can not do otherwise" of Luther, and Gandhi's "still, small voice." In such situations of moral conflict, purely utilitarian considerations, even from disinterested motives, will not be sufficiently strong to establish man's liberty.

No one has described the essense of conscience with deeper understanding than Nicolas Berdyaev when he emphasized that it "is not a special department or function of human nature but the wholeness of man's spiritual being, its center or its heart in the ontological and not in the psychological sense of the term." Therefore, "pure conscience is precisely what is meant by freedom from the world, which is the true freedom of the human spirit and is prior to freedom *in* the world." That is the reason why "conscience is disturbed by social environment; and most of all, perhaps, it is distorted by economic dependence...." Here lies the danger of the phenomenon of *false* conscience which we so often found in the form of fanaticism in the history of political murder. "Fanaticism is one of the most painful distortions of conscience. It almost completely destroys its freedom and the capacity for pure and first hand moral calculations, though fanatics may be pure, idealistic, disinterested people and frequently complete ascetics."[7]

In the light of these considerations, the acts of conscience are not the disharmony between different "behavior patterns," "rationalizations" in favor of some strong subconscious motive, or a kind of illusion or self-deception, but signify the really high points of individual and collective history. Without struggles originating in conscience, human progress would cease. Only out of those struggles appear those great men whom Bergson calls "moral creators," individuals who through their creative actions in thought, feeling, or community life bring us nearer to the realization of our highest values.

This age-old feeling of conscience is disappearing in the world. In his powerful book, *The Brave New World,* Aldous Huxley has convincingly shown how a purely mechanically and technologically interpreted universe would necessarily destroy the foundations of our Western civilization, the continuous fight for a pattern of values which can not be demonstrated either experimentally or historically. The first victim of this brave new world was conscience. For the cynic, the sceptic, the sophist, the positivist, and the scientist for whom science is panacea, conscience as a basis for the profoundest decisions in the tragic hours of inner conflict is pure self-deception. Under this hypothesis there is no other explanation for martyrdom and self-sacrifice than the irrationalism of an abnormal human being whose fixed ideas have gained dominance over his mental or moral elasticity. He is simply a *dégénéré supérieur.* Under this hypothesis real moral individuality disappears. There is only the conflict of rival *mores.*[8]

It is not surprising but significant that modern social science has practically eliminated the whole problem of conscience, although it is manifest that it underlies some fundamental decisions of social and political action. When conscience becomes an act of mechanism instead of one of conscious dynamism, a great amount of individual responsibility and creative effort disappears from the world. The ruling theory of an absolute moral relativity becomes an excuse for practically any policy, and statesmen feel themselves to be nothing more than the exponents of certain powerful interests, simple instruments of causality. In the light of the genesis of the new tyranny, we can not doubt that the victory of totalitarian despotism had one of its deepest causes in the moral training of a generation acting exclusively according to what they felt to be expedient for them. Lacking respect for traditional values, they created new ones to satisfy their appetites. The dictators used and increased this amoralism.[9]

To return, however, to the problem of tyrannicide: it would be erroneous to believe that every deep individual conviction is the voice of conscience. The history of political murder and of distortions of tyrannicide has amply shown that the so-called voice of conscience may often be the voice of a fanatic or of a man perverted by vicious political propaganda. At this point one feels very strongly the lack of any thoroughgoing investigation of this problem. But, following those who have dug most deeply into the foundation of moral sentiments, one might dare to say that conscience has two main sources. One is reason, although alone it is a dangerous guide. "Reflection can not be relied upon to keep up ... selflessness," wrote Bergson; "... the truth is that intelligence would counsel egoism first. The intelligent being will rush in that direction if there is nothing to stop him...."[10] Furthermore, pure reason is not a driving force in human history if it is not supported by a strong passion or emotion.[11]

Reason must, therefore, be liberated from its crudely personal and egotistic elements. Passion for truth may be enough to do this, but it will remain the privilege of some rare intellects. For the average man and even for philosophers, this act of purification lies in the other mighty source of conscience, which has been called pity, sympathy, or, in its accentuated form, love. Reason could never show the equal right and dignity of all men. Only reason supported by sympathy is able to liberate mankind from the narrowness of a closed society and pave the way for an increasingly open society. Therefore, a real act of conscience tries to build up unity between reason and love. One must keep reason clear and sympathy alive. A real act of conscience must be based on sympathy, but before we act we must also know the world in which we intend to introduce changes and reforms. From this perspective, an act of conscience is prospectively a creative act. Sympathy must drive men towards continuous enlargement of equality and reciprocity. But only reason can show us how far this drive may go within the limits of the social forces at our disposal.

The final justification of tyrannicide, then, is the conviction that the tyrant not only causes misery and the annihilation of rights previously acquired but ultimately destroys the foundation of the civilized society itself: the dignity of man and the very possibility of moral and spiritual progress. The tyrant's rule makes life valueless, even if it does not break it physically, because it creates a situation in which even those who do not come into open conflict with it lose life for the sake of living. It corrupts both rulers and ruled. Men cease to be men; they become mere instruments of the selfish ends of the tyrant. It is in such a situation that conscience acts.

The moral case for tyrannicide, properly defined, is so strong that many opponents of the doctrine attack it only from the angle of practical expediency. There are three general arguments of this kind. The first is the argument, already mentioned, of the great danger of a purely individual action. This is the reason for the recurrence, in the literature on active resistance, of the argument that the decision to resist should lie, not with the individual, but with representative bodies; or of the argument that the individual tyrannicide should follow the advice of "learned and grave men."[12] This caution in making the decision is amply motivated, since a single isolated individual, however pure his intention, can scarcely judge correctly the complexity of a tragic situation, especially under totalitarian dictatorship; and, as has been emphasized, there must be at least a relative probability that the tyrannicide will be successful and will not expose the tormented country to even greater suffering. Moreover, if we consider the role of fanaticism and of pathological individuals in the history of political murder, the danger of resting tyrannicide on individual decision can not be questioned.

Yet it remains true that in a state thoroughly corrupted by the tyrant the organs of popular representation can not function; if they could, the power of the tyrant would be at an end. Therefore in these tragic situations the decision on final action must necessarily depend on individuals. But the old concept of the tyrannicide as a single, isolated individual must be changed in consideration of the circumstances of totalitarian tyranny. There is small probability that an isolated individual could even meet the tyrant. And even if he could meet and kill him, in a rare moment unguarded by the praetorians, the system would continue as long as the leading organs of the dictatorship remained intact. This was the reason for the general conviction in the German resistance that the elimination of the tyrant must be connected with a widespread active resistance which, simultaneously with the tyrannicide, would conquer the most important military key positions. Animated by this conception, the German resistance developed into a silent conspiracy among many individuals for the realization of this aim. The failure of the attempt against the Führer made the carrying out of this policy impossible, but the conception of the resisters was surely a correct one. In a time when all constitutional organs are suppressed and silenced, such an initiative can come only from a group of free and determined men and women with a thorough knowledge of the tragic difficulties of the situation and of their military and moral power. The ultimate outcome of their revolt will still depend partly on unpredictable circumstances; but it will depend primarily on their wisdom, their influence, and their "ability to die."

A second, related line of argument emphasizes the importance of the ruler. Even aside from the principle of the sanctity of human life, is it not disastrous to society to expose legitimate rulers to the chance of assassination by pathological persons or fanatics misled by the tradition that gives even a narrowly restricted approval to tyrannicide? The danger certainly exists, as has been abundantly shown in this book. But it is greatest in the case of revolutionary movements, where the intensity of public indignation and the organization of an upheaval almost give safe conduct to pathological individuals. The existence of a real leader, supported by constitutional tradition and popular opinion, is the best safeguard against the plots of deranged persons. To reduce this argument to its proper proportions, one need only compare the police protection given Churchill or Roosevelt with that which surrounded Mussolini, Hitler, and Stalin.

Moreover, a general condemnation of tyrannicide by men of good will is not necessarily the best way to insure against the tragic abuse of the tradition. It rather serves to conceal the true meaning of the tradition and thus to blur the boundaries between the rare cases in which tyrannicide may be justified and the innumerable cases in which it is simply a mask for political murder.

The third practical argument against tyrannicide is the most important: the assassination of the tyrant will never accomplish the desired ends. Even if the tyrant is killed in spite of the efficiency with which he is guarded, the tyrannical machine will remain sufficiently strong to crush any attempt at revolt; a new tyrant will step into the boots of the old; the affair will end in a general bloodbath and a new wave of terrorism.

No general refutation of this argument can be given. This aspect of the problem is strictly a matter of the interpretation of the historical record. The practical results of the tyrannicide depend on the power of the tyrant, on the efficiency of his tyrannical structure, on the extent of servile obedience to him, on his charismatic influence, and on the amount of moral resources still remaining in the society. But it can be argued that some acts of tyrannicide have radically changed existing conditions for the better.[13]

The assassination of the Serb king Alexander caused a decisive change toward the liberation of popular forces. Even one of those who made some apologies for Queen Draga was driven to the conclusion:

... This is not a strictly moral universe, and it is not true that it is useless to kill a tyrant because a worse man takes his place. It has never been more effectively disproved than by the successor of Alexander Obrenovitch.... Peter Karageorgevitch was a great king. Slowly and soberly he proved himself one of the finest liberal statesmen in Europe....[14]

One might add that with the passing of Alexander the emancipation of the Slavs from Habsburg imperialism began. Similarly, in the case of Count Stürgkh the result of the assassination was almost immediate. In his trial Friedrich Adler could say:

This was the situation the twenty-first of October, 1916, then four revolver shots followed. Two days later, the conference under President Sylvester declared itself energetically for the reconvening of Parliament. Eight days later, the ministry of Koerber began to take shape and the whole of Austria asserted that [the previous condition] was a situation which had proved to be unbearable and impossible, and that something different had to come; and every man found it quite natural that a total change had occurred in all public relations.[15]

It can also be argued that the assassination of Darlan solved a dangerous and complicated situation. Though with characteristic neglect of the moral implications of the case, which, from the point of view of this treatise, are of primary importance, it was pertinently said of its practical results, "The assassination of Darlan was a free gift to the United States. Everyone felt this, no matter what he said publicly. Even the inevitable official denunciations had a hollow sound."[16] It can scarcely be doubted that the histories of the future will acknowledge the devastating influence of Darlan's quasi-dictatorship.

The story of the German resistance is not only the clearest case of a genuine attempt at tyrannicide; it is also replete with important practical lessons. One is a negative lesson. If the attempt had succeeded, "it would have spared the lives of millions of soldiers on all fronts who died during the months from July, 1944, to May, 1945, and those of the masses of civilians who died in extermination camps in Poland or in bombed German cities. In addition, the failure led to the wholesale elimination of German men and women who, like innumerable others, are now sorely missed in the task of reconstruction."[17] But even with the attempt unsuccessful, it can not be doubted that it shook the moral cohesion of the dictatorship, that it created in many souls that "oath-free situation" which numerous fighters regarded as necessary to annihilate the loyalty toward the Führer. It became evident that the power of the tyranny rested on naked violence and could be maintained only by disordered mass murder which destroyed the family life of many brave and decent people. Even the semblance of a legal order or of a national aim disappeared in the "justice" of the people's tribunals and in the extorted confessions in the torture chambers.

And, although it has been repeatedly emphasized that tyrannicide must not have a purely symbolic aim, one should also not forget that the effects of tyrannicide can not be measured solely by immediate, concrete results. On the positive side, the spirit of resistance, both active and passive, gave rise to a new solidarity of heroism and self-sacrifice, based on a clear moral vision of Germany's present and future. Who could measure the repercussions of the deed, the fresh hopes and the strengthening of resistance in the people, the slackening of the self-confidence of the tyrannical structure? The act and the self-sacrifice of the tyrannicide may produce a kind of moral tempest, purifying the oppressive political and moral atmosphere. There is no doubt that the German active resistance had exactly this effect, and that a kind of new symbol of liberation grew in the minds of many people and is still living even after their defeat.

All things considered, it is evident that the situation that justifies tyrannicide is an extremely rare one. It is also evident that tyrannicide can never be a remedy in itself; it can, at best, only create a situation favorable to the application of the necessary reforms. For tyranny is never exclusively the work of a ruthless man. The tyrannical situation arises from a deep economic and moral crisis of society in which envenomed class and group antagonisms can not be bridged by compromise, and in which traditional values no longer have command over embittered masses.

But even in totalitarian tyranny there can be, as the German resistance has shown, a part of society still uncorrupted, capable of resolute and considered self-sacrifice at the command of conscience. And so long as this remains true, it remains possible that the killing of the tyrant may stir fresh moral energies into life and open the way to the regeneration of the society.

The totalitarian dictatorship always tries to combine the most varied and antagonistic depositories of power, coalescing divergent interests and ideologies through the appeal of its messianic prophecies. As it is unable to satisfy in the long run these contradictory tendencies, jealousy and hatred among the underlings are inevitable. Moreover, it is in the very nature of the rule that the circle of the tyrant can not consist of noble-hearted men. Those who at the beginning may have clung to him, fascinated by the emotionalism and mysticism of the issue, abandon him as they realize how the totalitarian machine makes all genuine endeavors —except power and rapine—impossible. And, as the tyranny reveals itself more and more clearly as a structure of naked force, it may produce, as it did in Germany, a counter-movement of resistance based on a strengthened loyalty to the values of free men.

In such a situation, the killing of the tyrant may arouse an enormous repercussion. It may stir fresh revolutionary energies into life everywhere. Even though no revolution immediately results, the tyrannical structure may be profoundly weakened. The whole system is so deeply dependent on the magic principle of The One that no adequate substitute for him may be found. The jealousies and hatreds of the underlings will be set free, and in the resulting struggle for power, the regenerative forces of society—if they are sufficiently strong—may find their opportunity.

And here lies the most significant lesson taught by the German resistance. No active resistance against modern tyranny can be successful without the participation of a number of key military men in it. A purely civil resistance would be immediately crushed. There is no possibility of barricades any longer, without the assistance of military forces. However, to arouse a sufficiently extended and efficient military revolt, the moral structure of the totalitarian dictatorship, whose center is the charismatic influence of the supreme leader, must be shaken. The men of the German resistance clearly understood this. They were continually handicapped by the vicious legend of Hitler and the oath given to him. Thus they felt his annihilation absolutely necessary for the extension of active resistance and to gain the support of hesitating elements.

These conclusions on the possible function of tyrannicide need a strong qualification. The results of tyrannicide would be quite different in the changing phases of the dictatorial rule. Speaking more concretely, one of the best experts on Italian Fascism was firmly convinced that the assassination of Mussolini at the time of the Matteotti crisis would have made the continuation of the Fascist experiment impossible. Later, its effects would have been far more doubtful; later still, the disappearance of the Duce would simply have precipitated the German occupation of Italy. Similarly, one could argue that in the hectic weeks of the blood purge of 1934 the elimination of Hitler would have shaken the whole system at its foundations. In the period when the prestige of Hitler was at its height, an assassination might well have produced simply a new edition of the stab-in-the-back legend. On the other hand, it can be argued that the attempt of July, 1944, if it had succeeded in its first objective of killing Hitler, would have led to an overthrow of the totalitarian regime.

In default of individual action, there is only one other possibility for the destruction of totalitarian dictatorships. What actually put an end to the tyrannies of Mussolini and Hitler, as to many lesser tyrannies of the past, was war. It is in the nature of tyranny that its drive towards militarism and expansion, its hazardous foreign policy, its threat to the security and stability of the surrounding world, may produce this nemesis. But can one say that this alternative conclusion is clearly preferable to tyrannicide?

XXI   THE FUTURE

AT THE CLOSE of this study, a last question claims consideration. Will the future before which we stand show an enlargement and intensification of the ideas and practice of tyrannicide, or will they fade away as anachronistic memories of barbarous ages? It is evident that the application of violence in individual and in international relations would lose its significance and meaning if we could expect, as optimistic people at the beginning of the twentieth century confidently expected, a growth of human rights and constitutionalism, the free development of human personality, a diminishing pressure of population on the satisfaction of human needs, and the victory of mutual aid and collaborative organization over the age-old methods of control through conquest and force. Both world wars were fought with this hope, supported by the solemn promises of the victorious statesmen. But just the opposite happened. The general conditions which had caused the wars and were created by them proved stronger than the ideology of democracy and peaceful cooperation.

The postwar world is a world of fear and suspicion, of intensified nationalism and intensified racial antipathies. There are high-flown declamations about the approaching world state, there are attempts at limited goals of international organization, but the overwhelming fact remains that the world is militarized as never before. It is a world in which we are seriously told that our best security against extermination by nuclear weapons must lie in the hope that they are too terrible to be used. It is a world, also, of economic instability. It is a world in which abject poverty and literal hunger are the lot of millions of people who through colonial exploitation or entrenched monopoly are deprived of access to sufficient land for their subsistence. It is a world of neo-mercantilism; of the steady extinction of the independent middle classes; of the advance of the collective state in its various forms, less and less controlled by political supervision and an independent public opinion. It is a world in which people are being drilled by collectivism in habits of accepting the state as the supreme director of individuals and the distributor of favors and punishments. It is a world in which a new mass migration—suggestive of the *Völkerwanderung* which marked the end of ancient civilization, but in this instance a planned migration, ruthlessly forced by victorious powers in the name of national unification or proletarian control—has caused untold misery and death and created a class of perpetual refugees, counted in many millions, uprooted from their native soil, a proletariat alienated alike from its homelands and from the countries which grudgingly receive it.

The world of the new *Völkerwanderung* is in a far worse situation than that of the first, which found at least a support and moral guidance in the traditions of the Roman Empire and in the spiritual force of the Christian church. There is at present no political or spiritual power strong enough to make an end to chaos and fill the hearts of men with a higher hope. Christianity, weakened by the Reformation, by the nation-states, and by the growth of materialism and scepticism, has far less attraction to the masses now than it once had, though its influence over peoples crying for salvation is continuously growing again. The victory of democratic Christian parties in the West is highly significant; and one should not forget that the English Labor Party is rather a Christian party than a Marxian one.

But the fact remains that Soviet Russia, the second greatest power in the world in economic and military strength, is the only one that has elaborated an ideology and a creed through which it can extend its influence. This creed is near to the thinking capacity and the subconscious aspirations of the uprooted, hungry, and despairing masses and the underdeveloped parts of the world. The lesson which it preaches to them is cogent in its extreme simplicity. It does not need to be presented with the subtleties of Marxian dogma, which are beyond the comprehension of the untrained masses; it can be expressed in the robust and brutal terms of apparent fact combined with slogans which capture loyalty through promises of an assured Utopia.

This is the real danger that menaces Western civilization. On the one hand, there is no better material for Communism than people who can not sustain themselves. On the other hand, an exclusive emphasis on the economic bases of potential revolution, which have been recognized in the postwar policies of the democracies, is a great oversimplification, too Marxian in its spirit. In reality, the emotional and moral drive of sovietism is the determining force. The starving masses are not the dynamic agency. The small, directing political organ at the top and its new fifth columns are not hungry individuals. They are composed mostly of real or would-be intellectuals, who act in accordance with the sacred books. Professional revolutionists, greedy for power and realistically conscious of their personal interests, are well paid by the Russian Big Brother. But true idealists also swell the army of redemption, disgusted by the present world of injustice against which the Soviet claims to fight, but unable to penetrate deeply into the stereotyped Soviet arguments and irresponsible claims.

Thus one can say that the whole proletariat (in Toynbee's sense), both internal and external, remains liable to fall under the dominance of Soviet imperialism. And whenever and wherever a proletariat has gained power, it has immediately followed the Russian pattern of the totalitarian state. This is due only partly to the enormous prestige of the Big Brother and the great power of the supreme military and political general staff; it is due also to the fact that the very process of destroying capitalistic democracy leads inevitably to the abolition of free individual action and the control of bureaucrats, militarists, and the guardians of the sacred books and ceremonies; to the rule of tyrants under a supertyrant, who dominates and personifies the whole structure.

What has been the answer of the endangered democratic world to the continuing threat of Communist expansion? It has asserted and to some extent demonstrated its willingness to resist simple military aggression. It has devised programs to restore the shattered economies of the West and to develop the underdeveloped areas with the help of western, primarily American, technique and capital. It has attempted to induce and assist western democracies and the countries of southeast Asia to organize for common defense against aggressors. And it has attempted to rekindle faith in democratic values through propaganda and official declarations.

Nobody will deny the great importance of these endeavors, or their partial success. It seems clear that Soviet influence, both among intellectuals and workers, is declining in the European countries whose average culture is superior to that of Russia. In the countries where religion is strong, the dormant power of the Roman Catholic Church has been regalvanized. And the Soviet rule in the satellite countries has been a mighty object lesson in the falsity of Soviet propaganda, both for the unhappy people of those countries and for the western world. It is almost certain that western Europe can not be sovietized in a peaceful way, if economic life functions tolerably and the feeling of national unity is not offended. The present strength of anti-sovietism, however, is no guarantee that the long-run drive toward Communism can be checked.

The moral and political situation in the underdeveloped parts of the world is different. Here the chief motive force of evolution is the hatred against previous imperialistic systems and a passionate drive toward national unity. Untaught by past experiences, these peoples can not comprehend the ideological controversies between Marxism and human rights. And as Soviet propagandists do not stress these subtleties, but use only the coarsest formulas of class and racial struggles in promising these nations complete liberation and independence, they may be as easily captured as China has been by a distorted and simplified sovietism, if they can not be convinced that the West offers them a higher stage of individual freedom and national self-determination rather than a new form of colonial imperialism. Needless to say, further revolt in Asia could substantially change the situation in the Western countries which have partly freed themselves from the attraction of the Communist creed.

The program of the democratic world, so far, is not a sufficient answer to the continuing danger. Progress in the economic field is necessarily slow; progress in international organization is continually vitiated by the entrenched interests of national sovereignties. And propagandistic assertions of the virtues of democracy and the errors of Communism will not gain the hearts of the masses unless they can be based upon a rethinking of the liberal faith which can revive, in modern terms, the dynamism of its age-old values. The basic problem is not an economic or a military one, but moral and, in the deepest sense, political.

The enormous impetus of Marxism has been due to its successful combination of the deep-seated drive of the human heart toward Utopia with claims to scientific exactness and the dissolution of existing standards of right and wrong. With all its contempt for permanent values, for conscience and the moral law—a contempt which allows the utmost irresponsibility to its specialists in strategy—it nevertheless offers as its ultimate goal the age-old ideals and promises of discarded and discredited religions. Thus it has filled the moral vacuum created by the failures of liberalism.

Without a new moral *élan* in the West itself, it will not be able to kindle the enthusiasm for a better world which can effectively counter the distorted ideals of Communism. The doctrines of humanitarian liberalism—the unity of mankind, the guiding role of reason, and the permanence of fundamental values—have increasingly lost their attraction to dissatisfied masses and to intellectuals who have witnessed the falsification of the promises of liberalism by nationalism, imperialism, colonialism, and the meager results of parliamentary democracy. Moreover, the liberal faith has been itself undermined by the positivism and moral relativism associated with the rise of science as the only authority venerated in the modern world. The substitution of an amoral scientific empiricism for age-old values has enfeebled and crippled the democratic spirit. It fostered the advent of the modern tyrants; it fostered the confusion which kept many modern liberals from recognizing them clearly for what they were. On these principles of relativism and valueless empiricism we can not fight seriously for democracy. If democracy is a theory of relativistic expediency among many other theories, there is no longer any special dignity or moral justification in it. What Robert M. Hutchins said in 1940 remains true today:

> In order to believe in democracy we must believe that there is a difference between truth and falsity, good and bad, right and wrong, and that truth, goodness, and right are objective standards even if they can not be experimentally verified. Political organization must be tested by conformity to ideals. Its basis is moral. Its end is the good for man. Only democracy has this basis. If we do not believe in this basis, we do not believe in democracy. These are the principles which we must defend if we are to defend democracy. . . .

The economic side of humanitarian liberalism has also been shaky and inconsistent. The great tradition of liberalism towards the successive realization of an integrated world-economy with the elimination of all the institutions which hinder the free flow of goods, of men, and of ideas has been dismissed as a bloodless generalization. The fatal shrinking of production by the mute monopoly in land, the hereditary sin of our civilization, has been forgotten. And liberal fighters against communism have found no other remedy to propose than the dangerous one of liberal collectivism, controlled by experts and state officials, as a sort of homeopathic cure for totalitarian collectivism—a remedy which can itself lead steadily to the fatal disease.

We lack, in fact, a genuine political philosophy. The idea of the welfare state is a perfectly legitimate idea, a logical consequence of ethics, provided it is purged of certain accidental elements of the historical state which adulterate its real meaning. Our only choice is to work for a state based on ethical principles trying to elevate the economic, moral, and spiritual level of its members. If we regard the state as an amoral institution, separated from the postulate of individual morality, it will inevitably fall into an exploitative organization. Thus in the true liberal state, every extension of state power must be accompanied, as far as possible, by its devolution to local, autonomous groups; the development of the individual must be based primarily not on charity or state support but on mutual cooperation; and the chief aim of politics must be, not the strengthening of the state, but the strengthening of the individual under the moral law.

Many independent thinkers and responsible leaders are disturbed by the present weakness and confusion of liberal thought and are seeking a solution for the reconciliation of individual freedom with the needs of mass democracy. And many common people share the fear that their personal happiness and their hopes for the future may be frustrated by the trends that seem to dominate the modern world. The unusual repercussion aroused by George Orwell's novel, *1984,* seems to lie in the fact that many thinking persons felt in it a kind of apocalypse of our free Western civilization. The world depicted by Orwell impressed them, not as a terrifying Utopia or as a portrait of the alien Bolshevik regime but as an analysis of the mighty and widespread tendencies by which we and our children are dangerously menaced. His main problem was the same as that presented by the Grand Inquisitor of Dostoyevsky: that man would lose his freedom for the sake of a falsified happiness and security.

Only men with an exaggerated optimism will deny that the future of freedom looks very gloomy in the world we are approaching and that the economic, moral, and political climate is very propitious for dictatorships in the backward and underdeveloped areas of the world. These dictatorships will have an inevitably totalitarian character. In Russia and all the territories dominated by her system there can be no other outcome than the complete tyranny of a very small elite over the masses and the annihilation of the influence of any opposing individual or group. The pressure of this system will continually grow and the ever more burdensome centralization and militarization both of the West and of the East will increase international tension to the extreme. The situation will be far more acute than that provoked by the Fascist or Nazi dictatorships; and again there will be no other solution but war or successful revolt against the tyrants.

But the chances of active resistance will be very small, much smaller than against Hitler or Mussolini, since independent persons will be far more completely eliminated and the heroic temper will become extremely rare. Both the materialistic determinism of the Soviet ideology and the relativism of Western collectivism are mighty deterrents to individual action. And the conception of tyrannicide will lose a great deal of its old meaning, since the tyrant will become really a system and not a single individual. But, though the new tyranny has become institutional and impersonal, and the world is full of smaller tyrants, a deeper analysis still shows that, as the men of the German resistance clearly understood, it is ultimately contained by a symbolic force, the charismatic influence of the supreme leader. In the more uncritical, more hero-worshipping atmosphere of totalitarian Communism, the charismatic prestige of the successors of Stalin may be far greater than that of Hitler, and the need more imperative for what the German fighters called "an oath-free situation."

Both morality and reason dictate the right to resistance against unlawful pressure and the vicious misuse of sovereignty, seeking to restore a sufficient degree of individual liberty and the moral freedom without which life is worthless and the roads towards the higher values of the human community are blocked. Tyrannicide may be the last resort in a desperate situation in which other means of resistance offer no chances for the liberation of the community. We have seen repeatedly in this book all the dangers of the method and the mistakes committed even by noble souls. Yet, as long as arbitrary and criminal power continues to exist, the act of tyrannicide will remain the ultimate sacrifice which a human being can offer to an abused and ill-guided community for regaining the possibility of its moral and spiritual freedom. It will surely not remedy the corruption and devastations of a prolonged tyranny, but it may offer an opportunity not otherwise existent for atonement and reconstruction.

Thus the crucial point of our problem will remain the maintenance of a sufficient number of free men, fortified in their conviction that human dignity and the moral self-determination of the individual are superior to the aims of the state. But is this hope for the survival of free men not an Utopian one? With the full development of the tyrannical system, will it not be able to extinguish completely the type of *Homo Liber,* partly by killing it, partly by continuous training and education which will domesticate it and make it in a few generations unable to distinguish between freedom and slavery? If human personality is nothing but a bundle of vegetative appetites and reflexes conditioned by surrounding influences, can not the omnipotent state do whatever it likes with its human material, provided it can give satisfaction to its most elementary biological needs?

There are at the present time a great number of people who are haunted by this dilemma. Behind the Iron Curtain, I often met this argument in discussing the situation with those who in spite of terror, propaganda, and punishment, though miserably fed, remained loyal, at least in the silent intimacy of their lodgings, to their liberal-democratic conviction. These men often used the argument against me: "Well, our example does not prove that human nature will not succumb to the totalitarian temptation. We were educated under the old observance and the new behavior hurts us at every point. But look at these youngsters who, carefully separated from their families, are trained from morning to night in the new pattern and who know that the acceptance and assimilation of the dominant creed will mean for them the choice between opulence and misery, between power and slavery, between honor and contempt. And imagine further that the same routine will be continued for one or two generations, facing less and less resistance. Do you still think that the ideology of freedom will continue in a world which has no real idea of its meaning?"

What argument can be used against this prophecy? None, from the point of view of a mechanistic psychology. There are only three from another school of philosophy. All three were clearly anticipated by the great Frenchman whose words open this book. Étienne de la Boétie believed thoroughly in the ultimate victory of liberty, and his thought was based on the following arguments: first, "... There is in our souls some natural seed of reason which, when nourished by good advice and custom, blossoms into virtue, and, on the other hand, when unable to withstand the surrounding vices, suffocates and dies." But, second, even in this negative case, "always there remain some, better-born than the rest, who feel the weight of the yoke and can not refrain from shaking it off, who never become accustomed to subjection, and who ... can not refrain from looking upon their natural privileges and from remembering their predecessors and their natural being...." So freedom will inevitably reappear; the more so, because, third, the system of slavery is self-defeating and corrupts the rulers themselves: "When wicked men come together there is a conspiracy, not a companionship; they do not love each other, but fear each other; they are not friends, but accomplices." I think these are the only arguments for the victory of freedom. There are no others. But it seems to me that they are stronger than the arguments for the victory of servitude.

NOTES

Chapter I

1. See E. Zeller, "Über den Begriff der Tyrannis bei den Griechen," in *Kleine Schriften* (Berlin, 1910), vol. I, p. 399.

2. See Hans Friedel, "Der Tyrannenmord in Gesetzgebung und Volksmeinung der Griechen," *Würzberger Studien zur Altertumswissenschaft*, no. 11 (Stuttgart, 1937), p. 36. Friedel declares, "The blow of Harmodius and Aristogeiton . . . at the Pantheon celebration in 514 is the first practical example of the murder of a tyrant on Attic soil"; *ibid.*, p. 28. It should be noted, however, that in this famous incident it was not the tyrant who was killed, but his younger brother, and that the plot grew out of personal grievances. The less famous slaying of Clearch, tyrant of Heraclea, in a plot led by Chion and Leonides in 353 B.C., is a clearer case of an early tyrannicide; see H. G. Plass, *Die Tyrannis in ihren beiden Perioden bei den alten Griechen* (Bremen, 1852), vol. I, p. 259.

The popular drinking-song honoring Harmodius and Aristogeiton who "laid the tyrant low and liberated our Athenian land" can be found in the *Oxford Book of Greek Verse in Translation*, pp. 243 ff.

The story of Harmodius and Aristogeiton is given by Thucydides and by Aristotle, both of whom tried to correct the popular version: see Thucydides, VI, 5, 4-59; *Aristotle's Constitution of Athens*, ed. K. von Fritz and E. Kapp (New York, 1950), pp. 86 f. (ch. 18), and the editors' notes, pp. 20, 160.

3. W. W. How and J. Wells, *A Commentary on Herodotus* (Oxford, 1912), vol. I, p. 278.

4. Herodotus, III, 80. The translation is taken from R. B. Godolphin, *The Greek Historians* (New York, 1942), vol. I, p. 199.

5. Xenophon, "Hiero," IV, 5, in *Scripta Minora* (Loeb Classical Library ed., 1925), p. 27. The idea that the tyrant is the most wretched and miserable of men recurs continually in the literature on tyranny. Xenophon elaborates this idea in his dialogue and then explains how the tyrant, by becoming less a tyrant, can reenter the fellowship of men; *ibid.*, pp. 27 ff. For Xenophon on tyranny see the scholarly essay of Leo Strauss, *On Tyranny: An Interpretation of Xenophon's Hiero* (Glencoe, Ill., 1948).

6. See Malcolm MacLaren, Jr., "Tyranny," in *The Greek Political Experience: Studies in Honor of William Kelly Prentice* (Princeton, 1941).

See also How and Wells, *op. cit.*, vol. II, pp. 338-347, for discussion of the ill-repute of tyrants and of their actual policies, which did not always substantiate the "dark pictures" of tyrants drawn by Herodotus and later writers.

In *The Origins of Tyranny* (Cambridge, 1922), pp. 302 f., P. N. Ure writes, "Originally [the word 'tyrant'] was used in a colorless sense as a synonym for king or monarch. It is still so used in the tragedians and frequently in Herodotus. But wherever the tyrant is spoken of in contradistinction to the king it is always in terms of detestation." Ure discusses the commercial bases of Greek tyranny and defends the thesis that the general hatred of the tyrants arose from the fact that their power was based upon commerce and wealth.

There are also brief comments on the early Greek attitude toward tyranny in Mason Hammond, *City-State and World State* (Cambridge, Mass., 1951), ch. I; T. R. Glover, *Democracy in the Ancient World* (New York, 1927), pp. 40-48.

7. "Monarchy," said Socrates, according to Xenophon, "is legal rule resting on the will of the people; tyranny is that which is exercised contrary to the will of

the governed and not according to legal norms, but according to the pleasure of the ruler": Xenophon, *Mem.*, IV, 6, 12, quoted Zeller, *op. cit.*; see also Plass, *op. cit.*

8. See Plass, *op. cit.*; J. A. R. Marriott, *Dictatorship and Democracy* (Oxford, 1935), ch. II; the books referred to in n. 6 above also deal with this point. W. Jaeger discusses the cultural policy of the tyrants in his *Paideia: The Ideals of Greek Culture*, tr. G. Highet (Oxford, 1939), vol. I, ch. XI.

9. *Aristotle's Constitution of Athens*, p. 82 (ch. 14).

10. *Ibid.*, p. 83 (ch. 16).

11. *The Politics of Aristotle*, tr. Ernest Barker (Oxford, 1946), p. 138 (1285 a).

12. Plato, *Republic*, IX, 577-580.

13. *Politics* (Loeb Classical Library ed.), IV, 2, 2 (1289 a, 38 ff.); cf. V, 8, 1 ff. (1296 a, 3 ff.).

14. *Republic* (Jowett translation), IX, 587.

15. *Ibid.*, VIII, 565-567.

16. *Statesman*, 293, 300, 301. See Zeller, *op. cit.*; also Gerhard Heintzeler, "Das Bild des Tyrannen bei Platon," *Tübingen Beiträge zur Altertumswissenschaft*, no. 3 (Stuttgart, 1927).

17. *Politics* (Loeb ed.), IV, 8, 3 (1295 a, 15); III, 5, 4 (1279 b, 5); V, 8, 6 (1311 a); *Ethics*, VIII, 12.

18. In addition to the quotations given above, see *Politics*, III, 9, 4 (1285 a, 25). See also Zeller, *op. cit.*, pp. 404 f.

19. *Politics*, V, 9, 2-6 (1313 a-b).

20. *Ibid.*, V, 9, 8 f. (1314 a). A second method of maintaining tyranny, said Aristotle, was to make it less and less tyrannical until it came to resemble benevolent monarchy, retaining of tyranny only the characteristic of force, so that the ruler could govern with or without the consent of his subjects: *ibid.*, V, 9, 10-21 (1314 a, 30–1315 b, 10). But it was in the former way that most tyrants held their power: *ibid.*, V, 9, 2 (1313 a, 34).

21. See the significant comparison between Aristotle's picture of tyranny and the initial stages of Nazi dictatorship in C. L. Sherman, "A Latter-Day Tyranny in the Light of Aristotelian Prognosis," *American Political Science Review*, XXVIII (1934) 424 ff.

22. *Republic*, VIII, 566 f.

23. *Politics*, II, 4, 8 (1267 a, 14); V, 8 (1311 a, 22 ff.).

24. *Politics*, V, 10, 26-27 (1312 a) (Barker translation).

25. See C. L. Rossiter, *Constitutional Dictatorship* (Princeton, 1948), ch. II; H. R. Spencer, "Dictatorship," in *Encyclopedia of the Social Sciences*, vol. V, pp. 133 ff.

26. *De Republica*, I, 25.

27. *Ibid.*, III, 22. The translation is from G. H. Sabine and S. B. Smith, *On the Commonwealth: Marcus Tullius Cicero* (Columbus, 1929). Sir Frederick Pollock expressed the opinion that this passage, preserved by Lactantius, probably had more influence upon the medieval history of the law of nature "than any one passage in the jurists"; "History of the Law of Nature," *Essays in the Law* (London, 1922), p. 39, n. 1. On Cicero's role in the development and transmission of the theory of natural law see Hammond, *op. cit.*

28. *De Officiis*, III, 4.

29. *Ibid.*, III, 6. See the discussion of tyranny in Cicero's *Commonwealth*, I, 42-45; II, 26-29; III, 31.

30. *De Beneficiis*, VIII, 20, cited Alfred Coville, *Jean Petit: la question du tyrannicide au commencement du xv⁰ siècle* (Paris, 1932), pp. 185 f.

31. "*Nulla fere sit Deo acceptior hostia tyranni sanguine.*" This wording is not Seneca's, but was probably based on a quotation from one of his tragedies. "*... Victima haud ulla amplior Potest magisque opima mactari Jovi Quam rex iniquus...*": *Hercules Furiosus*, 38, v. 922-924, cited Coville, 186.

32. *The Histories of Polybius*, tr. E. S. Schuckburgh (London, 1889), II, 59 (vol. I, p. 155).

33. *Ibid.*, II, 56 (vol. I, p. 152).

34. In his essay "Of Fate," *Plutarch's Morals*, tr. W. W. Goodwin (Boston, 1870), vol. V, p. 298. In his *Lives*, Plutarch takes it for granted that, since liberty is to be cherished, tyranny is a misfortune for any people. In his life of Aratus he describes the wretchedness of the tyrant who must constantly be on guard against the violence of outraged subjects, and here he makes the often-repeated observation that there are few tyrants who have not died a violent death. In his very laudatory life of Brutus he ascribes Brutus' participation in the plot against Caesar to the highest impersonal motives. Plutarch's "Timoleon" was also a source of inspiration to those who opposed tyranny by deed or word, since here he went so far as to condone Timoleon's participation in the assassination of his own brother.

35. *Sénèque Le Rheteur, Controverses et Suasoires*, ed. M. H. Bornêque (Paris,

1902), III, 6; IV, 7; IX, 4. Note the similar use of the theme of tyrannicide by Quintilian, *Institutio Oratoria*, XII, 1, 40.

36. *Satires*, VII, 151. Juvenal himself said elsewhere, "Few kings go down without slaughter and wounds to Ceres' son-in-law. Few tyrants die a bloodless death": *Satires* X, 112, 113. This passage was frequently quoted later.

37. *Codex*, I, 14, 4; cf. other refs. cited Hammond, *City-State and World State*, p. 177, n. 8.

38. *Inst.* I, 2, 6; cf. *Digest*, I, 4, 1.

39. For brief accounts of the early development of the theory of natural law, see Sir Frederick Pollock, *op. cit.*; James Bryce, "The Law of Nature," in *Studies in History and Jurisprudence* (New York, 1901), vol. II, pp. 556 f.

Stoicism could, of course, lead also to an attitude of complete indifference towards the tyrant. Epictetus frequently lists the tyrant with other evils—fever, storms, robber bands, disease—that ordinarily come upon men: *The Discourses as Reported by Adrian* (Loeb Classical Library ed., New York, 1926), III, 24; IV, 1, 92-93. But the man who has achieved complete freedom by the renunciation of worldly goods and physical comforts can have only contempt for the tyrant, who is powerless to deprive him of anything of value. "But the tyrant will chain—What? Your leg. But he will cut off—What? Your neck. What, then will he neither chain nor cut off? Your moral purpose"; *ibid.*, I, 18. "For when the tyrant says to a man, I will chain your leg, the man who has set a high value on his leg replies, Nay, have mercy on me, while the man who has set a high value on his moral purpose replies, If it seems more profitable to you to do so, chain it.... I do not care ... But if you wish me to say that I pay attention to you too, I tell you that I do so, but only as I pay attention to my pot." *Ibid.*, I, 19. Such an attitude could scarcely give support to any form of resistance; on the other hand, it could give little support to the dignity of rulers.

40. See R. W. and A. J. Carlyle, *A History of Mediaeval Political Theory in the West* (New York, 1903 ff.), vol. I, p. 157.

41. "I will give thee a king in my anger...": Hosea 13: 11; "Who makes a hypocrite to reign on account of the sins of the people": Job 34: 30 (Vulgate).

42. *De Civitate Dei*, ed. J. E. C. Weldon (London, 1924), V, 21.

43. *Ibid.*, V, 19.

44. *Ibid.*, I, 21.

45. "It is not always wrong not to obey a command; for when a lord orders those things which are opposed to God, he should not be obeyed," quoted Fritz Kern, *Gottesgnädentum und Widerstandsrecht im früheren Mittelalter* (Leipzig, 1914), p. 205, n. 384.

46. *Libri moralium in Job*, XXII, 24; quoted Carlyle, *op. cit.*, vol. I, p. 153, n. 1.

47. See Judges 3: 15-30; Judges 4: 17-22; Judith 10-14; II Kings 9: 22-24, 30-35.

48. C. H. McIlwain, *Growth of Political Thought in the West* (New York, 1932), pp. 152 f.

49. George Buchanan, *De Jure Regni apud Scotos* (1579), secs. 63-69; Buchanan's views are discussed below, ch. VI. John Milton, *The Tenure of Kings and Magistrates*, in *Works* (New York, 1939), vol. V, pp. 15-16; Milton's views are discussed below, ch. VII.

50. *Etymologiae*, IX, 3.

51. *Epistolae*, 68 (a. 864, Migne, PL. 119, 888 A B), quoted Kern, *op. cit.*, p. 398. For other statements see Kern, Appendix, pp. 396 ff.

Chapter II

1. J. E. E. Dalberg-Acton, *The History of Freedom and Other Essays* (London, 1907), pp. 39, 44.

2. Medieval thought on resistance is discussed in Otto Gierke, *Political Theories of the Middle Age*, tr. F. W. Maitland (Cambridge, 1927), pp. 34 f. and *passim;* R. W. and A. J. Carlyle, *A History of Mediaeval Political Theory in the West* (6 vols., London, 1903-1936), *passim;* Fritz Kern, *Gottesgnädentum und Widerstandsrecht im früheren Mittelalter* (Leipzig, 1914); C. H. McIlwain, *The Growth of Political Thought in the West* (New York, 1932), *passim;* Ewart Lewis, *Medieval Political Ideas* (2 vols., London and New York, 1954), *passim,* esp. pp. 246-253, 269-271; W. Parsons, "The Mediaeval Theory of the Tyrant," *Review of Politics*, IV (1942), 129-143.

3. Bracton, *De Legibus et Consuetudinibus Angliae*, ed. Woodbine (4 vols.,

New Haven, 1915-1942), vol. II, p. 33; ed. Travers Twiss (6 vols., London, 1878-1883), bk. I, ch. 8, sec. 5.

4. C. H. McIlwain, *Constitutionalism, Ancient and Modern* (Ithaca, 1940), ch. IV.

5. Aquinas, *Summa Theologica, Ia IIae*, q. 93, a. 3; q. 96, a. 4.

6. See selections tr. Lewis, *op. cit.*, pp. 111, 116, 130-133, 295, 308-310, 321 f., 326.

7. Bracton, *op. cit.* (Woodbine), vol. II, pp. 305 f.; (Twiss), bk. III, ch. 9; see Lewis, *op. cit.*, p. 283.

8. *The Statesman's Book of John of Salisbury*, tr. John Dickinson (New York, 1927), bk. IV, ch. 1 (p. 3).

9. *Ibid.*, bk. VII, ch. 17 (p. 335).

10. *Ibid.*, Dickinson's intro., pp. lxvii f.; see also Kern, *op. cit.*, p. 400.

11. *The Statesman's Book...*, bk. VII, ch. 17 (pp. 335, 339).

12. Aquinas, *De Regimine Principum* (Leyden, 1643), bk. I, ch. 1.

13. Occam, *Dialogus*, in Goldast, *Monarchia s. Romani Imperii...*, vol. II (Hanover, 1612), pt. III, tr. 1, bk. 2, ch. 6 (pp. 794 f.); see Lewis, *op. cit.*, p. 302; cf. Aegidius Romanus, *De Regimine Principum* (Rome, 1482), bk. III, pt. 2, ch. 2: "If, however, that one ruler does not intend the common good, but, through civil power oppressing others, has ordained all things to his own private good, he is not a king but a tyrant."

14. Occam, *op. cit.*, pt. III, tr. 1, bk. 2, ch. 6 (pp. 794 f.); see Lewis, *op. cit.*, p. 301.

15. Natural law, for Aquinas, was a structure of norms inherent in human nature, prescribing that man should fulfil the potentialities of his species as a rational being; *Summa Theologica, Ia IIae*, q. 94, a. 2. Such self-fulfilment of human nature was, Aquinas believed, possible only through the organized society of the state, where the specialization of human activities and their coordination by the ruler would create the conditions of the good life: *De Regimine Principum*, bk. I, ch. 1.

16. Aquinas, *De Regimine Principum*, bk. I, ch. 15; cf. Aegidius Romanus, *op. cit.*, bk. III, pt. 2, ch. 8 on "What is the office of the king?"

17. Aegidius Romanus, *op. cit.*, bk. III, pt. 2, ch. 10; cf. also chs. 6 f.

18. *Ibid.*, bk. III, pt. 2, ch. 11.

19. See Walter Ullmann, *The Medieval Idea of Law as Represented by Lucas de Penna* (London, 1946), pp. 188 f.

20. Bartolus, *De Tyranno*, ch. VIII, tr. E. Emerton, *Humanism and Tyranny* (Cambridge, 1925); Bartolus attributed the description to Plutarch, but, as Emerton points out, p. 141, n. 1, it seems obviously to come from Aegidius.

21. *Ibid.*, p. 144.

22. The Aristotelian list of the signs of tyranny as summarized by Aegidius apparently became common; cf., e.g., the identical list in *Somnium Viridarii*, written 1376 or 1377, in Goldast, *Monarchia...*, vol. I), pt. I, ch. 134.

23. Wyclif, *De Officio Regis*, ed. A. W. Pollard and C. Sayle (London, 1887), ch. I (pp. 5, 8); ch. VIII (p. 201). Even those who admitted the propriety of some sort of resistance might often agree with this position so far as to say that the surest weapon against the tyrant was prayer to God for relief; thus John of Salisbury, *op. cit.*, bk. VIII, ch. 20 (p. 373); Aquinas, *De Regimine Principum*, bk. I, ch. 6.

24. Aeneas Sylvius, *De Ortu et Auctoritate Imperii Romani* (in Goldast, *Monarchia...*, vol. II), chs. XVI, XIX-XXIII; see Lewis, *op. cit.*, pp. 321-325.

25. Occam, *Dialogus*, pt. III, tr. 2, bk. 2, chs. 20, 28 (pp. 917 f., 933 f.); see Lewis, *op. cit.*, pp. 302-304, 307 f.; Aquinas, *Commentum in IV Libros Sententiarum Magistri Petri Lombardi* (in *Opera Omnia*, Paris, 1873, vol. VIII), bk. II, di. 44, q. 2, a. 2.

26. For feudal revolt see Carlyle, *op. cit.*, vol. III, pp. 56-59, 65 f.; for revolt against the king, see *ibid.*, pp. 62 f., 108-113, 130-132.

27. *Manegoldi ad Gebehardum Liber*, ed. K. Francke in *M. G. H., Libelli de Lite* (Hanover, 1891), vol. I, at p. 365.

28. This important maxim was stated as a principle of natural law by Florentinus, *Digest*, I, 1, 3, and by Isidore of Seville, *Etymologiae*, bk. V, ch. 4; Isidore's words were incorporated in the *Decretum*, c. 7, di. 1.

29. Gerson, *Libellus de Auferibilitate Papae ab Ecclesia* (in *Opera Omnia*, Antwerp, 1706, vol. II, pp. 209-223), consid. X; see Lewis, *op. cit.*, p. 404.

30. Aquinas, *Summa Theologica, IIa IIae*, q. 104, a. 6; cf. *Commentum in IV Libros Sententiarum, loc. cit.*

31. *The Statesman's Book...*, Dickinson's intro., p. lxxviii.

32. *Ibid.*, bk. VIII, ch. 17 (p. 336).

33. *Ibid.*, bk. VIII, ch. 18 (p. 356).

34. See Ullmann, *op. cit.*

35. *The Statesman's Book...*, bk. VIII, ch. 20 (pp. 372 f.).

36. *Ibid.,* bk. VIII, ch. 20 (p. 373).
37. *Ibid.,* bk. VIII, ch. 21 (p. 375).
38. *Ibid.,* bk. VI, ch. 18; cf. also bk. VIII, ch. 21.
39. Dickinson has found the distinction suggested by an imperialist writer at the end of the eleventh century, and he finds what he regards as a suggestion of it in one passage of the *Policraticus: ibid.,* intro., p. lxxiv, n. 254.
40. Aquinas, *Commentum in IV Libros Sententiarum,* bk. II, di. 44, q. 2, a. 2. ....
41. Aquinas, *De Regimine Principum,* bk. I, ch. 6.
42. Cf. McIlwain, *Growth of Political Thought...,* pp. 328-334, and Lewis, *op. cit.,* pp. 249-253, for further comment on the interpretation of this passage and its relation to the controversial question of Aquinas' concept of kingship.
43. Bartolus, *De Tyranno,* in Emerton, *op. cit.,* p. 132.
44. Salutati, *De Tyranno,* in Emerton, *op. cit.,* pp. 78 f.
45. *Ibid.,* pp. 89, 93.
46. *Ibid.,* p. 90. In discussing Julius Caesar he rejected the usual condemnation of Caesar as an usurper. Caesar, he said, was not a tyrant, because his defect of title had been wiped out by the people's acceptance of him and by his eminent rule. In spite of the authority of Cicero, then, it might be said that Caesar's assailants "not lawfully, but by abuse of law, laid accursed hands upon the father of their country." They "sinned against the state in the most serious and damnable way possible by kindling the rage and fury of civil war in a peaceful community": *ibid.,* pp. 100 f. Dante had properly placed Brutus and Cassius in the lowest depth of hell with Judas Iscariot: *ibid.,* ch. V.
47. Alfred Coville, *Jean Petit: la question du tyrannicide au commencement du* xve *siècle* (Paris, 1932), p. 220.
48. *Ibid.,* pp. 183 f.; 213-218. For example, he attributed to Aristotle a clearcut defense of tyrannicide which is not to be found in his works, and he selected from Aquinas the single statement from his commentary on the *Sentences,* which, taken alone, misrepresents his opinion on the subject.
49. The statement condemned was as follows: "Every tyrant can and should rightfully and properly be slain by any of his vassals or subjects, even through treachery and ambush and subtle lures and flattery, regardless of any oath or compact which has previously been made with him, and without waiting for the sentence or command of any judge": Gerson, *Opera,* vol. V, p. 385; cited Coville, *op. cit.,* p. 522.
50. Gerson, *Vivat Rex,* a sermon preached before Charles VI of France in the name of the University of Paris in 1405, in *Opera,* vol. IV, pp. 599 f.
51. The total list includes the following conditions as well: the tyrant must not be killed insidiously and suddenly to the detriment of his soul, when it could be done otherwise; means bad in themselves, such as false oaths, must not be used; he must not be killed by a priest or in a sacred place; it must be improbable that he could be killed by someone else.
52. Gerson, Sermon against the assertions of Jean Petit, in *Opera,* vol. V, pp. 364-368.
53. *Disputatio vel Defensio Paschalis Papae* (1112), in M. G. H., *Libelli de Lite,* vol. II, at p. 665.
54. Manegold, *Ad Gebehardum,* XLVIII, quoted Carlyle, *op. cit.,* vol. III, pp. 164 f.
55. Innocent IV, Condemnation of Frederick II at Council of Lyons, 1245, in Carl Mirbt, ed., *Quellen zur Geschichte des Papsttums und des römischen Katholizismus* (4th ed., Tübingen, 1924), pp. 196 f.; for additional illustrations see Kern, *op. cit.,* pp. 398-400; for types of papal action against rulers see *ibid.,* pp. 402-405.
56. Cf. McIlwain, *Growth of Political Thought...,* pp. 231 ff.
57. *Ibid.,* pp. 196 f.
58. Occam, *Octo Quaestiones* (in Goldast, *Monarchia...,* vol. II), II, 7.
59. *Ibid.,* II, 8.
60. Gerson, *De Auferibilitate Papae,* consid. 12; see Lewis, *op. cit.,* p. 406.
61. Cf. the discussion of Marsiglio in McIlwain, *Growth of Political Thought...,* pp. 300 ff.; C. W. Prévité-Orton, *The Defensor Pacis of Marsilius of Padua* (Cambridge, 1928), intro.
62. Marsiglio did not attempt any detailed explanation of how the corporate community should be organized for action, but Prévité-Orton suggests that he was probably thinking in terms of the procedures actually established in some Italian city-states for controlling the *podestà* or the ruling committee of the city: *ibid.,* p. 99, n. 4. Marsiglio said that if the offense committed by the ruler was something covered by law, it should be corrected according to law. If it was

not covered by law, then punishment or correction must be determined according to the discretion of the *legislator* (the corporately-organized community), but it ought to be determined by law as far as possible; *Defensor Pacis, dictio* I, ch. 18, secs. 3 f.; see Lewis, *op. cit.*, pp. 298 f.

Chapter III

1. J. C. L. de Sismondi, *A History of the Italian Republics* (one-volume ed., London, 1832), p. 88.
2. Jacob Burckhardt, *The Civilization of the Renaissance in Italy*, tr. S. G. C. Middlemore (New York, 1935), p. 25; cf. J. A. Symonds, *Renaissance in Italy: The Age of the Despots* (London, 1898), pp. 83 ff.
3. See Sismondi, *op. cit.*, chs. VIII-IX; Burckhardt, *op. cit.*, pt. I, ch. V.
4. Sismondi, *op. cit.*, pp. 201 f.; Burckhardt, *op. cit.*, p. 33.
5. Machiavelli, *The Prince*, ch. VII.
6. Sismondi, *op. cit.*, pp. 198 f.
7. *Ibid.*, p. 265.
8. Symonds, *op. cit.*, pp. 130 f.
9. Machiavelli, *History of Florence*, bk. VII, ch. VI. Sismondi relates the story more briefly: *op. cit.*, ch. XII.
10. W. Roscoe, *The Life of Lorenzo de Medici* (4th ed., London, 1800), vol. II, pp. 411-421; cf. also vol. III, appendix LXXXIV.
11. P. Villari, *The Life and Times of Niccolò Machiavelli* (London, 1891), vol. II, p. 30; cf. Burckhardt, *op. cit.*, pp. 80 f., 510 f. The name of Machiavelli was found in a list of citizens among whom the conspirators had hoped to find support. Machiavelli was imprisoned and tortured but found innocent of knowledge of the plot: Villari, *op. cit.*, vol. II, pp. 29-34.
12. *Ibid*, p. 31.
13. Boccaccio, *De Casibus Virorum Illustrium*, bk. II, ch. XV, quoted Burckhardt, *op. cit.*, p. 76.
14. Guicciardini, *Reggimento di Firenze* quoted Symonds, *op. cit.*, p. 132.
15. Machiavelli, *Discourses on the First Ten Books of Titus Livy*, tr. L. J. Walker (2 vols., New Haven, 1950), I, 10.
16. *Ibid.*, I, 10 (vol. I, pp. 236 f.).
17. *Ibid.*, I, 10 (vol. I, pp. 237-239). In a later *Discourse*, Machiavelli declared that, whereas the ills of a popular government could be set right by suasion, there was no remedy for the bad prince except the sword: I, 58 (vol. I, p. 345).
18. *Ibid.*, III, 6 (vol. I, p. 472).
19. *Ibid.*
20. Burckhardt, *op. cit.*, p. 440.
21. Symonds, *op. cit.*, pp. 92 f.
22. *Ibid.*, pp. 131 f., n. 2; p. 312, n. 1.
23. *Ibid.*, pp. 311 f.; cf. Machiavelli, *History of Florence*, VIII, 2.
24. See the review of V. Lamansky, *Sécrets d'état de Venise* (St. Petersburg, 1814), in *Edinburgh Review*, CLXVI (1887), 35 ff.
25. See, e.g., Symonds, *op. cit.*, pp. 132 f., and passages cited in n. 22 above.

Chapter IV

1. Luther, *Von weltlicher Oberkeit, wie man ihr Gehorsam schuldig ist*, in *Werke* (Weimar ed.), vol. XI, pp. 246, 247, 267, 268.
2. Luther, *Ermahnung zum Frieden auf die Zwölf Artikel der Bauerschaft in Schwaben*, in *Werke*, vol. XVIII, pp. 293, 294; cf. *Von weltlicher Oberkeit*, p. 270.
3. Luther, *Ermahnung zum Frieden...*, p. 329.
4. Luther, *Eine treue Vermahnung zu allen Christen, sich zu hüten vor Aufruhr und Empörung*, in *Werke*, vol. VIII, pp. 680 f. The following statement illustrates very well Luther's interesting combination of the argument based on utility and the argument based on scriptural authority: "Insurrection is futile and never leads to the desired reform. For insurrection is devoid of reason and usually strikes the innocent harder than the guilty. Therefore no insurrection is ever right, however good its cause. The harm resulting from insurrection is always more than the amount of reform accomplished. . . . For this reason temporal powers are ordained and the sword put into their hands that they may punish the wicked and protect the godly, and that insurrection may not be necessary, as St. Paul says in Romans 13 and St. Peter in I Peter 2. But when Herr *Omnes* breaks loose he can not distinguish the wicked from the good; he strikes at random and then horrible injustice results. . . . I hold and will always hold with those against whom insurrection is made, however wrong their cause; and I am against those who make insurrection, however right their cause. For insurrection can not occur without the shedding

of innocent blood or wrongs inflicted upon the innocent."

5. Before trying to rule the world in a Christian fashion, first take heed to fill it with real Christians, said Luther. "The masses are and always will be unchristian, though they all be baptized and be called Christian": *Von weltlicher Oberkeit*, pp. 249-251.

6. Luther, *Wider die räuberischen und mörderischen Rotten der Bauern*, in *Werke*, vol. XVIII, p. 359.

7. *Ibid.*, p. 358.

8. Luther, *Ob Kriegsleute auch in seligem Stande sein können* (1526), in *Werke*, vol. XIX, pp. 633-635.

9. Luther, *Tischreden* #2749, in *Werke* (Erlangen ed.), vol. LXII, p. 207; H. G. Schmidt maintains that this is the only such statement in the whole of Luther's writings: *Die Lehre vom Tyrannenmord: ein Kapitel aus der Rechtsphilosophie* (Tübingen, 1901), p. 53. It would be a tedious job to verify Schmidt's assertion.

10. Luther, *Von weltlicher Oberkeit*, p. 267.

11. In the last quarter of the fourteenth century, the English reformer, John Wyclif, had anticipated the theory of the divine right of kings. Like Luther, he had been impelled to elevate the king by his opposition to the church. Perverse kings, even tyrants, while lacking full *dominium*, still had their power from God and must be obeyed. See above, p. 23.

12. Calvin, *Institute of the Christian Religion*, tr. H. Beveridge (Edinburgh, 1845), b. IV, ch. XX, sec. 4.

13. *Ibid.*, bk. IV, ch. XX, secs. 6, 19.

14. *Ibid.*, bk. IV, ch. XX, sec. 23.

15. *Ibid.*, bk. IV, ch. XX, sec. 22.

16. *Ibid.*, bk. IV, ch. XX, sec. 27.

17. *Ibid.*, bk. IV, ch. XX, sec. 31.

18. Calvin, *Opera*, vol. XVIII, pp. 426-427; cf. discussion of Calvin's doctrine of non-resistance in J. W. Allen, *A History of Political Thought in the Sixteenth Century* (New York, 1928), pp. 52 ff.

19. P. Hume Brown, *John Knox* (London, 1895), vol. I, p. 73.

20. *Ibid.*, vol. I, pp. 156 f.

21. Knox, *Works*, ed. Laing, vol. IV, pp. 365 ff., at p. 416.

22. *Ibid.*, p. 411.

23. *The Appellation of John Knox from the cruel and most unjust sentence pronounced against him by the false bishoppes and clergie of Scotland, with his supplication and exhortation to the nobilitie, estates, and communaltie of the same realm*, in *Works*, vol. IV, pp. 467 ff., at p. 496.

24. *Ibid.*, p. 507.

25. Knox, *History of the Reformation in Scotland*, in *Works*, vol. II, p. 282.

26. Allen, *op. cit.*, p. 115.

27. Knox, *A Faithful Admonition to the Professors of God's Truth in England*, in *Works*, vol. III, p. 309; cf. *ibid.*, p. 329; cf. *Works*, vol. IV, p. 506.

28. Andrew Lang, *John Knox and the Reformation* (New York, 1905), p. 49.

29. The full title was *How Superior Powers Ought to be Obeyed of their Subjects: and wherein they may lawfully by God's worde be disobeyed and resisted* (Facsimile reproduction of Geneva, 1558, ed., New York, 1931). Professor McIlwain in his biographical note in this edition classes Goodman's treatise with the two Knox works and with John Ponet's *Treatise of Politicke Power* as one of the books which "really mark the first shift of opinion under the pressure of religion away from the doctrines of almost unlimited obedience which characterize the political thought of the first half of the century." For a brief analysis of Goodman see Allen, *op. cit.*, p. 116.

30. Ponet, *A Shorte Treatise of Politike Power, and of the true Obedience which subiectes owe to kynges and other civile Governours, with an exhortacion to all true naturall Englishemen* (1556). Ch. VI, from which this summary is taken, deals with the question, "Whether it be lawful to depose an evil governor, and kill a tyrant." A facsimile reproduction of the *Shorte Treatise* is included in W. S. Hudson, *John Ponet: Advocate of Limited Monarchy* (Chicago, 1942). The passage quoted will be found here at pp. 111 f. Ponet's treatise was reprinted in 1639 and again in 1642.

31. R. H. Murray, *The Political Consequences of the Reformation* (Boston, 1926), p. 188. Robert H. Kingdon has recently shown that in his *De haereticis comburendis* (1554) Beza had suggested resistance by inferior magistrates to protect the true religion: "The First Expression of Theodore Beza's Political Ideas," *Archiv für Reformationsgeschichte*, XLVI (1955), 88-99.

32. Beza, *De iure magistratuum in subditos, et officio subditorum erga magistratus*, in Stephanus Junius Brutus Celta, *Vindiciae contra tyrannos* (1589), pp. 230-331, questions VI and VII.

33. *Ibid.*, question VI.

34. *Ibid.*, question V.

Chapter V

1. This *Baptistes*, written about 1539 and printed in 1578, was printed in English translation anonymously in London in 1643 under the interesting title, *Tyrannicall-Government Anatomized, or a Discourse concerning Evil-Counsellors*. It was probably translated by Milton, who had a keen and understandable interest in the whole literature on tyranny and tyrannicide. See J. T. T. Brown, "An English Translation of George Buchanan's Baptistes Attributed to John Milton," in *George Buchanan: Glasgow Quatercentenary Studies, 1906* (Glasgow, 1907), pp. 61 ff.
2. Harold Laski, intro. to his ed. of *A Defense of Liberty against Tyrants* (New York, n.d.), p. 5.
3. Buchanan, *De Jure Regni apud Scotos*, in *Rerum Scoticarum Historia* (Aberdeen, 1762), secs. 9-12.
4. *Ibid.*, secs. 15, 18-22, 27, 57.
5. *Ibid.*, secs. 58, 72.
6. *Ibid.*, secs. 52-72.
7. *Ibid.*, secs. 45-47.
8. *Ibid.*, secs. 63-67.
9. *Ibid.*, sec. 86.
10. *Ibid.*, sec. 87.
11. *Ibid.*, secs. 88, 89.
12. *George Buchanan: Glasgow Quatercentenary Studies, 1906*, pp. 30, 451-456.
13. All quotations from the *Discourse* are taken from an English translation in manuscript by Oscar Jászi from the edition by Paul Bonnefon, *Oeuvres complètes d'Estienne De La Boétie* (1892).

Chapter VI

1. R. H. Murray, *The Political Consequences of the Reformation* (Boston, 1926), p. 201.
2. Hotman, *Franco-Gallia* (Eng. tr., London, 1711), p. 45.
3. *Ibid.*, p. 63. "It is plain that this most valuable liberty of holding a Common-Council of the nation is not only a part of the people's right; but that all kings, who by evil acts do oppress or take away this sacred right, ought to be esteemed violators of the law of nations; and being no better than enemies of humane society, must be considered not as kings but as tyrants": *ibid.*, pp. 71-72. The extensive powers which Hotman ascribed to the Common-Council included "the creating and abdicating of their kings," "the declaring of peace or war, the making of all public laws," and "all such matters as in popular speech are commonly called affairs of state": *ibid.*, pp. 77-78. The authority of the Common-Council prevailed for 1100 years, and "it is not yet a hundred years since the liberties of Francogallia and the authority of the annual General Council flourished in full vigor": *ibid.*, p. 122. It would be easy to read much more into Hotman's argument than is actually there. We must remember that the argument is essentially medieval rather than modern, and that there is nothing democratic about it.
4. *Ibid.*, pp. 63-65.
5. There has been a long controversy over the question whether the author was Hubert Languet or Philippe Duplessis-Mornay, an adviser of Henry IV. For a summary of the controversy, see Harold J. Laski's intro., pp. 57-60, to his ed. of *A Defence of Liberty against Tyrants: A Translation of the Vindiciae contra Tyrannos by Junius Brutus* (New York, n.d.) and Ernest Barker in *Cambridge Historical Journal*, III (1930), 164 ff.
6. *A Defence of Liberty against Tyrants: A Translation of the Vindiciae contra Tyrannos*, ed. Laski, pp. 7 f.; the translation reprinted by Laski was that published in London in 1689.
7. *Ibid.*, pp. 26-33.
8. *Ibid.*, pp. 34, 37, 48.
9. *Ibid.*, pp. 42, 56.
10. *Ibid.*, p. 51 f.
11. *Ibid.*, p. 58.
12. *Ibid.*, p. 89.
13. *Ibid.*, p. 113.
14. *Ibid.*, p. 129.
15. *Ibid.*, p. 121.
16. *Ibid.*, p. 137.
17. *Ibid.*, p. 146.
18. *Ibid.*, pp. 133 f.
19. *Ibid.*, pp. 122-126.
20. It was reprinted seven times before 1608; translations appeared in England in the significant years 1648 and 1689 and it was reprinted in whole or in part eight times in England before 1689.
21. See Laski, *op. cit.*, intro., p. 60; Murray, *op. cit.*, p. 209. It would be tempting to trace a direct line of descent from the *Vindiciae* through Milton, Harrington, and Sidney to Locke and the

theorists of the American Revolution. But there are important differences between the doctrines of the *Vindiciae* and those of the modern contract theorists. In the first place, the people could act only through their officers, who were not necessarily elected by them, so that the right to resist supported the privileges of an established aristocracy and of the urban and provincial magistracy. There is here not even popular sovereignty in the sense in which John Adams would have thought of popular sovereignty in 1775. As J. W. Allen explains in *A History of Political Thought in the Sixteenth Century* (New York, 1928), p. 325, "the people is sovereign in the sense that all government action must be referred to the general welfare; and because political authority can only be conceived as originating in its needs and resting on its recognition." This is the familiar medieval conception of popular sovereignty, but it is natural that seventeenth- and eighteenth-century revolutionists should have interpreted it as meaning what they wanted it to mean.

In the second place, the governmental contract described in the *Vindiciae*, while thoroughly secular, is not that eighteenth-century contract which rational men can make and remake at will. It is rather a medieval natural-law method of expressing the proper relationship that should exist in every state between the community and its ruler. It naturally lacks that emphasis upon the wills of a multitude of individuals which made the latter idea of the social contract such a potent weapon for change.

22. Boucher, *De justa Henrici tertii abdicatione....* (Paris, 1589; reprinted 1591).

23. Rossaeus, *De justa reipublicae in reges impios auctoritate. . . .* (Paris, 1590).

24. Boucher, *De justa Henrici tertii abdicatione....* (1591 ed.), I, 19, cited R. W. and A. J. Carlyle, *A History of Mediaeval Political Theory in the West*, vol. VI (London, 1936), p. 391, n. 2.

25. See J. W. Allen, *A History of Political Thought in the Sixteenth Century* (London, 1928), pt. III, ch. VI; A. T. Tilley, "Some Pamphlets of the French Wars of Religion," *English Historical Review*, XIV (1899), pp. 451-470; M. C. Labitte, *De la démocratie chez les prédicateurs de la Ligue* (Paris, 1841).

26. Labitte, *op. cit.*, p. 80.

27. L. Ranke, *History of the Popes*, Bk. V, ch. 13.

28. Labitte, *op. cit.*, pp. 93 f.

29. *Ibid.*, pp. 94 f.

30. *Ibid.*, pp. 96 f.

31. *Ibid.*, pp. 301 f. Labitte summarizes Boucher and Rossaeus in detail.

32. Laski, *op. cit.*, p. 52.

33. Mariana, *De Rege et Regis Institutione* (1605), bk. I, ch. VIII (p. 69).

34. *Ibid.*, bk. I, ch. VI (p. 57).

35. Suarez, *Defensio Fidei Catholicae*, bk. VI, ch. IV, secs. 7-9, cited J. Laures *The Political Economy of Juan de Mariana* (New York, 1928), p. 68, n. 1.

36. Suarez, *Tractatus de Legibus ac de Legislatore*, bk. III, ch. X, secs. 7, 8, summarized Murray, *op. cit.*, p. 231.

37. Mariana, *De Rege...*, bk. I, ch. V (pp. 48-50).

38. *Ibid.*, bk. I, ch. VI (p. 51).

39. *Ibid.*, bk. I, ch. VI (pp. 54-58).

40. *Ibid.*, bk. I, ch. VI (pp. 58-61, 53).

41. P. Hume Brown, *George Buchanan* (Edinburgh, 1890), p. 291. Englishmen attributed the anonymous *Vindiciae Contra Tyrannos* to a Jesuit, who, writing under the name of Doleman in 1594, had argued for a Catholic successor to Elizabeth, and the suspicious mind of James I came to the conclusion that the pamphlet had been written by an emissary of the papacy to discredit the Protestant cause: E. Armstrong, "Political Theory of the Huguenots," *English Historical Review*, IV (1889), 39.

42. Bodin, *The Six Books of the Commonweale* (English tr., London, 1606), bk. II, ch. IV (p. 210); spelling modernized.

43. *Ibid.*, bk. II, ch. IV (pp. 212 f.).

44. *Ibid.*, bk. II, ch. V (p. 219). Bodin argued further that confirmation of a usurper's title by a subsequent vote of the people could not legitimize his title, since the people would be acting under compulsion. If the tyrant were first to quit his power, so that the people might act freely, this would be a different situation (p. 219). Bodin was willing to concede that long prescription, for example one hundred years of rule by usurpation, would serve to legitimize the title for the descendants of the usurpers (p. 220).

45. *Ibid.*, bk. II, ch. V (p. 222). Bodin refers here specifically to the sovereign authority of the kings of France, Spain, England, and Scotland.

46. *Ibid.*, bk. II, ch. V (p. 225).

47. Allen writes that Pierre du Belloy (*Apologie Catholique*, 1585) was "the first in France to expound with any fullness a theory that may conveniently be called, par excellence, the theory of the divine right of kings": *op. cit.*, p. 383.

48. Barclay, *De regno et regali potestate adv. Buchananum, Brutum, Boucherium, et reliquos monarchomachos libri sex* (Paris, 1600).

49. See summary by Allen, *op. cit.*, pp. 387 ff.

50. Barclay, *De regno* ..., p. 268, quoted Lossen, *op. cit.*, p. 36, n. 59.

Chapter VII

1. Tyndale, *The Obedience of the Christian Man* (1528) (1582 ed.), p. 32 (1888 ed., pp. 90-92), quoted J. W. Allen, *A History of Political Thought in the Sixteenth Century* (New York, 1928) p. 128.
2. See above, p. 50.
3. A. O. Meyer, *England and the Catholic Church under Queen Elizabeth*, tr. McKee (1916), p. 271, quoted J. B. Black, *The Reign of Elizabeth, 1558-1603* (Oxford, 1936), p. 144.
4. Black, *op. cit.*, ch. X.
5. Allen, *op. cit.*, p. 131.
6. *Homily*, "Against Disobedience and Wilful Rebellion" (1571), quoted Allen, *op. cit.*, p. 127.
7. Jewel, *Apology*, pt. 4, quoted G. P. Gooch, *English Democratic Ideas in the Seventeenth Century* (2nd ed., Cambridge, 1927), p. 34.
8. Preface to *The Anarchy of a Mixed Government*, quoted Figgis, *The Divine Right of Kings* (2nd ed., 1922), p. 184.
9. *The Political Works of James I*, ed. C. H. McIlwain (Cambridge, 1918), pp. 248, 307, 333.
10. *Ibid*, p. 66.
11. Quoted *ibid.*, p. xc.
12. *Ibid.*, p. 40.
13. *Ibid.*, p. 74.
14. *Ibid.*, pp. 71 ff.: "An Apology for the Oath of Allegiance."
15. *Ibid.*, p. 177.
16. *Ibid.*, pp. 213 ff.
17. *Ibid.*, p. 243.
18. *Ibid.*, pp. 205 f.
19. Clarendon, *History of the Rebellion and Civil Wars in England* (7 vols., Oxford, 1849), vol. I, p. 37 (I, 32).
20. Accounts of the assassination and of the circumstances immediately preceding it will be found in Clarendon, *op. cit.*, vol. I, pp. 33 ff. (I, 48 ff.); Ranke, *A History of England* (Oxford, 1875), vol. I, ch. IX; S. R. Gardiner, *The First Two Stuarts and the Puritan Revolution, 1603-1660* (New York, 1890), ch. III, sec. IV; *Dictionary of National Biography*, articles on John Felton and George Villiers, first Duke of Buckingham.
21. One statement which Felton prepared in advance for his defense was a quotation: "That man is cowardly and base and deserveth not the name of a gentleman or soldier that is not willing to sacrifice his life for the honour of his God, his king, and his country." Another was of his own composition: "Let no man commend me for the doing of it, but rather discommend themselves as the cause of it, for if God had not taken away our hearts for our sins, he would not have gone so long unpunished": *Dictionary of National Biography*, "John Felton."

22. Quoted G. M. Trevelyan, *England Under the Stuarts*, (New York, 1930) p. 146, n. 1.

23. S. R. Gardiner, ed., *The Constitutional Documents of the Puritan Revolution, 1628-1660* (Oxford, 1889), pp. 1-9; 17-31.

24. Quoted S. R. Gardiner, *The Fall of the Monarchy of Charles I 1637-1649* (2 vols., London, 1882), vol. II, p. 27.

25. Gooch, *op. cit.*, p. 106.

26. Selden, *Table Talk, King; King, Prerogative;* quoted Gooch, *op. cit.*, p. 103.

27. Rutherford, *Lex Rex: The Law and the Prince. A Dispute for the just Prerogative of King and People* (London, Oct. 7, 1644), Q. XIII. On Rutherford's book, Gooch quotes the Bishop of Dunkeld who complained that "every one had in his hand Rutherford's new book, *Lex Rex*, stuffed with questions that in the time of peace would have been judged damnable treason, but were now so idolized that, whereas in the beginning Buchanan was looked on as an oracle, he was now slighted as not antimonarchial enough": *op cit.*, p. 98.

28. Rutherford, *op. cit.*, Qs. I, IV, VII, IX-XI.

29. *Ibid.*, Q. XIV.

30. *Ibid.*, p. 106.

31. *Ibid.*, Qs. IX, XXII, XXIV, XXVIII, XXXI. Rutherford's method of reasoning seems to follow fairly closely that of the *Vindiciae* at numerous important points: as, for example, in his discussion of the contractual relationships existing between God, king, and people (cf. Q. XIV).

32. See Gooch, *op. cit.*, pp. 99 f.

33. The following summary appears on

the title page of Lilburne's *Regall Tyrannie Discovered* (London, 1647): "A Discourse, showing that all lawfull (approbational) instituted power by God amongst men, is by common agreement, and mutual consent. Which power ... ought always to be exercised for the good, benefit, and welfare of the Trusters, and never ought otherwise to be administered: Which, whensoever it is, it is justly resistable and revokable; it being against the light of Nature and Reason, and the end wherefore God endowed man with understanding, for any sort or generation of men to give so much power into the hands of any man or men whatsoever, as to enable them to destroy them, or to suffer such a kind of power to be exercised over them, by any man or men, that shall assume it unto himselfe, either by the sword, or any other kind of way." Cf. Richard Overton, *An Appeal from the Commons to the Free People* (1647), in A. S. P. Woodhouse, ed., *Puritanism and Liberty* (London, 1938), pp. 323 ff.

34. For an account of the Strafford case, see Gardiner, *The Fall of the Monarchy of Charles I, 1637-1649*, vol. II, chs. X, XII.

35. W. C. Abbott, *The Writings and Speeches of Oliver Cromwell* (Cambridge, 1937-   ), vol. I, p. 744.

36. Quoted Abbott, *op. cit.*, p. 719.

37. See, for example, Charles's speech proroguing Parliament in 1628: "I must avow, that I owe the account of my actions to God alone": Gardiner, *Constitutional Documents ...*, p. 8; Charles's later speech on the same subject: "Princes are not bound to give account of their actions, but to God alone ...": *ibid.*, p. 17; Charles's refusal to recognize the jurisdiction of the high court of justice in 1649: "No earthly power can justly call me (who am your king) in question as a delinquent...": *ibid.*, p. 284.

38. "Thus you see that I speak not for my own right alone, as I am your king, but also for the true liberty of all my subjects, which consists not in the power of government, but in living under such laws, such a government, as may give themselves the best assurance of their lives, and property of their goods; nor in this must or do I forget the privileges of both Houses of Parliament...": *ibid.*, p. 285.

"But it is not my case alone, it is the freedom and liberty of the people of England; and do you pretend what you will, I stand more for their liberties. For if power without law may make laws, may alter the fundamental laws of the kingdom, I do not know what subject he is in England, that can be sure of his life, or anything that he calls his own...": *State Trials and Proceedings for High Treason ...* (6 vols., London, 1742), vol. I, p. 1022; cf. pp. 988, 1043.

39. *Ibid.*, vol. I, pp. 987, 1019. When a group of the king's judges was put on trial in 1660, after the Restoration, the chief defense of those who chose to defend themselves was that they had acted on the authority of Parliament, which was at the time the only legal authority in the country: see *ibid.*, vol. II, pp. 320, 327, 332, 336, 393. In his trial for treason in 1662, Sir Henry Vane developed the same argument at length: *ibid.*, vol. II, pp. 436-438.

40. *Ibid.*, vol. I, p. 1018. The charge is included in Gardiner, *Constitutional Documents ...*, pp. 282 ff.

41. *State Trials*, vol. I, p. 1037; Gardiner, *Constitutional Documents ...*, p. 289.

42. *State Trials*, vol. I, p. 1003. Sir Henry Vane had refused to participate in the trial of the king, but in his defense against the charge of treason brought against him in 1662, he justified resistance to the king as resistance to tyranny and argued the case for the supremacy of Parliament during the Commonwealth on the basis of natural law, which "is part of the law of England, as is evident by all the best received law books.... This is the law that is before any judicial or municipal law, as the root and fountain whence these and all governments, under God and his law, do flow": *ibid.*, vol. II, pp. 446 f.

43. From *Might and Right Well Met*, 1649, reprinted in A. S. P. Woodhouse, ed., *Puritanism and Liberty*, pp. 212 ff., at p. 216.

44. Quoted Abbott, *op. cit.*, vol. I, p. 746.

45. *Ibid.*, vol. II, p. 337.

46. John Milton, *The Tenure of Kings and Magistrates* (1649), *Works* (New York, 1932), vol. V, pp. 8-14.

47. *Ibid.*, pp. 10 f.

48. *Ibid.*, p. 14, pp. 18 f.

49. *Ibid.*, pp. 19 ff.

50. *Ibid.*, p. 7. Milton's views on the subject are elaborated but remain essentially unchanged in his bitter reply to Salmasius, to the preparation of which he devoted the last months before his blindness, *Defense of the People of Eng-*

268   NOTES TO PAGES 84-107

land Against Claudius Anonymous, Alias Salmasius (1651), *Works*, vol. VII.

51. Hobbes, *Leviathan*, II, 19 (Everyman ed., p. 174).

52. R. S. Gardiner, *History of the Great Civil War: 1642-1649* (4 vols., London, 1893), vol. IV, p. 329.

53. C. H. Firth, *Oliver Cromwell* (London, 1901), p. 438.

54. Miles Sindercombe, Sexby's paid confederate, after failing to find a suitable opportunity to shoot Cromwell, finally tried in 1657 to burn down Whitehall. The Whitehall plot was exposed at the last minute, and Sindercombe, tried and condemned, died by suicide in the Tower while awaiting execution. In 1654 two conspirators had been put to death for a Royalist plot to assassinate Cromwell. An otherwise obscure cooper named Venner led a small group of Fifth Monarchy Men in a plot against Cromwell and the Protectorate government. Venner was hanged four years later for a plot against Charles II. On the plots against Cromwell, see C. H. Firth, *The Last Years of the Protectorate: 1656-1658* (2 vols., London, 1909), vol. I, pp. 33-40; 113-119; 219-236.

55. The authorship of the pamphlet, usually attributed to Sexby, has been disputed. It is Firth's opinion that Sexby planned the pamphlet, but that he was assisted in its writing by Captain Sileus Titus: *ibid.*, p. 224, n. 1.

56. *Killing No Murder* (1689 ed.), pp. 2 f.

57. *Ibid.*, pp. 5, 6-8.

58. *Ibid.*, p. 23.

59. *Ibid.*, p. 25.

60. The text of the pamphlet, including this preface, can be found in H. Morley, *Famous Pamphlets* (London, 1886), pp. 83 ff.

61. *State Trials*, vol. II, p. 320.

62. Lord Russell said, "I...would have suffered any extremity, rather than have consented to any design to take away the king's life...": *ibid.*, vol. II, p. 753; cf. statements by Russell, *ibid.*, p. 726; Wolcot, p. 699; Sidney, p. 811.

63. "In 1683, on the day of Lord Russell's execution, a convocation of the University of Oxford solemnly condemned the doctrine that power comes from the people and that, obedience being conditional, resistance to a ruler was under certain circumstances permissible. The convocation then ordered books containing the pernicious doctrine to be burned. Books by Hobbes, Milton, Knox, Bellarmine, Buchanan, and others were assigned to the flames": R. Lodge, *The History of England from the Restoration to the Death of William III* (London, 1910), p. 225.

Chapter IX

1. *The Political Works of James I*, ed. C. H. McIlwain (Cambridge, 1918), pp. 278, 309.

2. Adolph Damaschke, *Geschichte der Nationalökonomie* (Jena, 1909), p. 80.

3. Jean Jacques Rousseau, *A Discourse on the Origin of Inequality* (Everyman ed.), p. 226.

4. John Locke, *Of Civil Government*, 202 (Everyman ed.), p. 219.

5. *Ibid.*, 207, p. 222.

6. *Ibid.*, 220, p. 228; cf. 243, p. 242.

7. *Ibid.*, 232, pp. 234 f.

8. *Ibid.*, 230, p. 233.

9. *Ibid.*, 220, p. 228.

10. *Ibid.*, 240, 241, p. 241.

11. Dumas Malone, *Jefferson and His Times*, vol. I (Boston, 1948), p. 242.

12. This was a passage in a private letter, written from France; Jefferson's intention was not to stir up a spirit of rebellion but to point out that it was a lesser evil than the European despotism of which he had become very much aware: see Malone, *op. cit.*, vol. II (Boston, 1951), pp. xvii, 165-167.

13. "The tree of liberty grows when it is watered with the blood of the tyrants"; quoted F. Guizot and Mme. Guizot de Witt, *France* (New York, 1898), vol. VI, p. 133.

14. *The Federalist* (Modern Library ed.), #48, p. 321.

15. *Ibid.*, #47, p. 313.

16. Quoted *ibid.*, #48, p. 324.

17. *The Works of Voltaire*, ed. E. R. Dumont (1901), pp. 134, 137.

18. *Oeuvres complètes de Diderot* (Paris, 1875), vol. III, pp. 24, 84, 392.

19. First ed., Amsterdam, 1770; definitive ed., Geneva, 1780; it was translated into most of the European languages; an English ed. was published in London in 1777.

20. Anatole Feugère, *Un précurseur de la Révolution, L'Abbé Raynal (1713-1796)* (Angoulême, 1922), pp. 259 f.

21. Egon Friedell, *Kulturgeschichte der Neuzeit* (Munich, 1928), vol. II, p. 498.

22. Alphonse Lamartine, *History of the Girondists* (New York, 1849), vol.

III, pp. 77, 79.
23. Albert Mathiez, "French Revolution," in *Encyclopaedia of the Social Sciences*, vol. VI, at p. 482.
24. Clarence Crane Brinton, *The Jacobins, An Essay in the New History* (New York, 1930), pp. 204 f.
25. Quoted Jean Jaurès, *La Convention*, vol. II (vol. IV of his *Histoire socialiste*) (Paris, n.d.), p. 916.
26. Quoted Guizot, *op. cit.*, vol. VI, p. 120.
27. Quoted Jaurès, *op. cit.*, vol. II (IV), p. 950.
28. Quoted *ibid.*, p. 961.
29. *Ibid.*, p. 962.
30. Mathiez, *op. cit.*, at p. 481.
31. Quoted Jaurès, *op. cit.*, vol. I (III), p. 568.
32. Quoted J. Salwyn Schapiro, *Condorcet and the Rise of Liberalism* (New York, 1934), pp. 97 f.
33. *The Rights of Man* (Everyman ed.), p. 20.

Chapter X

1. *Anarchical Fallacies* (1791), in *Works* (ed. Bowring), vol. II, pp. 489-534, at p. 501.
2. *Fragment on Government*, ed. F. C. Montague (Oxford, 1931), ch. I.
3. Élie Halévy, *The Growth of Philosophic Radicalism* (London, 1934), pp. 143-145.
4. *Fragment on Government*, ch. I, sec. 43.
5. *An Introduction to the History of the Science of Politics* (London, 1935), p. 107.
6. *Dissertations and Discussions* (London, 1859), vol. I, p. 333.
7. In his appeal to the National Convention of France, *Emancipate your Colonies!* (1793), *(Works)*, vol. IV, pp. 407-418), in which he tried to popularize the doctrine of Adam Smith concerning the economic and political disadvantages of the colonial system, we hear a passionate and sometimes ironical protest against the treason of the masses, who were beginning to assume the old role of the despots. "You abhor tyranny," he exclaimed. "... You abhor the subjection of one nation to another. You call it slavery. You gave sentence in the case of Britain against her colonies: Have you so soon forgot that sentence: Have you so soon forgot the school in which you served your apprenticeship to Freedom?" It is no argument for maintaining the colonial system that it is a part of the empire: "Yes, you have or have had it; but when came it to you? Whence, but from the hand of despotism? Think how you have dealt by them. One common Bastille inclosed them and you. You knock down the jailor, you let yourselves out, you keep them in, and put yourselves into his place. You destroy the criminal, and you reap the profit, I mean always what seems to you profit, of the crime...." This policy will poison the new system of freedom both economically and morally: "In the event of a rupture with Spain, you have designs, I think, in favour of her colonies. With what view? ... To keep them? Say so boldly, and acknowledge yourselves worthy successors of Louis XIV. To give them independence? Why not give it then where it is already in your power to give it ... ?" There is no escape from tyranny under the colonial system: "What a mountain of arguments and calculations must you struggle under, if you persevere in the system of colony-holding with its monopolies and counter-monopolies! What a cover for tyranny and peculation ... !"
8. See pp. 55-57 above.
9. Cf. quotations from Tolstoy collected in Paul Eltzbacher, *Anarchism* (New York, 1908).
10. Quoted René Fülop-Miller, *Leaders, Dreamers, and Rebels* (New York, 1935), p. 274.
11. *The Social Contract*, bk. II, ch. XI (Everyman ed., p. 45). Even more than *The Social Contract*, the *Discourse on Inequality* expressed the main teaching of Rousseau and foreshadowed the main trend of radicalism in the coming century.
12. Rousseau, *Oeuvres et correspondence inédites*, ed. Streckeisen-Moulton (1861), p. 100, quoted Émile Durkheim, *Le socialisme* (Paris, 1928), p. 67.
13. From a speech by August Bebel, Berlin, November 2, 1898, in Bebel, *Assassinations and Socialism* (New York, n.d.), pp. 17, 29.
14. Karl Kautsky, *Terrorismus und Kommunismus, Ein Beitrag zur Naturgeschichte der Revolution* (Berlin, 1919), p. 100.
15. I doubt the sincerity of these statements and regard them as tactical utterances because they are in sharp contradiction to the whole revolutionary trend of Marx's political thought.
16. Quoted Kautsky, *op. cit.*, p. 121.

Chapter XI

1. Vittorio Alfieri, *Della Tirannide* (Bari, 1927), p. 9.
2. Gudence Megaro, *Vittorio Alfieri, Forerunner of Italian Nationalism* (New York, 1930), p. 47.
3. *Ibid.*, p. 95.
4. *Ibid.*, p. 148.
5. Wilhelm Röpke, *Die Gesellschaftskrisis der Gegenwart* (Erlenbach-Zürich, 1942), pp. 66 f.
6. H. A. Korff, *Geist der Goethezeit* (Leipzig, 1923), vol. I, pp. 211-214.
7. Friedrich von Schiller, *Wilhelm Tell*, act V, scene I.
8. G. W. Spindler, *The Life of Karl Follen* (Chicago, 1917), p. 41.
9. Quoted *ibid.*, p. 40.
10. Quoted *ibid.*, p. 41.
11. Carl Wittke, *Karl Heinzen* (Chicago, 1945), *passim*.
12. Ferdinand Freiligrath, *Ca Ira!* (1846), *Gesammelte Dichtungen*, vol. III (Stuttgart, 1871), p. 127.
13. *Ibid.*, p. 123.
14. Friends of the author assert that this crude old song could still be heard in Vienna in the revolutionary days of 1918-1919.
15. Alexander Petöfi, "Akasszátok föl a királyokat" ("Hang the Kings"), Collected poems, Centennial ed. (Budapest, 1923), p. 532.
16. *The Works of Walter Landor, Poems*, ed. Stephen Wheeler (London, 1935), vol. III, pp. 61 f. The original edition, now very rare, containing also the prose address suppressed later, was published in Bath for the benefit of the Hungarians in America.
17. Quoted Sidney Colvin, *Landor* (English Men of Letters series, New York, n.d.), p. 197.
18. Bolton King, *Mazzini* (London, 1902), p. 165.
19. John Foster, *Walter Savage Landor* (London, 1895), pp. 121 f.
20. *Spectator*, LV (August 9, 1890).
21. See below, pp. 207 f.
22. Giuseppe Mazzini, *Scritti editi ed inediti* (Ed. Nazionale), vol. LXXVII, pp. 167 f.
23. *Ibid.*, vol. LV, pp. 156 f.

Chapter XII

1. Quoted "Babeuf," in *Encyclopaedia Britannica* (11th ed.).
2. Quoted Belfort Bax, *The Last Episode of the French Revolution, Being a History of Gracchus Babeuf and the Conspiracy of the Equals* (Boston, n.d.), p. 98.
3. Babeuf apologized for the men of the September terror, saying, "They are simply priests, the sacrificers of a just immolation for the public security. If anything is to be regretted, it is that a larger and more general second of September did not sweep away all starvers and all despoilers": quoted H. A. Taine, *The French Revolution* (New York, 1885), vol. III, p. 224.
4. Quoted Bax, *op. cit.*, pp. 146, 149.
5. Quoted Bax, *op. cit.*, p. 149.
6. Quoted F. H. Aulard, "Babeuf," in *La grande encyclopédie*.
7. A. Espinas, *La philosophie sociale du xviiie siècle et la révolution* (Paris, 1898), p. 196.
8. Quoted George Sencier, *Le Babouvisme après Babeuf* (Paris, 1912), p. 127.
9. Quoted Maurice Dommanget, *Blanqui* (Paris, 1924), p. 49.
10. Quoted *ibid.*, p. 64.
11. Quoted *ibid.*, p. 93.
12. Quoted Max Nomad, *Apostles of Revolution* (Boston, 1939), p. 68.
13. Quoted Dommanget, *op. cit.*, p. 93.
14. Quoted Mark Hovell, *The Chartist Movement* (Manchester, 1925), p. 147.
15. Quoted *ibid.*, p. 152; cf. p. 104 above.
16. M. Beer, *A History of British Socialism* (London, 1929), vol. I, pp. 291 f.
17. Especially in theatrical literature one grasps the emotions of the heroic days of the Bolshevik Revolution. Among the great variety of examples collected by René Fülop-Miller in his *Geist und Gesicht des Bolschewismus* (Vienna, 1926), one, given on pp. 247 ff., seems particularly significant. The "Liberation of Labor" was performed by thousands of soldiers in addition to professional actors at the May Festival of 1920 in Leningrad. The official scenario describes the themes of the play.

One sees on the stage a great wall, in the middle of which there is a colossal golden door. From behind the wall one hears gay music, and glaring lights are visible on the horizon. The wall hides a world of gay life. Before the closed door are cannon which forbid entrance into this happy realm of freedom, equality, and fraternity. On the staircase in front of this door there are slaves occupied in hard work, chased by overseers with long knouts. One hears from all sides sighing and groaning, the clanking of chains and the whistling of the knouts, cursing and screaming, and the ironic laughter of the overseers. The slaves interrupt their work to listen to the joyful music behind the wall, and express the desire to enter there. But the overseers again crack their knouts, and the labor is resumed. Soon fanfare announces the approach of the masters, of the exploiters. They are surrounded by guards, by jesters, by priests and priestesses, by hangmen, servants, astrologers, dancers, and singers. Behind them walks, supported by attendants, a stout, overfed king with animal-like features. After him comes a plantation-owner with a large stick in his hand. Then the king of the stock-exchange appears in a black suit and a silk hat and with jewel-bedecked fingers. A fat clergyman advances with an accordion in his hand. The splendid company does not care for the workers, but the masses begin to murmur, while the music starts with the tones of the future world. The masters are terrified when the slaves toss aside their working tools and announce the struggle against the exploiters. Violent scenes occur, but the guards restore order. Armed peasants also are repelled from entering the golden door. Priests come to appease the masses, who again begin to accept their traditional burden. But very soon the blazing star of the Red Army appears and the first Red troops engage in the battle. The golden door is forced open. The day of peace, liberty, and joyful work begins to dawn. One sees the colossal tree of liberty adorned with red ribbons. The Red Army throws away its weapons and picks up the working tools. All the people join in a gay dance and the *International* swells out.

Is this not a striking vision of the modern tyrant?

18. Quoted *ibid.*, p. 309.
19. Edward S. Mason, "Blanqui and Communism," *Political Science Quarterly*, XLIV (1929), pp. 498-527, at p. 527.
20. Buonarotti, *Conjuration des Égaux*, p. 93, quoted Mason, *op. cit.*, p. 527.

Chapter XIII

1. D. P. Mirsky, *Russia: A Social History* (London, 1932), p. 260.
2. Quoted A. Yarmolinsky, "Nihilism," in *Encyclopaedia of the Social Sciences*.
3. The essence of the doctrine was old. Long before the appearance of the Nihilists, the German philosopher, Max Stirner, had expressed the whole credo of violent anarchism. The only help for the masses, he taught, was "violent insurrection against the condition that has hitherto existed." The problem of property could be solved only "by the war of all against all"—not with the implication of revolutionary upheaval, but with direct reference to individual action. "Put your hand to it and take what you need...." "The power over life and death, which Church and State reserve to themselves, this too I call mine...." Quoted Paul Eltzbacher, *Anarchism* (New York, 1908), pp. 111, 113.
4. Tolstoy, the third of the great Russian anarchists, rejected violence and advocated a return to original Christianity; see p. 113 above.
5. Quoted A. P. Maximoff, ed., *The Political Philosophy of Bakunin: Scientific Anarchism* (Glencoe, Ill., 1953), p. 34.
6. Quoted Eltzbacher, *op. cit.*, p. 122.
7. Quoted K. Diehl, *Sozialismus, Kommunismus, Anarchismus* (4th ed., Jena, 1922), p. 100.
8. Quoted Max Nomad, *Apostles of Revolution* (Boston, 1939), p. 231.
9. Quoted Eltzbacher, *op. cit.*, p. 151.
10. Alexander I. Spiridovitch, *Histoire du terrorisme russe 1886-1917* (Paris, 1930), p. 412.
11. Quoted Eltzbacher, *op. cit.*, p. 174.
12. Quoted J. B. S. Hardman, "Terrorism," in *Encyclopaedia of the Social Sciences*.
13. Karl Oldenberg, *Der russische Nihilismus von seinen Anfängen bis zur Gegenwart* (Leipzig, 1888), pp. 110 f.
14. Quoted Thomas G. Masaryk, *The Spirit of Russia* (London, 1919), p. 545.
15. Quoted Manya Gordon, *Workers before and after Lenin* (New York, 1941), p. 457.
16. Quoted W. H. Chamberlin, *The Russian Enigma* (New York, 1943), p. 77.
17. E. A. Vizetelli, *The Anarchists* (New York, 1911), p. 52.
18. Quoted Paul Liman, *Der politische Mord im Wandel der Geschichte* (Berlin, 1912), p. 211.
19. Benedetto Croce, *History of Eu-*

rope in the Nineteenth Century (Eng. tr., New York, 1933), pp. 311 f.
20. Quoted Liman, op. cit., p. 228.
21. Quoted Vizetelli, op. cit., p. 145.
22. H. G. Schmidt, Die Lehre von Tyrannenmord (Tübingen and Leipzig, 1901), p. 140.
23. G. Sorel, Réflexions sur la violence (7th ed., Paris, 1930), p. 56.
24. Ibid., p. 433.
25. Lenin, "Our Program," in E. Burns, ed., A Handbook of Marxism (London, 1935), p. 573.
26. Lenin, "What Is To Be Done," in A Handbook of Marxism, p. 587.
27. Ibid., pp. 590 f.
28. Ibid., pp. 603 f.
29. Ibid., p. 606.
30. Ibid., p. 608.

Chapter XIV

1. Henri Bergson, The Two Sources of Morality and Religion (New York, 1935), p. 268.
2. A good, though purely factual introduction is Paul Liman, Der politische Mord im Wandel der Geschichte (Berlin, 1922); an interesting and more penetrating essay is Fr. v. Bezold, "Zur Geschichte des politischen Meuchelmordes," in Beilage zur allgemeinen Zeitung (Munich, 1899), nos. 92, 93.
Though P. A. Sorokin has devoted an enormous amount of space in his Social and Cultural Dynamics to the topic of social disturbances, he alludes only occasionally to the problem of political murder; and his fundamental generalization does not grasp the essence of the problem. "The phenomena of social disturbances are fundamentally like phenomena of criminality. The main difference is in scale. When a few individuals kill, steal, or rob others, the isolated cases are called 'crimes.' When the same actions are perpetrated on a large scale and by the masses, the phenomena are called 'riots,' 'disturbances,' 'revolutions,' and so on. Accordingly, most of the 'disturbances' spring from, and develop in, exactly the same sort of situation as does criminal demoralization among individuals. The determining factor in each case is the condition of the sociocultural network of values and relationships": vol. III (1937), p. 501.
Nobody will deny the close connection between criminality and revolution. Both theoretical observers and active revolutionaries have been impressed by the role of pathological and unbalanced persons in cases of violent social transformations; but an identification of revolution with criminality eliminates essential points of difference, above all the whole moral aspect of the revolutionary phenomena, which also lies at the bottom of tyrannicide.
3. Liman, op. cit., pp. 51 ff.
4. P. 4 above.
5. D. S. Margoliouth, "Assassins," in Encyclopedia of Religion and Ethics, vol. III.
6. Von Bezold, op. cit.
7. For details see Gaetano Salvemini, Carlo and Nello Rosselli (London, 1937).
8. Charles Benoit, Le machiavellisme avant Machiavel (Paris, 1907).
9. J. K. Pollock and H. J. Heinemann, eds., The Hitler Decrees (Ann Arbor, 1934), p. 86.
10. See ch. III above.
11. P. 121 above; both Stapsz and Sand had the motivation of tyrannicides; but neither Napoleon nor Kotzebue were tyrants.
12. See p. 129 above.
13. Quoted R. C. Carr, "The Cult of Assassination," The Nineteenth Century and After, no. DCXCI (Sept., 1934).
14. Quoted Liman, op. cit., p. 164.
15. Stoyan Pribichevich, World without End (New York, 1939), p. 118.
16. Robert J. Donovan, "A Demonstration at Blair House," The New Yorker, July 19, 1952.
17. Salvemini, The Fascist Dictatorship in Italy (New York, 1927), p. 155.
18. E. I. Gumbel, Vier Jahre politischer Mord (Berlin-Friedenau, 1922); see also Hans Kilian, Der politische Mord (Zürich, 1936).
19. Quoted Kilian, op. cit., p. 24.
20. Independent lawyers clearly understood the danger of this new interpretation. One of them, Hugo Sinzheimer, wrote almost prophetically of a similar judgment in 1929, "This judgment legalizes political murder. If it is correct, we have no right any longer to keep the murderers of Rathenau in custody, because Rathenau was a traitor to the country. And if in the near future the Reichstag should be blown up by an infernal machine, we should be reluctant to arrest the perpetrators of the deed. For they would have acted only from negligence, because they would be surely

'convinced' that the acceptance of the Young Plan by the Reichstag was, according to the teaching of the Nazis, a treason to the country." The legal literature is still very illuminating in regard to the situation in Germany before the advent of the Nazis. See, among others, Sinzheimer, "Die Legalisierung des politischen Mordes," *Die Justiz* (Berlin, 1929), vol. V, no. 2; Gustav Radbruch, "Zum Fehmemordprozess Schulz," *ibid.* (1928), vol. IV, no. 1, and "Staatsnotstand, Staatsnotwehr und Fehmemord," *ibid.* (1929), vol. V, no. 3.

21. Quoted Konrad Heiden, *Der Fuehrer* (Boston, 1944), p. 485.
22. Kilian, *op. cit.*, pp. 35 ff.
23. Robert H. Jackson, *The Case against the Nazi Criminals* (New York, 1946), pp. 4 f.
24. *Ibid.*, p. 35.
25. Quoted *ibid.*, pp. 63 ff.
26. These figures are taken from statistics presented in Günther Weisenborn, ed., *Der lautlose Aufstand* (Hamburg, 1953), pp. 13 f., 259.
27. Bogdan Raditsa, "Yugoslavia's Tragic Lesson to the World," *The Reader's Digest* (Oct., 1946).
28. E. L. Palmieri and J. Kobler, "What Happened to Mussolini's Millions," *Life*, Jan. 17, 1949.
29. His immediate predecessor had been murdered by Nazi sympathizers.
30. *Manchester Guardian Weekly*, Dec. 30, 1948.
31. See Arthur Koestler, *Thieves in the Night: Chronicle of an Experiment* (New York, 1946), p. 247.
32. As their speeches before the Cairo tribunal were withheld from publication, the case needs further clarification: *The New York Times*, Jan. 11, 1945.
33. The foregoing chapter is an expansion of the author's article, "The Stream of Political Murder," *American Journal of Economics and Sociology* (1944), 335-355.

Chapter XV

1. Nicolai Hartmann, *Ethics* (New York, 1932), vol. I, pp. 90 f.
2. See p. 70 above.
3. Chapter XVI below.
4. From the viewpoint of his "scientific" amoralism, Karl Marx described the terrorists as "thoroughly sound men, without melodramatic pose, simple, objective, heroic. . . ." Terrorism was "a specifically Russian, historically inevitable method of action, about which there is as little to moralize—for or against—as there is about the earthquake in Chios": quoted Solomon F. Bloom, *The World of Nations: A study of the National Implications in the Work of Karl Marx* (New York, 1941), p. 94.
5. These cases are analyzed by Emil Ludwig, *The Davos Murder* (London, 1937), pp. 86 ff.
6. Herman Wendel, *Der Kampf der Südslawen um Freiheit und Einheit* (Frankfurt, 1925), pp. 432 ff.
7. Harold W. V. Temperley, *History of Serbia* (London, 1919), p. 280.
8. R. W. Seton-Watson, *Sarajevo: A Study in the Origins of the Great War* (London, 1925), pp. 149 f.
9. *Ibid.*, p. 145.
10. Quoted Viktor Bibl, *Der Zerfall Osterreichs* (Vienna, 1922), vol. II, p. 475.
11. *Le procès de Rosa* (Paris, 1930), p. 25.
12. *Ibid.*, pp. 48 f.
13. *Ibid.*, p. 93.
14. Ludwig, *op. cit.*, p. 62.
15. *Ibid.*, p. 127.
16. Tisza was killed, two years later, by a band of returned soldiers.
17. Friedrich Adler, *Vor dem Ausnahmegericht* (Jena, 1923); the quotations in the text are taken from this pamphlet, pp. 45 ff.
18. A friend of the author, who had closely observed the proceedings from the journalists' bench, is the source of this statement.
19. Quoted Forrest Davis, *Huey Long: A Candid Biography* (New York, 1935), pp. 42 f.
20. Harnett T. Kane, *Louisiana Hayride: The American Rehearsal for Dictatorship* (New York, 1941).
21. *Ibid.*, p. 6.
22. *Ibid.*, pp. 135-137.
23. *Ibid.*, pp. 134 f.
24. Davis, *op. cit.*, postscript.
25. Some private inquiries by the author through reliable friends indicate that the assassination of the dictator was, so to speak, in the air. One of Huey Long's close associates remarked, "At that time state politics were seething so that people went to every gathering, every political consultation, every convention, fully armed. . . ." Another source, which seems reliable, mentioned that a few days before the assassination a big meeting took place to discuss the means for controlling Long. Someone at the meeting remarked that "if Long went on as he did, someone would shoot him." Similar remarks were made

all over the state. Of course such facts are no evidence on the question of tyrannicide; they indicate only that hatred of the dictator was widespread.

26. Robert Penn Warren, *All the King's Men* (New York, 1946), p. 418.
27. *The New York Times*, Sept. 30, 1941.
28. Walter Lippman's column, Aug. 29, 1941.
29. *The New York Times*, Dec. 25, 26, 27, 1942.
30. *Ibid.*, Dec. 26, 1942.
31. The reader may be interested to know that the analysis to this point was written immediately after the event.
32. *The New York Times*, Dec. 23, 1943.
33. *Ibid.*, Dec. 26, 1943.

Chapter XVI

1. It is ironic that Hitler himself included in *Mein Kampf* (42nd, unabridged ed., Munich, 1933), p. 609, a comment on tyrannicide, which he regarded as an anachronism, of no practical use in the modern struggle for power: "The danger of secret organization lies today . . . in the fact that its members completely misunderstand the greatness of the task, and instead of this the opinion develops that the destiny of a people could be really determined for the better by a sudden assassination. Such an opinion may have its historical justification, particularly when a people is smarting under the tyranny of some oppressor of genius of whom it is known that his overwhelming personality alone guarantees the firmness and horror of the inimical oppression. In such a case a self-sacrificing man may suddenly arise from the people to plunge the steel into the breast of the hated one. And only the republican conscience of small scoundrels, conscious of their guilt, will regard such an action as the most odious, whereas the greatest bard of freedom of our people has dared to give a glorification of such an act in his *Tell*."
2. H. R. Trevor-Roper, *The Last Days of Hitler* (New York, 1947), p. 223.
3. Alan Bullock, *Hitler: A Study in Tyranny* (London, 1952), p. 736. Bullock's richly documented analysis is the best portrait of the man who was, as he says, "the most remarkable of those who have used modern techniques to apply the classic formulas of tyranny" (p. 735). Bullock presents Hitler as both fanatic and calculator, both charismatic leader and "astute and cynical politician" (p. 343).
4. Karl Bonhoeffer, "Führerpersönlichkeit und Massenwahn," an unpublished memorandum written in the fall of 1945; Karl Bonhoeffer's two sons, especially Dietrich, played important parts in the resistance.
5. Quoted Bullock, *op. cit.*, p. 707. Speer, who was one of the ablest of Hitler's collaborators, worked out early in 1945 a plan to kill him by introducing poison gas into the ventilating system of his underground bunker: *ibid.*, p. 671.
6. Quoted Trevor-Roper, *op. cit.*, p. 31.
7. Bonhoeffer, *op. cit.*
8. According to Hans Rothfels, *The German Opposition to Hitler* (Hinsdale, Ill., 1948), p. 165.
9. Published materials on the history of the resistance include the narratives of survivors more or less intimately involved, letters and other documents left by the participants, memoirs written by friends or relatives of those who perished, accounts of Allied Intelligence officers, and some official documents. Early books of particular importance for the understanding of the conspiracy of July 20 are Fabian von Schlabrendorff, *Offiziere gegen Hitler* (Zürich, 1946); an abridged English adaptation under the title *They Almost Killed Hitler*, prepared and edited by Gero v. S. Gaevernitz (New York, 1947) (references below apply to the English version); Hans B. Gisevius, *To the Bitter End* (Eng. tr., Boston, 1947); Rudolf Pechel, *Deutscher Widerstand* (Zürich, 1947); Allen W. Dulles, *Germany's Underground* (New York, 1947). Schlabrendorff was deeply involved in the conspiracy of July 20; Gisevius, an active underground worker and an important source for Dulles' interpretation, was connected with some of the participants but not admitted to the inner circle; Rudolf Pechel, former editor of the *Deutsche Rundschau*, had wide connections with various aspects of the resistance; Dulles was the OSS chief who established contact with the German underground.

These and other early publications were the basis of the excellent study by Hans Rothfels, *The German Opposition* to Hitler (Hinsdale, Ill., 1948), a careful treatment of the factual and psychological aspects of the conspiracy, against the general background of the resistance movement, to the extent of the data then available. An excellent recent treatment of the conspiracy, which analyzes particularly the moral conflicts in the consciences of the army group, is Eberhard Zeller, *Geist der Freiheit: Der zwanzigste Juli* (Munich, n.d.).

A bibliography of over 300 books on the resistance in general is included in Günther Weisenborn, ed., *Der lautlose Aufstand: Bericht über die Widerstandsbewegung des deutschen Volkes, 1933-1945* (Hamburg, 1953). This important book, which grew out of a published appeal by the poet-historian Ricarda Huch for data on the lives and work of martyrs of the resistance, is an impressive collection of personal and official documents, selected and edited with an intention of scrupulous objectivity, abundantly demonstrating the breadth of the movement, its steady growth, the important role of religious, socialist, and communist workers' organizations, and the extent of resistance in the rank and file of the army. It effectively answers the often-made assertion that the resistance in Germany was insignificant.

A work of symbolic value is *Das Gewissen Steht Auf: 64 Lebensbilder aus dem deutschen Widerstand 1933-1945* (Berlin, Frankfurt, Main, 1954) —photographs and brief memoirs of martyrs of various aspects of the resistance, collected by Annedore Leber, widow of the socialist leader Julius Leber who was a member of the conspiracy of July 20. Pictures and text unforgettably express the unity of the movement and the strength of the moral conviction on which it was based.

An important collective work published too late for use in this study is *Die Vollmacht des Gewissens*, hrsg. von der Europaischen Publikation e. V., I (Munich, 1956); besides discussions of the theory of resistance, it includes detailed historical analyses of successive periods in the military resistance, 1933-1945, by Helmut Krausnick, Kurt Sendtner, and Theodore Heuss, and an extensive bibliography compiled by Georg Stadtmüller.

10. *A German of the Resistance: The Last Letters of Count Helmuth von Moltke* (2nd, enlarged ed., London, 1947), p. 29.

11. The details of this tragic story are given in the touching book, *Die weisse Rose* (Frankfurt, 1952), by Inge Scholl, sister of the two young organizers of the movement.

12. Rothfels, *op. cit.*, pp. 53 f.
13. Quoted Bullock, *op. cit.*, p. 523.
14. Trevor-Roper, *op. cit.*, p. 11; a list of ten attempts from 1939 to 1944 is given in Weisenborn, *op. cit.*, pp. 23 f.
15. Rothfels, *op. cit.*, pp. 60-63, 130-157.
16. Quoted Leber, *op. cit.*, p. 228.
17. Weisenborn, *op. cit.*, p. 141, puts the deaths immediately resulting from the affair at 160 to 180, on the basis of the research of the "Special Commsision on the 20th of July." Earlier estimates were much higher; cf. Rothfels, *op. cit.*, p. 9.

Some responsible writers suggest that Rommel's death in October, which was announced as due to illness, should be counted among the casualties of the conspiracy, of which Rommel was toward the end an adherent. According to the story, Hitler did not wish to risk the public trial of such a noted figure; he accordingly had him poisoned and arranged an impressive state funeral, at which Rommel's loyalty to Hitler was extravagantly eulogized; for the details, and the sources cited, see Zeller, *op. cit.*, pp. 280-283.

18. Quoted Dulles, *op. cit.*, p. 116.
19. Quoted Rothfels, *op. cit.*, p. 87.
20. Quoted Zeller, *op. cit.*, p. 9.
21. From the notes of a lady who lived through these tragic events and knew intimately many actors of the drama.
22. Quoted Friedrich Meinecke, *Die deutsche Katastrophe* (Wiesbaden, 1946), p. 145.
23. Countess Marion Dönhoff, "Den Freunden zum Gedächtnis," privately circulated MS (Hamburg, n. d.).
24. Quoted Schlabrendorff, *op. cit.*, p. 103.
25. *Ibid.*, pp. 83 ff.
26. Paulus von Husen, "Der 20, Juli 1944 und die deutschen Katholiken," *St. Josephs-Blatt* (St. Benedikt, Oregon), Oct. 28, 1946; on the constitutional and social ideas of the conspiracy, see also Rothfels, *op. cit.*, pp. 100-111.
27. One of the conspirators has called Moltke's main idea "a directed defeat": Gisevius, *op. cit.*, p. 435. The term is too narrow and misleading; cf. Rothfels, *op. cit.*, pp. 112-130.
28. So far as the author knows, these

notes have never been published.
29. Quoted Schlabrendorff, *op. cit.,* p. 94.
30. Quoted *ibid.,* p. 127.
31. *A German of the Resistance* ... ; Moltke had been arrested in January, 1944, for warning a friend wanted by the Gestapo; he was thus, as he wrote to his wife in the letter quoted, removed from the danger of being drawn into active preparation for an uprising and was enabled to fulfill his mission of representing the absolute opposition between Nazism and the Christian soul itself.
32. Quoted Schlabrendorff, *op. cit.,* p. 120.
33. But individual members of the Intelligence were, as Rothfels points out, *op. cit.,* pp. 21 f., among the first to break the cloak of secrecy that had concealed the extent of the resistance.
34. Meinecke, *op. cit.,* p. 150.
35. Dönhoff, *op. cit.*
36. Quoted Weisenborn, *op. cit.,* p. 9.

Chapter XVII

1. The analysis of some Catholic opinions in this chapter should not be taken to imply the exclusive role of Catholicism in the fight against Hitler. A full evaluation of the comparative influence of the Protestant and the Catholic resistance movements remains to be made. But the most significant fact is that, as the resistance took form toward the end of the Hitler regime, its actual leaders included both Protestants and Catholics working together. There were supporters and opponents of tyrannicide among the adherents of both creeds.

Two important books, published while this study was in press, illustrate current rethinking of the problem of resistance, among leaders of German thought. *Die Vollmacht des Gewissens,* hrsg. von der Europaischen Publikationen e. V., I (Munich, 1956), includes a deeply-probing symposium on the right of resistance, by a group of distinguished public officials, army officers, jurists, Protestant and Catholic theologians, and professors of history and philosophy; and three significant essays on aspects of the problem: Hermann Weinkauff, "Die militäropposition gegen Hitler und das Widerstandsrecht"; Max Pribilla, "Der Eid nach der Lehre der katholischen Moraltheologie"; and Walter Künneth, "Die evangelisch-lutherische Theologie und das Widerstandsrecht." *Widerstandsrecht und Grenzen der Staatsgewalt: Bericht über die Tagung der Hochschule für Politische Wissenschaften, München, und der Evangelische Akademie, Tützing, 18.-20. Juni 1955...,* ed. Bernhard Pfister and Gerhard Hildmann (Berlin, 1956), comprises a number of significant papers on the history of the theory of resistance and its present status; the many participants include noted historians, political theorists, and Catholic and Protestant theologians.

2. Reinhold Schneider, *Gedenkwort zum 20, Juli* (Freiburg im Breisgau), 1947.
3. Paulus von Husen, "Der 20, Juli 1944 und die deutschen Katholiken," *St. Josephs-Blatt* (St. Benedikt, Oregon), Oct. 28, 1946. Von Husen was a member of the Kreisau Circle.
4. 10th ed., 1927.
5. Max Pribilla, S.J., "An den Grenzen der Staatsgewalt," *Stimmen der Zeit, Monatsschrift für das Geistesleben der Gegenwart,* CXLII (1948), 410-427.
6. Romans 13: 1-4.
7. It should be noticed, however, that the classic medieval discussions of the right of resistance and tyrannicide treat the subject purely in terms of reason and natural law, without any allusion to the possible role of the pope; cf. pp. 24-30 above.

Chapter XVIII

1. Élie Halévy, *L'Ère des tyrannies; Bulletin de la Société française de philosophie* (Paris, 1936), p. 247.
2. On the definition of dictatorships see Carl Schmitt, *Die Diktatur* (Munich and Leipzig, 1928).
3. See pp. 99-101 above.
4. Cf. J. N. Figgis, *The Divine Right of Kings* (Cambridge, 1922), esp. pp. 256-266.
5. Edmund Burke, *Letters on a Regicide Peace,* in *Works* (1872 ed.), vol. V, at p. 254, quoted Alfred Cobban, *Dictatorship: Its History and Theory* (New York, 1939), pp. 165 f.
6. József Rédei, *Magyar tragédia*

száz év elött, Lovassy László pere és rabságának titkos iratai (Budapest, 1938).
7. Cobban, *op. cit.*, p. 33.
8. H. A. L. Fisher in *Cambridge Modern History*, vol. IX, at p. 162.
9. Quoted H. A. L. Fisher, *ibid.*, vol. IX, at p. 763.
10. Quoted Cobban, *op. cit.*, pp. 98 f.
11. Albert Guérard, *Napoleon III* (Cambridge, 1943), pp. 245 f.
12. For further details see F. B. Artz, "Bonapartism and Dictatorship," *South Atlantic Quarterly*, XXXIX (1940), 37-49.
13. See pp. 3-7, 35-37 above.
14. These analogies were carefully elaborated by Charles L. Sherman, "A Latter-Day Tyranny in the Light of the Aristotelian Prognosis," *American Political Science Review*, XXVIII (1934), 424 ff.
15. Cobban, *op. cit.*, p. 263.
16. *New York Times*, Apr. 14, 1927. Similar statements were made by many influential writers and diplomats. The *"trahison des clercs"* must be regarded as an important factor, not only in encouraging the establishment of the Fascist and Nazi tyrannies but also in blunting the forces of internal resistance when they had been established. The conciliatory treatment of the new tyrannies by the democratic powers and, above all, the peace flights of Neville Chamberlain in 1938 contributed effectively to the demoralization of German public opinion. "Who can be surprised," asked a keen historian of the Third Reich, "that the broad masses, who were unable to look behind the scenes, were strengthened in their belief that basically all was in order, when they saw the leading statesmen of the western democracies at Munich arm in arm, as it were, with Hitler and Mussolini?" Erich Kordt, *Wahn und Wirklichkeit: Die Aussenpolitik des Dritten Reiches* (Stuttgart, 1947), p. 395.
17. Wilhelm Röpke, *International Economic Disintegration* (New York, 1942), pp. 246 f.
18. Quoted Antonio Ferro, *Salazar: le Portugal et son chef* (4th ed., Paris, 1934), pp. 324 f., 147 f.
19. Quoted Cobban, *op. cit.*, p. 186.
20. Quoted above, p. 6.
21. Quoted H. Heller, *Rechtstaat oder Diktatur* (Tübingen, 1930), p. 13.
22. Above, pp. 159, 161.
23. See above, p. 56.
24. See Hans Gerth, "The Nazi Party, Its Leadership and Composition," *American Journal of Sociology*, XLV (1940), 517-541. Before the annexation of Austria and the Sudetenland there were in Germany 33 gauleiters, 760 subdistrict leaders, 21,354 leaders of local groups, about 70,000 leaders of party cells, and 400,000 leaders of block units. The *Blockwarte* made the private life of every individual, his apartment and its equipment, his nearest friends and relatives thoroughly known to the party; they contributed more to the consolidation of the Nazi system than the constant fear of the Gestapo; see Erich Kordt, *op. cit.*, p. 44.
25. Max Weber, *Wirtschaft und Gesellschaft* (Tübingen, 1922), pp. 140 ff.
26. See the excellent remarks on the *"Bild des Führers"* in Kordt, *op. cit.*, p. 48.
27. Quoted Konrad Heiden, *Der Fuehrer: Hitler's Rise to Power* (Boston, 1944), p. 758.
28. Perhaps never has a group of men so deeply grasped the meaning of the words put into the mouth of the Grand Inquisitor by Dostoyevsky as did the Nazis. The Grand Inquisitor reproaches Jesus for having made uncounted millions of men hungry and miserable by his gift of spiritual freedom, which these base creatures can not use to their real advantage. The Inquisitor is about to take away this pernicious freedom in order to give men bread and to unite them in a common and mysterious creed: ". . . For who can rule men if not he who holds their conscience and their bread in his hands? We have taken the sword of Caesar, and in taking it, of course, we rejected Thee. . . . Oh, ages are yet to come of the confusion of free thought, of their science and cannibalism. But then the beast will crawl to us and lick our feet and spatter them with tears of blood. And we shall sit upon the beast and raise the cup, and on it will be written, 'Mystery.' But then, and only then the reign of peace and happiness will come for men. . . ." *The Brothers Karamazov* (Modern Library ed.), p. 316. But the Inquisitor remained a humanitarian, though a devilish one; the Nazis discarded the very idea of peace and happiness for the mystery of the Superman and racial domination.
29. Heiden, *op. cit.*, pp. 255 f.
30. Many Nazi leaders also exalted homosexual relations. They felt that heterosexual love might become a dangerous element: the omnipotence of the state could be confronted by the values

of family relationships. "The friendship relation has a connection with the state, the erotic relation has not...." Quoted *ibid.*, pp. 294 f.

31. Christopher Dawson, *The Judgment of the Nations* (New York, 1942), pp. 154 f.

32. Franz Neumann, *Behemoth: The Structure and Practice of National Socialism* (New York, 1942), pp. 438 f.

33. Max Scheler, *Wesen und Formen der Sympathie* (3rd ed., Bonn, 1931), p. 39.

34. The analysis of old Sparta by Schiller, the poet-historian, gives almost the impression of a prophecy of the Nazi state:
"One single virtue was practiced in Sparta while all others were neglected; that was patriotism.... The most natural and most beautiful human feelings were sacrificed to this artificial drive.... Political merit was gained at the expense of all moral feelings. In Sparta there was no conjugal love, no maternal love, no filial love, no friendship; there existed nothing but citizens and civic virtue....

"Even more repulsive was the way in which the spirit of humanity was killed in Sparta; and the essence of all duties, the respect for the human species, was completely lost. A state law made inhumanity towards the slaves a duty.... Spartan law preached the dangerous principle that men should be considered as means and not as ends in themselves; in this way the foundations of natural law and morality were undermined by law...." Friedrich von Schiller, "Die Gesetzgebung des Lykurgus und Solon," *Sämmtliche Werke*, vol. XX (Augsburg, 1827), at pp. 77 f.

Cf. Arnold J. Toynbee, *Civilization on Trial* (New York, 1948), pp. 255 f.: "*Individuality* is a pearl of great moral price, which was the most radically suppressed in the Spartan way of life, the Ottoman Sultan's slave household, and the totalitarian regimes."

Chapter XIX

1. Leon Trotsky, *Stalin: An Appraisal of the Man and His Influence* (New York, 1946), p. 383.

2. Cf. Eduard Heimann, "Marxism: 1848 and 1948," *The Journal of Politics*, XI (1949), 523-531.

3. Lenin, *The State and Revolution*, ch. II, sec. 1 (Vanguard Press, New York, 1929), p. 133.

4. The profoundly antidemocratic nature of Lenin, Trotsky, and Stalin has been clearly shown by Bertrand D. Wolfe, *Three Who Made a Revolution: A Biographical History* (New York, 1948). Wolfe's study differs from many analyses of the period in its awareness of the significance of moral values in the development of tyranny. David Shub, *Lenin* (New York, 1951) also shows effectively that Stalinism was already present in its essentials in Lenin's ideas and policies. That the differences between Stalin and Trotsky were in the area of tactics rather than of fundamental conceptions also appears clearly in I. Deutscher, *The Prophet Armed: Trotsky, 1879-1921* (Oxford, 1954).

5. Merle Fainsod, *How Russia Is Ruled* (Cambridge, Mass., 1953), pp. 116 f.; the whole book is a searching and astute explanation of both the sociological and the psychological aspects of the Russian tyranny.

6. *Ibid.*, p. 478.

7. *Ibid.*, p. 485.
8. *Ibid.*, pp. 485, 486.
9. *The Bolshevik*, January, 1950, quoted W. W. Kulski, *The Soviet Regime: Communism in Practice* (Syracuse, 1954), pp. 683 f.
10. Quoted Kulski, *op. cit.*, p. 125.
11. Fainsod, *op. cit.*, p. 485.
12. *Pravda*, June 28, 1946, quoted Fainsod, *op. cit.*, p. 494.
13. Deutscher, *op. cit.*, p. 494.
14. N. D. Kazantsev *et al.*, *Kolkhoznoe Pravo* (Collective Farm Law) (Moscow, 1947), quoted Kulski, *op. cit.*, p. 652.
15. Fainsod, *op. cit.*, p. 887.
16. Victor Kravchenko, *I Chose Freedom: The Personal and Political Life of a Soviet Official* (New York, 1946), p. 476.
17. Konrad Heiden, *Der Fuehrer* (Boston, 1944), pp. 760 ff.
18. Trotsky, *op. cit.*, pp. 378 f.
19. I. Deutscher, *Stalin: A Political Biography* (Oxford, 1949), p. 358; cf. Boris Souvarine, *Stalin* (New York, 1939), p. 657.
20. Trotsky, *op. cit.*, p. 412; the sheer opportunism and plagiaristic eclecticism of Mussolini's ideas and program is well brought out in A. Rossi, *The Rise of Italian Fascism, 1918-1922* (London, 1938); cf. also "The History of Fascism," (London) *Times Literary Supplement*,

December 4, 1953, a review of Luigi Salvatorelli and Giovanni Mira, *Storia del fascisme d'Italia del 1919 al 1945* (Rome).
21. Quoted Hal Lehrmann, *Russia's Europe* (New York and London, 1947), p. 149.
22. *Ibid.*, p. 303.
23. The foregoing six sentences are taken from a report by the author to the Social Science Research Council and the American Philosophical Society, who had assisted him to revisit in 1947 some of the satellite countries: "Danubia, Old and New," *Proceedings of the American Philosophical Society*, XCIII (1948), at p. 31.
24. Pp. 207 f. above.
25. Benjamin Constant, *L'esprit de conquête* (Paris, 1918), p. 35.
26. Maurice Joly, *Dialogue aux enfers entre Machiavel et Montesquieu ou la politique du Machiavel au xixe siècle* (Brussels, 1868).
27. *Ibid.*, pp. 228 f.
28. *Ibid.*, pp. 238 f.

Chapter XX

1. Henri Bergson, *The Two Sources of Morality and Religion* (New York, 1935).
2. P. 54 above.
3. William Godwin, *An Enquiry Concerning Political Justice*, ed. R. A. Preston (New York, 1926), vol. I, pp. 149-151.
4. See pp. 202 f. above.
5. P. 27 above.
6. P. 126 above.
7. Nicolas Berdyaev, *The Destiny of Man* (New York, 1937), pp. 213-217. Another element of conscience, from a religious point of view, was acutely analyzed by Max Scheler; he stated that "the revolutionary force of the moral world is not the Utopia, but repentance," in which the feeling of collective responsibility is as important as the feeling of personal responsibility. The promptings of conscience point towards an invisible order of our soul and our relation to the creator of this order; they are spontaneous and do not need our interpretation: *Vom Ewigen im Menschen*, vol. I, *Religiöse Erneurung* (Leipzig, 1921), pp. 12, 13, 42, 45, 50. Nicolai Hartmann has elucidated the problem of conscience from different angles; it is the central point of his monumental *Ethics*. Following Pascal and Scheler, he has renewed the concept of "an order of the heart" or "a logic of the heart" and supplemented the formalistic law of Kant with the dictates of the individual conscience, saying, "Never act merely according to a system of universal values, but always at the same time in accordance with the individual values of thine own personal nature": *Ethics* (New York, 1932), vol. II, p. 357.
8. "We can state immediately how man has become cheaper, how the individual has fallen in his value, since people believe in the discovery that the tribunal of personal conscience is a dischargeable institution": Herrmann Steinhausen, *Die Rolle des Bösen in der Weltgeschichte* (Stockholm, 1939), p. 51; the reader will also find many illuminating remarks in this connection in John Middleton Murry, *The Free Society* (London, 1948).
9. Even before the catastrophe came, the best Germans, both in the resistance movement and outside, realized that the chief destroyer of Germany was not the political system of the Nazis but its moral and spiritual implications. This was the main point in the argument of Karl Jaspers in his famous speech on the occasion of the reopening of the medical school of the University of Heidelberg, August 15, 1945: "Each individual is essentially infinite. No scientific concept can grasp him as a whole. . . . Man's unfathomableness is the veil which conceals the innermost nature of man from scientific knowledge. The freedom of man is his most decisive reality."
10. Henri Bergson, *op. cit.*, p. 199.
11. Cf. W. T. Stace, a philosopher of a different camp from Bergson, *The Destiny of Western Man* (New York, 1942), p. 146: "Bare reason alone implies the infinite value of the individual. But reason, though it may in some sense control and direct men, does not contain in itself any actual impulse to action."
12 Cf. pp. 52, 63, 70 above.
13. For the details of these cases, see ch. XV above.
14. Rebecca West, *Black Lamb and Grey Falcon* (New York, 1941), vol. I, p. 1112.
15. Friedrich Adler, *Vor dem Ausnahmegericht* (Jena, 1923) p. 96.
16. Freda Kirchwey in *The Nation*, January 2, 1943.
17. Hans Rothfels, *The German Opposition to Hitler: An Appraisal* (Hinsdale, Ill., 1948), p. 164.

INDEX

absolute monarchy, nature of: 17, 18 f., 27, 43 f., 59, 73, 77 f., 81, 99-101, 205-207, 267
Acton, Lord: 17, 184
Adams, John: 64, 265
Adler, Friedrich: 173-175, 243
Aegidius Romanus, 22, 260
Aeneas Sylvius, 23
Alexander II, Czar of Russia: 133, 169
Alexander, King of Yugoslavia: 158
Alexander Obrenovich, King of Serbia: 170 f., 243
Alfieri, Count Vittorio: 119 f.
Allen, J. W.: 49, 76, 263, 265 f.
anarchism, anarchists: 113, 117, 135-140, 141 f., 219, 235, 271
anti-Semitism, 162-164, 166, 214 f.
Aquinas, Thomas: 18 f., 21, 23 f., 26 f., 28-31, 34 f., 38 f., 67 f., 201, 209, 237, 260 f.
Aristogeiton, 3
Aristotle, 4-9, 12, 15, 21 f., 25, 29, 39 f., 53 f., 63, 69, 85, 209, 257 f., 260 f., 276
Armstrong, E.: 265
Arrow Cross, 163
Artz, F. B.: 276
Atatürk, Kemal: 211
Augustine, 13 f., 15
Aulard, F. H.: 270

Babeuf, François-Noel: 106, 127-129, 132, 270
Babington Plot, 76
Babouvism, 127-130, 132 f., 141
Bakunin, Mikhail A.: 129, 135 f., 141
Barclay, William: 73
Barère de Vieuzac, Bertrand: 104, 108

Barker, Sir Ernest: 264
Barthou, Louis: 158
Bartolus, 22, 27 f.
Bax, Belfort: 270
Beaton, Cardinal: 48
Bebel, August: 116
Beck, Ludwig: 190 f., 193
Beer, M.: 131
Bellarmine, Robert: 78, 268
Belloy, Pierre du: 265
Benes, Eduard: 165
Benoit, Charles: 272
Bentham, Jeremy: vii, 111 f., 117, 269
Berdyaev, Nicolas, 239
Bergson, Henri: 149, 234, 239 f.
Bernadotte, Count Folke: 166
Beza, Theodore: 51 f., 263
Bezold, Fr. von: 152 f., 272
Bismarck, Prince Otto von: 155
Black, J. B.: 266
Blanqui, Auguste: 129-132
Bloom, Solomon F.: 273
Boccaccio, 29, 39
Bodin, Jean: 72 f., 100
Bolsheviks, 108, 154, 219
Bolshevism, 127 f., 130-132, 146, 226-230, 270 f.; see also Lenin
Bonhoeffer, Dietrich: 189, 274
Bonhoeffer, Karl: 184
Booth, John Wilkes: 156 f.
Borgia, Cesare: 36, 153, 170, 220
Boscoli, Pietro Paolo: 38 f.
Boucher, Jean: 65-68, 73
Bracton, 17 f., 32, 75, 78
Brinton, C. Crane: 269
Brown, J. T. T.: 264
Brown, P. Hume: 263, 265
Brutus, Marcus Junius: 9, 11 f., 38 f., 106 f., 121, 125 f., 258

INDEX

Brutus, Stephen Junius, *pseud.*: see *Vindiciae contra Tyrannos*
Bryce, James: 259
Buchanan, George: 14, 17, 53-55, 64, 68, 71, 73, 77, 80, 83, 92, 94, 236, 266, 268
Bukharin, N. I.: 220
Bullinger, Heinrich: 48
Bullock, Alan: 274
Buonarotti, P.: 271
Burckhardt, Jacob: 36, 40
Burke, Edmund: 206
Butler, Nicholas Murray: 210

Caesar, Julius: 8, 10, 105 f., 261
Calvin, Jean: 46-49, 51
Carlyle, R. W. and A. J.; 259 f.
Carnot, President of the French Republic: 142, 169
Carr, R. C.: 272
Casablanca Conference, 188
Chamberlain, Neville: 277
Charles I, King of England: 78-82, 84, 86 f., 267
Chartists, 131
Chrysostom, 14
Cicero, 8-10, 12, 26, 29
Clarendon, Earl of: 266
Clément, Jacques: 65-71
Cobban, Alfred: 209, 276 f.
Coligny, Admiral: 47, 51
Collette, Paul: 179
Collins, Michael: 158
Colvin, Sidney: 27
Condorcet, Marquis de: 110
conscience, 44, 83, 85, 91, 126, 146, 167-169, 188, 190, 199 f., 230, 237-241, 279
Constant, Benjamin: 231
constitutionalism, v f., 4, 32 f., 43, 59 f., 80-82, 86 f., 94, 102, 104 f., 110-112, 264
contract theory, 23 f., 51 f., 54, 60-63, 65, 67, 80 f., 103, 111, 265 f.
Council of Ten, 40 f., 152
Corday, Charlotte: 106 f., 138
Coville, Alfred: 258, 261
Croce, Benedetto: 140, 272
Cromwell, Oliver: 81, 83-86, 207, 268

Damaschke, Adolph: 268
Dante, 261
Danton, 108
Darlan, Admiral François: 179-181, 243 f.
Davis, Forrest: 273
Dawson, Christopher: 216
Declaration of Independence, 104
deposition, 27 f., 30-32, 48-50, 53, 60, 66, 68, 70, 78, 80 f., 83, 90
Deutscher, I.: 224 f., 278
Dibelius, Otto: 203
Dickinson, John: 260 f.
dictatorship, distinguished from tyranny: vii, 8, 205, 207 f., 210 f.
dictatorships, totalitarian: vii, 162-165, 185, 208-210, 212-232, 237, 245 f., 249, 252-255, 277 f.
Diderot, Denis: 105
Diehl, K.: 271
disobedience, 13, 23 f., 46, 48 f., 52, 54, 90, 259
Disputatio vel Defensio Paschalis Papae, 261
divine right of kings, 13, 43-45, 47, 73, 75-78, 81, 100, 109, 206, 263, 265, 267; *see also* absolute monarchy, non-resistance
Dommanget, Maurice: 270
Dönhoff, Countess Marion: 197
Donovan, Robert J.: 272
Dostoyevsky, Feodor: 134, 277
Dulles, Allen W.: 274
Duplessis-Mornay, Philippe de: *see also Vindiciae contra Tyrannos*

Ehud, 12, 14
Elisabeth, Empress of Austria: 116, 142, 169
Elizabeth I, Queen of England: 74-76, 78
Encyclopedists, 105, 129
Engels, Friedrich: 116 f., 220
Epictetus, 259
Erzberger, Matthias: 159
Espinas, A: 270
Ezzelino, 35 f., 124

Fainsod, Merle: 221 f., 278
Fascism, 212-218, 225-229, 278
Fascists, 153, 159

INDEX

Fayau, deputy to the Convention: 108
Fehme tribunals, 159
Felton, John: 79, 266
Fenian Brotherhood, 156
Ferro, Antonio, 277
Feugère, Anatole: 268
Fieschi, Giuseppe: 129, 156
Figgis, J. N.: 266, 276
Filmer, Sir Robert: 76
Firth, C. H.: 268
Follen, Karl: 122
Francis Ferdinand, Archduke: 171
Frankfurter, David: 172 f.
Franklin, Benjamin: 104
Freiligrath, Ferdinand: 123
Friedel, Hans: 257
Friedell, Egon: 268
Frunze, M.: 227
Fülop-Miller, René: 269-271

Gallenga, Antonio: 125 f., 238
Gandhi, Mahatma: 166, 238
Gardiner, S. R.: 266
Garfield, James A.: 138, 151
German Resistance, viii, 168, 185-197, 237, 242, 244-246, 253
Gerson, Jean: 24, 29 f., 32, 78, 261
Gerth, Hans: 277
Gierke, Otto: 259
Gisevius, Hans B.: 274 f.
Glover, T. R.: 257
Godwin, William: 236
Goerdeler, Karl: 190-193
Goering, Hermann: 184, 214
Gooch, G. P.: 266
Goodman, Christopher: 50, 263
Goodwin, John: 82
Gregory I, the Great: 13 f., 23
Grynszpan, Herschel: 169 f.
Guérard, Albert: 208
Guicciardini, Francesco: 39
Guise, Francis, Duke of: 51, 64-66
Guizot, F. P. G.: 268 f.
Gumbel, E. I.: 159 f.
Gunpowder Plot, 71, 77
Gustlof, Wilhelm: 172 f.

Halem, Nicolaus von: 195
Halévy, Elie: vii, 205
Hammond, Mason: 257, 259
Hardman, J. B. S.: 271

Harmodius, 3, 12, 126
Harrington, James: 64, 264
Harrison, Thomas: 85
Hartmann, Nicolai: 168, 279
Heiden, Konrad: 273, 277
Heimann, Eduard: 278
Heintzeler, Gerhard: 258
Heinzen, Karl: 122 f.
Heller, H.: 277
Henderson, Sir Neville: viii
Henry III, King of France: 65 f., 69 f., 72
Henry IV, King of France (Henry of Navarre): 66 f., 71 f., 74, 264
Herodotus, 3 f.
Heuss, Theodore: 275
Hildmann, Gerhard: 276
Himmler, Heinrich: 163, 184
Hitler, Adolf: viii, 154, 161, 163, 183-185, 187-194, 196, 206 f., 214 f., 221, 225, 227 f., 242, 246, 274 f.
Hlinka Guardists, 163
Hobbes, Thomas: 84, 149, 268
Hödel, Emile: 139
Homilies, 76
Hooker, Thomas: 64
Horthy, Admiral Miklós: 152, 158
Hotman, Francis: 59 f., 73, 264
Hovell, Mark: 270
How, W. W.: 257
Huch, Ricarda: 197, 275
Hudson, W. S.: 263
Hugo, Victor: 156
Huguenots, 51 f., 57, 59-64
Humbert, Prince of Piedmont: 172
Husen, Paulus von: 200, 276
Hutchins, Robert M.: 251
Huxley, Aldous: 239

Innocent IV, pope: 31
insurrection, *see* revolt
Iron Guard: 159, 163
Isidore of Seville, 14, 260

Jackson, Robert H.: 162 f.
Jacobinism, 127, 129, 131 f., 145
Jacobins, 106-109
Jaeger, W.: 258
James I, King of England (James VI of Scotland): 15, 53, 71, 76-78, 86, 99 f., 265

INDEX

James III, King of Scotland: 54
Jaspers, Karl: 279
Jaurès, Jean: 109, 156
Jean Petit, 29 f., 78
Jefferson, Thomas: 104 f., 209, 268
Jehu, 12, 14, 49
Jesuits, 67-71, 76, 78, 265; *see also* Bellarmine, Mariana
Jewel, John, Bishop of Salisbury: 266
John of Salisbury, 19 f., 22, 25, 28, 35, 68, 260 f.
Joly, Maurice: 231
Jovanovitch, Dragoljub: 229
Judith, 14, 39, 126
Jukiĉ, 171 f.
Juvenal, 11, 259

Kane, Harnett T.: 176 f.
Kautsky, Karl: 116 f.
Kerensky, Alexander: 157
Kern, Fritz: 259, 261
Kilian, Hans: 272 f.
Killing No Murder, 84 f.
King, Bolton: 270
Kingdon, Robert M.: 263
King Steam, 114
Knox, John: 17, 48-50, 52 f., 77, 268
Koestler, Arthur: 273
Kordt, Erich: 277
Korff, H. A.: 120 f.
Kotzebue, August von: 121, 155, 272
Krausnick, Helmut: 275
Kravchenko, Victor: 226
Kropotkin, Prince: 135-137
Kulski, W. W.: 278
Künneth, Walter: 276

Labitte, M. C.: 265
La Boétie, Étienne de: v f., 55-57, 113, 214, 254 f.
Lamansky, V.: 40 f.
Lamartine, Alphonse: 268
Landor, Walter Savage: 124 f.
Lang, Andrew: 263
Languet, Hubert: 264; *see also Vindiciae contra Tyrannos*
Lapua, 158
Laski, Harold J.: 53, 64, 67
Laures, J.: 265
Laval, Pierre: 179
law of nature, *see* natural law

Leader, the: 56, 214, 222 f., 253
Leber, Annedore: 275
Leber, Julius: 190, 275
Lehndorff, Count Heinrich: 195
Lenin, 131-133, 138, 144-146, 158, 220-223, 278
Lessing, Gotthold Ephraim: 121
Lessing, Theodor: 153
Leuschner, Wilhelm: 189
Lewis, Ewart: 259
Levellers, 81
Liebknecht, Karl: 159
Lilburne, John: 81, 267
Lincoln, Abraham: 156 f.
Liman, Paul: 271 f.
Lippmann, Walter: 179
Locke, John: 53, 64, 102-104, 209, 235, 264
Lodge, R.: 268
Long, Huey: 175-178
Louis Philippe, King of France: 129, 155 f.
Louis XIV, King of France: 101
Louis XVI, King of France: 101, 107-110
Lovassy, László: 206
Lucas de Penna, 22, 25 f.
Luccheni, Luigi: 116, 142
Ludwig, Emil: 273
Luther, Martin: 44-46, 52, 75, 238, 262 f.
Luxemburg, Rosa: 159

Machiavelli, Niccolò: 36, 38-41, 44, 85, 149, 153, 262
Maclaren, Malcolm M., Jr.: 257
Madison, James: 104
Magna Carta, 20
Malone, Dumas: 268
Manegold of Lautenbach, 23 f., 31
Manin, Daniel: 124, 126
Margoliouth, D. S.: 272
Mariana, Juan de: 29, 67-71, 80, 83, 92-94, 168, 241
Marriott, J. A. R.: 258
Marsiglio of Padua: 19, 32 f., 261 f.
Marx, Karl: 116 f., 141, 143, 220, 269, 273
Marxism, 107, 115-117, 129, 131 f., 135, 140 f., 143-145, 219 f., 250; *see also* Revisionism

Masaryk, Jan: 165
Masaryk, Thomas G.: 271
Mason, Edward S.: 271
Mathiez, Albert: 107, 109
Matteotti, Giacomo: 154, 159, 246
Mazzini, Giuseppe: 124-126, 156, 238
McIlwain, C. H.: 14, 259-261, 263
McKinley, William: 169
Medici, Alessandro de': 38
Medici, Catherine de: 57, 59, 62
Medici, Lorenzino de': 38
Megaro, Gudence: 270
Meinecke, Friedrich: 197
Meyer, A. O.: 266
Mill, John Stuart: 112, 209
Milton, John: 14, 60, 64, 83 f., 104, 264, 267 f.
Mirsky, D. P.: 271
Moltke, Count Helmuth von: 186, 193-195, 275 f.
monarchomachs, 15, 67, 73, 104
Montani, Cola de': 38
Montesquieu, Baron Charles de: 104, 106
Moslem Brotherhood, 166
Most, Johann: 139
Moyne, Lord: 166
Munich Conference, 191, 277
Murray, R. H.: 263-265
Murry, John M.: 279
Mussolini, Benito: viii, 116, 153, 159, 165, 206, 210, 212 f., 227 f., 242, 246, 278

Napoleon I, 155, 207 f., 231, 272
Napoleon III (Louis Napoleon), 125, 156, 207 f., 231
Narodniki, 134 f.
nationalism, 75, 95, 120 f., 125, 155-157, 166, 171, 213, 223 f., 228 f., 250
natural law, 8 f., 11 f., 15, 18 f., 21, 23, 27, 29, 32 f., 51, 67, 80-82, 90 f., 102 f., 107, 111, 131 f., 143, 201-203, 236, 258, 260, 267
Nazis, 153, 159-164, 277, 279
Nazism, 185, 212-218, 225-229
Nechaev, Russian anarchist: 134, 136
Nero, 10, 13, 25, 220
Neumann, Franz: 216
Nicholas I, pope: 14 f.

Nietzsche, Friedrich Wilhelm: 149
Nihilism, 133 f., 271
Nobiling, Karl: 139
Nokrashy Pasha, 166
Nomad, Max: 270 f.
non-resistance, 13-15, 23, 45-48, 76, 87, 94, 263
Nürnberg Trial, 162 f.

Occam, see William of Occam
O'Higgins, K.: 158
Oldenberg, Karl: 271
Orsini, Felice: 125, 156
Orwell, George: 252
Overton, Richard: 267

Paine, Thomas: 110
Parsons, W.: 259
passive resistance, 56 f., 113
Paul, the Apostle: 12, 14-16, 54, 201, 262
Pavlov, Russian anarchist: 137
Pazzi conspiracy, 40
Pechel, Rudolf: 274
Peter, the Apostle: 12, 14 f., 262
Petliura, Simon: 169
Petöfi, Alexander: 124
Pfister, Bernhard: 276
Phoenix Park murders: 156
Pisarev, D. I.: 134
Pisistratus, 4
Pius V, pope: 75 f.
Plass, H. G.: 257 f.
Plato, 4-9, 85, 101, 209
Plehve, Viatscheslaf: 169
Plutarch: 11 f., 106 f., 152, 258, 260
Politiques, 72 f., 100
Pollock, Sir Frederick: 112, 258 f.
Polybius, 11
Ponet, John: 50, 80, 263
pope, as definer of tyranny: 20 f., 30 f., 65, 71, 75 f., 203, 276
Potempa murder, 161
Prévité-Orton, C. W.: 261
Pribichevich, Stoyan: 272
Pribilla, Max: 200-204, 237, 276
Princip, Gavrilo: 171
Proudhon, Pierre Joseph: 208
Prynne, William: 80 f.

Quintilian, 259

INDEX

Radbruch, Gustav: 273
Radich, Stepan: 158
Raditsa, Bogdan: 273
Ranke, L.: 265 f.
Rathenau, Walter: 159 f., 272
Ravachol, French anarchist: 141 f.
Ravaillac, 71
Raynal, l'abbé: 105 f.
Rédei, József: 276
Regicides: 83, 85, 267
Reinsdorf, German anarchist: 139
resistance, see disobedience, non-resistance, passive resistance, resistance by inferior magistrates, resistance by private citizens, revolt, revolution, self-defense, tyrannicide.
resistance by inferior magistrates, 47-49, 52, 61-63, 202, 241, 263
resistance by private citizens, vi, 17, 19, 25, 28, 33, 50, 52, 54, 61-63, 66, 68, 70, 84-87, 91-93, 95 f., 102 f., 200-204, 241 f., 253
Resistance, German: see German Resistance
Revisionism, 139, 141 f., 144 f.
revolt, right of: 17, 23 f., 48 f., 54, 68, 70, 80 f., 102-104, 111, 262, 271; see also revolution
revolution, concepts of: vi, 91, 101-104, 115 f., 128-132, 140-146, 235
Revolution, the American: 99, 104 f., 235, 265
Revolution, the English (Puritan): 80-84, 86 f., 99, 101
Revolution, the French: 99, 101, 106-110, 127-129, 207 f., 235
Revolution of 1688, 102 f.
Robespierre, Maximilien: 108
Röhm, Ernst: 154, 227
Roman law, 11, 19 f., 28 f., 43, 59; see also "vi vim repellere . . ."
Rommel, Erwin: 275
Roosevelt, Franklin D.: 180, 242
Röpke, Wilhelm: 120, 277
Rosa, Fernando de: 172
Rosenberg, Alfred: 163
Rossaeus, 65-67
Rosselli, Carlo: 153
Rossi, A.: 278
Rossiter, C. L.: 258

Rothfels, Hans: 274-276, 279
Rousseau, Jean Jacques: 100 f., 106, 114 f., 269
Russell, Lord: 268
Rutherford, Samuel: 80 f.
Rye House Plot, 86, 102

Salazar, Antonio de Oliveira: 211 f.
Salutati, Coluccio: 27
Salvemini, Gaetano: 272
Sand, Karl: 121 f., 155, 272
Sarajevo, 171
satellite states, viii, 164 f., 229 f., 249, 254
Scheler, Max: 216, 279
Schiller, Friedrich von: 121, 274, 277 f.
Schlabrendorff, Fabian von: 187-189, 195, 274
Schmidt, H. G.: 142, 263, 272
Schmitt, Carl: 205
Schneider, Reinhold: 199
Scholl, Inge: 275
sedition, see revolt
Selden, John: 60, 80
self-defense, right of: 24, 28, 46, 80 f., 102 f., 200, 236
Sencier, George: 270
Sendtner, Kurt: 275
Seneca, Lucius Annaeus: 10 f., 12, 39, 83, 106, 258
Seneca Rhetor, 11
Seton-Watson, R. W.: 171
Sexby, Edward: 84 f.
Sforza, Francesco: 37
Sforza, Galeazzo Maria: 37 f.
Sherman, C. L.: 258, 276
Shub, David: 278
Sidney, Algernon: 60, 64, 104, 264
Sindercombe, Miles: 268
Sinzheimer, Hugo: 272 f.
Sismondi, J. C. L. de: 37, 262
Sixtus V, pope: 66
Social Democrats, see Revisionism
Socrates, 238, 257 f.
Sorel, Georges: 129, 142 f., 145 f.
Sorokin, P. A.: 272
Souvarine, Boris: 278
Spectator, vi
Speer, Albert: 184, 274
Spencer, Henry R.: 258

INDEX

Spencer, Herbert: 217
Spengler, Oswald: 149
Spindler, G. W.: 270
Spiridovitch, Alexander I.: 271
Stace, W. T.: 279
Stalin, Joseph: 219-228, 242, 278
Stamboliski, Alexander: 158
Stapsz, Friedrich: 155, 272
Stauffenberg, Count Claus von: 188, 191, 195, 200
St. Bartholomew, Massacre of: 51, 53, 64
Steinhausen, Herrmann: 279
Stern Gang, 166
Stirner, Max: 271
Stoicism, 7, 9-11, 15, 259
Stolypin, Peter: 169
Strafford, Thomas Wentworth, First Earl of: 79-81
Strauss, Leo: vii f., 257
Stürgkh, Count Carl von: 173-175, 243
Suarez, Francisco: 67 f., 71
Swinburne, Algernon: 125
Symonds, J. A.: 40
syndicalism, *see* Sorel

Taine, H. A.: 270
Tell, William: 105, 121, 126, 175, 195, 274
Temperley, H. W. V.: 170
Thomas Aquinas, *see* Aquinas
Thucydides, 257
Tilley, A. T.: 265
Tisza, Count Stephen: 173, 273
Tkatchev, P. N.: 131
Tolstoy, Leo: 113, 117, 271
Toynbee, Arnold: 249, 278
"tree of liberty ..., the": 104, 131, 268
Tresckow, Henning von: 192, 195 f.
Trevor-Roper, H. R.: 274 f.
Trotsky, Leon: 219-221, 224 f., 228, 278
Trott zu Solz, Adam von: 189
Truman, Harry S.: 157
Turgenev, Ivan: 134
"Turkish St. Bartholomew": 155
Tyndale, William: 75

tyrannicide, condemnation of: vi, 26 f., 29, 45 f., 61, 71-73, 142, 233, 235 f., 241-243, 261 f., 274
tyrannicide, meaning of: vi, 41, 149, 167-169, 192, 236, 238
tyrannicide, praise of: 3, 7, 10 f., 12, 14, 25, 38 f., 50, 54, 66 f., 69 f., 72, 76, 84, 105-107, 120, 122 f., 124-126, 274
tyrannicide, theory of: vii f., 25-30, 45 f., 50, 54 f., 68 f., 72 f., 73 f., 77 f., 84 f., 90-96, 101 f., 125 f., 167-169, 194-196, 199 f., 204, 233-246, 253
tyranny, concepts of: vii, 3-7, 12, 14 f., 20-22, 52, 55-57, 60, 62-66, 69 f., 72-74, 82, 89, 91 f., 99 f., 102, 104 f., 109 f., 111-115, 119 f., 140, 144 f., 167, 205-207, 212-218, 225 f., 230-232, 237, 245, 253-255, 257 f., 260, 270 f.
tyranny, two kinds of: 7, 26-28, 34, 38 f., 52, 54, 62 f., 68, 70, 72 f.

Ullmann, Walter: 260
Ulyanov, Alexander: 138 f.
Ure, P. N.: 257
Ustashi, 158

Vaillant, August: 142
Vane, Sir Henry: 267
Venner, Thomas: 268
Victoria, Queen of England: vi, 169
Villari, P.: 262
Villiers, George, First Duke of Buckingham: 78 f.
Vindiciae contra Tyrannos, 51, 60-65, 73, 80, 264-266
Visconti, Gian Galeazzo: 36
"*vi vim repellere ...*", 24, 28, 32, 236
Vizetelli, E. A.: 271 f.
Vollmacht des Gewissens, Die: 275 f.
Voltaire, François Marie Arouet de: 105, 120, 136

Wallenstein, Albrecht von: 154
Warren, Robert Penn: 178
Weber, Max: 214, 277
Weinkauff, Hermann: 276
Weisenborn, Günther: 273, 275

Weiss, Carl A.: 177 f.
Wendel, Herman: 273
West, Rebecca: 279
White Rose, the: 187
Widerstandsrecht und Grenzen der Staatsgewalt, 276
Wilhelm I, Kaiser: 139
William II, King of England (William Rufus): 20
William of Occam, 21, 23, 32
William of Orange (the Silent): 71, 74, 76

Windhorst, Ludwig: 155
Wittke, Carl: 270
Wolfe, Bertrand D.: 278
Wyclif, John: 23, 263

Xenophon, 3 f., 40, 257 f.

Yarmolinsky, A.: 271

Zassulich, Vera: 138
Zeller, E.: 257 f.
Zeller, Eberhard: 275